LATE BEETHOVEN

LATE BEETHOVEN

MUSIC, THOUGHT, IMAGINATION

MAYNARD SOLOMON

UNIVERSITY OF CALIFORNIA PRESS
BERKELEY · LOS ANGELES · LONDON

*The University of California Press
gratefully acknowledges a subvention from the
Music Endowment Fund of the University
of California Press Associates.*

University of California Press
Berkeley and Los Angeles, California

University of California Press, Ltd.
London, England

Some of the chapters in this book were previously
published; they are listed in the Acknowledgments.

Library of Congress Cataloging-in-Publication Data

Solomon, Maynard.
   Late Beethoven : music, thought, imagination /
Maynard Solomon.
      p.   cm.
   Includes bibliographical references and index.
   ISBN 0-520-23746-3 (alk. paper)
   1. Beethoven, Ludwig van, 1770–1827—Last
years. 2. Composers—Austria—Biography.
3. Beethoven, Ludwig van, 1770–1827—Criticism
and interpretation. I. Title.
ML410.B4 S655 2003
780'.92—dc21   2002013906

Manufactured in the United States of America

12 11 10 09 08 07 06 05 04 03
10 9 8 7 6 5 4 3 2 1

For Eva, again

CONTENTS

ACKNOWLEDGMENTS

A project that began twenty years ago as a book on Beethoven and Romanticism gradually ramified into a more ambitious book on late Beethoven and especially on some of the hallmarks and sources of his late style. While the book can be read as a collection of separate studies, it is intended as a series of diverse but related perspectives on the imaginative world within which Beethoven dwelt during his last fifteen years and on the ways in which his thought and music may be interrelated.

All of the chapters were written with this book in mind. Seven of them— the prologue and chapters 4, 5, 6, 9, 10, and 12—are previously unpublished in any form. Four of them have appeared, or will appear, in somewhat different form in Festschriften and memorial volumes honoring my dear friends and cherished correspondents Lewis Lockwood, Robert L. Marshall, the late Alan Tyson, and the late Harry Goldschmidt. The previously published chapters have been considerably revised and expanded and now represent my latest thinking on their respective topics.

Friends and colleagues who by their comments, suggestions, and information have improved one or another chapter include Wye J. Allanbrook, Mark Evan Bonds, Sieghard Brandenburg, Bruce Cooper Clarke, Marianne Goldberger, Grita Herre, Joseph Kerman, Richard Kramer, Thomas J. Mathiesen, the late Max Rudolf, Heinz Schuler, Stephen Moore Whiting, and Robert S. Winter, along with Messrs. Lockwood, Marshall, and Tyson. I am deeply grateful to each and every one of them. Warm thanks also to the eager and challenging participants in my seminars as a visiting professor at SUNY Stony Brook and at Columbia, Harvard, and Yale universities, and since 1998 as a member of the graduate faculty of the Juilliard School, where several of the book's leading ideas were first conceived and formulated.

Several of the chapters were presented in whole or in part at various conferences: the *Fidelio/Leonore* Symposium, Princeton University, 1982; "Probleme der symphonischen Tradition im 19. Jahrhundert: Internationales Musikwissenschaftliches Colloquium," Bonn, 1989; "Current Issues in the Interpretation of Mozart's Instrumental Music," Stanford University, 1991; "The Political and Aesthetic Education of Romanticism," conference of the North American Society for the Study of Romanticism, Duke University, 1994; "Rethinking Beethoven's Late Period: Sources, Aesthetics, and Interpretation," Harvard University, 1996; "Biographie und Schaffensprozess bei Beethoven," Berlin, 1999; and the "International Beethoven Festival-Conference on the Sonatas for Violin and Piano," Boston University/ Harvard University, Boston, 2000. Still others were given as lectures at Yale University, the University of Michigan, the University of Pennsylvania, Princeton University, Harvard University, the Phi Beta Kappa Society of Hunter College of the City University of New York, the Andiron Club, the Center for Cultural and Historical Studies at Columbia University, the Society of Fellows at New York University, and the Juilliard School.

The main libraries that I consulted, whose librarians unfailingly welcomed and responded to my queries, included the Research Libraries of the New York Public Library; Columbia University Libraries; Österreichische Nationalbibliothek; Deutsche Staatsbibliothek zu Berlin, Preußischer Kulturbesitz; Beethoven-Archiv, Bonn; the Bobst Library of New York University; the Library of Congress; the New York Society Library; the Livingston Masonic Library, New York; the Morgan Library; and the libraries of Harvard, Yale, and Princeton universities.

I am grateful to the editors and publishers of journals or books in which some of my chapters have previously been or are scheduled to be published.

"The Ninth Symphony: The Sense of an Ending," *Critical Inquiry* 17 (1991); also, an earlier version in *Probleme der symphonischen Tradition im 19. Jahrhundert. Internationales Musikwissenschaftliches Colloquium Bonn 1989. Kongreßbericht,* ed. Siegfried Kross et al. (Tutzing: Schneider, 1990).

"Beyond Classicism" in *The Beethoven Quartet Companion,* ed. Robert S. Winter and Robert Martin (Berkeley: University of California Press, 1994).

"Some Romantic Images" in *Haydn, Mozart, and Beethoven: Essays in Honour of Alan Tyson,* ed. Sieghard Brandenburg (Oxford: Oxford University Press, 1998); and, abridged, in *The Lessons of Romanticism,* ed. Robert F. Gleckner and Thomas Pfau (Durham: Duke University Press, 1998).

"The Diabelli Variations: The End of a Beginning," *Beethoven Forum* 7 (1999).

"The Masonic Thread" and "The Masonic Imagination" under the title "Beethoven, Freemasonry, and the Tagebuch of 1812–1818," *Beethoven Forum* 8 (2000).

"Beethoven's Seventh Symphony and the Rhythms of Antiquity" is to be published, abridged, in *Kunstwerk und Biographie: Gedenkschrift für Harry Goldschmidt,* ed. Hans-Werner Heister and Silke Wenzel (Bockel Verlag, forthcoming).

"Beethoven's Violin Sonata in G, op. 96: Rhetoric and Structure" is to be published in the proceedings of the International Beethoven Festival-Conference on the Sonatas for Violin and Piano of Ludwig van Beethoven, ed. Lewis Lockwood and Mark Kroll (University of Illinois Press, forthcoming).

"Reason and Imagination: The Aesthetic Dimension" is to be published in *Reading Texts: Essays in Honor of Robert L. Marshall,* ed. Stephen Crist, Roberta Marvin, and Michael Marissen (University of Rochester Press, forthcoming).

Shepherding this book into print has been a gratifying process, for which I owe thanks to my intrepid and esteemed literary agent, Georges Borchardt, the University of California Press, its resourceful music editor Mary Francis, and its skilled production team—designer Jessica Grunwald, copy editor Tony Hicks, music setter Ernie Mansfield, proofreader Annelise Zamula, indexer Roberta Engleman—headed by senior editor Rose Vekony, who solved a host of substantive problems with apparent effortlessness and infinite patience. The piano reductions of the symphonic music examples are by Jan Brandts Buys (Universal-Edition).

As always, my wife, Eva, has been my keenest and most reliable editor. My deepest gratitude goes to her, our children, and our grandchildren.

New York, 2003

A SEA CHANGE

It is well recognized that during his last years, especially from 1817 on, Beethoven's music underwent a transformation that redefined his legacy and in a series of powerful masterstrokes forever enlarged the sphere of human experience accessible to the creative imagination. Some may disagree about the precise dates of the inception of the late style, differ over the extent to which it emerged from immanent or external sources, and struggle to describe its characteristics in a coherent and meaningful way, but few have disagreed about the existence of the phase itself, let alone its seismic character or its chief examples—the late sonatas and string quartets, the "Diabelli" Variations and the bagatelles, the Ninth Symphony and *Missa solemnis*. And many Beethovenians have called attention to adumbrations of particular aspects of the late style in keynote works written between about 1810 and 1816, seeing in the solo and string sonatas, chamber music, song cycle, and symphonies of those years signs of transition towards an emerging set of paradigms.

Students of Beethoven have wondered whether and how the phenomenon of the late style may be linked to the changing circumstances of his life. Many conceivable connections have been proposed and elucidated, often with fruitful results, for it is clear that no single perspective can exhaust the style's sources. Prominent among biographical factors are his state of mind, his descent into almost total deafness by 1818, and his increasing vulnerability to the aging process. Psychologically, of course, this was an era of enormous stress for Beethoven, and his inner conflicts have been thought to be somehow connected to the emergence of the late works. Attention

is inevitably drawn to the failure of his marriage project by his early for-
ties, followed by his renunciation of the possibility of domestic happiness,
and his increasing tendency to isolate himself from the world. Here, one
cannot overlook that the onset of the late style roughly coincided with the
harrowing legal struggle over the guardianship of his nephew Karl. Historical and cultural factors also play their part: the close of a dramatic period
in European history, climaxed by the end of the Napoleonic Wars and the
consolidation of coercive regimes in the chief continental monarchies, exemplified by the autocratic Habsburg state under Emperor Franz II and
Prince Metternich.

There is a conspicuous fusion of retrospective and modernist tendencies
in Beethoven's late style, but the relative absence of contemporary musical
influences confirms the weight of Beethoven's originality, his expanded
rhetorical vocabulary, his formulation of unprecedented ways of representing
states of being that flourish beyond the boundaries of ordinary experience,
and his transformations of Classical structural models, preparing the way for
their eventual dissolution. The exhaustion of the vaunted "heroic style" and
its descent into self-parody in *Wellington's Victory* and other propagandist
pièces d'occasion written in connection with the victory over Napoleon and
the subsequent convening of the Congress of Vienna made it imperative
that Beethoven locate a hitherto unimagined musical *problématique*. It was a
time of many endings—historical, philosophical, biographical, stylistic—a
period of flux in which old habits of mind needed to be reconsidered and
the most deeply held beliefs subjected to scrutiny.

Without minimizing the importance of diverse efforts at reconstructing
the multiple contexts within which the last works came into being, this book
will focus on what appears to be a striking metamorphosis in Beethoven's
system of beliefs, proposing that a thoroughgoing transformation was well
under way by the years around 1810, gaining momentum as the decade proceeded, and that this eventually amounted to a sweeping realignment of his
understanding of nature, divinity, and human purpose, constituting a sea
change in Beethoven's system of beliefs. Signs of this realignment may be
found in Beethoven's letters and conversation books, but they are especially
distinct in his Tagebuch, the intimate diary he kept between 1812 and 1818,
to which he confided his inmost feelings and desires.[1] My aim is to encourage
the inquiry into the connections—at least, the analogies—between Beethoven's thought and his later works.

II

In the wake of personal disappointments and as the consciousness of his own mortality cast a lengthening shadow, Beethoven was acutely aware that he would not have sufficient time to complete his creative endeavors. He thought he deserved a period of grace precisely for that purpose, writing: "before my departure for the Elysian fields I must leave behind me what the Eternal Spirit has infused into my soul and bids me complete. Why, I feel as if I had hardly composed more than a few notes."[2] But he had little hope of divine intervention on his behalf; he agreed with Homer's calculation that "To men are allotted but a few days" (Tagebuch no. 170; *Odyssey*), and though he yearned for Pliny's "fame and praise and eternal life" (no. 114) and hoped against hope that he might live on, "even if by artificial means [*Hilfsmitteln*], if only they can be found!" (no. 40), he knew that he was in a race against time.

Thus, Beethoven had to decide how he was to spend his remaining time on earth, whether to try to fill the dwindling days with simple pleasures or to pursue his dedication to great artistic challenges, or even to raise the stakes in his creative exertions. Predictably, but not without scorching conflicts, he opted for art against life, and this answer is written large and repeatedly throughout his Tagebuch, beginning with its very first entry in 1812: "You must not be a *human being, not for yourself, but only for others;* for you there is no longer any happiness except within yourself, in your art" (no. 1). Another entry sounds the same theme: "Live only in your art, for you are so limited by your senses. This is nevertheless the *only existence* for you" (no. 88). He renounced ordinary conceptions of personal gratification; he abandoned the dream of "a shiftless life, which I often pictured to myself" (no. 3). Sacrifice became the order of the day: "Everything that is called life should be sacrificed to the sublime and be a sanctuary of art" (no. 40); "Sacrifice once and for all the trivialities of social life to your art" (no. 169). These ideas of self-abnegation for the sake of music became an abiding belief; in 1824 he wrote, "Only in my divine art do I find the support which enables me to sacrifice the best part of my life to the heavenly Muses."[3]

Beethoven's choices were designed to enhance his creativity and to provide favorable conditions within which it could flourish. He set in motion a process of stripping down to essentials, eliminating whatever he perceived to be superfluous and trivial, even renouncing the possibility of love and marriage and setting limits on his affectionate and social interactions. Knowing that the time remaining to him was sufficient for the working out of only a relative handful of his ideas, he steeled himself for the task ahead: to "develop everything that has to remain locked within you" (no. 41). This sacrificial stance was more than an abstract reflection of a moralizing creed; his later years were marked by an increasing withdrawal into inwardness, into a state very like the extended ritual silence of Brahman novices that he remarked upon in the Tagebuch (no. 94c). He considered retreating still further, into the quasi-monastic solitude of rural life, removed from the hurly-burly of the city. Perhaps he was hoping somehow to accomplish the impossible—to slow things down by constructing universes where events might move at a slower rate, thus to expand the time available to him.

Contemplating the encroachments of time and mortality, Beethoven set his priorities, determined which compositions he would write, and eventually laid out an ambitious program. By 1817–18 at the latest, when he was writing the closing entries of his Tagebuch, he had settled on a series of compositions, works that constituted the components of a vast creative effort. (Indeed, with the exception of the late quartets, the great works of the last decade were all actually begun in 1817–18.) In his last sonatas he chose to work out possible reconfigurations of musical form and to sound unplumbed depths of expressivity; he explored the possibility of describing a devotional journey in his "Diabelli" Variations—a Divine Comedy or Pilgrim's Progress in tones; he wrote a song cycle in the form of a Romantic circle—a wreath, a *Liederkreis*—so tightly woven that its constituent elements cannot be separated out; he composed a colossal symphony that presumed to dissolve boundaries between language and music, thus perhaps to restore the union of the arts rumored to have existed in ancient ritual drama; in that symphony and in a prodigious and learned Mass he aimed also to dissolve boundaries between religions and to locate some of the common denominators of every faith. He had many more works in mind than he had time for. In a process of compositional triage, he abandoned or postponed ideas for setting Goethe's *Faust* and *Claudine von Villa Bella;* Grillparzer's *Melusine;* an oratorio for the Gesellschaft der Musikfreunde to a libretto by Karl Bernard; and another oratorio, on Saul, to a text by Christoph Kuffner, that was intended to utilize music of the ancient Hebrews and the old modes. Also thrown overboard were a hybrid choral-symphonic Adagio Cantique, a Tenth Symphony, the Requiem he had promised his patron Wolfmayer, an orchestral overture on the letters B–A–C–H, a string quintet, a piano concerto, and doubtless a large number of other works. In view of his endless ambitious and even grandiose projects, he obviously had time for only a very small number of potboilers, written mostly in the aftermath of strenuous accomplishment.

He had set his creativity in opposition to his needs for consolation and pleasure, his longings to become a husband and a father, and his yearnings for a simple life, however trivial such an existence might have seemed in comparison to his art. It is fortunate, then, that Beethoven's art did not become his adversary, for one might think it inevitable that he would eventually lash out against a sacrificial imperative that insisted on his exclusive devotion to his artistic mission, as though he were an instrument of some unforgiving moral precept. And, perhaps, such a revolt did occur when he moved to seize control of his nephew Karl from the boy's mother, for it was an act through which he imagined that he had at last established the family that had been forbidden him, thereby fulfilling what he termed his "longing for domesticity" (no. 3). The torturing struggle to win the guardianship of his nephew revealed Beethoven's inability to sustain a renunciatory position. The desire for kinship overwhelmed both his defenses and his better judgment, even threatened to undermine his dedication to art. But in the end the creative and familial constellations reinforced one another, for Beethoven understood his action to become the boy's sole guardian as another form of self-denial, a burden undertaken by him as an acolyte of divinity: "Regard K[arl] as your own child," he wrote, "disregard all idle talk, all pettiness for the sake of this holy cause. . . . Your present condition is hard for you, but the one above, O He is, without Him is nothing. In any event the sign has been accepted" (nos. 80–81).

III

Beethoven searched world literature, mythology, art, philosophy, and religion for creeds that would justify so extreme a set of restrictions on ordinary human activity, to confirm the rightness of his choices. His readings in Homer, Schiller, Kant, and Herder, in the ancient classical writers and the modern Romantics, and in Brahman and Masonic texts provided a mosaic of ideas that gave voice to his own sentiments, offering guidance, wisdom, and the solace necessary for one who has accepted a stoical solution to the unyielding existential questions. Determined to leave his mark upon the world, he accepted the exhortation of the *Bhagavad-Gita:*

> Let not thy life be spent in inaction. Depend upon application, perform thy duty, abandon all thought of the consequence, and make the event equal, whether it terminate in good or evil; for such an equality is called *Yōg,* attention to what is spiritual.

(no. 64b)

Blind Homer, as always, remained an inspiring mentor to the deaf composer:

> Let me not sink into the dust unresisting and inglorious,
> But first accomplish great things, of which future generations too shall hear!

(no. 49; *Iliad* 22.303–5)

Herder warned of the dangers attendant on such great endeavors, prescribing courage: "Risk everything, then! What God has granted to you, nobody can rob you of. Indeed, he granted it to you, to you, brave man" (no. 56; "Das Leben der Menschen"). The Masonic-Catholic dramatist Zacharias Werner enjoined him to seek "The great good of self-completion in creating! / You are the mirror image of the Eternal" (no. 60d; *Die Söhne des Thals*).

Also copied into his Tagebuch are extracts from Sir William Jones's vedic "Hymn to Narayena," with its appeal to the supreme deity to raise the poet's soul to heights of ecstasy:

> Oh! Guide my fancy right,
> Oh! raise from cumbrous ground
> My soul in rapture drown'd,
> That fearless it may soar on wings of fire.

(no. 62)

Thus, Beethoven chose art over life precisely because, for him, art provided plentiful compensations here and hereafter that were unavailable by other means. Music, though its creation required great sacrifices, was not itself a sacrificial burden. Rather, it offered innumerable strategies of prolongation to fend off forebodings of a darkening horizon. Through music Beethoven could locate and limn realms of permanence, constantly renewable, impervious to forces of decay and disintegration. Through music he could create impregnable, unified structures; describe endless forms of transcendence over hostile energies; inscribe narratives of return, refinding, and rebeginning; forge a channel between himself and a forbearing deity; invoke the healing powers of music. He could guarantee felicitous outcomes, overcome extreme odds, declare himself—and us—victors in every deadly game. In his music Beethoven could create ecstasies so powerful that they momentarily eradicated fear—or at least made it endurable. That some might regard such matters as merely symbolic, and therefore both illusory and transient, might well be immaterial to a true believer, to one who had experienced the full might of music as a palpable reality.[4]

IV

At the same time, out of sight, a deep transformation of Beethoven's world outlook was under way, accompanying or preparing the way for the transformations of music's capabilities that were emerging in his mind. The sea change in Beethoven's thought affected every facet of his intellectual, ideological, and spiritual temperament. Politically, this involved his turn from a fairly conventional radical humanism, shaped by the Josephinian *Aufklärung,* the French Enlightenment, and antityrannical currents in literature and philosophy, to a less sanguine view (famously touched by disillusion) of princely or imperial saviors and political solutions. As an artist, Beethoven revealed an increasing affinity with some of the dominant categories and preoccupations of early Romanticism, an affinity strikingly exemplified in his adoption of certain of Romanticism's imaginative tropes and phenomenological metaphors. One may also find in the fragmentary aesthetic pronouncements and comments that are sprinkled throughout Beethoven's letters and conversation books a rough tapestry of neoclassical, classical, and romantic ideas that increasingly highlight his participation in romantic expressive theories and his deep identification with such central concepts of Romanticism as the infinite, yearning, nostalgia, and inwardness.

The tension between Beethoven's Classicist and Romanticist tendencies can be viewed as beginning with a detachment from an Olympian, Winckelmannian conception of Classicism, in place of which Beethoven, in the major works of his "heroic" style, constructed a restless Classicism now imbued with a broad range of extreme images centering on death, struggle, memorialization, elegy, and festal celebration. In his music Beethoven implied—perhaps even argued—the necessity of restoring to Classicism the fusion of Apollonian decorum and Dionysian violence that Schiller and Friedrich Schlegel had shown to have been thoroughly commingled in the ancient world, a fusion to which Nietzsche—in good part via his reading of Beethoven's Ninth Symphony—was to give its lapidary expression later in the nineteenth century. Beethoven's conception of pastoral, too, as exemplified especially in the G-major Violin Sonata, op. 96, may be interpreted as moving toward a restoration of the full range of classical pastoral experience that Virgil, Bion, and Theocritus had known, including its Elegiac and Bacchic strains, thereby rescuing musical pastoral from its ongoing slide into a picturesque, devitalized celebration of the bucolic. I will propose that Beethoven was deeply involved in a quest to preserve essential qualities of the ancient world, that this quest for a renovated Classicism is itself a defining characteristic of Romanticism, and that participation in this endeavor may qualify Beethoven as a representative of a "Renaissance impulse" in music. Thus, for example, the Seventh Symphony's deployment of a variety of musical analogues of classical poetic rhythms and meters arguably is a token of his participation in the Classic-Romantic revalidation of the cultural, ethical, and aesthetic premises of Antiquity.

Of equal interest are many striking indications of Beethoven's participation in the ideas of Speculative Freemasonry, a loose agglomeration of moral, philosophical, pseudoscientific, mythic, and religious doctrines associated with an arcane symbolism and drawn in large measure from universal features of the world religions, past and present. My identification of some hitherto obscure passages in his Tagebuch revealed Beethoven's surprising familiarity with and espousal of remote and ancient religious conceptions, documenting his interest in esoteric ritual practices of the religions of the East and the Antique, and his fascination with amorphous descriptions of the attributes of a supreme being. His erudition may be somewhat more apparent than real, for the core imagery and practices of the exotic religions were widely described in the literature of the Freemasons and other advanced fraternal societies such as the Order of Illuminati. Still, the range of Beethoven's references—some fleeting, some more extensive—to the mystery religions of the East and the

Mediterranean is impressive, touching as they do on the Egyptian-Saitic-Osirian, Orphic-Eleusinian, Cabiric-Samothracian, Brahman-Indian, Delphic, and Bacchic-Dionysian. These seem to add up to an ecumenical, Deistic view of the sacred that opens up the spectrum of feelings that accompany ideas of initiation into ever higher states of being or of entry to a sacrosanct place—feelings of awe, the uncanny, the supernatural, and other untranslatable extreme states usually identified with mystical and ecstatic varieties of religious experience. That may be why some of his Tagebuch entries—along with references to exotic and Eastern religions in his correspondence and conversation books—can be read as the chronicle of a conversion, and Beethoven's most affecting outcries in the diary as signs of a convert's struggle to be relieved of sin by providing proof of his striving for righteousness.[5]

V

I have stressed Beethoven's interest in two overarching and sometimes intersecting constellations of thought—Romanticism and Freemasonry, but there are many other perspectives from which to view Beethoven's sea change, and all of them taken together are surely insufficient to understand so momentous a turn in the workings of his mind. There is no identifiable main ingredient in these new departures, which draw from a heady mixture of sources, including comparative religion, mythology, classical and contemporary literature, and survivals of fragmenting Enlightenment thought systems. Considerable weight should nevertheless be given to the mediation of Freemasonry and of the emergent Romantic school and its main representatives, for they were prime conduits for the conveyance of many transformative ideas and images derived from ritual, initiation, and the sacred.

Beethoven is not to be regarded as the sum of his intellectual influences; his sources are themselves fluid, constantly evolving, reciprocally open to influence. He himself generates ideas and is a wellspring of creative imagery, an essential source of Romanticism itself, and not merely of Romantic music. For better or worse, he is one of those who poses the crucial questions and provides the normative prescriptions of what the arts can achieve or ought to say. He creates important aspects of the Romanticist view of the world; in his person he exemplifies the survival of the Illuminist moral-political ideal, disconnected from its historical context, and long after the suppression and fragmentation of the Order that had given rise to it. In the aftermath of the Enlightenment, he became an active agent in the configuration of a deeply individual, and utterly vital, world outlook.

The more interesting challenge, then, is not simply to locate the sources of Beethoven's intellectual and spiritual enrichment in his last years but to try to grasp the expansion of his productive powers afforded by his increased accessibility and receptivity to a broad repertory of highly imaginative conceptions. Beethoven had gained access to a bottomless pool of imagery with which to depict the hitherto undescribed, to enlarge the expressiveness of musical rhetoric and the communicative potentialities inherent in musical form itself, even to invent structures both organicist and dissociative whose very configurations were themselves laden with significance. A multitude of productive images had been placed in the service of music by a mysterious process operating within the alembic of his creativity. They provided kindling for the blaze of Beethoven's imagination.

This book will offer evidence of a reshaping of Beethoven's way of experiencing and thinking about the world as he moved into his full maturity. It will also try to draw some possible implications for the music, with extended treatments of selected late compositions and others that are transitional to— or in search of—the late style. There is no attempt to treat the late works systematically or exhaustively; rather, discussions of them are used primarily to highlight signs of the dovetailing of Beethoven's thought and creative imagination during this period of their rapid mutual expansion and metamorphosis. The discussions are also intended to remind us of alternative implications, of the almost limitless range of interpretations and of their capacity for coexistence. My aim is to open the subject for further inspection, to offer some fragmentary ideas of potential directions that may be worth exploring rather than to foreclose or preempt the course of the investigation.

Whether the metamorphosis in Beethoven's thought was a necessary precondition of his late style is a subject for serious reflection. Certainly, it remains to be fully demonstrated that Beethoven's post-1810 intellectual and spiritual preoccupations were, for him, permanent and transformative possessions, and that his encounter with the initiatory dimension was a crucial factor in expanding his imaginative reach. But it would be shortsighted to believe that the far-ranging shifts in Beethoven's late musical style, rhetoric, and conceptions of form were wholly unrelated to the seismic shifts in his system of beliefs.

CHAPTER ONE

THE END OF A BEGINNING:
THE "DIABELLI" VARIATIONS

For Lewis Lockwood

Now may be an appropriate time to reexamine an old notion in the literature on the "Diabelli" Variations, namely that Beethoven, initially scornful of so impoverished a theme, was persuaded to use it despite its triviality, and went on to demonstrate what implications could be drawn from such unpromising material. To give two examples out of many: in his classic book on Beethoven, Walter Riezler found the theme to be "entirely insignificant," but "expounded with incredible versatility";[1] and in his exemplary monograph on the "Diabelli" Variations, William Kinderman described Opus 120 as Beethoven's "only major work to have found its origin in the commonplace, a static, repetitious, and thoroughly banal theme," underscoring "the apparent absurdity of building a monumental edifice upon such slight foundations."[2]

Naturally, the contrast between the theme and Beethoven's elaboration of it was observed from the very beginning, with Adolf Bernhard Marx writing in 1830 that "a sort of mischievousness or high spirits" had "led [Beethoven] to grasp a wholly agreeable but nevertheless wholly insignificant waltz and to use the same as a veritable mine of new ideas."[3] Even the publishers' announcement in the *Wiener Zeitung* in 1823 stressed that "this work is the more interesting because of the fact that it is elicited from a theme which no one would otherwise have supposed capable of a working-out of that character in which our exalted Master stands alone among his contemporaries."[4] Diabelli, however, saw no reason to apologize for his theme; quite the contrary—the announcement declares, "We are proud to have given occasion for this composition." It was, then, left to Beethoven's notoriously unreliable biographer, Anton Schindler, to inaugurate the legend that

Beethoven himself regarded Diabelli's waltz as trivial or even ludicrous. Schindler claimed that the composer initially declined to participate in a collective set of variations on it because he felt that the theme, with its "cobbler's patches"—exact transpositions of a sequence up one step, called rosalias or *Schusterflecken*—"would leave the contributors open to ridicule."[5] Nevertheless, "not long after this categorical refusal," Schindler recalled, Beethoven asked him to find out how much Diabelli was willing to pay for a full set of variations on the theme, and he reported that the composer was so "happily surprised" at the prospect of receiving the "unusually high price" of eighty ducats that he reversed himself, and even became eager "to demonstrate what could be done with an ordinary waltz, and even with a 'rosalia.'"[6] But Beethoven's top asking price, documented in a letter to the publisher, was actually only half that amount;[7] and Schindler's account is defective in every other respect as well, misstating the planned number of variations as well as both the time and the place of composition, and getting the date of the project's initiation wrong by more than four years.[8] Clearly, he had no firsthand knowledge of the work's genesis, so his unsupported claim that Beethoven viewed the theme with contempt may safely be written off as an invention.

Of course, the theme has also had its eminent defenders, beginning with the very first reviewer, writing in 1823, who perceived "something simply remarkable in its construction and working out,"[9] continuing with Heinrich Rietsch's observation that because of the theme's "simple, clear construction, the lightly imprinted harmonic sequences provide a welcome playground for further creative fantasy,"[10] and culminating in Donald Francis Tovey's famous observation that the theme is "rich in solid musical facts from whatever point of view it is taken," cast in "reinforced concrete," as he put it, a prosaic theme that "sets the composer free to build recognizable variations in every conceivable way."[11] Despite Tovey's authority, the primary narrative about Opus 120 that we have inherited continues to deny the seriousness, not only of the work's theme, but of Beethoven's purposes. Told from Schindler's unimaginative, narrow perspective, this story trivializes Beethoven's motives, which are reduced to a composer's vanity, whimsy, and greed, and we are foreclosed from asking about the significance of the theme and how it may be essential to alternative ways of understanding the work. Perhaps, given a statement of aesthetic assumptions, Diabelli's theme really can be shown to be trivial, banal, or musically defective, or even all three. The more fruitful issue, how-

EXAMPLE 1.1.   Theme of "Diabelli" Variations, op. 120.

ever, is not its perceived triviality, but what it may be capable of representing. Looked at more closely, it may turn out to be as rich in symbolic implications as Tovey found it to be in musical facts. We may eventually come to see it as an unusual waltz, pellucid, brave, utterly lacking in sentimentality or affectation.[12] At the least, it represents a beginning, a point of departure, and this, in itself, may be a matter of some importance (ex. 1.1).

II

We know Beethoven by his beginnings—by themes, figures, rhythmic patterns, harmonic motifs, and sonic textures that instantly establish something essential about the character of a composition, that set out a range of possibilities for what is to follow, that arouse expectations that will be fulfilled or frustrated, that provide apertures of particularity through which we may glimpse, enter, and begin to explore worlds we never knew, let alone made. I use a geographical image here, for there is an inimitable, metaphorical way in which music may evoke geographies, terrains, locations, places. Partly, this has to do with the ways in which musical genres, even apart from their use of conventional topics and characteristic styles, may remain associated with their original social functions and conditions of patronage. Thus, the opening of a Mass or requiem has the capability of conveying us in imagination to those enclosures in which sacred music is customarily performed; the first measures of a serenade tell us that we are outdoors, that it is evening, that we are celebrating a ritual occasion in a pastoral locale; the first notes of a string quartet or keyboard sonata move us indoors—into a connoisseur's salon or, later, a concert hall; the rhythmic gesture of minuet and gavotte, contredanse and waltz bring to mind a great variety of spaces, from court, theater, band shell, and ballroom to the bourgeois interior.

Sometimes a beginning may connect us to something much less tangible even than a suggested sense of place, but its connective powers are nevertheless fully in play. Such openings tell us to expect nothing more than that the work is to be an example of a particular style. Even here, we are "placed": we find ourselves on familiar terrain simply because we are reminded of the sound of another composer; we are "in" Haydn or "in" Mozart, or perhaps "in" a denoted, recognizable subdivision of Classical style, therefore set within the borders of a tradition. Parody, quotation, and stylistic imitation are ways of locating us in time, or space, or tradition, ways of affirming or denying connections to the already existent, to the known. Analogously, the start of a work—say, the Sonata in C minor, op. 111, or the Grosse Fuge, op. 133—may bear the inimitable stamp of the hand that wrote it, summoning up images of the real or rumored workshop of its own composer, inviting us to use biographical knowledge (or legend) as a compass.

It is a question of orientation: the imagination is set in motion, taking the hint, seeking to find its bearings, asking directions, aiming to convert a mysteriously fluid stream of sound into some semblance of solid ground or recognizable terrain. Of course, it goes without saying that these are imaginary landscapes. Nevertheless, they make it possible for us to situate ourselves, to fulfill our need to know where we are in order to offset the sense of the uncanny that comes from the shock of crossing a threshold to another world. And even if we do not know where we are, we need some signpost by which we can estimate our distance from the known. It is a matter of being either at home or away, or—sideslipping into a different set of metaphors—safe or imperiled, celebrating one's own traditions or witnessing strange rituals. That may be why many listeners often feel an impulse to invent programs and literary prototypes for musical compositions—somehow to diminish the anxiety, terror, and loneliness that may be aroused by the musical evocation of an unrecognizable time and place.

In the openings of certain of his greatest works, Beethoven deliberately eradicates the implication of a safe haven. Instead, reckless of his listeners' comfort, he turns from validating the expected to inventing places where no one has ever gone before, in beginnings that suggest heightened, altered, and anxious states. These imply not safety but terror; not the comfort of an earthly pastoral but the remote sublimity of the immeasurable heavens; not the warm Arcadian greensward but distant, astral, or enigmatic regions, as for example in the opening of the Symphony No. 4 in B-flat, op. 60 (ex. 1.2).

We can hereafter forgo the geographical simile—which has perhaps been stretched a bit beyond its appropriate limits. For by now Beethoven has shifted the metaphorical terrain from recognizable locations in nature or society to unplumbed reaches of the universe and to those "psychical localities" that are the scene of action of dreams, fantasies, and every representation of the imaginary.[13] He does this, for example, in the openings of the Fourth, Fifth, Seventh, and Ninth symphonies, not to affirm the chaotic and the strange but to demonstrate more powerfully the importance of overcoming them, in scenarios of desire, estrangement, and humiliation that eventuate in fulfillment, reconciliation, and convalescence.

Such works often are structured according to the ineluctable logic of clarification and familiarization. In stark contrast, most sets of classical variations open in the sphere of the recognizable, the familiar. The theme is given, taken for granted. When we hear the opening of a work like the Six Variations in G on Paisiello's "Nel cor più non mi sento," WoO 70, or the Variations in E-flat for Cello and Piano on Mozart's "Bei Männern, welche

EXAMPLE 1.2.   Symphony No. 4 in B-flat, op. 60, Adagio, mm. 1–14.

Liebe fühlen," WoO 46, we already know this music, whether it is as a folk song or a popular aria from a fashionable opera; the drawing card of such works is usually a melody already pleasantly engraved in our minds, as in all of Beethoven's sets of variations from the 1790s (ex. 1.3).

Or, at least, we know its type; so that when Beethoven unfolds his "wholly new manner" in 1802, opening his Opus 34 Variations with a nostalgic Adagio instead of a hit tune, or his Opus 35 with the skeletal bass of a Haydnesque theme that has yet to materialize, or, later on, his C-minor Variations, WoO 80, with a dramatic variant of "La Folia," we do not experience these original themes as alien or disruptive, even though we recognize the daring of the composer having abandoned thematic ready-mades, fresh off the rack.

From this admittedly restricted standpoint, we may say that, embedded in the formal structures of Beethoven's late works are two great arcs of experience, in both of which he sought to inscribe, from opposite perspectives, chronicles of illumination and achievement. One arc begins from a dangerous—at least, unfamiliar—territory or state of being and makes its way to safety by a circuitous route; the other takes its point of departure in

EXAMPLE 1.3.   Six Variations for Piano on Paisiello's "Nel cor più non mi sento," WoO 70, mm. 1–8.

the familiar, which is then disassembled, chaoticized, deconstructed, and de-familiarized before it, in turn, rediscovers an ultimate state of concord.

It is evident to which of these arcs the "Diabelli" Variations belongs. Thus, it should not be a surprise that this set of variations opens with a familiar theme-type—a German dance or waltz, or *Ländler*—one that is redolent of the commonplace, the here and now, the solidly present, the factual rather than the fanciful. And it should not occasion surprise that Beethoven chose to use such a theme for a major experimental work of his last period. The theme designates a beginning, launched from the terrain of the familiar. More closely, it can be seen to represent a special kind of reference to the quotidian. The issue now becomes whether we are able, with more specificity, to come closer to the meaning of this particular embodiment of the quotidian.

III

I already have touched on how a composer may signify the familiar as a referential musical image. In doing so, Beethoven may have been appropriating to his purposes an idea of the familiar as a trope of poetic invention that was widespread among his contemporaries. The English Romantic poets, especially, were much concerned with dichotomies between the familiar and the unknown, defining the role of the poet as aiming to reveal the latter through an exploration of the former. In "A Defence of Poetry," Shelley wrote that poetry strips the veil of familiarity from the world, and lays bare the naked and sleep-ing beauty, which is the spirit of its forms. . . . It makes us the inhabitants of a world to which the familiar world is a chaos. It reproduces the common universe of which we are portions and percipients, and it purges from our inward sight the film of familiarity which obscures from us the wonder of our being. It compels us to feel that which we perceive, and to imagine that which we know. It creates anew the universe, after it has been annihilated in our minds by the recurrence of impressions blunted by reiteration.[14]

It is not only a question of defamiliarization, but of discovery and renewal, for in addition to lifting the veil from "the hidden beauty of the world," poetry "awakens and enlarges the mind itself by rendering it the receptacle of a thousand unapprehended combinations of thought."[15] But where can the poet locate those familiar objects? Wordsworth's famous prescription was to turn to the "humble and rustic," and there "to choose incidents and sit-uations from common life, and to . . . throw over them a certain colouring of imagination, whereby ordinary things should be presented to the mind in an unusual aspect."[16]

Similar ideas were part of the fabric of German thought as well. Novalis described the need for chaos to "shimmer through the regular veil of order-liness" and referred to the "delight in revealing in the world what is beyond the world."[17] It is only a short step to Wordsworth's "humble and rustic" from Herder's conception of poetry as a reflection of immediate life, his valorization of the folk and of folk art, his view that a vital national litera-ture and language should keep "one foot on German earth."[18] If the idea of the familiar opens on the quotidian, the sphere of the quotidian itself opens, not only on the humble, the popular, the rustic, and every manifes-tation of the ordinary, but on larger issues of identity as well. That such ques-tions may be implicated in the "Diabelli" Variations may come to seem more probable when we look at some details of the origination and publication of Beethoven's Opus 120.

IV

Sometime between early 1819 and early 1821, Diabelli conceived the idea of commissioning variations on his waltz as a collective project involving

numerous Viennese composers. Beethoven proceeded on his own, well before the collective set was under way, working without any commitment to
Diabelli, and composed almost two-thirds of his variations by mid-1819; he
revised and completed the work in late 1822 and early 1823 shortly after
concluding an agreement for its publication. Entitled "Thirty-Three Variations on a Waltz for Pianoforte," and dedicated to his intimate friend Antonie Brentano, Beethoven's "Diabelli" Variations was rushed into print in
June 1823 as a separate work, Opus 120, from the house of Cappi and Diabelli. One year later, on publication of the set of fifty variations on the
theme by fifty composers, Beethoven's opus was republished as part 1 of a
two-volume set bearing the unusual and cumbersome heading, "Vater-
ländischer Künstlerverein." The newspaper advertisement described the set:

> *National Association of Artists*
> Variations for the Pianoforte,
> on a Given Theme,
> Composed by the Most Excellent Composers and Virtuosi
> in Vienna and the I. & R. Austrian States.
> Part I, containing 33 Variations by L. van Beethoven, op. 120 . . .
> Part II, containing 50 Variations on the same theme by the following
> composers . . . [19]

The announcement explained that "all the noted living national composers
and piano virtuosos, fifty in number, had joined together for the purpose of
each writing one variation on one and the same theme placed before them."
In the context of such an appeal to national pride one aspect of the theme's
significance becomes somewhat clearer, for a waltz, interchangeably called
"Ein Deutsche" or "Deutscher Tanz," is a plain musical product of German
soil. Beethoven's first reference to the set in his correspondence described
it as "Große Veränderungen über einen bekannten 'Deutschen'"—"Grand
Variations on a well-known German dance."[20]

On an uncomplicated level, then, the theme, composed by Diabelli in
contemporary German musical vernacular and taken as the point of departure of Beethoven's variations, represents the homeland through its native
language. And this is consistent with Beethoven's attraction to conceptions
of a national culture in the years following his disillusionment with France
and its First Consul. As early as 1812 he exalted creative artists as "teachers

of the nation,"[21] and after 1815 he began increasingly to use German-language expression marks and titles in place of the customary Italian, including designations like *Hammerklavier* for his Piano Sonatas opp. 101, 106, and 109, and *Veränderungen* rather than the Italian-derived *Variationen* for the "Diabelli" Variations.[22] I do not mean to suggest, however, that nationalist or patriotic motives are more than peripheral to Beethoven's intentions, for it is clear enough that the formulation of the collective project was Diabelli's rather than Beethoven's. After all, he worked independently of Diabelli in drafting his own set, and the first and post-1824 editions of Opus 120 make no reference to the Künstlerverein.[23] What interested Beethoven more deeply, I suspect, are issues flowing from the very idea of representing the quotidian and, in particular, the possibilities of utilizing an image drawn from the German vernacular as a point of departure for a metaphysical exploration.

V

In Diabelli's German dance, his "Deutsche," Beethoven happened upon a subject that was drawn from "common life" in Wordsworth's sense, and embodied the national in Herder's sense. But Diabelli's theme has both a more extensive and a more elusive kind of referentiality, quickly exhausting the kinds of simple denotation suggested by Wordsworth or Herder, and expanding through a nebula of associations that rise from the initial moment of referentiality and overflow boundaries in all directions. Thus, to dip randomly into this reservoir of possibilities, Diabelli's theme conveys ideas, not only of the national, the commonplace, the humble, the rustic, the comic, but of the mother tongue, the earthly, the sensuous, and, ultimately, perhaps, of every waltzing couple under the sun.

The bedrock of this ordinariness may be in its implied celebration of the merely human, which Diabelli's theme is perfectly suited to symbolize because it is the approximate equivalent in music of what Erich Auerbach once described in connection with Dante's language as the "humblest vernacular."[24] As such, the theme has the potentiality to designate all those who are in need of redemption, all who are unnoticed, disinherited, or in quest of plenitude. We may number among those who are signified by these thirty-two bars, then, the shepherd, the child, the good soldier, the pilgrim, Parsifal, Tyll Eulenspiegel, the minstrel called "der lieber Augustin," Pirate Jenny,

Leporello and Zerlina, and the widest assortment of clowns, simpletons, and ordinary stiffs who, because of their place at the bottom of the heap, have the capacity of surviving and of trying to set things right. And to these we can add the lowly "cobbler" himself, the much-maligned shoemaker who manufactures those boots and shoes so vital to walkers on the road of life, and whose clumsy "Schusterflecken," Beethoven once wrote laughingly, have the potential to be turned into works of art, if only one knows how—and, presumably, if one has the wit and the capacity to stick to one's last.[25]

In other words, by virtue of its ordinariness, not to be mistaken for triviality, this theme, this beginning that Beethoven chose for his Opus 120, is suited to unpacking issues of firstness and lastness and their interchangeability. The purpose of this vernacular beginning may be to show us a lastness that calls not only for variation and metamorphosis but for transvaluation and reversal. The "Diabelli" Variations may be a version of pastoral in William Empson's sense, in which—to use Kenneth Burke's bold paraphrase—is designated "that subtle reversal of values whereby the last becomes first. They do this, not by assuming the qualities of the first, but by suggesting the firstness implicit in their lastness." Those who have been cast down may be uplifted, "not by renouncing their humbleness, but by affirming it, until out of it there arises the prophetic truth."[26]

By its utter indestructibility, its imperviousness to perpetual attempts to dismantle it, Diabelli's theme comes to stand for the unwearying tenacity of every individual, and gives token of assurance of a permanent place in the order of things. The "Diabelli" Variations is not a conjurer's trick demonstrating how an unlikely edifice can be built upon an absurd foundation. It is a demonstration of a different kind: how one thing can be radically transformed into another—or split into many—without itself being annihilated; it is an essay on creative metamorphosis and a promise of endurance.

VI

Many of Beethoven's memorable beginnings are declarations of discontinuity. Consider the first measures of the *Eroica*, Fifth, Seventh, Eighth, and Ninth symphonies, and of the "Pathétique," "Appassionata," and "Hammerklavier" sonatas, to name only some of the more obvious examples. But Beethoven is not always interested in rhetorical initiating gestures or world-

EXAMPLE 1.4.   String Quartet in A minor, op. 132, Assai sostenuto, mm. 1–8.

birthing starts. Frequently in the late sonatas and quartets he wants us to join him in overhearing events that are already ongoing; he is the brooding observer, inviting us to share what he has seen, to let this music enter us, unresisting. Such works may begin imperceptibly, creeping into existence, gradually emerging from stillness, as in the opening of the String Quartet in A minor, op. 132. In these beginnings, Beethoven slips into a parallel universe, which unfolds without demanding either a break or a confrontation (ex. 1.4).[27]

It may be that the Diabelli theme blends both kinds of beginnings. It offers both a continuation and a new start. Yes, it has suddenly sprung into existence, but it has not required any forcible event, let alone a shock, to announce its presence. It is *there* because its very nature is to be present. Perhaps it has always been there. It inaugurates activity, it sets things in motion; it sets the scene. It authorizes us to begin. In this sense it is a prologue rather than—or as well as—a beginning; in other words, it is a beginning before a beginning.

Well, then, for better or worse, we may have made a beginning. We now know a bit more about how this music starts, where it comes from, and even something of what the theme may signify. But a beginning also demands a continuation and a goal. What, then, is the end of this beginning? In asking this question, we perhaps approximate Beethoven's own question, one that took him four years to settle. In the "Diabelli" Variations, Beethoven knows the beginning right from the start, and he is in search of something beyond it—implication, potentiality, something worth searching for. The point of departure ought somehow to make possible the discovery of a point—a moment, or a locus—of arrival.

VII

On reflection, it seems to me that the philosopher Ernst Bloch was only partially right when he wrote in the opening words of his *The Principle of Hope,* "We begin empty *[Wir fangen leer an]*."[28] If my reading of Diabelli's theme has any validity, it suggests that we can also begin in a limited state of plenitude, imbued with the earth's simple pleasures, unaware, however, of such things as beauty and spirit, passion, despair, and death; which is to say, all those things that lie beyond a state of undisturbed innocence, real or imagined. The "Diabelli" Variations tells of dissatisfaction with qualified pleasures and simplicities, urges the necessity of going further, of delving and plunging and climbing and seeking in realms that do not appear in the lives or the dreams of thoroughly contented folks (or of ordinary music). It is not a willed dissatisfaction; rather, it rises from the essential nature of those—Faust, Don Giovanni, Egmont, Beethoven—who are driven to go further, even as it causes them enormous pain, even as it opens onto dangers of unnecessary journeys and brings them face to face with mortality.

From innocence to knowledge, earth to Paradise, the human to the infinite. These are some of the metaphors that are put into play by Beethoven's Opus 120. I don't believe, however, that its overarching metaphor is just a variant of Schiller's and Rousseau's scenarios of alienation and reconciliation; Beethoven doesn't here seek a return to nature or the classic, he seeks wisdom, ecstasy, the empyrean, whatever the cost. He will not settle for a bustling waltz, even with all that it symbolizes. Nor will he reject it. Rather, he will use it, seeing in the cobbler's patches—which propel us unceremoniously up the scale with neither preparation nor apology—the emblems of emergence, of ascent, of every potential upward pathway, however daunting, that leads from the quotidian to the celestial.

He uses it because this theme, this beginning, sets up the possibility of mobilizing every conceivable metaphor of maximum contrast—the miniature and the boundless, the blade of grass and the starry vault, the earthly and the unearthly, the profane and the sacred, the lowliest and the divine. Diabelli's theme and its fraternal twin, Leporello's buffo "Notte e giorno

EXAMPLE 1.5.   "Diabelli" Variations, no. 22, mm. 1–8.

EXAMPLE 1.6.   "Diabelli" Variations, no. 24, mm. 1–9.

faticar"—not coincidentally, the "beginning" of *Don Giovanni,* act 1, scene 1—are accorded equal time with a devotional fughetta that might have issued from Bach's Goldberg Variations (exx. 1.5, 1.6).

By the use of extreme registral contrasts, Beethoven extends to its furthest limits the distance between the theme and its spiritualized metamorphosis. And he accelerates the animated character of the theme in a variety of prestos, vivaces, and allegro assais, which convey the sense of hastening toward a desired destination, as in variation no. 10. But as the narrative continues, we also begin to encounter moments in which the action is greatly decelerated, approaching ever closer to motionlessness in such later variations as no. 20.

In the end, this set of variations abandons none of the terrain it has traversed, the terrain that lies between Diabelli's humble "Deutsche" and a composer's astonishing vision of a transfigured universe. All of it is necessary; no part of it is sufficient. It describes a long journey, this Pilgrim's Progress on a Biedermeier waltz (as I once called it).[29] A voyager pauses on his way, reflects, looks back whence he came, measures the distance from his starting point and estimates the distance yet to be covered. The implied protagonist of Beethoven's "Diabelli" Variations looks back to the theme, which is the link to the home that he left in favor of an arduous pursuit of every conceivable metaphor for a desired goal—toward God, Paradise, reason, wisdom, order, peace, achievement, perfection, healing, and love. Setting aside inexact poetic analogies, however, we may want to say that although Beethoven's Opus 120 may be about many things, it is always a set of studies in musical transformation. Beethoven called it "Veränderungen"—implying changes, metamorphoses, rather than *Variationen*—with good reason.

One might expect that ultimately it is about the transformation of a waltz into a fugue, in Variation 32; and this would be appropriate as the traditional way of ending a work in the learned style, of marking an arrival, and of reinforcing its sacred implications. But Beethoven defeats the traditional expectation and chooses to close with a wordless song, a spectral dance in tempo di menuetto, moderato, marked *grazioso e dolce.* In the long run, then, the "Diabelli" Variations seems to be about the transformation of an earthly waltz into a celestial minuet. From a seemingly inconsequential starting point, Beethoven's wayfarer entered the ascending path, reached toward perfection, encountered loss and the prospect of death, and was overcome by homesickness for the beginning as the last days came dimly into view. The

EXAMPLE 1.7.   "Diabelli" Variations, no. 33, mm. 1–5.

thirty-third variation is introduced by a Poco adagio that breaks the fugue's agitated momentum and finally takes us to the brink of utter motionlessness, providing a curtain to separate the fugue from the minuet and serving to introduce the final image—of a tender, songful, profound nostalgia, a vantage point from which we can review the purposes of the entire journey (ex. 1.7).

CHAPTER TWO

BEYOND CLASSICISM

It was once presumed to be common knowledge that Beethoven was a founder of the Romantic movement in music, and that his works influenced most of the Romantic composers and were the models against which nineteenth-century Romanticism measured its achievements and failures. However, the issue of Beethoven's place in the turn from Classicism to Romanticism not only has been the subject of some controversy but has undergone several extreme pendulum swings over the course of time. The question is by no means settled, and it may be helpful to take stock of it, for it has an important bearing on whether we perceive and perform his works primarily as outgrowths of eighteenth-century traditions and performance practices or as auguries of fresh traditions in the process of formation.

The initial articulation of Beethoven's romanticism was in large part the work of nineteenth-century composers and literary figures: it was through the writings of E. T. A. Hoffmann, Bettina Brentano von Arnim, Alphonse de Lamartine, Victor Hugo, Hector Berlioz, and Richard Wagner that Beethoven came to be viewed as the originator of the Romantic movement in music and as its most representative and influential composer. Even during the nineteenth century, however, informed musical opinion increasingly came to stress Beethoven's adherence to Classical techniques and structural principles, so that, by the end of the century, the influential theorist and historian Hugo Riemann defined the Romantics as those composers who "came after Beethoven."[1] For others the issue became a standoff, at best. "In [Beethoven's] works," wrote Tovey's teacher, Hubert Parry, "the classical type of sonata found its ripest perfection, and the romantic impulse, which finally superseded the sonata, found its first decisive expression."[2]

Nevertheless, Hugo and Wagner were rather more influential than the sober music historians, and the view of Beethoven as a Romantic was widely taken for granted, a perception that has persisted in much popular literature on music. But the loose and poetic formulations of French and German Romantics appeared to dissolve under the first sustained examination. This took place in 1927, the centenary year of Beethoven's death, with the publication of Arnold Schmitz's *Das romantische Beethovenbild,* which thoughtfully reconstructed the evolution of the Romantic image of Beethoven and subjected the musical and biographical evidence of his romanticism to close and skeptical scrutiny. Together with several chapters of Ludwig Schiedermair's somewhat earlier *Der junge Beethoven* and a subsequent massively documented monograph by Jean Boyer, *Le 'romantisme' de Beethoven,* Schmitz overturned the accepted notion of Beethoven's romanticism and established the dominant modern view of him as the inheritor of twin traditions—ideologically those of the Enlightenment and musically those of European, especially Viennese, Classicism.[3] Beethoven was seen in both instances as the child of these eighteenth-century traditions rather than as someone who departed from them in some radical or disruptive way.

It was not difficult to uncover Beethoven's roots in the eighteenth century. He grew to maturity in the Habsburg dominions, which were imbued with the spirit of the German *Aufklärung,* a movement fed by a variety of currents, including Enlightenment and Kantian philosophy, and by the ideological outlook of enlightened despotism in its rationalist phase. Beethoven was proud of his adherence to the central tenets of this so-called Josephinian Enlightenment, named after Emperor Joseph II—its idealization of reason, furtherance of reform, critique of superstition, and altruistic commitment to virtue. And, of course, there is much evidence of his pride in belonging to an ongoing musical tradition, one whose roots were mainly in the eighteenth century; he especially worshipped Handel, Bach, Gluck, Mozart and Haydn, intending to place their portraits on his walls.[4] It is scarcely surprising that Beethoven scholarship has been able to accumulate voluminous materials on his sources and influences; or that it has succeeded in demonstrating that a thoroughly assimilated, lucid, and highly structured Classicism persists even in his most adventurous works.

Schmitz used several effective strategies. He showed that Romantic conceptions of Beethoven were riddled with misconceptions and errors. And he found an easy target in the extravagant programmatic interpretations of

Beethoven's music by enthusiastic Romantic writers and musicians. Mainly, however, his strategy was to present a simplified view of Romanticism, portrayed as an irrational and morbid movement, one irrevocably hostile to form. By these yardsticks, Beethoven surely was no Romantic, for he linked art with science as redemptive activities, he neglected no opportunity to praise the powers of reason, he scorned the gravitation of Viennese Romantics to a highly eroticized, mystical Catholicism, and he dissociated himself from the dogmas of the church in both its conventional and revivalist forms.

Just as some Romantics purveyed a myth of the "shallow Enlightenment," chroniclers of Romanticism such as Schmitz purveyed an unmediated conception of an "irrational Romanticism," a conception whose criteria were primarily derived from the more nocturnal characteristics of late Romanticism. That the founding Romantics, especially those centered in Jena, Berlin, and Heidelberg, were drawn to the mysterious, the fantastic, and the irrational, is, of course, not in question; but early Romanticism maintained a precarious balance between rational and arcane views of existence, taking up arms against a diluted and dogmatic pseudorationalism. As Friedrich Schlegel observed in one of the *Lyceum* fragments of 1797, "What's commonly called reason is only a subspecies of it; namely, the thin and watery sort."[5]

So persuasive was Schmitz's critique—and so congruent was it with the historicizing temper of early twentieth-century *Musikwissenschaft*—that the Romanticist position soon was virtually bereft of significant defenders. "The deeper we delve into the essence of Beethoven's music," wrote Walter Riezler in 1936, "the more obvious it is that it belongs to the classical world, and the more clearly it is divided from the romantic."[6] "To count him among the Romanticists," wrote Paul Henry Lang in 1940, "amounts to a fundamental misreading of styles, for Beethoven grew out of the eighteenth-century. . . . What he did was to make a new synthesis of classicism and then hand it down to the new century."[7] Most of the other leading critics of the first half of the twentieth century—including so unlikely a figure as the supposed archromantic Romain Rolland—followed Schmitz's lead. Even where music historians saw in Beethoven impulses toward Romanticism, or Romantic experiments and gestures, or foreshadowings of Romantic developments, they tended to regard him as responding in a fragmentary, unsystematic way to an emergent movement from which he himself remained aloof.

Perhaps the most influential recent elaboration of the Classicist position is in Charles Rosen's *The Classical Style* (1970) and *Sonata Forms* (1980). Surveying Beethoven's stylistic evolution with his customary insight and sensibility, Rosen suggests that although Beethoven's earlier Viennese compositions were written "now in a proto-Romantic style and now in a late and somewhat attenuated version of the classical style" he soon "returned decisively to the closed, concise, and dramatic forms of Haydn and Mozart, expanding these forms and heightening their power without betraying their proportions." For Rosen, Beethoven's harmonic practice "enlarged the limits of the classical style beyond all previous conceptions, but he never changed its essential structure or abandoned it . . . even while using it in startlingly radical and original ways." Contrary to most historians, Rosen finds "no line that can be drawn" between Beethoven's "first and second periods"; he suggests that the *Eroica* Symphony's innovative significance lies in extending "the range of hearing in time" and in carrying Classical procedures "to the outer limits beyond which the language itself would have had to change."[8]

Rosen observes that Beethoven occasionally experimented with Romantic tonality and proportions, especially in several works written during the years of transition to the late style. But he regards these Romantic ventures either as unworthy or, in the case of *An die ferne Geliebte,* op. 98, the song cycle that "stands as the first example of what was the most original and perhaps the most important of romantic forms," as "a sport among his forms." The "Diabelli" Variations, op. 120, is seen as "an investigation of the language of classical tonality," and, in his late music, Beethoven's most "startling innovations" are regarded as taking place "comfortably within the sonata style."[9] Beethoven, then, is best understood as one who extended the musical styles and structures of others—chiefly Haydn and Mozart—and who exercised only marginal influence on the immediately succeeding musical generation because of the highly organized Classical style in which he worked: "The Romantic style did not come from Beethoven, in spite of the great admiration that was felt for him, but from his lesser contemporaries and from Bach."[10]

Lest we misunderstand his powerful argument, one worked out with considerable flexibility and in full awareness of the counterindications, Rosen presents his conclusion aphoristically: "I have treated Beethoven throughout as if he were a late eighteenth-century composer," he writes in *Sonata Forms.*"[11] Joseph Kerman has taken exception to this view, which dislodges Beethoven from many of his contexts and tends to minimize his innovative contributions to musical rhetoric and expressive form.[12] It also tends to make sonata form so dependent on the Classical style that it cannot "be squared with the evolving style or styles of musical romanticism."[13] Nor can Rosen's belief that Beethoven is "intelligible only as a part and extension of the eighteenth-century tradition of sonata style" be easily reconciled with his own observation that the emotional and ideological "climate of his music is that of Napoleonic and post-Napoleonic eras."[14] Kerman objects that "In a symphony called 'heroic' the emotional climate cannot, I believe, be separated off from form and style as clearly as Rosen would like."[15]

Rosen's brief for Beethoven's Classicism tacitly—and rather precariously—depends on his definition of Classical form as the contrast between dramatic tension and stability whose outcome is "the symmetrical resolution of opposing forces"; the reconciliation "of dynamic opposites is at the heart of the classical style."[16] But this is a dialectical formula that Rosen himself suspects is "so broad as to be a definition of artistic form in general."[17] Its capaciousness tends to erase distinctions among works that may well fit comfortably within so accommodating an archetype even though they belong to different universes in other important respects. Of course, no global definition of either Classicism or Romanticism has ever proven wholly satisfactory. Theorists have always been disconcerted to discover that the properties, tropes, and conventions thought to be uniquely characteristic of a given style period are also present in other style periods. Classical, Romantic, Baroque, Mannerist, Modern—every style period has been thrown into question. And each such term is a contested one. A striking example of style-period deflation is what Erwin Panofsky called the "Renaissance-Dämmerung," the increasing tendency by early-twentieth-century medievalists "to contest the very existence of the Renaissance, either *in toto* or in part."[18] In music history, some have concluded from the evidence of cultural continuity that there is no disjunction between Classicism and Romanticism.

Codifying positions earlier formulated by Lang and others, Friedrich Blume held Classicism and Romanticism to be an indivisible phase in music history, "two aspects of the same musical phenomenon just as they are two aspects of one and the same historical period."[19] Within the unified style period that Blume dubs "the Classic-Romantic," Beethoven "occupies but one of the many intermediate positions in the continuing development of this antinomy."[20] Therefore, the question whether Beethoven "should be counted among the Classics or the Romantics, becomes meaningless," for "he was simply both in his own personal way, just as all creative musicians were."[21] Although stressing continuity rather than change, Blume is aware of the novel characteristics of German musical Romanticism. So it remains an open question whether he actually succeeded in abolishing the traditional Classic/Romantic dichotomy or merely in displacing it into two phases of a more extended historical period.

Many continue to see a world of differences between the Classical and the Romantic, discriminations that can be sensed even if they cannot be completely mapped and analyzed.[22] Still, for those who are vexed by apparently unresolvable terminological disputes, Blume's point of view is an attractive one. However, it is because the issues far transcend terminology and nomenclature that the debate over Beethoven's romanticism has thus far been so extraordinarily fruitful. The antiromantic view of Beethoven and his music has enabled us to strip away many of the accretions and falsehoods of extravagant, heroizing biographies; it has given us a more accurate insight into Beethoven's political and ideological outlook and uncovered the complexities of his attitudes toward authority, revealing the irreconcilable tension in his personality between obedience and rebellion. And, in viewing the Beethoven style as a personal fusion of preexistent styles, traditions, and procedures rather than as a demonic or divinely inspired creation *ex nihilo,* it has placed the evolution of his musical style in clearer perspective.

On the debit side, the unqualified view of Beethoven as a Classicist has tended to close off serious consideration of his intellectual and musical receptivity to post-Classical and post-Enlightenment ideas and imagery, thus tending to downplay investigation of the expressive content and symbolic implications of his music. Especially, it has given rise to the tendency to see Beethoven primarily as an inheritor of tradition rather than as a forceful agent in music's evolution. Of course, we can only understand Beethoven's music by documenting its manifold origins; but knowledge of origins cannot exhaust meaning. Moreover, the quest for origins is never-ending precisely because sources have their own sources, and the productive contexts of a complex work of art cannot be fully itemized. Classicizing scholars have collapsed Beethoven's innovations into a few subsets of his music's potential sources, thereby diminishing his uniqueness while simultaneously magnifying the originality of his predecessors, whose own influences are not always subjected to equally close scrutiny. The "heaven-storming" Beethoven thus yields to a more subdued, even a docile Beethoven.

To emphasize in Beethoven the traditional rather than the new, the compliant rather than the disruptive, the origins of his style rather than its originality, has had unexpected consequences, for the question of Beethoven's classicism versus his romanticism, whatever its intrinsic merit, has served as a compact metaphor for the way we perceive his music. The apparently abstract issue turns out to be the surface of an array of aesthetic and ideological subtexts. Thus, refuting Beethoven's romanticism enabled Schmitz to conclude that Beethoven "never created the calling of the free musician in a revolutionary sense. . . . He did not revolutionize the art of music, invented no new artistic methods, laws, or forms, [and] dispensed with the traditional rules of music neither for himself nor for others."[23] Here, Schmitz was adding his voice to a persistent theme of conservative German cultural criticism, a theme already sounded by Wagner, who, at least on one occasion, refused to see Beethoven as a revolutionary composer: "The German nature . . . remodels the form from within, and is thus relieved of the necessity of externally overthrowing it. Germans, consequently, are not revolutionary, but reformist."[24] In our own time, Classicist and formalist views of Beethoven converge with archaicizing trends in performance practice and various commercializations of Beethoven's works to anesthetize us to the impact of his music.

II

Such conservative perceptions of Beethoven would have come as a great surprise to both his supporters and his adversaries in his own time. Contemporary critiques of Beethoven were typically written from the standpoint of what we would now call Classicism—though it was not yet defined as such—reproaching him for perceived violations of normative precepts of order, unity, balance, and decorum. The early reports of Haydn's dissatisfaction with his pupil's Trio, op. 1, no. 3, and his inability to appreciate Beethoven's post-1800 works, may bear on this point, but the professional reviewers were the first to sound this note in print.[25] From the late 1790s they showed keen sensitivity to Beethoven's departures from tradition, especially to his extended tonal trajectories and harmonic idiosyncrasies. In the very first volume of the Leipzig *Allgemeine musikalische Zeitung,* the violin sonatas, op. 12, were said to reveal Beethoven's "search for rare modulations, an aversion to customary [harmonic] relationships"; the reviewer concluded that "Beethoven goes his own path; but what a bizarre and thorny path it is!"[26] Later, in a notorious review, the *Eroica* Symphony was described as "losing itself entirely in lawlessness," containing "too much that is glaring and bizarre, which greatly hinders one's grasp of the whole."[27] A subsequent review of the same work suggested that it urgently required abridgment as well as "more light, clarity and unity."[28] The Allegro assai of the Sonata in F minor, op. 57 ("Appassionata"), was found to be filled with "oddities and bizarreries *[Wunderlichkeiten und Bizarrerien]*"; Beethoven, the critic noted, "has once again unleashed many evil spirits."[29] Expectedly, many of Beethoven's later works were described in similar terms, with the Cello Sonatas, op. 102, held to be "most singular, most strange."[30]

Reviews of Beethoven quartets fairly represent the Classicist perspectives of Beethoven criticism during his lifetime. In August 1801, the *Allgemeine musikalische Zeitung* took note of the first installment of the Opus 18 quartets, which had appeared in Leipzig two months earlier, stressing their learned style and difficulty of execution: "Among the works that have recently appeared . . . three quartets give a conclusive indication of his artistry; however, they must be played frequently, since they are difficult to perform and are in no way popular."[31] The three String Quartets, op. 59 ("Razumovsky"), received only a few inauspicious lines in the *Allgemeine musikalische Zeitung;* the reviewer found them "very long and difficult" and predicted that, with the possible exception of the C-major quartet, they "will not be intelligible to everyone."[32] By 1811, an *Allgemeine musikalische Zeitung* critic, whatever his view of Opus 18 might have been a decade earlier, had now come to regard Beethoven's first six quartets as Classical models, distinguished by "unity, utmost simplicity, and adherence to a specific character in each work . . . which raise them to the rank of masterworks and validate Beethoven's place alongside the honored names of our Haydn and Mozart."[33] In contrast, however, the critic saw the "Razumovsky" quartets as "indulging without consideration in the strangest and most singular whims of [Beethoven's] ingenious imagination," and the String Quartet in E-flat ("Harp"), op. 74, which Breitkopf & Härtel had published in November 1810, as a powerful blend of the bizarre and the fantastic, an amalgam of heterogeneous elements pervaded by a somber and even lugubrious spirit. He reproached Beethoven for trying to express in this quartet sentiments alien to what he conceived to be the nature of the genre, one "which indeed is capable of sweet earnestness and lamenting melancholy but which should not have the goal of celebrating the dead or of picturing feelings of despair; rather, it ought to gladden the heart through the mild, comforting play of the imagination."[34] Clearly, the issue of classical decorum had now spilled over its customary boundaries of concern with issues of formal symmetry, balance, and proportion to disclose its underlying preoccupation with music's expressive content and rhetoric.

Inevitably, Beethoven's late quartets met with great resistance, although by the later 1820s his reputation was such that many reviewers merely alluded to the difficulty of understanding, performing, and appraising his music, tasks they were grateful to leave for their successors. Critics balanced their attacks on Beethoven with obligatory bows to his genius. For example, the *Allgemeine musikalische Zeitung* reviewer of the String Quartet in B-flat, op. 130, described the odd-numbered movements as "grave, mysterious, somber, although also certainly bizarre, harsh, and capricious," and the second and fourth movements as "full of mischief, gaiety, and cunning." But the trite charge of bizarrerie was found insufficient to describe the same critic's disorientation on hearing the Grosse Fuge, which was found to be "incomprehensible, like Chinese," a "confusion of Babel"; and, in a phrase that would have delighted the Dadaists, the concert as a whole was held to be one that "only the Moroccans might enjoy."[35]

The Classicist critique of Beethoven in his own time was scarcely limited to music journalists. Many eminent contemporaries had negative or conflicted reactions to Beethoven's music, including such writers as Goethe, Hegel, and Grillparzer and such composers as Haydn, Zelter, Weber, Spohr, Cherubini, and even Beethoven's greatest—but, for a time, most reluctant—disciple, Schubert. Spohr dismissed the Fifth Symphony with the remark: "Though with many individual beauties, yet it does not constitute a classical whole."[36] Weber felt certain that Beethoven could rise to true greatness "if he would only rein in his exuberant fantasy."[37] "For Goethe," observed Rolland, "Beethoven was the abyss"; upon hearing Mendelssohn play the first movement of the Fifth Symphony on the piano, Goethe was "strangely moved" and said, "It is stupendous, absolutely mad. It makes me almost fear that the house will collapse. And supposing the whole of mankind played it at once!"[38] The young Schubert's rejection of Beethoven turned precisely upon the issues of Classical unity and restraint: an 1816 reference to Beethoven in his private papers disowned the "eccentricity which joins and confuses the tragic with the comic, the agreeable with the repulsive, heroism with howlings and the holiest with harlequinades, without distinction."[39] In a similar vein, Hegel compared the "bacchantic thunder and tumult" of modern music with the "tranquility of soul" to be found in the compositions of the great masters, of whom he mentions none later than Mozart and Haydn. In their music, by way of contrast to Beethoven's, "the resolution is always there; the luminous sense of proportion never breaks down in extremes: everything finds its due place knit together in the whole."[40] Only a few years after his moving oration at Beethoven's funeral, Grillparzer entered in his Tagebuch an indictment of Beethoven's "unfortunate" influence, with particular stress upon the composer's transgressions of "all conception of musical order and unity," his "frequent infractions of rules," and his subordination of beauty to the "powerful, violent, and intoxicating."[41]

In all of these critiques Beethoven's music was measured against an implicit Classical standard whose ideals included lawfulness, objectivity, and moderation; and he was denounced for excessive fantasy, the mingling of styles and affects, and the infringement of traditional rules. Even Beethoven's most loyal students and disciples were placed on the defensive by his perceived iconoclasm. Ignaz Moscheles described how he eventually reconciled himself to Beethoven's "unlooked-for episodes, shrill dissonances, and bold modulations" and admonished that Beethoven's "eccentricities . . . are reconcilable with *his* works alone, and are dangerous models to other composers."[42] Similarly, Carl Czerny wrote that the "so-called irregularities of harmony found in certain of Beethoven's works can be justified and explained on aesthetic grounds. . . . They are suitable only in those places where Beethoven used them"; but he disclaimed such passages as the dissonant horn entrance preceding the recapitulation in the first movement of the *Eroica* Symphony and the development of the *Thème russe* in the scherzo of the String Quartet, op. 59, no. 2: "They are the children of an ingenious love of mischief and a bizarre frame of mind, which often got the better of him."[43]

Of course the later Beethoven also had his Romanticist defenders, who freely acknowledged and rejoiced in his subjectivity, in the free play of his imagination, and in his new organizing conceptions of musical form. Writing in Schlesinger's journal, the *Berliner allgemeine musikalische Zeitung,* which promoted a Romanticist aesthetic, poet Ludwig Rellstab praised the "exaltation and fervor" of the String Quartet in E-flat, op. 127, seeing in it the soul of "the genius who desires only self-realization," whose struggle to express his sufferings evoked "the manly anguish of a Laocoon."[44] In the same journal Adolph Bernhard Marx predicted that future generations would easily learn to comprehend the string quartets in A minor and F, opp. 132 and 135, "in the same way that our contemporaries no longer have difficulties" with Haydn quartets.[45] The Belgian music critic François-Joseph Fétis realized that Beethoven's aims represented a definitive break with those of his predecessors: "He had a different object than to charm the ear by the successive development of some principal phrase, by happy melodies or by beautiful harmonic combinations." Beethoven, he concluded, "found the ordinary forms of music too symmetrical, too conventional, and too proper" to encompass his thought adequately.[46]

It follows that during his own time Beethoven was widely regarded as a radical modernist, whose modernism was seen to distinguish him sharply from the Classical standards established, in the main, by Mozart and Haydn. Of course, they too had their share of hostile notices before they were elevated to canonical status; but the classicizing critiques of Beethoven were too vehement and pervasive to be regarded as merely the usual, provisional resistance to modifications of cultural traditions. His contemporaries— including many of his advocates—saw him as subverting Classical principles and procedures, as radical, iconoclastic, and eccentric—and as an artist representative of his own time. They did not regard him as an eighteenth-century composer.

The question naturally arises whether this modernism can be defined as Romanticism. No simple answer is possible, for the Classic-Romantic dichotomy in the arts, like the Enlightenment-Romantic polarity in philosophy, appears *post festum*. None of the early Romantic poets in England saw themselves as belonging to a Romantic movement; in Germany, even the Schlegels, observed René Wellek, "were not conscious of forming or founding a romantic school."[47] But most of those whom we now call Romantics did have a sense of participating in an important modernist project, one with serious ideological overtones—whether aesthetic, philosophical, political, or religious.

And, paradoxically, this sense coexisted—indeed was inextricably blended—with an unswerving devotion to the ideals of classicism. The early German Romantics rarely repudiated Hellenic concepts of order, measure, and harmony, or classical notions of aesthetic coherence, proportion, and moderation, even when their writings were most transparently dedicated to the overthrow of these concepts. They did not consider themselves in conflict with classicism; rather they aspired to be its heirs. That is why the first definitions of Romanticism are not manifestos of dissidence but of adherence to a dynamic tradition. "Romantic poetry is a progressive, universal poetry," reads Friedrich Schlegel's *Athenaeum* fragment 116 (1798), in which the term "Romantic" was applied to the new poetry for the first time; but, he continues, it is a poetry that "opens up a perspective upon an infinitely increasing classicism."[48]

The interpenetration of Classical and Romantic characteristics in Beethoven was first formulated in print in 1810 by E. T. A. Hoffmann, in his review of the Fifth Symphony. He acknowledged that Beethoven's works were usually viewed as the "products of a genius who ignores form and discrimination of thought and surrenders to his creative fervor and the passing dictates of his imagination."[49] By way of refutation, however, his essay offered a lengthy analysis of the Fifth Symphony's thematic and structural unity.[50] Hoffmann's achievement was to define as Romantic the profoundly modern elements of Beethoven's music and, in the same breath, to reconcile those elements with the rhetoric, styles, and forms of Classicism. Casting his net perhaps wider than was necessary, he designated Mozart, Haydn, and even Bach and Palestrina as Romantic, but he allowed for a variety of romanticisms, thus giving the widest latitude to each composer's individuality. He pictured Beethoven's adherence to the rules as the riskiest kind of musical Romanticism, one that sought to bind in aesthetic form fearful and perilous subject matter: "Beethoven's music," he wrote, in what was to become one of the most famous passages in the history of music criticism, "sets in motion the machinery of awe, of fear, of terror, of pain, and awakens that infinite yearning which is the essence of romanticism."[51] The greatest exponent of a Romanticist music aesthetic, the philosopher Arthur Schopenhauer, eventually transposed Hoffmann's formulation into a universal dialectic of nature:

[A] symphony of Beethoven presents us with the greatest confusion which yet has the most perfect order as its foundation; with the most vehement conflict which is transformed the next moment into the most beautiful harmony. It is *rerum concordia discors* [the discordant concord of the world], a true and complete picture of the nature of the world, which rolls on in the boundless confusion of innumerable forms, and maintains itself by constant destruction.[52]

German idealist aestheticians were well aware of the hazards of the unbridled Romantic imagination, which, as August Wilhelm Schlegel acknowledged, had a "secret attraction to a chaos which lies concealed in the very bosom of the ordered universe, and is perpetually striving after new and marvellous births."[53] Earlier, Schiller too had warned, "The danger for the sentimental [i.e., Romantic] genius is, . . . by trying to remove all limits, of nullifying human nature absolutely . . . [and] passing even beyond possibility."[54] Thus, Hoffmann's defense of Beethoven was a bold one in that it did not minimize Beethoven's attraction to chaos. Rather, he declared that Beethoven's music enters "the realm of the colossal and the immeasurable," opening upon a labyrinthian cosmos, highly individual and utterly fantastic, and giving free play to extreme emotions such as terror, longing, ecstasy, and awe. Uncompromising, Hoffmann held Beethoven's extravagant imagination to be wholly consistent with his control of Classical form.

III

Beethoven is sui generis. He never joined any movement, despite his early, loose affiliation with Freemasonry and the Bonn Lesegesellschaft, his youthful passion for the French Revolution's ideals, his tilt toward German nationalism after 1804, his lifelong adherence to the reform program of Emperor Joseph II. Mozart joined the Freemasons; so did Haydn, who also after several rebuffs at last gained membership in the Tonkünstlersocietät; Schubert was elected to the Gesellschaft der Musikfreunde. But Beethoven, though he took pride in his honorary citizenship of Vienna and his election to several musical societies abroad, remained aloof from organizational ties. Similarly, whatever the power of Romanticism's pull upon his imagination, he never became an adherent of any specific Romantic tendency. Nor, even apart from his rejection of the irrational and the sentimental, could he consciously yield to Romanticism's most dangerous blandishments—its often undisguised eroticism, its mystical view of death as the doorway to life, its tendency to convert systematic thought into aphorism. Of course, these were Beethoven's preoccupations too, but he tried to subject them to strict control and sublimation: his lovers are never united, except, at the close of *Fidelio,* in conventional conjugal fidelity; "Joyfully I go to meet death," he wrote in his Heiligenstadt Testament, but this was hardly his "Hymn to the Night," for he added, "Should it come before I have had an opportunity to develop all my artistic gifts then . . . I certainly would like to postpone it";[55] and though his Bagatelles, op. 126, and many of the individual "Diabelli" variations are supreme embodiments of the Romantic aphorism, Beethoven urgently forges them into larger designs—a "Cycle of Bagatelles" and, in the "Diabelli" Variations, the most coherent variation cycle since Bach. Similarly, the interlocking structure (and inseparability) of *An die ferne Geliebte*'s component songs suggests that Romantic openness impelled Beethoven toward ever more profound formal integration. Much to the alarm of the publisher, Schott's Sons, Beethoven mischievously described the seven-movement String Quartet in C-sharp minor, op. 131, as pieced together from a variety of pilfered materials; yet the quartet's carefully ordered series of subdominant relationships and the thematic integration of its corner movements show it to be a paradigm of large-scale architectural cohesion.[56] Romanticism may have given Beethoven license to represent the forbidden and the boundless; but his will to form—his classicism, if you like—enabled him to set boundaries on the infinite, to portray disorder in the process of its metamorphosis into order, to transform suffering, tragedy, and death into healing, hope, and affirmation. It is in this larger sense that Rosen's is a persuasive model of Beethoven's development, for it aims at a reconciliation of Beethoven's "startlingly radical and original ways" with his continuing adherence to Classicism and its ideals.

Although it is tempting once again to sidestep the issue of Beethoven's Romanticism and to revert to the more transparent one of his modernism, which was so plainly recognized in his own time, it may be preferable to leave the issue open. We cannot really know whether Beethoven's unprecedented expressive, technical, and formal innovations, his simulation of narrative forms in instrumental music, his drive to expand the denotative power of musical sound, his creation of new styles to express propulsive, heightened, and transcendent states would have emerged without at least the partial stimulus of Romantic ideas, images, and art, which were so conspicuous in Beethoven's intellectual milieu. He owed an irredeemable debt to many classicisms—those of Mozart and Haydn, Schiller, revolutionary and Napoleonic France, and most of all to the classicism of ancient Greece and Rome. Still, it seems certain that Beethoven's creative outlook was immeasurably enriched by images, ideas, and ways of perceiving the world that were central to the Romantic sensibility. His kinship with Romanticism is no less authentic even if we make allowance for the possibility that his appropriation of Romantic conventions, metaphors, images, and designs is also a special case of his receptivity to the manifold forms of the imaginative, exemplifying his endless quest for materials useful to an urgent creative project.

Such a quest, of course, may itself be an essential ingredient of Romanticism, of its Faustian drive to transcend the given, its yearning for the unreachable, its rebellious temper. However, as those of Beethoven's contemporaries who were nurtured on Schiller's aesthetics understood, this drive is actually predicated upon the existence of the classical, which holds out unsurpassable models of the ideal in every potential embodiment—promises of liberation, fraternity, reconciliation with nature, eternal life, fusion with the Godhead, the achievement of pure joy, the experience of beauty. Schiller had posed the tormenting but ecstatic dilemma of the modern artist: to represent in art an unreachable ideal—unreachable because "nothing can satisfy whilst a superior thing can be conceived," and because the ideal that had existed in Eden and will exist once again hereafter can never exist in the present moment.[57] Thus, it follows that the quest for the classical ideal is a task for Tantalus, or for one endowed with the will, the restlessness, and the Romantic temperament of a Beethoven.

CHAPTER THREE

SOME ROMANTIC IMAGES

For Alan Tyson

THE TALKING TREES

Always impatient with the written word and ever eager to return to his music, Beethoven was prone to slips of the pen. Quill flying, mind wandering, he would place on his letters such improbable dates as "1089" and "1841"; two documents of 1802 are misdated "1782." He would render the village of Heiligenstadt as "Heiglnstadt." Or, responding to a dear friend who felt that he had been neglected, he would write, "You believe that my goodness of heart has diminished. No, thank Heaven, for what made me behave to you like that was deliberate, premeditated wickedness on my part."[1] Fortunately, he looked over that letter before mailing it to Franz Wegeler and modified the word "deliberate" by an interlineated "no."

Such errors provide a happy hunting ground for those of us who like to turn up interesting new confirmations of the quirky operations of the unconscious in everyday life. Thus, I was pleased but not at all surprised when, in the course of investigating Beethoven's religious outlook, I found what appeared to be a clear mental error—what Freud's translators used to call a "parapraxis" or "symptomatic action." Such actions, wrote Freud, "give expression to something which the agent himself does not suspect in them, and which he does not as a rule intend to impart to other people but to keep to himself."[2] On a leaf of sketches dated late September 1815 Beethoven addressed himself to God: "Almighty in the forest! I am happy, blissful in the forest: every tree speaks through Thee [*Jeder Baum spricht durch Dich*]."[3] Surely, I thought, Beethoven meant to say, "Thou speakest through every tree." Perhaps, but a closer look at some other evidence of Beethoven's worship of nature showed that he more than once referred to the plant and mineral kingdoms in a religious tone. In his "farewell" letter to Therese Malfatti, whom he courted unsuccessfully in 1810, he described the "childish excitement" with which he anticipated his summer holiday:

> How delighted I shall be to ramble for a while through bushes, woods, under trees, through grass and around rocks. No one can love the country as much as I do. For surely woods, trees and rocks produce the echo which man desires to hear.[4]

The reference to the "echo" of nature may seem conventional enough; but its place in our sequence becomes clear with a more explicit marginal notation of 1815 or 1816: "It is indeed," he wrote in stammering phrases, "as if every tree in the countryside spoke to me [als ob jeder Baum zu mir spräche], saying 'Holy! Holy!' In the forest, enchantment! Who can express it all?"[5]

Well, then, perhaps this was no slip of the pen; perhaps Beethoven really did mean to describe the tree as some superior form of deity. Momentarily dissatisfied with Freud, my thoughts turned to Sir James Frazer and I wondered whether Beethoven, like Frazer, had spent some imagined moments in Diana's sacred grove and sanctuary at Nemi. How interesting it would be to demonstrate that Beethoven's nature worship was so deeply rooted that it sometimes bordered upon more primitive forms of belief. Perhaps, I thought, what I had taken as something close to childlike gullibility in Beethoven was really a carefully controlled streak of primitivism, existing in a tension with his indestructible adherence to reason.

This brought to mind a curious passage in the diary of Beethoven's friend, Therese von Brunsvik. She recalled Beethoven's visits to her family's Hungarian estates in the years after 1800, where he was initiated into what she termed the "circle of chosen spirits who formed our social republic," these spirits being the Brunsvik siblings and their dearest friends. She described the scene:

> A circular place in the open was planted with tall linden trees; each tree bore the name of a member of the society. Even when we mourned their absence we spoke with their symbols, conversed with them and let them teach us. Very often, after bidding the tree good morning, I would question it regarding this and that, whatever I wished to know, and it never failed to make reply![6]

The sober historian within me finally sprang to life, objecting that such rituals could not have been merely a sentimentalized kind of phallic worship; they must have derived, at least in part, from the "freedom tree" plantings by Republicans, Jacobins, and latter-day Rousseauists of that era. After all, the Brunsviks, like Beethoven, were adherents of Republican ideals and enlightened thought: Brunsvik père was an enthusiast of the American Revolution and Therese Brunsvik recalled, "I was brought up with the names of Washington and Benjamin Franklin."[7] But how could one ignore the overtones of pagan ritual that seemed to lie on the surface of her story? Vaguely my thoughts turned to the "Cosmic Tree" that Mircea Eliade's primitive initiates climb as they seek the center of the world, the "sacred pole" that some call the Tree of Life and others equate with the Cross on Calvary. Or was Therese Brunsvik merely emulating Schiller's Maid of Orleans?

For hours together I have seen her sit
In dreaming musing 'neath the Druid tree.

(act 1, sc. 2)

Clearly I was caught in a traffic jam of overly luxuriant interpretations. Seeking a quick exit, I yielded to a sudden access of skepticism. Perhaps Beethoven's verb, "to speak," was only intended to express his belief that the majesty of God finds expression in every one of his creations. Perhaps what he really meant was something quite conventional, such as: "Through Thy power every tree is endowed with a particle of Thy Being." Well, yes, "every tree speaks through Thee" could be interpreted in that way; but it would be difficult to read the phrase, "Every tree in the countryside spoke to me," in that way.

Unable to resolve the issue, I let it rest for several years. But the subject was later revived when I opened Novalis's novel *Heinrich von Ofterdingen* (1802) and read its hero's initial musings:

Once I heard tell of the days of old, how animals and trees and cliffs talked with people then. I feel as though they might start any moment now and I could tell by their looks what they wanted to say to me.[8]

Later, Heinrich realizes that it is the poet's calling to restore the peaceable kingdom by taming ferocious animals, arousing gentle inclinations in humans, and awakening what he called "the secret life of the woods and the spirits hidden in trees."[9] And I soon learned that Novalis had no monopoly on this secret life. A few more hours of research disclosed the friendly speech of trees in many German works published not long after 1795, including Tieck's *William Lovell* and Friedrich Schlegel's *Lucinde,* as well as writings by Hölderlin, Caroline Günderode, and E. T. A. Hoffmann, to say nothing of the brothers Grimm. "The mute forest speaks its maxims," writes Hölderlin, "giving lessons to the mountains."[10] "The woods reply not," writes Schiller, as though in counterpoint, "and the ocean, / Unheeding, churns th' eternal foam."[11]

There is no need to multiply examples. It seems that I had stumbled upon one of the image-metaphors through which certain of Beethoven's contemporaries conveyed their beliefs, particularly their views of divinity and nature. What had appeared to be a curious personal image, an idiosyncratic phrase, or even a slip of the pen, turned out to be a sign of Beethoven's kinship with wider cultural and philosophical currents; a simple metaphor opens on a network of shared beliefs and patterns of thought. It also appeared to be a possible indication that some of Beethoven's intellectual and spiritual interests can be more centrally located in certain trends in German Romanticism than has usually been allowed, for these soulful trees are but one aspect of Romanticism's desire to achieve a fusion of humanity with nature by deciphering the language of mere matter. As the scholar Walter Wetzels has observed, Romantic natural science investigated the electrophysiology of plants, seeking not only to understand the speech of flowers, but to establish a "magical unification" of man and the inorganic parts of nature, thus to reestablish "the ancient link between man and nature, which had been buried since the Golden Age."[12] That is why Novalis wrote: "If God could become man, He can also become stone, plant, animal, and element, and perhaps there is in this way a progressive redemption in nature."[13]

Beethoven's close kinship to Romanticism was already clear in his attraction to many of its dominant categories, especially those centering on extreme alternatives—death and resurrection, freedom and necessity, Arcadia and Elysium, the individual and the cosmos, permanence and change. Moreover, in his choice of texts as well as in his radical reformulation and expansion of the expressive capabilities of music, it seems apparent that he participated in some of German Romanticism's most crucial interests— the description of such states of being and feeling as *Das Unendliche* (the infinite), *Sehnsucht* (yearning), *Heimweh* (nostalgia), and *Innerlichkeit* (inwardness). If there is an overriding metaphor in Romanticism, it probably is to be sought at the intersection of these interests, in the representation of infinite longing for an ideal state of being; that is, the image in all its potential manifestations of the gulf between desire and fulfillment.

A kinship to Romanticism is also apparent in Beethoven's impulse to enlarge the sphere of musical denotation through a variety of compositional practices—tonal allegory, implied narratives, expression marks, literary titles, experiential allusions, and other "resonating signposts," as I have elsewhere called them, that "vibrate with an implied significance that overflows the musical scenario, lending a sense of extramusical narrativity to otherwise untranslatable events."[14] Of course, such efforts had precedents in ancient and neoclassical precepts of the imitative character of art; but the early Romantic aesthetic included a novel proposal, enthusiastically advocating an intermingling of the arts, the transfer of formal and technical principles from one art to another. Novalis called for poetry "without sense and connection . . . and an indirect effect like music";[15] and August Wilhelm Schlegel asked his compatriots "to bring the arts closer together and seek for transitions from one to the other. Statues may quicken into pictures, pictures become poems, poems music, and (who knows?) in like manner stately church music may once more rise heavenward [like] a cathedral."[16] E. T. A. Hoffmann described the unfolding of his novel *Die Elixiere des Teufels* in sections that could be marked *grave sostenuto, andante sostenuto e piano,* and finally, when his hero "goes forth into the most colorful world; this is where the *allegro forte* begins."[17] Ludwig Tieck luxuriated in the prospect of breaching outmoded boundaries:

What has been separated by divine jealousy
The goddess of fancy here reunites.
Sound knows its color
And through every leaf the sweet voice shines.
One family all are color, fragrance, song.[18]

Earlier, Rousseau, Herder, and Schiller had foreshadowed this Romantic call for a restoration of an ancient and original fusion of the arts that presumably had existed long ago. Schiller wrote: "Music in its highest perfection must become form and affect us with the quiet power of antiquity; plastic art in its highest perfection must become music and move us by its immediate sensuous presence. . . . The perfect style of each art is manifested when it knows how to remove its specific limitations and to assume a more general character by a wise use of its peculiarity, without, however, giving up its specific advantages."[19] Across the continent, Wordsworth described the relation of *The Prelude* to *The Recluse* as that of "the Ante-chapel . . . to the body of a Gothic Church."[20] The enthusiasm for intermingling the arts at last became a subject for parody: Hoffmann's Kapellmeister Kreisler described how he once bought a coat in the key of C-sharp minor, which so alarmed his friends that he hastily had sewn onto it a collar in the more decorous key of E-flat major.[21]

The early Romantics hoped to dissolve boundaries, those that separated art, philosophy, and myth, and those that walled off one art-form from another. Each art was to overcome its innate limitations by emulating the properties of the other arts. Pater's memorable late-Romantic formulation, "All art constantly strives towards the condition of music," had ample earlier precedent, something Pater understood well: "Each art may be observed to pass into the condition of some other art, by what German critics term an *Anders-streben*—a partial alienation from its own limitations, by which the arts are able, not indeed to supply the place of each other, but reciprocally to lend each other new forces."[22] Mozart arrived on the scene a decade too early to be self-consciously theoretical about issues of musical representation, but Beethoven may have had some such thing in mind when in his later years he repeatedly referred to himself as a "tone-poet *[Tondichter]*."[23] His most thorough expression in prose of this aspiration to intermingle the characteristics of the arts—along with serious trepidation about its potential for vulgarization—is recorded in the marginal notations in the sketchbook and other autograph materials for the *Pastoral* Symphony (see p. 94 and p. 261, n. 17). We will have further occasion to witness the conflict between Beethoven's striving for greater communicativeness via denotational devices and his desire to achieve maximum expressivity by strictly nonverbal and nonpictorial means.

Although Beethoven's creative mind was stimulated by many other imaginative metaphors and tropes that were elaborated by his romantic contemporaries, it is not altogether self-evident that these may be taken as simple indications of Beethoven's receptivity to Romanticism. An increased understanding of Romanticism in recent decades has not brought us closer to a universal or synoptic definition of the movement; indeed, the term is itself of so Protean a character, so ridden with contradictions, and so filled with richness of significance, that ultimate agreement on its definition is improbable and even undesirable, for most interesting concepts elude definition. That is why Jorge Luis Borges was so fond of quoting St. Augustine on the nature of time: "What is time? If you don't ask me, I know; but if you ask me, I don't know."[24]

Furthermore, although we have seen a gradually emerging scholarly consensus as to the pervasiveness of certain archetypal tropes and images that were among the aesthetic and ideological preoccupations of the new sensibility, it has also become apparent that none of these has been shown to be exclusive to Romanticism. And if the tropes of Romanticism are not unique to Romanticism, but can be found in other style periods—in mannerism, the baroque, among the ancients, and especially in classicism and neoclassicism—then it seems to follow that the essence of Romanticism can no more be reached by an uncovering of its shaping tropes than by the older, unsatisfactory method of listing its characteristics. M. H. Abrams was well aware of this difficulty: "Taken singly," he wrote, the archetypal images " . . . all are older than recorded history: they are inherent in the constitution of ancient languages, are widely current in myth and folklore, and make up some of the great commonplaces of our religious tradition."[25] He was concerned that archetypal criticism may undermine "the properties of the literary products it undertakes to explicate" by collapsing works of art into "such unartful phenomena as myth, dreams, and the fantasies of psychosis."[26]

Nevertheless, it is arguable that the tropes are qualitatively changed when they appear in a Romantic context and that it is their distinctiveness in that context that may be decisive. If the tropes participate in universal archetypes, they perhaps do not do so intractably, because they are subject to transformation under pressure from historical and cultural forces. We can thus identify "Romantic mutations" of the underlying, archaic images and metaphors.[27] And, however exclusive they are to Romanticism, a shared palette of such images may at least be an indication of the strong pull exerted by the Romantic sensibility on Beethoven's imagination.

THE CORRESPONDENT BREEZE

In the first version of *Fidelio,* written in 1804–5, Florestan's aria closes with a backward glance to the time before his separation from Leonore:

> Ah, those were beautiful days
> When my glance clung to thine,
> When, seeing thee,
> My heart happily began to throb.
> Dearest, moderate your lamentations,
> Travel your path in peace;
> Tell your heart
> That Florestan was a worthy man.

These rather stiff sentiments were dear to Beethoven's own heart, for he was accustomed to recommend resignation as an anodyne for life's vicissitudes, and especially as a remedy for separated lovers. But in the 1814 revision he and his new librettist Georg Friedrich Treitschke sensed a somewhat more dramatic possibility—Florestan's vision of Leonore arriving to release his soul to eternity (ex. 3.1).

> Do I not sense a mild, murmuring breeze?
> Like an angel in golden mists
> Coming to my side to console me;
> An angel . . . leading me to freedom in heavenly realms.

Leonore's presence is heralded by a gentle movement of air, a breeze that is a harbinger both of liberation and of reunion. It is an image that recurs elsewhere in Beethoven's vocal music during his fourth decade. In the text of his song cycle, *An die ferne Geliebte,* op. 98, written apparently to Beethoven's order by a young Romantic poet, the murmuring breeze again reappears as an emblem of yearning for and symbolic reunion with a distant beloved (ex. 3.2).

> Silent West Wind, as you drift
> Yonder to my heart's chosen one,

EXAMPLE 3.1.   *Fidelio*, act 2 (no. 11), Florestan's aria, Poco allegro, mm. 1–8.

EXAMPLE 3.2.   *An die ferne Geliebte*, op. 98, no. 3, Allegro assai ("Stille Weste, bringt im Wehen"), mm. 134–37.

Bear my sighs, which die
Like the last rays of the sun.

(trans. Philip L. Miller)

The west wind is the lover's surrogate, which "will drift playfully about your cheek and bosom, blow through your silken hair." And in Beethoven's song cycle the arrival of spring, the time of love and of nature's rebirth, is announced by the breeze:

May comes again, the meadows are in bloom,
The breezes stir so gently, so warmly.

The wide presence of this pastoral image in Romantic writings of the early nineteenth century, and the argument that it may justly be identified as a distinctively Romantic metaphor was explored by Abrams in "The Correspondent Breeze." There he held that the image's remarkably widespread use by "poet after poet, in poem after poem, all within the first few decades of the nineteenth century" is itself sufficient to flag it as Romantic, despite "ample precedent in myth, religion, and the poetry of religious meditation."[28] Mainly, however, he showed how the image of the breeze was subjected to a Romantic transformation: the Romanticists' breeze, which on its surface is linked with the "outer transition from winter to spring, is correlated with a complex subjective process: the return to a sense of community after isolation, the renewal of life and emotional vigor after apathy and a deathlike torpor, and an outburst of creative power following a period of imaginative sterility."[29] This was Beethoven's plain intention in combining two poems by Goethe as a text for his miniature cantata, *Calm Sea and Prosperous Voyage,* op. 112, in which Aeolus "unlooses the strings" of the zephyr to relieve the "deathlike stillness" that lies upon the immense waters. Invisible yet palpable, mild yet capable of raging force, the movement of air represents the emanations of the human spirit as a regenerative force.[30] And it is in this same capacity that Florestan's breeze is foreshadowed in the Chorus of the Prisoners:

Oh what joy to breathe the scent of open air:
Only here, here is life.

This is a quite different breeze from the one in Ilia's aria in *Idomeneo:*

Gently flowing breezes,
Oh, fly to my beloved,
And tell him that I adore him.

In Mozart's libretto the breeze is a conventional messenger of love, an incorporeal Cupid; there is no stirring of the soul to wakefulness, no sense of an awakening or of a passage from dormancy to animation. In *Fidelio*, however, the caressing breeze is both a breath of life and a sign of release from bondage. This is so not merely in an abstract, metaphorical sense but because, isolated, helpless, and immobile, all of Florestan's senses have been systematically starved—of food, water, light, air, sound, and human contact. He has been deprived of every form of sensory and spiritual nourishment. The correspondent breeze enters the dungeon as both a reminder and a promise—of Florestan's beloved, of the bountiful greenness of the earth, and therefore of the potential for emergence into the air and light. That is why Florestan's "murmuring breeze" is close kin to the west wind's "azure sister of the Spring," in Shelley's ode, who sounds her "clarion o'er the dreaming earth," and to Wordsworth's "gentle breeze / That blows from the green fields and from the clouds / And from the sky."[31]

THE STARRY SKIES

From decoding the hieroglyphics of the inorganic to reading the mysteries of the celestial vault was only a short step for the Romantics, who believed in a continuum connecting the earth's natural elements and creatures with the stars in the heavens. Novalis and his friend, the once-influential Johann Wilhelm Ritter, sought to formulate a new Romantic physics that would provide evidence of "a secret correspondence between man and the stars";[32] as Wetzels noted, they thought that through our "spiritual powers" we can "communicate with all forms of nature" and are capable of influencing the physical world if only we are in "harmony with its rhythms, its laws, its soul."[33] Beethoven was sufficiently attracted by Kant's astrological speculations about the determining influence of the heavenly bodies upon life in the solar system that he copied into his Tagebuch several passages on this subject from the philosopher's early cosmological essay, *Allgemeine Naturgeschichte und Theorie des Himmels.*[34] And Goethe wrote,

> The superstition of astrology has its origin in our dim sense of some vast cosmic unity. Experience tells us that the heavenly bodies which are nearest us have a decisive influence on weather, on plant life and so forth. We need only move higher, stage by stage, and who can say where this influence ceases? . . . Man, in his presentiment, . . . will extend such influence to the moral life, to

happiness and misfortune. Such fanciful ideas, and others of the same kind,
I cannot call superstition; they come naturally to us and are as tolerable and
as questionable as any other faith.[35]

Like the Correspondent Breeze and the Talking Trees, the Starry Skies is
an image of a nature animated by a numinous power, an all-embracing image of the boundless space within which everything unfolds, an active space
that in some way is also a manifestation of the deity. Celestial imagery becomes a prime metaphor of the "sense of identity with a larger power of
creative energy" that Northrop Frye observed to be so characteristic of Romantic culture.[36] Romanticism's model of astronomical unity was no longer
tied to the mechanical, synchronized clockwork of Newtonian physics.

In clusters of images centering upon the starry skies, the mysteries of
space, the turnings of the heavenly spheres, the attributes of the deity against
the backdrop of the celestial vault, the immensity of the night, Beethoven
seems to have found a natural outlet for his feelings of awe and wonder. Apparently he was predisposed to such imagery wholly apart from any literary
or religious influences, for his neighbors recalled that in Bonn the child often retreated to the solitary attic of the Fischer house in which he lived so
that he could gaze into the distance through two telescopes that were kept
there.[37] The texts of several of his earlier lieder sound the motif of the starry
skies. But the references in "Adelaide," op. 46 (1794–95), to "the field of
stars" are grounded in pastoral, serving as gentle contrast to the "golden
clouds of sinking day." And lines from the "Gellert" Lieder, op. 48, written
in 1801 or 1802, show a lingering Enlightenment conception of a Christian God as watchmaker of the universe, setting "the numberless stars in
their places" with mechanical, un-Romantic precision. This conception is one
that Beethoven never wholly abandoned; in his copy of an 1811 edition of
Christoph Christian Sturm's *Reflections on the Works of God in Nature* he noted
many passages describing the rational designs of nature as crafted by a divine artisan, particularly underscoring paragraphs praising God for the
magnificence of his creation:

. King of heaven! Sovereign Ruler of worlds! Father of angels and men! O that
  my ideas were as vast and sublime as the extent of the heavens, that I might
  worthily contemplate thy magnificence! O that I could raise them to those
  innumerable worlds, where thou dost manifest thy glory even more than on

our globe; that as I walk at present from flower to flower, I might then go from star to star, till I came to the august sanctuary where thou sittest upon the throne of thy glory! But my wishes are useless, as long as I am but a traveler on this globe. I cannot fully know the beauty and magnitude of these celestial worlds, till my soul be freed from this gross body. In expectation of this, as long as I shall live, I will lift up my voice, and invite men to celebrate the glory of the Lord.[38]

Beethoven frequently invoked the celestial to symbolize the rarefied spheres of beauty and pure feeling, and he was fond of telling correspondents how he preferred to dwell in an untrammeled, lofty sphere. "My kingdom is in the air," he once remarked.[39] However, his references to the astral regions increasingly became filled with a sense of the numinous and mysterious. He told Carl Czerny that the idea of the Molto adagio of the second "Razumovsky" Quartet, op. 59, came to him when he was "contemplating the starry sky and thinking of the music of the spheres";[40] Karl Holz also heard this story and retold it with more emphasis on the Romanticism of the imagery, recalling that the Adagio was inspired on a night when "the clear stars illuminated the heavens" and Beethoven, wandering through the fields of grain near Baden, glanced upward "questioningly, longingly, into the infinite expanse"[41] (ex. 3.3).

References to the boundlessness of the heavens occur in greater profusion in Beethoven's later writings and in his choices of texts for setting. Some of these remain steeped in the pastoral mode, where, despite occasional storms, we retain the memory of a peaceable kingdom, the blessings of nature, the beneficence of God. A sense of divine purpose and order pervades even the most nocturnal of Beethoven's lieder, "Abendlied unterm gestirntem Himmel" (Evening Song Beneath the Starry Heaven), WoO 150, of 1820, to a poem by Heinrich Goeble:

> When the sun sinks down,
> And day draws to its close,
> When Luna, gently, kindly, beckons,
> And the night descends;
>
> When stars in splendor shimmer,
> When a thousand sunbeams glitter,

EXAMPLE 3.3.   String Quartet in E minor, op. 59, no. 2 ("Razumovsky"), Molto adagio, mm. 16–20.

So great the soul then feels
And from the dust breaks free.

So gladly gazes at those stars,
As if toward its native land,
Gazes at those bright far ones,
And forgets earth's vanity.

(trans. George Bird
and Richard Stokes)

Pastoral imagery remained central to Beethoven's outlook throughout his creative life, for pastoral style—even when used in instrumental works for which there are no literary or programmatic indications—may safely be taken to symbolize an achieved return to nature, and even a recapture of the

Golden Age.[42] Of course, I would not quarrel with a reading of the pastoral finales in the Violin Sonata in G, op. 96, and the String Quartet in F, op. 135, as Romantic irony—the frank confession that we can never wholly satisfy our metaphysical longings and thus must settle for simpler, more finite satisfactions. In many of his lieder, ranging from his six separate settings of three different texts entitled "Sehnsucht," to *An die ferne Geliebte,* Beethoven used the pastoral mode to express the prototypically Romantic sense of yearning, evoking warm, earthly landscapes framed in clouds and sunshine. *Sehnsucht,* whatever its metaphysical implications, also exists on a human scale—as the desire for love, for creative fulfillment, for tranquil communion with nature.

By way of powerful contrast, however, in imagery of the starry vault Beethoven located an "antipastoral" essence in which the condition of alienation is taken to be almost insuperable. The astral regions are cold, dark, sublime, infinite, chaotic, more than human. They are of the night. ("The night is sublime, the day is beautiful," wrote Kant.)[43] Their gods are many, exotic, drawn from all the world's mythologies or from figments of pantheistic fantasy such as those excerpts from Brahman theology that Beethoven copied into his Tagebuch in 1815: "Brahm, His spirit, is enwrapped in Himself. He, the Mighty One, is present in every part of space. . . . You sustain all things. Sun, ether, Brahma."[44] Ultimately, in the finale of the Ninth Symphony, Schiller's text combines astral imagery with utopian strivings for the improbable rewards of infinity: "Brothers, beyond the starry firmament there surely dwells a loving father." The contrast with the *Pastoral* Symphony is instructive, since both symphonies are constructed around implied mythic scenarios of reconciliation. But where the one symbolizes the restoration of an earthly Arcadia, the later symphony pictures the supernal striving for a celestial Elysium. One is enwrapped in memory, the other in dream, in discovery of utopian possibility rather than in recovery of a primal unity.

The metaphor of the starry skies is capable of representing that which cannot be represented—infinity, boundlessness, metaphysical longing— precisely because it embodies the idea of division within nature. Thus, the vault of the heavens is simultaneously an object of wonder and worship, and of disorder striving for order. Perhaps that is why the heavens provoke the sense of "tranquillity tinged with terror" that Edmund Burke saw as characteristic of sublime objects in general.[45] And why, as Northrop Frye wrote,

"The circling of the stars symbolized the perfection of obedience which would be man's perfect freedom."[46] These contending implications pervade Sir William Jones's "Hymn to Narayena," several verses of which Beethoven transcribed into his Tagebuch from J. F. Kleuker's translation:

Spirit of Spirits, who, through ev'ry part
Of space expanded and of endless time,
Beyond the stretch of lab'ring thought sublime,
Badst uproar into beauteous order start.
Before Heaven was, Thou art:
Ere spheres beneath us roll'd or spheres above,
Ere earth in firmamental ether hung,
Thou sat'st alone; till, through thy mystick Love,
Things unexisting to existence sprung,
and grateful descant sung[47]

And all of these simultaneous implications reverberate in Beethoven's most frequently cited allusion to the starry skies—his reference in a conversation book of 1820 to a famous passage in Kant: "Two things fill the mind with ever new and increasing awe and admiration the more frequently and continuously reflection is occupied with them; the starry skies above me and the moral law within me."[48] In Beethoven's abridgment of early 1820, this came to read: "'The moral law in us and the starry heaven above us.' Kant!!!"[49] Surely, Beethoven felt the starry heaven in what Rudolf Unger called its "double aspect: in the secret-filled incomprehensibility and infinity of its perpetual distance and in the comforting immutability and reason-filled order of its perpetual present."[50] Or, in Kant's own formulation: "the sublime is to be found in an object even devoid of form, so far as it immediately involves, or else by its presence provokes, a representation of *limitlessness*, yet with a super-added thought of its totality."[51]

THE ROMANTIC SOLITARY

To intensify Florestan's isolation, Beethoven and his librettist have even confiscated Leonore's portrait, which, in the original French text by J. N. Bouilly, had served to console the prisoner. Such total deprivation is intended to represent, not merely Pizarro's vengefulness or the inhumanity of tyrants in general, but the existential state of a familiar Romantic figure—the solitary hero. He appears in a wide variety of guises, from the landscapes of Caspar David Friedrich and the historical paintings of Géricault to the poetry of Wordsworth and Byron and the image of Napoleon on Elba; his figure—for he is almost always male—dominates the novels of Novalis, Schlegel, Tieck, Jean-Paul, and Goethe, as well as the narrative and autobiographical poetry of the English Romantics; we see him sometimes as a Promethean rebel, sometimes as a Satanic or Faustian figure, sometimes as a wanderer in the exotic geographies of nature. We encounter him in Beethoven's *Pastoral* Symphony—as a sensitive Romantic observer journeying in search of a lost time, a Rousseauist time when mankind and nature were united, a time that was the mythic equivalent of an idealized childhood, under the protection of a forbearing father and a bountiful mother. His persona is adopted by Beethoven himself in his pantheistic rambles through the Austrian countryside. He is the observer of immensity in the Molto adagio of the "Razumovsky" Quartet, op. 59, no. 2, the "Abendlied" of 1820, and in the "starry vault" of the Ode to Joy.

And we also meet him in *Christ on the Mount of Olives* (1803), a work suffused with the conception of the solitary hero, one whose isolation is both an effigy of Christ's capacity for endurance and a foreshadowing of his death. As Alan Tyson has observed, Beethoven's Christus resembles Florestan in several respects, both men being resigned to death, both equally helpless, suffering, and solitary.[52] But Christ sees himself as abandoned by God; his meekness does not altogether mask his desolation:

> I suffer greatly, my father!
> Oh look, have pity on me . . .
> Fear overtakes me at the nearness of death. . . .
> Father . . . , Thy son beseeches Thee.
> With Thy might everything is possible;
> Take this cup of sorrow from me!

Florestan is incapable of such entreaty, perhaps because he still retains a glimmer of hope, feels the stirring of the correspondent breeze. But, like Christ, Florestan is reduced to an observer in the midst of tumultuous action, cannot take up arms in his own defense. Similarly, Count Egmont remains incarcerated while the sounds of the people's army outside gradually rise into a "Symphony of Victory [Siegessymphonie]." Apparently, Beethoven was not prepared to unite the solitary, reflective hero with the death-defying man of action, either here or elsewhere.

THE ROMANTIC PRISON

In the gallery of solitary heroes who peopled the Romantic imagination, the prisoner occupied a special place as a symbol of loneliness, persecution, deprivation, and yearning, and it is as an embodiment of these that he appears in Fidelio as well as in Egmont, Goethe's drama for which Beethoven provided incidental music. The locus of confinement—whether a castle dungeon or a fortress—is also a condensed image that has accumulated a variety of symbolic implications. In an exemplary paper, Aileen Ward has traced this evolution in British poetry, from Edmund Spenser, in whose works the castle is the abode of "the allegorical action, usually with sinister overtones" and Shakespeare, whose castles are "the scenes of violent historic action—rebellion, imprisonment, murder, regicide," to the writers of the later eighteenth century, for whom "the dungeon, the dark underside of the castle, was an obvious symbol for all that was evil in the ancien régime."[53] Ward observes that with the passing of the revolutionary crisis the "imagery of castle and prison was depoliticized," and in both Wordsworth and Blake, transformed "into a wider symbolism of the human condition itself."[54] For Wordsworth, the castle was no longer a symbol of despotism but had become "a refuge, a source of strength, later described as an emblem of 'righteousness,' 'venerable,' 'time-cemented,' 'firm'," while for Blake, "the manacles that bind humanity are mind-forged."[55] But these later developments were not central to Beethoven's imagery, which remained focused on the antityrannical aspects of the metaphor: "And just as the ocean breaks through the dikes, so you will smash through the bulwark of tyranny and sweep it out of your land" (Egmont); and "No longer kneel down like slaves; Tyrannical force is banished here" (Fidelio).

Nevertheless, for Beethoven, as for the Romantics in general, the symbol of the prison is scarcely limited to the ideological purposes of the Sturm und Drang dramatists and postrevolutionary idealists or Jacobins. His prisons also exemplify what has been called the "Romantic prison," a multivalent image that connotes both a place of punishment and a place of re-demption. Despite its apparatus of coercion and sadism, its crypts, snares, and secrets, it is simultaneously the "happy prison," conceived, in Victor Brombert's description, as "the protected and protective space, the locus of reverie and freedom," a place for poetic and religious meditation.[56] And because Beethoven and the Romantics were imbued with a wide range of notions of salvation through suffering, the prisoner came to be regarded as somehow a privileged personage, one who deserves deliverance precisely because he has suffered. Of course, such issues also absorbed the pre-Romantic eighteenth century—in Piranesi's etchings, the Gothic novel, and the antityrannical dramas of Alfieri, Schiller, and Goethe. However, as Brombert informs us, the "carceral images in 19th-century literature . . . correspond to fundamental Romantic concerns and obsessions. The di-alectical tensions between the finite and infinity, between fate and revolt, between oppression and the dream of freedom, between victimization and vengeance, are repeatedly given a symbolic setting in the context of soli-tary confinement."[57]

For the Romantics the prison possesses an uncanny quality because it car-ries mythic echoes of the underworld, of Hades, of the abyss, the labyrinth, the secret place. Rocco says, "I am under the strictest orders never to let anyone" enter "the underground chambers. . . . And there is one cell into which I can never let you go, no matter how much I trust you." But like any normally inquisitive mythological heroine Leonore insists on entering the inner sanctum, on opening the forbidden door. By engaging such mythic resonances, the prison is able to stand for polarities of innocence and crim-inality, good and evil, darkness and light, death and rebirth, separation and reunion. Imprisonment becomes a locus of *Sehnsucht* in an infinity of forms, from the longing of Leonore and Florestan for each other to Florestan's hunger for all the insignia of survival: for light, air, wine, bread, and love. In their own ways, even Pizarro and Rocco are consumed by unfulfillable desires—Pizarro for revenge and Rocco for gold. If *Fidelio* has a dramatic weakness it is that its celebratory finale largely deprives us of the sense of continuing longing and expectation so central to Romanticism's preoccu-pation with incompletion. Only the music for "O Gott, welch' ein Au-genblick" preserves the memory of loss, the sorrow of separation; without it, the tragic residue so fundamental to the Romantic outlook might have been altogether sacrificed in the general jubilation.

THE CONVALESCENT SOUL

As usual, the biographical and universal implications of Beethoven's imagery contend for our attention, considering that he was a deaf composer, painfully confined within an ever-darkening inner space.[58] "I was soon obliged to seclude myself and live in solitude," he wrote in the Heiligenstadt Testament; "I must live quite alone and may creep into society only as often as sheer necessity demands; I must live like an outcast."[59] And again, to Wegeler: "My poor hearing haunted me everywhere like a ghost; and I avoided all human society."[60] Ultimately, to retreat from the world became a workable way for Beethoven to adapt to adversity, as well as a way of providing for the needs of his creativity.

However, it is not only actual prisoners or deaf composers who are hemmed in, "cabin'd, cribb'd, confin'd." "O'er my thoughts / There hung a darkness, call it solitude / Or blank desertion" (Wordsworth, *The Prelude*, [1850], bk. 1, ll. 393–95). Whatever its potential for redemption may be, every spiritual alienation or sense of dejection takes place within a metaphorical enclosure. And, sometimes, there may be little hope for a meaningful redemption, nothing left but "les derniers soupirs" of star-crossed lovers, as in "the scene in the burial vault" that Beethoven tried to picture in the Adagio affettuoso ed appassionato of his String Quartet in F, op. 18, no. 1.[61]

In the *Malinconia* movement of the sixth quartet of the same set, Beethoven designated as his subject someone trapped within a different kind of darkness, stricken with melancholia, endlessly mourning, unable to rid himself of grief. And Beethoven signals confinement of an even more oppressive kind in his designation, "Beklemmt," at the most emotional moment of the Cavatina of the String Quartet in B-flat major, op. 130. We are not forced to choose among the multiple meanings of the word—"confined," "straitened," "oppressed," "weighted down," "anxious," "constricted," and even "suffocated"—for all of these at once may bear on Beethoven's intention.[62] Together, they imply a crisis that calls out for resolution, for breaking out of an oppressive circle, either by way of a modernist Grosse Fuge or a high-spirited, classical rondo.

The Molto adagio of the String Quartet in A minor, op. 132, is headed "Holy Song of Thanks by a Convalescent to the Divinity, in the Lydian Mode *[Heiliger Dankgesang eines Genesenen an die Gottheit in der lidischen Tonart]*." The invalid is another kind of prisoner, afflicted and weary, in whom there is a need to cross a threshold, or to awaken from a frightening dream. The invalid, too, yearns for an open space, looks upward to the presumed realm of the deity. Beethoven's sufferer—later convalescent—prays for deliverance more from a sickness of the soul than of the body. Alienated, he or she is cut off from nature by an unhappy consciousness. The possibility of redemption involves a severe trial, an illness, through which to find one's way back to love, to nature, to God, to the community. ("Romantic meditations," writes Abrams, "often turn on crises—alienation, dejection, the loss of a 'celestial light' or 'glory'. . . —which are closely akin to the spiritual crises of the earlier religious poets.")[63]

THE PEASANT HUT

Of course, not all enclosures are oppressive: an enclosure may be an object of desire, a protected good place, an Eden, Oasis, or Happy Island carved out of the wild, the desert, or the ocean; it may be what Auden described as "a place of temporary refreshment for the exhausted hero, a foretaste of rewards to come or the final goal and reward itself, where the beloved and the blessed society are waiting to receive him into their select company."[64] One such image had a particular resonance for Beethoven: over the years he repeatedly told of his desire to live an isolated life in close contact with the soil. "If my trouble persists, I will visit you next spring," he wrote to his old friend Wegeler in 1801; "You will rent a house for me in some beautiful part of the country and then for six months I will lead the life of a peasant."[65] The prospect of Beethoven returning to the soil is daunting—at first, one wonders if it is merely a pose, or an enthusiastic declaration to a Bonn compatriot of continuing adherence to a once-shared Rousseauist sentimentalism. But later on we find the same hope expressed in Beethoven's private musings: "A farm, then you escape your misery!" he wrote in his Tagebuch in 1815;[66] and on the leaf containing one of his invocations of the enchanted forest, he wrote, "If all else fails, there remains the country, Baden, Lower Brühl, even in winter. It would be easy to rent a lodging from a peasant."[67] And in a conversation book of late September 1824 Beethoven urgently renewed this ancient wish: "Go to Vösslau or another place. In winter, away, away, far from the city [and from] people. Behind the garden in Vösslau a *peasant* house in which you may create solely for the infinite."[68] Here again, Beethoven sees the taking of a simple country house as a merger with nature and as a way of serving "the Infinite," as though by stripping himself of the worldly he would be able to reach the divine.

> Hither come and find a lodge
> To which thou may'st resort for holier peace,—
> From whose calm centre thou, through height or depth,
> May'st penetrate, wherever truth shall lead.

> (Wordsworth, *The Excursion,* book 3, ll. 106–9)

Beethoven's urge to retreat to conflict-free surroundings frequently has religious overtones. "Bitte um innern und äußern Frieden" (plea for inner and outer peace), he wrote as a heading to the Allegretto vivace of the Dona nobis pacem of the *Missa solemnis,* op. 123. He elaborated this salient idea in notations in other sketchbooks for the *Missa solemnis,* thereby indicating his intention to find musical equivalents for these thoughts: "Calm and gaiety issue from peace," he wrote in one sketchbook, and in another, "In the upper registers, the soprano, too, can demonstrate inner calm and joy as the evidence of peace."[69] Calm, joy, the infinite, and nature are threaded like beads on an unbroken strand of associated ideas. Only through inner peace, discovered in the peaceful seclusion of nature, can one find joy, and enter her dwelling in Elysium. "Tranquillity and freedom are the greatest treasures," he wrote in his Tagebuch.[70] "Oh Providence," he pleaded in his Heiligenstadt Testament, "do but grant me one day *of pure joy* — For so long now the inner echo of real joy has been unknown to me — Oh when, — oh when, Almighty God — shall I be able to hear and feel this echo again in the temple of Nature and in contact with humanity?" Beethoven's retreat to Heiligenstadt in the fall of 1802 had not fulfilled "the hope I cherished . . . of being cured."[71] But despite the Plutarchian tone of the Testament, his hopes had not faded altogether, and his convalescence always remained a potentiality, even in his last years.

THE DISTANT BELOVED

The image of a distant beloved is most famously represented in Beethoven's Romantic song cycle, *An die ferne Geliebte,* op. 98, written in 1816:

Now I am far from you,
Mountain and valley separate us
From each other, from our peace
From our happiness, from our sorrow.

All of nature's agents vainly conspire to unite the lover with his beloved: the light sailing clouds, the birds, the quiet west wind, the ripplets of the brook. Ultimately, however, what brings them closest is music—the lover's songs, which, when sung by the beloved, shall assuage their longing even though they may not overcome their literal separation: "What has separated us until now / succumbs to these songs. / And a loving heart is reached / by what a loving heart has hallowed."

Joseph Kerman has observed that the figure of a distant beloved "turns up in what would appear to be more than a statistically fair share of Beethoven's song poems," including "Adelaide," "An den fernen Geliebten," "Sehnsucht," "Lied aus der Ferne," "Andenken," "Der Jüngling in der Fremde," "Ruf vom Berge," and "Gedenke mein."[72] And he quotes Paul Bekker to the effect that "Beethoven's whole lyric output might almost be regarded as a series of variations upon the *An die ferne Geliebte* theme."[73] Patently, the image was one with special gravity for Beethoven, inasmuch as he had sufficient experience of separation, loss, and loneliness, and these stimulated in him the usual Romantic sentiments—of emptiness, longing for reunion, and the desire for forgetfulness, all of these exemplified in his letters to beloved women. "[S]ince you all left Vienna," he wrote to Therese Malfatti, "I feel within me a void which cannot be filled and which even my art, which is usually so faithful to me, has not yet been able to make me forget."[74] In his loneliness, he took comfort in whispers and visions; he wrote to Countess Deym: "A thousand voices are constantly whispering to me that you are my only friend, my only beloved. . . . Wherever I happened to be, your image pursued me the whole time."[75] To Marie Bigot (and her husband), after a painful misunderstanding: "I went last night to the Redoute in order to amuse myself, but in vain; visions of all of you pursued me everywhere."[76] The beloved's image, however distanced, tempers his loss. This was an ingrained pattern of adaptation; as a boy of sixteen, he tried to repair the death of his mother by visualizing "the dumb likenesses of her which my imagination fashions for me."[77] Turned away by Therese Malfatti, he almost automatically reverted to the image of *die Entfernte*, quoting an apt line from Goethe's *Egmont:* "People are united not only when they are together; even the distant one, the absent one too is present with us."[78]

Ultimately, it seems, Beethoven was willing to settle for the image. He desperately wanted to unite with the woman he called his Immortal Beloved—"Oh God, why must one be separated from her who is so dear"— but he confessed that he prefers to retain her as a distant beloved: "Your love has made me both the happiest and the unhappiest of mortals — At my age I now need stability and regularity in my life." Accepting permanent separation, he weaves a daydream that he will become an eternal wanderer, who will return from exile to his beloved only at life's end, and then, "enfolded in your arms can let my soul be wafted to the realm of blessed spirits — alas, unfortunately it must be so."[79]

Whatever the biographical symmetries, however, Beethoven utilized the distant beloved to address more universal issues in his art. As Egmont's Clara, she is transmuted into a Goddess of Liberty: "Divine Liberty disclosed herself, taking the face and form of my beloved one. With bloodstained feet she approached me." In Florestan's vision, Leonore becomes "an angel appearing in garments of light." Beyond the literal evocations of parted lovers, the Romantic image of the distant beloved represents all those things—including the past, memory, freedom, and youth itself—which have been lost and have yet to be regained, or rather, which have the potential to be found again. For the Romantics, the distant beloved is a symbol of estrangement, of longing, of homesickness, of the eternal feminine. For Novalis, "The beloved is an abbreviation of the universe."[80] She occupies the space between absence and presence, between wanting and having. Hovering beyond reach, she is the source of motion, she generates activity, she is the ideal, she is *telos*. Ultimately, it is her very unreachability—even a certain chimerical quality— that is essential to the Romantic temperament. In that sense, Schiller's and Beethoven's "Freude, Töchter aus Elysium" is deeply anti-Romantic, for she holds out the imminent promise of fulfillment (Wir betreten feuertrunken, / Himmlische, dein Heiligtum!) and she herself is capable of action to bring together what had been splintered and separated (Deine Zauber binden wieder, was die Mode streng geteilt). In essential contrast, the "ferne Geliebte" exalts hunger into a state of permanence, seeking eternally to sustain desire without surrendering to finite satisfactions. We hear a spectral

EXAMPLE 3.4. *An die ferne Geliebte,* op. 98, no. 6, Andante con moto, cantabile ("Nimm sie hin denn, diese Lieder"), mm. 258–67.

Nimm sie hin denn, die - se Lie - der,

EXAMPLE 3.5. Cello Sonata in D, op. 102, no. 2, Adagio con molto sentimento d'affetto, mm. 1–9.

Adagio con molto sentimento d'affetto

EXAMPLE 3.5 *(continued)*

prefiguration of the song-cycle's closing melody (including its characteristic turning figure) in the slow movement of the Cello Sonata in D, op. 102, no. 2, of 1815, marked Adagio con molto sentimento d'affetto. Reduced to a skeletal essence and slowed to a somnambulistic tempo it seems to emanate from some metaphysical dimension in which archaic memory is itself the measure of desire's boundlessness (exx. 3.4, 3.5).

THE VEIL OF ISIS

The image of a distant beloved is closely related to another prevalent Romantic metaphor, that of the Veil of Isis. Both are images of women, both are shrouded, one literally, the other by her remoteness in space and time. Both are objects of desire, but where the beloved awakens feelings of tenderness, the goddess at Sais summons feelings of rage. If yearning is the invariable and essential Romantic attitude toward the Distant Beloved, the Romantics took a more aggressive stance toward the veiled Isis. "It's time to tear away the veil of Isis and reveal the mystery," wrote Friedrich Schlegel; "whoever can't endure the sight of the goddess, let him flee or perish."[81] Novalis agreed, writing, "He who does not wish to lift the veil is no worthy disciple of Sais."[82] The frustrations engendered by an unappeased yearning for a distant beloved apparently need to be discharged. To make the erotic implications more explicit, and somehow to blame the desired object for arousing sexual desire, Schlegel added, "Mysteries are female; they like to veil themselves but still want to be seen and discovered."[83]

Of course, although they preached philosophies of love, the early Romantics and their forerunners preferred to interpret the rending of the veil
of Isis as a metaphor of a quite different type, one that describes the culminating moment of a quest for truth.[84] As Schiller put it in "The Veiled
Statue at Sais" (1795):

> A youth there was who, burning with a thirst
> For knowledge, to Egyptian Sais came
> In hopes the wisdom of the Priests to learn. . . .
> To his wonderment the youth observed
> An image deeply veiled, of giant size.
> And turning to his guide: "What," he demands,
> "Does yonder veil beneath its folds conceal?"
> "The truth," is the reply.—"What," cried the boy,
> " 'Tis nothing else but Truth that I pursue,
> And must I find that just that Truth is veiled?"

Consumed with an "eagerness *to know,*" the youth defies the priests of Isis,
draws the veil, and dies:

> Whatever he saw, whatever then he learned,
> His lips have never told. . . .
> Woe be to him who seeks for Truth through sin!
> For truth so found no happiness will yield.[85]

Like Schiller, Wackenroder urged restraint and resignation upon truth-
seekers: "They have endeavored to unveil the secrets of Heaven and to place
them amongst the objects of this earth."[86] In Novalis's fragments of a novel
entitled *Die Lehrlinge zu Sais* (The apprentices at Sais), Hyazinth "left his fa-
therland and those he loved, and in his passion he did not heed the grief of
his betrothed." Lifting the veil, "He saw, wonder of wonders, himself."[87]
The quest for truth terminates as a platitude of achieved self-knowledge, in
a caricature of Romantic *Innerlichkeit.*
    We cannot altogether know what led Beethoven to copy, frame, and keep
in full view upon his desk during his later years a German translation of the
famous inscriptions about the Veil of Isis:

I am that which is.

I am everything that is, that was, and that shall be. No mortal man has
lifted my veil.

He is unique unto himself, and it is to this singularity that all things owe
their existence.[88]

Beethoven's interest in these inscriptions from ancient Egyptian and Orphic
ritual sources demonstrates his attraction to a symbol that was appropriated
in the rites of Freemasons and Illuminists (see below, pp. 146–50). At Bonn,
Beethoven's freethinking teachers and Illuminist associations had permanently
undermined his adherence to conventional religion. But his profound religious feelings perpetually sought an outlet: he was thus both ready and eager
to accept the Romantic explorations of Eastern and classical myths and rites;
he luxuriated in the idea of the oneness of humanity and its manifold deities;
he delighted in every expression of the polytheistic imagination. Once he even
dreamed of circumnavigating the world's religions, an oneiric quest through
India and Arabia, culminating in Jerusalem.[89] But it is also possible that he
sought in Isis a quasi-initiatory process of purification and resurrection; at least,
this is implied in a letter of 1815 to Countess Erdödy in which he describes
the Temple of Isis as a place of rebirth, "where the purified fire may swal-
low up all your troubles and you may awake like a new phoenix."[90]

Finally, somewhere within a network of overlapping meanings, the Veil
of Isis trope may well tap the underside of Beethoven's conscious idealization of *die ferne Geliebte*. Perhaps the perplexities of the feminine and the
mysteries of sexuality here found an opaque outlet in an occult symbol. Perhaps, after all, when Beethoven's contemporaries spoke of knowledge they
did not exclude its sexual meaning. That may be why Schiller's Cassandra
wants to remain blind:

Is it well, impending terror
To expose, the veil to raise?
Human life is nought but error,
Knowledge only Death conveys.[91]

Of course, there remained still another possibility, of finding a real beloved
beneath the veil of Isis. In his retreat at Walden Pond, Thoreau wrote: "The

oldest Egyptian or Hindoo philosopher raised a corner of the veil from the statue of the divinity; and still the trembling robe remains raised, and I gaze upon as fresh a glory as he did, since it was I in him that was then so bold, and it is he in me that now reviews the vision."[92] One wonders if Beethoven would have appreciated Thoreau's elegant proposal for a solution to the twin riddles of the Distant Beloved and the Veil of Isis.

CHAPTER FOUR

PASTORAL, RHETORIC, STRUCTURE: THE VIOLIN SONATA IN G, OP. 96

As a reminder of a harmonious world that once was and that still persists in memory, pastoral style is classicism's primary image of simple contentment. But insofar as it is also the vehicle of love, loss, and longing, expressive of those things that remain forever beyond our grasp, it is central to the nostalgic concerns of Romanticism. That is why poets and composers often have recourse to the pastoral genres as those best able to represent both classical serenity and Romantic turbulence and to suggest ways in which these may be interrelated.

So, when a composer employs the language of pastoral it is not only to evoke picturesque scenes and legendary figures frozen in graceful and often vacuous poses, not only about lovelorn swains, the felicities of rustic life, the recognition of the dignity of toil, the evidence of nature's bounty and profligacy, though it may often be about these as well, for, of course, these are crucial images of pastoral. Equally crucial, however, in the pastoral poetry of the ancient world—whether the Greek and Roman myths as set down by Ovid and Hesiod or the idylls and eclogues of Virgil, Theocritus, and Bion—is a sense that the idyllic state is a precarious one, vulnerable to being lost. From the start, pastoral style has been a global metaphor for an extensive range of affects and images, including burdensome issues and unsettling states of being. Oedipus himself started life as a pastoral hero, one of countless mythological highborn sons who were abandoned by their parents and secretly raised by shepherds or nurtured by gentle animals. Ancient pastoral poetry did not shrink from violence and death. For example, Bion's "Lament for Adonis":

Low on the hills is lying the lovely Adonis, and his thigh with the boar's tusk, his white thigh with the boar's tusk is wounded, and sorrow on Cypris he brings, as softly he breathes his life away.

His dark blood drips down his skin of snow, beneath his brows his eyes wax heavy and dim, and the rose flees from his lip, and thereon the very kiss is dying, the kiss that Cypris will never forgo.[1]

As a set of musical tropes pastoral mirrors an unbounded universe, and it provides copious means of sounding the main themes of a deeply felt existence within that universe. In its serenades, with their simulated guitar or lute accompaniments, it is the genre of love and, by extension, of every form of longing; in its echoes of forest murmurs and its evocation of pleasant landscapes it is the image of solitary contentment and of silent worship; as a mode of celebration of the ritual occasions of life, it is a music that magnifies both the individual and the community, and their reciprocal sense of shared traditions. Through its repertory of traditional dances it tells not only of love and courtship but of the body, the self, of abstract motion and the infinite degrees of velocity. Encoded in those dances—as Wye J. Allanbrook has shown—is data about distinctions of rank and divisions of class as well, but pastoral tends toward the amelioration of such differences, bridging lower and higher, firstness and lastness.[2] In the elegiac mode of its andantes and adagios it has to do with loss, mourning, homage, and consolation. Its scherzos often unfold within a satiric or dithyrambic dimension: they enter a festive world, heralding resurrections. And its rondo-finales deliver on implied promises, illustrating the varieties of halcyon finality.

Pastoral is surely the quintessential style for chronicling scenarios of an initial state of harmony, its subsequent rupture, the yearning for its restoration, and that restoration itself, transformed by the intervening experiences. That is why, in an era that prized classical texts and images, the deployment of pastoral mode was very often understood as an elaboration of the lineaments of a lost Arcadia, which, of all the imaginings of a paradisiac realm, was the utopian space perhaps most favored by refined sensibilities in the age of Mozart and Beethoven, a realm endlessly explorable, filled with activity and motion, while simultaneously gratifying sensuous and aesthetic longings for tranquility and beauty.

Arcadian imagery is thus a potent metaphor of a life that is fully experienced up to the moment of its extinction—and beyond, in historical memory. In the Arcadian mode we are at one with nature in all the turnings of its seasons and days, from spring to autumn, summer to winter, morning to evening, noon to midnight. Inevitably, then, Arcadia knows melancholy as well as joy, division as well as harmony, final sleep as well as first awakening.

Over the course of time, pastoral imagery in music increasingly focused on representations of idyllic existence, lives lived in nature's open realms, and uncomplicated amorousness. Pastoral style tended to become an unproblematical, conventional set of procedures appropriate to music imitative of the sounds of nature and picturing the supposed pleasures of rural life. At the extreme, pastoral's archaic power to disturb was set aside in favor of a burlesque commentary on rural life, featuring cheerful and picturesque subjects—say, Leopold Mozart's "Peasant Wedding," "Sleigh Ride," and "Sinfonia burlesca" or the boy Mozart's own pastoral quodlibet, *Gallimathias Musicum*—and utilizing naturalistic, imitative techniques that project a kind of lighthearted rustic stance. Often, in pastoral music of the eighteenth century, the disruption of an idyll is represented merely as a misunderstanding between lovers or the arrival of bad weather—tempests, storms, lightning and thunder—soon followed by the return of calm. At the loftiest level of this process, Haydn's oratorios *The Seasons* and *The Creation* are versions of a rational Enlightenment pastoral that locates harmonious patterns everywhere in a divine hierarchical arrangement of the universe.

In his Salzburg years Mozart developed a pastoral-style vocabulary to speak about love, beauty, nature, and connectedness—in the serenades, notturnos, and divertimentos that accompanied the ceremonies through which the community honored its leading citizens, celebrated its own achievements, and congratulated itself on its benevolence and wisdom, pretending—even believing—for a day that it had recovered the Golden Age of antiquity. Subsequently, except for a handful of Vienna-period serenades in which pastoral style predominates, Mozart used it in individual movements or extended sections of multimovement compositions, as one so-called characteristic style among many—military, heroic, pathetic, serioso, learned, churchly—thereby heightening its dramatic effect but tending to narrow its range of potential representation. Thereby he crafted musical counterparts of the idyllic or bucolic poetic interludes that the literary critic Renato Poggioli named "pastoral oases," where the poet evokes a secluded spot, a secret garden, or another fleeting vision of an Arcadian haven within a nonpastoral universe:

> Pastoral poetry makes more poignant and real the dream it wishes to convey when the retreat is not a lasting but a passing experience, acting as a pause in the process of living, as a breathing spell from the fever and anguish of being.[3]

Oases of this kind are frequently encountered in arias, serenades, romances, and rustic interludes in Mozart's operas. Allanbrook offers a profound pastoral reading of *Le nozze di Figaro*, seeing its pastoral as limning "a place out of time, where Eros presides." This, of course, is also the pastoral of Virgil and Watteau, but Allanbrook recognizes that pastoral is not bound by its mythological parameters and can take up residence in interior spaces as well. "[T]he very unreality of Mozart's pastoral place," she writes, " . . . is a guarantee of its possibility. It is merely a state of mind, called into being by a tacit understanding and defined by a nostalgic and otherworldly musical gesture."[4]

Beethoven initially took his cue from Mozart's later instrumental practice, however, and in many of his works pastoral style is reserved for the minuet/scherzo or finale movements, the latter often cast in rondo form. A few examples of such finales include the "Pastoral" Sonata in D, op. 28, the "Spring" Sonata in F for violin and piano, op. 24, the first two piano concertos, and the Violin Concerto. In them, as also in the opening scene of *Fidelio,* the pastoral style, rather than serving as a comprehensive and versatile descriptive rhetoric, usually constitutes a contrasting episode in a larger, nonpastoral, design. Nostalgia and felicity are the main features of such an episode; in a swift stroke it can serve as a recognizable token of wistful longings or as shorthand for a state of well-being. The trio of a scherzo or minuet may evoke a pastoral setting—whether aristocratic, bucolic, mythological, or an Edenic equivalent—that once was, that is well remembered, and that may come again. Pastoral finales are usually assured, hopeful, imbued with a confident expectation that the lost harmony between humanity and nature has been reestablished, or, if not already present, is not far off.

Pastoral is Beethoven's preferred voice only in his lieder, where it predominates, from such early Vienna songs as "Adelaide" and "Seufzer eines

Ungeliebten" to the most characteristic songs of his maturity, including the Eight Songs, op. 52, Six Songs, op. 75, Three Goethe Lieder, op. 83, and the valedictory "Abendlied unterm gestirnten Himmel," WoO 150, of 1820. The texts and musical gestures of his song-cycle, *An die ferne Geliebte* (1816), are replete with pastoral imagery, the whole indissolubly woven together as a symbol, not only of the reunion of parted lovers, but of their unity with nature and all of nature's creatures.

Apart from his dances for the Redoutensaal and music for the ballet *The Creatures of Prometheus,* op. 43, however, there is surprisingly little pastoral in Beethoven's early instrumental music. Evidently he had more momentous issues in mind—certainly the large-scale signature works of his heroic period were better suited to a more dynamic, heaven-storming rhetoric. Sometimes, nevertheless, he set out to fuse pastoral and heroic styles as contending perspectives on the rupture in modern consciousness and as alternative ways of healing that rupture—either by recovering an Apollonian equanimity or by unloosing a Dionysian impulse. On one conspicuous occasion he unveiled a pastoral moment at the very instant of its fracture by disruptive forces. The two crashing chords that open the *Eroica* Symphony introduce a flowing pastoral negotiation of the common chord, a shepherd's yodel or an alphorn call that lasts less than two measures (it may be no accident that it echoes the yodeling figure at the opening of Mozart's *Bastien und Bastienne,* a pastoral singspiel derived from a text by Rousseau), until it is tipped into disequilibrium by a decisive descent through D to C-sharp at measures 6–7. In a half-step, Arcadia has been lost, thus launching a pro-longed heroic narrative that will revert to the pastoral mode only in its contredanse finale.[5] But in two instrumental works written toward the close of the heroic period—and in *An die ferne Geliebte*—Beethoven deployed pastoral style throughout entire large-scale compositions rather than using individual pastoral topics as quick references to Arcadian states. The first of the instrumental works is the *Pastoral* Symphony, written in 1808; the second is his tenth and last Sonata for Violin and Piano in G, op. 96, written mainly in 1812–13.

The Sixth Symphony, of course, is replete with pastoral signifiers, includ-ing its main title, the famous programmatic movement descriptions, and a clutch of musical *topoi*—homophonic style, imitations of nature sounds, shepherd calls, folk instruments, and country dances—drawn from the roomy storehouse of such devices inventoried by eighteenth-century theorists and by scholars of our own time.[6] Beethoven, worried that he might have crossed the line into programmatic reductionism and perhaps hesitant to provide a target for snobbish critics, tried to reassure himself on this issue, writing on the sketches: "Pastoral Symphony—no [tone-]painting, rather something in which the emotions that are aroused in people by the pleasures of the countryside are expressed, in which some of the feelings of country life are portrayed"; and on the back of a first violin part, he wrote the subtitle, "More the expression of feeling than painting" (see also chapter 5, p. 94).[7] He eventually overcame his qualms and retained the descriptive titles in the *Pastoral* Symphony, but he followed his own advice to the letter in the Opus 96 Sonata, which is devoid of literary allusions and permits listeners to find its pastoral signifiers for themselves.[8]

Each of the movements of the G-major Sonata elaborates a distinctive version of pastoral, the whole constituting a series of sharply etched illustrations of the range and purposes of pastoral experience. The first movement, Allegro moderato, though untitled, is unabashedly an idyll, replete with bird calls, alpine horn arpeggios, drone basses, and figures that simulate the rustling, murmuring, and busy profusion of nature's sounds. The opening birdsong—resembling that of a skylark (*Feldlerche; Alauda arvensis*), noted for its song in upward flight—is a summons at daybreak, or an awakening of spring. A voice sounds, another responds, signaling that it is time to begin, for contact has been established. The heart also responds, overflows with joyful, confident, exultant feelings. The instrumental interplay is reminiscent of the conversational character of an eclogue: at the outset, the violin and piano echo one another's motifs and then dovetail their efforts in long, soaring, arpeggiated lines in parallel motion (mm. 10–19) before embarking on another round of playful imitations, calls, and responses. Collaborating, the instruments genially traverse an agreed route: they are of one mind; neither needs to develop a separate perspective, let alone to advocate a contending view of experience. Instead, external concord finds inner confirmation, with each instrument completing, ratifying, and reinforcing the other (ex. 4.1).

Pastoral topics take turns displaying their wares: a D-major subsidiary theme in mock-processional style (mm. 41–58) laughingly skitters downward, landing in the center of a sequence of bagpipe drones at measures 58–59, which in turn gives way to an extended trill, crescendo, at measures

EXAMPLE 4.1. Violin Sonata in G, op. 96, Allegro moderato, mm. 1–25.

EXAMPLE 4.2.   Allegro moderato, mm. 116–22.

63–72. Those among Beethoven's contemporaries who viewed the world through lenses of alienation scenarios crafted by Rousseau and Schiller would have known that all this is too good to last. Melancholia and thoughts of loss and mortality will sooner or later break this spell. Indeed, we may even imagine that there is already a touch of mortality at the very opening, a latent *mal du pays* in the bird call itself. So it is no surprise when a melancholy strain makes its entrance, foreshadowed at measures 87 and 91–94, and then, in the development, expressed in a series of brooding ostinatos on a sighing motif that dominate the texture until measures 116–26, when the instruments, no longer sighing in place or pressing to find an upward escape route, find relief in an echoing triplet figure that gracefully skims the depths of sadness (ex. 4.2).

Melancholic reflections give way to pizzicati and trills simulating more bird calls (mm. 139–41), but the return to the G-major opening lasts for only a moment before a shift into the parallel minor (mm. 148–49) transports the action to a mysterious landscape; the colors darken, and the movement drifts further into dream and dislocation. The twilight-hued G minor prepares the way for a transition into E-flat (mm. 161–70), which looms large as a secondary key here and throughout the sonata. Seemingly, E-flat major has been designated as the key in which the idyll is yet to be regained, which is to say it appears to stand for a lost or misplaced aspect of Arcadia. In the course of the recapitulation and coda the melancholic strain is reactivated: the ostinato sighing motif returns for a full eight measures (mm. 230–38), issuing into a muted metamorphosis of the opening idyll. Despite the constantly renewed song of the lark, alone, in duet, or in an avian concert of cascading trills (mm. 262–67), and despite the insistently affirmative crescendo, ascending scale, and unequivocal cadence at the close, the ethereal modulations of the Allegro's last page continue to reverberate even if they do not have the last word, bespeaking the precariousness of an ending which acknowledges that night must fall, even in Arcadia.

Whereas the Allegro moderato may bring to mind musical analogues of such venerable Arcadian poetic genres as the idyll or the eclogue, the slow movement, Adagio espressivo, in E-flat, speaks the eloquent language of pastoral's most plangent genre, the elegy. And just as G major has been firmly designated as expressive of idyllic states of being, both existent and recoverable, the key of E-flat is brought into play as a primary signifier of the elegiac mode, with its rhetoric of invocation, questioning, outcry, lament, consolation, and ultimate acceptance. Three themes create a tonal palette adequate to the scope and subtlety of the task. First, in legato phrases that move smoothly within the barlines, without suspensions, and in four-part harmony appropriate to congregational music, the piano intones a symmetrical eight-measure hymn to make known the mournful nature of the occasion, but without giving way to extremes of grief. At measure 9, the violin enters with a three-note motif, g–f–e♭, those notes outlining the "Lebewohl" (farewell) motto, reminiscent of the vanishing sounds of a posthorn, that Beethoven sometimes encoded into his music, for example in the coda of the finale of the Piano Concerto in C, op. 15, and that he identified so conspicuously in the opening measures of the "Lebewohl" Sonata in E-flat, op. 81a, as a pastoral-style signifier of leavetaking.[9] Only in retrospect do we realize that the motto had already been almost invisibly pre-echoed by the piano at measure 8, in the closing phrase of the hymn, which thus is simultaneously premature disclosure and prophecy (ex. 4.3).

Played sotto voce by the violin, the motto lasts but three measures, followed by an asymmetrical, lamenting, downward-pressing theme in the violin,

EXAMPLE 4.3.   Adagio espressivo, mm. 1–13.

Adagio espressivo

EXAMPLE 4.4.   Adagio espressivo, mm. 33–41.

a theme whose rapid figurations and exquisite chromaticisms offer a full measure of grief-laden affects before they run their course. Thus, the "Lebewohl" motto emerges from the hymn and then expands into a discourse on
lamentation, culminating in an ascending solo cadenza of sixty-fourth-note
figures that at last delivers its fervent query to the heavens.[10] It is only following the cadenza (mm. 32–37) that the violin at last is ready to lend its
voice to the hymn. In a gesture of compliance, the cadenza's closing
crescendo subsides into mezza voce, semplice, the violin thus completing
the transition from bleak questioning to acceptance of the opening hymn,
which it now makes its own (mm. 38–45) (ex. 4.4).

EXAMPLE 4.5.   Adagio espressivo, mm. 62–67.

To close the movement, the violin and piano in turn pursue a pastoral figure that curls gently downward from plateau to plateau (a counterbalancing response to the earlier cadenza's ascent?), perhaps seeking, without clamor, to reenter Arcadia; but having found what seems a resting place in a closing E-flat chord, played tremolo and *pianissimo* by the piano, the violin softly adds a prefiguring C-sharp as though to indicate that we are not yet done, that E-flat cannot serve as a satisfactory substitute for G major, that there is more to come, that the future, importunate, is demanding its prerogatives (ex. 4.5).[11]

The attacca joining the Adagio espressivo to the Scherzo offers a quick passage from interiority to outwardness. Acquiescence in the congregational conception of restrained grief authorized the Scherzo's almost magical shift from despondency to celebration, made possible an emergence from the elegiac mood of the Adagio espressivo. But though the audacious C-sharp lifted that mood with sleight-of-hand swiftness, the Scherzo does not by itself reestablish Arcadian harmony; rather, it constitutes an exhilarating moment en route to that restoration. Perhaps, by its nature and by its placement in classical-style structures, a scherzo necessarily has a transitional character; or

EXAMPLE 4.6.   Scherzo, trio, mm. 33–40.

perhaps the Opus 96 Sonata's narrative course cannot reach emergence all at once, but must go through several stages before eventually finding an outlet. Still, the restoration of the natural world and its simple delights is now within view, perhaps not yet here, but surely closer at hand, its nearness symbolized by an image of transparent earthly pleasure in the Trio at the Scherzo's very center—a flowing waltz in E-flat over a bagpipe drone bass, a superlative example of one of Poggioli's "pastoral oases." On the other hand, the Trio, like the scherzo of the Ninth Symphony, may not be a sign for Arcadia regained but for Arcadia's transience—a brief encounter and a quick disappearance (ex. 4.6).

Beethoven's most inimitable scherzos are disruptive, asymmetrical, propulsively unstable, undecorous, satiric, even demonic; as one anonymous critic, writing during Beethoven's lifetime in a Vienna music journal edited by his friends and unfailingly sympathetic to his efforts, noted of this Scherzo: "it has a kind of Satyric character, with a goat's spring . . . and a rich dose of malice."[12] The critic does not say whether the maliciousness resides in the G-minor tonality or in the sforzando-*piano* syncopating strokes strategically placed on the third beat of many of its measures. In any event, the coda of

EXAMPLE 4.7.   Poco allegretto, mm. 1–8.

this very brief Scherzo puts aside all malicious thoughts with a shift to G major that eases us into the fourth movement, Poco allegretto.

The Poco allegretto presents itself as an unproblematic set of variations on a playful, ambling theme in 2/4, a folklike dance tune alternating between the piano's treble register and the violin against a legato eighth-note pattern in the bass. It seems to be Beethoven's aestheticized version of a blustery buffo aria from a durable Viennese singspiel,[13] but it avoids any hint of burlesque rusticity, the swaying theme instead setting a tone of sublimated amorousness, dolce and *piano*, except for a gentle crescendo at measures 5–7 of each of its four eight-measure periods, which gracefully subsides at the close of each symmetrical phrase (ex. 4.7).

It is only after we pass the theme's double bar that we realize that we have glided into the first in a set of variations rather than a contrasting section of a finale rondo—a deceptive first impression reinforced by continuities of tempo and key as well as by the absence of a pause, let alone a full stop. Indeed, it seems that we have been lulled into thinking that there are no fur-

EXAMPLE 4.8. Poco allegretto, mm. 113–16.

ther serious obstacles to a felicitous outcome; we are apparently on an unobstructed path to a place of simple, unalloyed delight. Each of the first four variations offers a different mutation of the theme's dance character. Variation 1 features a gracefully advancing and receding pattern. Variation 2, played *sempre forte,* splits the dance figures into a stamping march rhythm in the bass and a quick-time contredanse in the treble. Variation 3 accelerates the tempo with a slithering bass melody in sixteenths against light syncopations in the upper voices. And variation 4 offers eight four-measure sequences, each alternating two measures of *forte* stamping with two measures of coquettish retreat, dolce, in which, to use Wilhelm von Lenz's phrase, "the dancers seek and flee one another" (ex. 4.8).[14]

Despite the conventional rhetoric of these variations, however, we should not take their unproblematic nature for granted; they are not quite as straightforward or lightweight as may appear on first hearing. The unexpected intertwinings of the theme with the first variation and of each of the first three variations with its next neighbor lend a sense of continual metamorphosis to the proceedings, like a smoothly-flowing relay race. The surface symmetry of the layouts is thrown into question by these intertwinings, for the closing measure of each section functions not only as an upbeat for the next but possibly as its opening as well, most strikingly where the overlapping measure seems to be integral to the rhetoric and structure of the incoming variation. The double function gives rise to some ambiguity as to the precise starting point of the new variation. It is a musical equivalent of an optical illusion or a Möbius strip (ex. 4.9).

Moreover, the theme and its first variations are dancelike but are not identifiable dances; rather they seem to be examples of those "[s]piritualized dance parodies" (Kerman) that Beethoven frequently constructed to create

EXAMPLE 4.9.   Poco allegretto, mm. 41–51.

a sense of disembodiment.[15] These tiny anomalies in structure and perception not only complicate the action but prepare for an unmistakable and dramatic event—even if half-expected—by which the finale's orbit will be thoroughly knocked off course and the structure of the sonata radically reconfigured. That moment arrives in the closing measure of variation 4, a passage in parallel motion flowing ritardando across a double bar into a section marked Adagio espressivo, thus breaking the mood, cutting the string of continuous action, and collapsing the temporal arc of the movement by a reversion to a superseded stage of the sonata's narrative trajectory—the identically titled slow movement. It is an allusion to an earlier, elegiac state of being rather than an actual repetition, creating an ambiguity that conveys a sense of the enigmatic. Consider, for example, the extent to which the sextuplet turning figures in thirty-second-notes at the end of this variation (mm. 149–63) share a density, shape, and crowded chromaticism with the sixty-fourth-note figures that close the sonata's second movement (mm. 58–64). We find ourselves within a quasi-reminiscence, recalling an earlier event, but not precisely. Through this sudden reversion to inwardness, the present is penetrated by memories we had thought to be safely in the past.

The Adagio espressivo was half-expected, deceptively opening as though it were a conventional slow variation, intended perhaps to preface a learned-style fugal ending, to set up a gratifying close, or to prepare for the return of the tempo primo. But the highly chromaticized piano cadenzas at measures 148 and 156—bracketed by fermatas, marked crescendo-diminuendo and *langsam*[16]—derail these expectations and instead shift the scene to hypnagogic territory, drifting into an unfamiliar, dreamlike universe. The possibility that this is just another variation in a linear succession vanishes. Instead, Beethoven gives us something more akin to an adagio movement, thus throwing into question the form of the finale. We have been lured into deep waters.

Lenz called attention to an aberrant feature of the cadenzas, observing that each cadenza consists of three sequences of seven thirty-second notes followed by a nineteen-note passage.[17] (Alternatively, they can be counted as four sequences of seven thirty-seconds, the fourth eventuating in a twelve-note sequence.) Pressing downward from the C two octaves above middle C in tightly packed chromatic steps, crescendo, they are obstructed in their first three tries; but the fourth attempt succeeds, descending diminuendo the rest of the way from the high F-natural to the F-sharp above middle C in an even twelve-note chromatic glide, which, after the fermata, elicits a dolce triplet passage from the violin—like a bird soaring into the open sky (ex. 4.10).

After a squarely symmetrical theme and four variations, each of which lasts thirty-two measures, variation 5 occupies nineteen measures, an irregular arrangement, even an enigmatic one, but one appropriate to a rhapsody-interlude that is heedless of exigencies of symmetry. Self-contained, a lengthy parenthesis, the Adagio espressivo variation has interrupted a story in progress, slipped into a paranormal state or hidden universe; now it is itself interrupted by two cadenzas—parentheses within a parenthesis—that cali-

EXAMPLE 4.10.   Poco allegretto, m. 148.

brate the depth of a hazardous descent into remote regions. Each cadenza's densely-packed chromaticisms and spider-like falling sequences speak to dislocation, asymmetry, the traversal of uncertain terrain: they suggest the presence of an obstacle to further descent, or the possibility of being trapped within a loop of repeating seven-note sequences. We have arrived at a threshold that is also a barrier to be surmounted. Having fallen into an unfamiliar universe, we now need to figure a way out.

An ending is often an ultimate object of longing, for it carries the possibility of restoration and healing. But desire cannot always decide whether it prefers a happy ending or a prolongation of the now, even if the latter carries with it a freight of suffering. One of Beethoven's late-style answers to this conundrum is to prolong the moment, thereby delaying the ending. In any event, for Beethoven, endings ought not to be too easily achieved, certainly not reachable by automatic default but only by determination, patience, and suffering, the merit badges of his Plutarchian heroism.

The burden of Beethoven's Opus 96 may be that the pastoral world is neither as harmonious nor as uncomplicated as had been imagined in Haydn's oratorios or in Beethoven's own *Pastoral* Symphony. Moreover, there is no easy way to lift humanity out of the dejected state of alienation into which it has descended. Arcadia and Eden cannot be recovered without a series of trials; they are accessible only to those who have gained wisdom through hard experience, who carry memories of expulsion and exile as proofs of worthiness. Nothing but a circuitous route is adequate to so momentous an undertaking, one not unlike that of ritual initiation, which involves risks, obstacles, an awareness of deadly surprises, and even a foreboding that in the end all may be lost. The quest for an appropriate and well-earned ending requires that, as the Boyg in *Peer Gynt* understood, "You must go round about." Or, as Frank Kermode once wrote, "The interest of having our expectations falsified is obviously related to our wish to reach the discovery or recognition by an unexpected and instructive route."[18]

Indeed, it requires more than a single interruption of this sonata's implied narrative to express the circuitousness of the Poco allegretto's route to realization, the density of the barrier, the twists and turns and blind alleys of the labyrinth. A crescendo-ritardando measure releases the music from the liminal sphere of the Adagio espressivo variation and returns it at measure 164 to the tempo primo, but in E-flat, which, by now, we have come to understand, is always transitory, whether as elegy, as Arcadian mirage, or perhaps in this instance as a marker to reassure us that the goal remains on the horizon of possibility even if the move remains premature, the ending still insufficiently prepared. In its seventh measure, the theme is abruptly suspended in midair and three additional measures of rhythmic gesture prepare to catapult us back into the variation sequence, variation 6 being a whirling, madcap, allegro dance, with sforzandos to mark the opening beats (ex. 4.11).

Later, at measure 205, the accent is shifted to the second beat, the syncopations hurtling the action forward; and then comes a learned-style fugato variation in G minor—whose first dozen notes are identical with the movement's main theme except for altered time values and the use of the minor mode[19]—to emphasize the gravity of the occasion, to imply that wisdom is a precondition for a deserved pastoral ending, and in further preparation for the now considerably postponed return to the main theme at measures 245–60.

With the return of the tempo primo in its original key, any reasonable listener would be confident that the music is ready to end. But after sixteen bars of literal recall of the main theme, without repeats, the music digresses into seven rushing measures of ascending and descending scales in contrary and parallel motion, preparing for one last postponement, a Poco adagio

EXAMPLE 4.11. Poco allegretto, mm. 164–75.

EXAMPLE 4.12. Poco allegretto, mm. 275–95.

EXAMPLE 4.12 *(continued)*

interlude (mm. 275–87) that offers a triple reminiscence—of the Adagio espressivo in this movement, which in turn is a reminder of the elegiac second movement, and, primarily, of the Poco allegretto's main theme, whose hitherto-concealed *tristesse* is now disclosed. The Poco adagio doesn't so much picture the ongoing uncertainty of the course, but rather the necessity of melancholia, the impermanence of life's pleasures, the contingency of life itself. Having delivered its cautionary message the music playfully scampers off into the sunset at measures 288–95 (ex. 4.12).

CHAPTER FIVE

REASON AND IMAGINATION:
THE AESTHETIC DIMENSION

For Robert L. Marshall

Beethoven left no connected writings on aesthetics, but his letters, diary, and conversation books contain a substantial number of aphoristic expressions that offer insight into his views on the nature of art, creativity, and the responsibilities of the artist. They reveal that he absorbed a surprising number of current aesthetic ideas, mixing them freely without apparent regard for consistency and without any thought of forming a systematic theory of art. These ideas, phrases, and fragments sometimes appealed to him as much for their sheer rhetoric as for their specific content. Furthermore, it remains open, especially in quotations drawn from Beethoven's letters, whether they are to be read as expressions of faith or primarily as conventional utterances intended to impress his correspondents with his devotion to high ideals in art. With due allowance for skeptical readings, however, it may be possible to find some order in this enthusiastic mélange of unelaborated ideas and, perhaps, to locate an evolutionary pattern in his conceptions of art and the artist.

As befits a socially committed composer who came to maturity in the 1780s and early 1790s in a Rhenish principality where the dominant perspectives among young and radical intellectuals were shaped in unequal parts by the *philosophes,* the Austrian *Aufklärung* of Emperor Joseph II, Freemasonry, the Order of Illuminati, and the precepts of Kantian thought and Schillerian drama, Beethoven consciously and automatically stressed the pragmatic and altruistic purposes of art, seen variously as intended to affect and instruct, elevate taste and morality, advance knowledge, improve the social order, and serve the divinity. Thus, he described his own purpose as "to raise the taste of the public and to let [my] *genius* soar to greater heights and even to perfection";[1] he hoped that a time would come when, as he said, "my art will be exercised only for the benefit of the poor";[2] and he avowed, "Since I was a child my greatest happiness and pleasure have been to be able to do something for others."[3] Chiding Goethe for delighting "far too much in the court atmosphere than is becoming to a poet," he declared that poets "should be regarded as the leading teachers of the nation."[4] He often paired "Kunst und Wissenschaft" (the latter here probably signifying "learning" rather than "science") as fundamental shaping forces, and he attributed to them manifold powers, including to "give us intimations and hopes of a higher life"; to unite "the best and noblest people"; and to "raise men to the Godhead [bis zur Gottheit]."[5] Consistently, through four decades, he connected his artistic purpose with a divine principle, seen as both the source and the goal of his creativity, affirming his faith in the transcendent purposes of art. For example, in 1792 or 1793 he wrote to his Bonn teacher, Christian Gottlob Neefe, of "my divine art";[6] to the publisher Breitkopf & Härtel in 1812, of "my heavenly art, the only true divine gift of Heaven";[7] and, in his last decade, to another publisher, Bernhard Schotts Söhne, alluding to "what the Eternal Spirit has infused into my soul and bids me complete."[8] Such acknowledgment of the godhead is not unmixed with a sense of the godlike nature of his own creativity: in 1815 he wrote to a friend, "Have you already heard in Courland about my great works? I call them great—but compared with the works of the All-highest all human works are small—";[9] nor is it untouched by Beethoven's competitive spirit, for he described himself not merely as the recipient of God's gift but as an active creator along divine lines. Ultimately, Beethoven settled for a creative partnership with the deity: "There is nothing higher than to approach the Godhead more nearly than other mortals and by means of that contact to spread the rays of the Godhead through the human race."[10]

Beethoven's aesthetic comments often center on what he viewed as an antagonism between the spiritual and material spheres: "Unfortunately," he wrote, "we are dragged down from the celestial [überirdische] element in art only too rudely into the earthly and human sides of life."[11] As for himself, he observed, "I much prefer the empire of the mind, and I regard it as the highest of all spiritual and worldly monarchies";[12] and again, "My kingdom is in the air. As the wind often does, so do harmonies whirl around me, and so too do things often whirl about in my soul."[13] It is noteworthy—and not without implications for his music—that these remarks are characterized by the use of spatial metaphors, and especially imagery of height and depth to represent value and judgment. He saw the conflict between the celestial and the earthly (and the subterranean as well) as a dialectic in which art attempts to escape from the world even as it is implicated in it. "A man's spirit, the active creative spirit, must not be tied down to the wretched necessities of life."[14] He imagined utopian havens where art could set up defenses against quotidian distraction, political censorship, and commercial necessity: "Art, when it is persecuted, finds asylum everywhere. Why, Daedalus when confined to the labyrinth invented the wings which lifted him *upwards* and out into the air. Oh, I too shall find them, these wings—."[15]

There is a suggestion in these remarks that music, by virtue of its ethereal natural medium ("the air"), occupies not merely a separate but a superior realm. Thus, although in his later years Beethoven dubbed himself a "Tondichter" (tone-poet) and infused musical form with unprecedented narrative and mythic strategies, he continued to see music as fundamentally distinct from the literary and pictorial arts: "The description of a picture belongs to painting. And in this respect the poet too, whose sphere in this case is not so restricted as mine, may consider himself to be more favored than my Muse. On the other hand my sphere extends further into other regions and our empire cannot be so easily reached—."[16] Similarly, even as he extended the imitative and symbolic potentialities of musical rhetoric, he continued to insist on their subordinate nature: "All painting in instrumental music is lost if it is pushed too far," he wrote in a sketchbook for the *Pastoral* Symphony; "Anyone who has an idea of country-life can make out for himself the intentions of the composer without many titles—Also, without any description, the whole will be recognized more as feeling than tone-painting."[17]

In his capacity as a working musician who was also an entrepreneur of his own musical commodities, Beethoven was preoccupied with the economics of art. "You know that I have to live entirely on the products of my mind," he wrote;[18] it was a condition that he resented because it forced him to expend his energies on business negotiations. "To hell with the economics of music," summed up his feelings on this score.[19] In an unguarded letter to a composer-publisher with whom he shared political sympathies, he proposed to resolve the "tiresome" issues of artistic commodity exchange through a solution derived from French utopian and Babouvist sources: "I wish things were different in the world. There ought to be in the world a *market for art [ein Magazin der Kunst]* to which the artist would only bring his works in order to take what he needed. As it is, one must be half businessman as well, and how can one be reconciled to that!"[20] In his enthusiasm for this utopian solution, Beethoven did not consider the possibility that economic independence might entail some cost in creative freedom. The influence of quasi-socialist concepts is apparent also in a draft introduction to a never-consummated complete edition of his works, in which he placed the issue of an author's compensation under the rubric of "human rights *[Menschenrechten]*" and reiterated his resentment of the "greedy brainpickers *[leckern Gehirnskoster]*" who line their pockets with profits from an author's work; he wrote: "The author is determined to show that the *human brain* cannot be sold either like coffee beans or like any form of cheese which, as everyone knows, must first be produced from *milk, urine* and so forth— The human brain is inherently inalienable *[Das Menschengehirn ist an sich unveräußerlich]*—."[21]

Throughout his life, Beethoven considered himself to be an adherent of Enlightenment rationalism, praising reason, abjuring superstition, and disdaining libretti on magic or supernatural subjects: "I cannot deny that on the whole I am prejudiced against this sort of thing, because it has a soporific effect on feeling and reason—."[22] But, on a simultaneous yet separate track, he was drawn to Romantic restlessness, to Faustian striving for an unreachable objective, unnamable and mysterious. "Every day brings me nearer to the goal which I feel but cannot describe. And it is only in that condition that your Beethoven can live. There must be no rest — I know of none but sleep."[23] The Romantic conception of unceasing striving or yearning for "the infinite" *(das Unendliche)* resonates throughout his conception of art: "The true artist has no pride. He sees unfortunately that art has no limits; he has a vague awareness of how far he is from reaching his goal; and while others may perhaps be admiring him, he laments the fact that he has not yet reached the point whither his better genius only lights the way for him like a distant sun."[24] If there were powerful neoclassicist undercurrents in his moralizing view of art's function and in his unswerving devotion to reason, an amalgam of these with Romantic conceptions was under way as early as the later 1790s, when he wrote about the need "to strive towards the inaccessible goal *[unerreichbaren Ziele]* which art and nature have set us —."[25] While the language may be reminiscent of remarks in Kant's *Critique of Judgment* about "the unattainability of the idea by means of imagination," there is no real reason to connect Beethoven's descriptions of the inadequacy of his strivings for artistic perfection with Kant's idea of the immeasurability and unreachability of the sublime.[26] Beethoven's obscure goal, although it may be sublime, is not the sublime, but creative achievement. Moreover, obscurity is itself an essential ingredient of the sublime, as Edmund Burke knew when he wrote that "in nature, dark, confused, uncertain images have a greater power on the fancy to form the grander passions, than those have which are more clear and determinate."[27]

Still, Beethoven viewed the unknowable, the unreachable, and the infinite as territories to be conquered by rationality, spirit, and the abundant powers of art and wisdom.[28] Accordingly, as is shown in 1802 in his correspondence with Breitkopf & Härtel concerning the piano variations, Opuses 34 and 35, he valorized originality as an essential ingredient of his art: "Both sets are really worked out in a wholly *new manner,* and each in a *separate and different way.* . . . I myself can assure you that in both these works the *method is quite new so far as I am concerned*—."[29] He was concerned about potential formal limitations on an oratorio that had been commissioned by the Gesellschaft der Musikfreunde: "I hope that I shall not be forbidden to deviate from the *forms which have been introduced until now into this type of composition.*"[30] Heedless of charges of "bizarrerie" that greeted his works in the classicizing music journals, he pursued the idea of the new in a multitude of formal, technical, and rhetorical innovations, insisting that each major work pose and solve a unique set of problems. It was reported by Karl Holz that when asked which among the String Quartets, opp. 127, 130, and 132, was the greatest, Beethoven responded with another Faustian remark, "Each in its way. Art demands of us that we shall not stand still." In these works, he continued, "You will find a new manner of part writing *[Stimmführung]* . . . and thank God there is less lack of fancy *[Phantasie]* than ever before."[31]

Beethoven's defiant skepticism about compositional rules and conventions is well documented. When Ferdinand Ries, citing the prohibitions of the musical theoreticians, pointed out parallel fifths in one of the string quartets, op. 18, Beethoven closed the argument with the words, "And I allow them thus!"[32] According to Carl Czerny, the composer Anton Halm once tried to justify his own violations of the rules by alluding to precedent in Beethoven's works, to which the latter responded, "I may do it, but not you."[33] In a conversation book of November 1823, the violinist Ignaz Schuppanzigh wrote, "[Carl Maria von] *Weber* says, As God pleases; *Beethoven* says, As *Beethoven* pleases!"[34] A passage in a draft letter to his Russian patron Prince Nikolas Galitzin gives this issue an almost Wordsworthian turn: "[W]hen feeling opens up a path for us, then away with all rules—."[35] A candid statement of Beethoven's aesthetic Caesarism surfaced as early as 1798, when he wrote to his friend Nikolaus Zmeskall von Domanovecz, "The devil take you, I refuse to hear anything about your whole moral outlook. *Power* is the moral principle of those who excel others, and it is also mine."[36]

Beethoven placed great value on the idea of progress in music; with Johann Sebastian Bach and Handel in mind, he wrote to Archduke Rudolph, "the older composers render us double service, since there is generally real artistic value in their works. . . . But in the world of art, as in the whole of our great creation, *freedom and progress* are the main objectives. And although we moderns are not quite as far advanced in *solidity* as our *ancestors,* yet the refinement of our customs has enlarged many of our conceptions as well."[37] Thus, closely associated conceptions of modernity and progress in the arts are fundamental to Beethoven's aesthetic. He was skeptical about the ability of broad audiences to grasp his innovations: "Even if only a few people understand me, I shall be satisfied," he wrote as early as 1796,[38] and at the end of his life, according to Ferdinand Hiller, he declared, "They say, 'Vox populi, vox dei'—I have never believed in it."[39] He once told Czerny that in Mozart's String Quartet in A, K. 464, which offers an unprecedented array of dissociated forms, chromatic textures, and contrapuntal techniques, "Mozart was telling the world: 'Look what I could do if you were ready for it!'"[40] In his own career, Beethoven composed music for a wide range of audiences: centrally, of course, for serious music-lovers and musicians of every kind, but also potboilers or easy pieces for the layman and amateur, classicizing diversions and ostentatious occasional pieces for imperial tastes, and modernist works for the avant-garde and the elite. Concerning one of his subtlest works, his String Quartet in F minor, op. 95, he wrote, uncompromisingly, "The Quartett is written for a small circle of connoisseurs and is never to be performed in public."[41] He defended his later works against charges of excessive difficulty, writing, "*what is difficult is also beautiful, good, great* and so forth. . . . [T]his is *the most lavish* praise that can be bestowed, since what is *difficult makes one sweat.*"[42] While striving to stretch the boundaries of musical discourse in his own time, the idea of reaching a future public had great appeal to him, for he saw it as providing the possibility of immortality. "*Continue to paint* and I shall *continue to write down notes,*" he wrote to a painter, "and thus we shall live for ever? yes, perhaps, for ever."[43]

There are several striking omissions in Beethoven's aesthetic remarks. He nowhere directly addressed issues of beauty or the sublime, the judgment of taste, the sensuous substratum of art. Kant's conception of disinterested beauty may have been antithetical to Beethoven's own creed, though surely not to his actual creative practice.[44] Evidently he did not see—or would not acknowledge—the disinterested creation of beautiful works as fundamental to his lofty purposes. More surprisingly, Beethoven did not adopt Schiller's modification of Kantian perspectives and particularly his proposal that beauty has the capacity to reconcile the rational and the sensuous, to serve as an ideal projection of freedom and transcendent possibility. Nor did he give much weight to views of art as a fusion of pleasure and instruction; the rendering of delight and pleasure to audiences was not crucial to his aesthetics, even though he did acknowledge once, in passing, that for the artist himself, "there is no more undisturbed, more unalloyed or purer pleasure" than that which comes from rising "ever higher into the heaven of art."[45] Perhaps he shared Schiller's idea, in letter 10 of the *Letters on the Aesthetical Education of Man,* that "the beautiful only founds its sway on the ruins of heroic virtues."[46] In letters of Beethoven's early and middle years there are occasional signs of an unmalleable earnestness, bordering on intolerance; and he was reported to have disapproved, on moral grounds, of the libretto to *Don Giovanni.*[47] To some extent, Beethoven shared the moralizing attitudes and the didacticism of post-Rococo aesthetics, with its critique of hedonism; but his high praise for *Die Zauberflöte* suggests his awareness that there is no unalterable requirement for the artist to trade delight for virtue, wonder for reason.

Beethoven rarely referred to formal or structural issues, but he seems to have been affected by widely prevalent conceptions of the artwork as a coherent whole. This is implied by his saying to a British admirer in 1815, "I have always a picture in my mind, when I am composing, and work up to it";[48] by his remark about *Fidelio* that "my custom when I am composing even instrumental music is always to keep the whole before my eyes";[49] and by his comment to Breitkopf & Härtel that, "once one has thought out a whole work which is based even on a bad *text,* it is difficult to prevent this whole from being destroyed if individual alterations are made here and there."[50] One ought not to conclude from such remarks that Beethoven privileged Goethean or Coleridgean conceptions of organicism in art. Still, the subject was not foreign to him: on the autograph title-page of his String Quartet in C-sharp minor, op. 131, which he sent to Bernhard Schotts Söhne for engraving in August 1826, Beethoven jokingly described this extremely original and tightly-structured quartet as "stolen together from a miscellany of this and that [zusammengestohlen aus Verschiedenem diesem u. jenem]"[51]— thus affirming that aesthetic wholeness may derive from heterogeneity, paying tribute to the potential for coherence that lies within the fragmentary, and to the capability of the imagination to represent the unprecedented through the redeployment or transmutation of already existing ideas and imagery.[52]

Although on one occasion he wrote to Prince Galitzin, "Nature is founded on Art and, again, Art is founded on Nature,"[53] conceptions of art as imitation and of the artist as a percipient agent reflecting the external world had little resonance for Beethoven even during his years of apprenticeship. In his last years he made explicit his belief in the primacy of a productive, shaping imagination, seen as a distinct faculty of the mind to set alongside reason and understanding, capable of anticipating reality, creating rather than reproducing, emulating or rivaling divine creation rather than deferring to the deity's prerogatives. "The imagination, too, asserts its privileges [die Phantasie will auch ihr Recht behaupten]," he reportedly remarked concerning his late quartets, "and today a different, truly poetic element must be manifested in conventional form."[54] To call upon several overworked metaphors, for him art was a beacon illuminating the chaotic reaches of as yet undiscovered worlds rather than a mirror of an ordered, mapped universe. In his later years, Beethoven began to see his creativity as an expression of both subjectivity and desire: "Gradually there comes to us the power to express just what we desire and feel; and to the nobler type of human being this is such an essential need."[55] Art involved self-revelation and implied an autobiographical dimension. Beethoven heard and responded to "the greater innate summons to reveal myself to the world through my works."[56]

Elsewhere in this book (see pp. 3–4 and 169–71) we itemize the signs of Beethoven's abiding belief that his personal creativity simultaneously involved and justified self-sacrifice, evidenced especially by multiple references to sacrificial imperatives in his intimate diary of 1812–18.[57] During those years, under the influence of a mixture of Brahman and Masonic ideas of salvation through self-denial, he began to take such conceptions as prescriptions for both life and art, so that he came to see the goal of his sacramental quest as a convergence of divinity and art.[58] In the course of time, the latter increasingly became the main purpose of his existence, and the purpose of art almost became, tautologically, the creation of art, as when he referred to "the most important object of my art, namely, the composition of great works."[59] We saw earlier, in another connection, that he was even willing to harness the demonic to his aesthetic mission: "I live entirely for my art and for the purpose of fulfilling my duties as a man. But unfortunately this too cannot always be done without the help of the powers of the underworld *[ohne die unterirdischen Mächte]*."[60] In a variant formulation Beethoven lamented the unfortunate circumstance that "the upward glance must also lose itself in the depths, there where the evil subterranean powers dwell."[61] Along related lines is a remark embedded in an overwrought letter to Nannette Streicher about the domestic disorder in his household: "In the sphere of art even swamp and slime are of more use to a man than all that damned nonsense *[Teufelszeug]*!!!—"[62] If this is read literally, it seems possible that Beethoven here credited primordial matter with generative powers or even that he glimpsed a pre-Bakhtinian dialectic in which hierarchical splits between perceived higher and lower spheres could be reconciled.

It may be that among Beethoven's most interesting aesthetic ideas are those that are not quite transparent and need to be understood in their poetic or musical implications. Another striking example appears in a literary quotation that Beethoven copied into a conversation book for 11 March 1820:

> The world is a king and desires flattery in return for favor; but true art is obstinate and will not yield to the fashions of flattery. Famous artists always labor under an embarrassment;—therefore their first works are the best, although they may have sprung from the dark womb. They say art is long, life is short—only life is long and art is short; may its breath lift us to the Gods—That is an instant's grace.[63]

One hesitates to impose too much of a sense of order upon such aphoristic and sometimes inchoate materials, to seek to reconcile Beethoven's conflicting ideas, or to situate his remarks within an evolutionary trajectory. Indeed, a more coherent set of aesthetic principles might well have become an impediment to his own creative efforts.

Nevertheless, taken as a whole, Beethoven's aesthetic remarks are neither haphazard nor capricious. They exhibit an internal development that roughly parallels the evolution of ideas coming into play against the backdrop of the Habsburg *Aufklärung,* the French Revolution, the Napoleonic era, and the post–Congress of Vienna years. They coincide with the emergence of Romantic tendencies among Beethoven's associates and contemporaries; it is possible to deduce a sympathy for Romantic music aesthetics from Beethoven's admiration for reviews of his works by E. T. A. Hoffmann and Adolph Bernhard Marx, as well as from his friendship with the composer-critic Friedrich August Kanne, an advocate of Schleiermacher's ideas; at the very least, there seems to be a discernible shift in his aesthetic stance toward Romanticist conceptions and imagery—emphasizing expression, inwardness, transcendental longing, and a drive to discover new ways of symbolizing extreme states of being. A Revolutionary Classicism gives way to an eclectic, unreified Romanticism, which, however, never supersedes Beethoven's commitment to art as a moral force.

Perhaps more fundamentally, the weight of Beethoven's aesthetic formulations eventually shifted from the primacy of reason to the primacy of the imagination. In his earlier years, a relatively unmediated adherence to reason and virtue acted as a powerful organizing principle of his creativity as well as an eventual constraint on its further development. In the course of time, as the so-called heroic style (ca. 1803–13) moved toward exhaustion, Beethoven found a collateral organizing principle in the idea of the imaginative, seen as an adjunct to reason, as an unfettered instrument of investigation with the power of representing a multitude of previously undescribed modes of being and strategies of transcendence.

CHAPTER SIX

THE SEVENTH SYMPHONY AND
THE RHYTHMS OF ANTIQUITY

For Harry Goldschmidt

From the start, devotees of Beethoven's music have been alert to the significance of the Seventh Symphony's rhythmic dimension. Richard Wagner designated this symphony "the apotheosis of the dance";[1] Paul Bekker called it a "new form," in which "the principle of rhythm . . . [rules] the form in every detail";[2] and Walter Riezler found in the sketches for the first movement "irrefutable evidence that for Beethoven this rhythm was the central idea of the movement, the starting-point," and summed up: "[I]n no other work are all the movements so dominated by rhythm."[3] Rhythm has long been seen as the Seventh Symphony's most salient feature, its substance, from which are derived its unusual rhetoric, as well as its melodies, its harmonic trajectories, and its structure.

Also, beginning early on, it was observed that some of the rhythms employed by Beethoven in the Seventh Symphony could be readily scanned according to the principles of stresses and syllabification codified in classical Greek prosody. Nottebohm's comment, in his essay on the Petter Sketchbook (1875), on the "dominant dactyl *[herrschende Daktylus]*" meter of the Vivace,[4] had been anticipated as early as 1816, when a Bonn essayist, Friedrich Mosengeil, called the first movement a "dactylic dance *[Daktylen-Tanz]*";[5] and, it seems, classically educated listeners could scarcely help noticing that the building blocks of the Allegretto are sequences of metrical units compounded of a dactyl and a spondee.[6] These and similar matter-of-fact observations were widespread in the critical literature, but, so far as I can tell, Carl Czerny, who was not only Beethoven's pupil but an eminent music theorist and pedagogue, was the first to see a more extensive use of Greek poetic meters in the symphony as a whole. He did so in a footnote to his

German translation of several treatises on composition by Anton Reicha, a footnote that had been consigned to obscurity until it was rescued in 1970 by Harry Goldschmidt, who saw in it potential support for a narrative or poetic interpretation of the symphony.[7] Reicha had tabulated the musical equivalents of the Greek meters and commented on their utility in writing vocal music. Czerny endorsed this view, and saw it as applicable to instrumental music as well:

> One can analyze many great instrumental compositions from this standpoint. Thus, for example, in Beethoven's truly great Seventh Symphony (in A major), the Introduction

> can be taken to have been written in weighty *spondees* [*schweren* Spondäen], ‿ _.
>
> The first Allegro with its wide range of dactylic figures

> is the image, as it were, of musical hexameter.
>
> The Andante [recte Allegretto] is formed from weighty *dactyls* and *spondees*.

> And this kind of poetic form can also be ascribed to the Finale.

> It isn't improbable that Beethoven, when he enthusiastically worked out this symphony in the years 1813–14 [recte 1811–12], really was thinking about the forms of heroic poetry and must have deliberately turned toward the same in his musical epic. In most of his compositions there resides, apart from their musical value, a deeper meaning, whose disclosure would indeed place them on a far higher plane.[8]

There appears to be room to expand on Czerny's synoptic insight, to explore in greater detail whether the use of Greek poetic meter extends to all of the movements of the symphony, and if that turns out to be so, what it might imply about Beethoven's compositional methods and the structure and significance of the work itself.

II

FIRST MOVEMENT: POCO SOSTENUTO

The lengthy introduction to the first movement, Poco sostenuto, opens with a broad sweeping pattern of sequences of four half-notes, corresponding to the poetic meter known as dispondaic ($----$), which is the tetrasyllabic version of the disyllabic spondaic meter ($--$) (fig. 6.1). Each four-note sequence lasts two measures and is initiated by an accented *forte* chord. A brief sighing figure in the oboes at measure 4 is in dactylic rhythm ($-\smile\smile \ -\smile\smile$), forecasting the many dactyls yet to come (ex. 6.1).[9]

The arpeggiated spondaic sequences are followed by—more accurately, alternate with—an ascending "running" figure of sixteenth-notes, which makes its appearance beginning at measure 10 (climbing and reclimbing—"like gigantic stairs," is the image that appealed to Sir George Grove).[10] It can be scanned either as proceleusmatic ($\smile\smile\smile\smile \ \smile\smile\smile\smile \ \smile\smile\smile\smile \ \smile\smile\smile\smile$) or, if we take into account the accent on the first note of each group of four, a variant of paeon primus (first paeon; $-\smile\smile\smile \ -\smile\smile\smile \ -\smile\smile\smile \ -\smile\smile\smile$), albeit without the expected long duration of the first beat. The running sixteenth-note sequences, four to the measure, may represent a reinterpretation of the arpeggiated half-notes, accelerating the action through the use of smaller note values.[11] With the *fortissimo* at measure 17, the two sequences are climactically and seamlessly combined, reminding us that among the ancients, one of the hallmarks of an accomplished poet was precisely the ability to mix and combine different rhythmic feet in a single meter, thereby creating a complex rhythmic texture.[12] The dolce countertheme introduced at measure 23—a lyricizing of the spondaic arpeggios—brings with it a set of new rhythmic ideas, scannable in various ways: its underlying rhythm seems dactylic ($-\smile\smile \ | \ -\smile\smile$), but it can be interpreted, with only a slight shift in perspective, as anapestic ($\smile\smile- \ | \ \smile\smile-$) or cretic ($-\smile- \ | \ -\smile-$) (ex. 6.2).

The sixteenth-note patterns return at measure 29, now as accompaniment, gathering strength for a *fortissimo* reprise of the rapturous spondaic-paeonic outburst (mm. 34–40). The Poco sostenuto closes only when all

Meter	Approximate duration represented through note values
I. Disyllabic	in $\frac{2}{4}$
1 ᵕ – iambus	
2 – ᵕ trochee	
3 – – spondee	
4 ᵕ ᵕ pyrrhic	
II. Trisyllabic	in $\frac{3}{8}$
1 – ᵕ ᵕ dactyl *light:*	
	in $\frac{2}{4}$
heavy:	
2 ᵕ – ᵕ amphibrach	
3 ᵕ ᵕ – anapest	
	in $\frac{6}{8}$
4 – – ᵕ bacchius	
5 – ᵕ – cretic	
6 ᵕ – – antibacchius	
	in $\frac{3}{4}$
7 – – – molossus	
	in $\frac{3}{8}$
8 ᵕ ᵕ ᵕ tribrach	
III. Tetrasyllabic	in $\frac{4}{4}$
1 ᵕ – ᵕ – diamb	
2 – ᵕ – ᵕ ditrochee	
3 – – – – dispondee	
4 ᵕ ᵕ ᵕ ᵕ proceleusmatic	
	in $\frac{2}{4}$
5 ᵕ – – – ⎫ first	
6 – ᵕ – – ⎪ second ⎫ epitrite	
7 – – ᵕ – ⎪ third ⎬	
8 – – – ᵕ ⎭ fourth ⎭	
	in $\frac{6}{8}$
9 – ᵕ ᵕ ᵕ ⎫ first	
10 ᵕ – ᵕ ᵕ ⎪ second ⎫ paeon	
11 ᵕ ᵕ – ᵕ ⎪ third ⎬	
12 ᵕ ᵕ ᵕ – ⎭ fourth ⎭	
	in $\frac{3}{4}$
13 – – ᵕ ᵕ ⎫ falling ⎫ ionic	
14 ᵕ ᵕ – – ⎭ rising ⎭	
	in $\frac{6}{8}$
15 – ᵕ ᵕ – choriamb	
	in $\frac{3}{4}$
16 ᵕ – – ᵕ antispast	

FIGURE 6.1.   Metrical chart translated from Anton Reicha, *Vollständiges Lehrbuch der musikalischen Composition*, German trans. Carl Czerny, 4 vols. (Vienna: Diabelli & Co., n.d. [1834]), vol. 2, pp. 472–73.

EXAMPLE 6.1. Symphony no. 7 in A, op. 92, Poco sostenuto, mm. 1–13.

EXAMPLE 6.2. Poco sostenuto, mm. 23–27.

EXAMPLE 6.3.   Poco sostenuto, mm. 54–62.

of the rhythms it has introduced have spent their energy and are ready to give way to the Vivace, at measure 63. The final measures summon up, condense, and reconcile the introduction's three main figures (the spondaic arpeggios, the dactylic sighing figure, and the proceleusmatic sixteenths), which are rapidly simplified to a single pitch across four octaves and to a drum tattoo that finds the simplest iambics at the moment of transition (ex. 6.3).

FIRST MOVEMENT (CONTINUED): VIVACE

To identify the essential material from which the Vivace of the Seventh Symphony is formed, Beethoven inscribed a simple rhythmic motif (dotted-eighth–sixteenth–eighth) on sketches for the main theme, first as a single bass line and then as a series of tonic triads (fig. 6.2). When it came to actually writing out the opening of the Vivace, he made his intention explicit with four measures of the motif in the winds, crescendo, unambiguously setting the section's organizing meter prior to unveiling his theme in the flutes at measure 67 (ex. 6.4). The motif thereby immediately establishes its precedence in the compositional hierarchy, always sounding in the theme's background, even when momentarily silent or not literally present.[13] It becomes evident that the theme is complete only when heard in com-

FIGURE 6.2.   Sketches, Vivace (Nottebohm, *Zweite Beethoveniana*, pp. 103, 105).

bination with the initiating motif, which moves to the strings, building a tension that is discharged at measure 89 in a ferocious, pounding eruption by the trumpets, lower strings, and timpani, marked *sempre fortissimo,* that reveals the theme to be a skeletal derivative, even an epiphenomenon, of the motif (ex. 6.5).

Hugo Riemann, perhaps scanning the opening measures from the up-beats instead of the downbeats, managed to find anapests where Czerny and Nottebohm had found dactyls.[14] Although music in triple time often lends itself to dactylic readings, it seems to me that the underlying rhythm and the melody itself have equal claims to be interpreted as cretic ($-\smile-$ | $-\smile-$). But none of these suggestions is altogether satisfactory. Riemann ignored the fact that the pulsating 6/8 figure demands stresses on beats 1 and 4 of each measure, and Czerny's and Nottebohm's dactyls are atypical inasmuch as the second and third beats of each foot are unequal.[15] By the same token, the foot is an uncharacteristic cretic, not only because it lacks the cretic's usual heavy tread, but because the first and the third long beats are of different lengths. What can be said is that the sequences are remindful of dactyls and cretics but do not fully align with either. The ambiguity underscores the difficulties of trying to find exact correspondences between musical and poetic meters if one looks only for patterns of duration instead of for a complex interaction of patterns of duration and patterns of stress. Such ambiguities are further compounded when music specifies swift tempos that are well beyond the speed at which poetry can be read or understood.

EXAMPLE 6.4.   Vivace, mm. 63–69.

EXAMPLE 6.5.   Vivace, mm. 88–93.

SECOND MOVEMENT: ALLEGRETTO

Throughout, except in its contrasting middle section, the Allegretto presents an unremitting dactylic-spondaic ostinato meter (ex. 6.6).

The exact outline of this sequence can be found among sketches for the second and third movements of the String Quartet in C ("Razumovsky"), op. 59, no. 3, which Beethoven completed in 1806 (fig. 6.3). In light of this sketch, Nottebohm thought it only a "natural supposition" that the Alle-

EXAMPLE 6.6.   Allegretto, mm. 1–10.

gretto had been conceived five years before the rest of the symphony was started and even that Beethoven "originally wanted to use it in that quartet in place of the present second movement."[16] Despite Riemann's demurral, this remains a reasonable deduction, suggesting that the theme may even have been an essential point of departure of the symphony as a whole.[17] Whether the latter is accepted or not, it is clear that the dactyl-spondee itself is the movement's central idea, the brick and mortar of its structure, from which its harmonic and melodic components are derived.[18]

In his instructions to the copyist, who had mistakenly marked the accents on several string parts only with dots, Beethoven insisted on clearly differentiating the dactyl and spondee of the sequence by the use of longer strokes to create a quasi-portamento effect in the dactyl and a lighter, more staccato effect in the spondee (fig. 6.4).[19]

The hypnotic effect of Beethoven's variations on this obsessive figure is relieved by the A-major middle section, marked dolce, which withholds the spondees but retains the dactylic rhythm, now sounded in the lowest strings; it is as though the music is "marking time" (Riezler) before returning to the ostinato processional path (ex. 6.7).[20]

A modified dispondaic figure in the winds (mm. 101–4, 110–11) appears to be a pastoral-style transformation of the opening measures of the Poco sostenuto, played against sinuously legato triplets in the first violins and the dactyls in the cellos and basses ($-\cup\cup$ $-\cup\cup$) until the rhythm is momentarily suspended at measure 145, precipitating a racing dactylic or tribrachic plunge down a grand ladder of tumbling triplets, staccato, eventuating in a fugal restatement of the opening section, pizzicato, as though to simulate the plucking of a great lyre.

FIGURE 6.3.   Sketch, String Quartet in C, op. 59, no. 3 (Nottebohm, *Zweite Beethoveniana*, p. 106).

FIGURE 6.4.   Instructions to copyist (Nottebohm, *Beethoveniana*, p. 108).

   The Allegretto is suspended between symmetrical representations of in-determinacy, famously framed by six-four tonic chords that serve, at the start, swiftly to draw a curtain, evoke a sense of restlessness, set a stage, dim the lights, descend in one quick exhalation of the winds from *forte* to *pianissimo,* opening a space within which the rhythmic action may commence. Rising from the nether registers of the orchestra, gradually increasing in volume and amplitude, the insistent pattern reaches climaxes in which the dactyl-spondee pulses lay claim to absolute hegemony, and others in which they are transubstantiated into learned-style fugato. In the Allegretto, Beethoven demonstrates that repetition can be a sign both for metamorphosis and for stasis; beyond the undeviating repetition of the basic meter we encounter

EXAMPLE 6.7. Allegretto, mm. 100–107.

dynamic intensification, transposition of the theme to ever higher registers, and an expressive countermelody that completes the musical fabric, along with crescendos, the fugato, and the final six-four chord. Whatever the movement's manifold implications, the sense of overhearing and being ineluctably drawn into an undulating ceremonial or ritual activity—an unfolding path to ecstasy or to an implied sacred realm—is not far from the surface. In the end, having written itself into existence, the Allegretto erases itself, disappears into the ambiguous harmonic cloud from which it had originated, into a region that cannot be measured in meters or feet. W. J. von Wasielewski saw it as "comparable to an enchantment formula in which the composer calls his phantasy picture into existence and then allows it to dissolve into nothingness."[21]

THIRD MOVEMENT: PRESTO

The Presto runs a virtuoso gamut of interlocking rhythms, both successive and simultaneous (ex. 6.8). Although it may be read in a variety of ways, the opening motif, which launches the action and plays a generative role throughout, is perhaps best understood as an amphibrach foot ($\smile - \smile \ \smile - \smile$), which is transmuted at measure 3 into a swiftly running dactylic ($- \smile\smile \ - \smile\smile$) or tribrachic ($\smile\smile\smile \ \smile\smile\smile$) pattern, both of these being typical of music in 3/4 time. But an alternative metrical narrative for the opening two measures is suggested by the unmistakably iambic meter ($\smile - \ \smile -$) of quarter-notes in the horns, lower strings, and timpani, the implied rhythm of which carries over into the subsequent measures, informing the entire scherzo. And a more extensive array of rhythmic figures quickly emerges, starting at measure 11, in a sequence of tribrach plus trochee two-bar phrases ($\smile\smile\smile \ - \smile \ | \ \smile\smile\smile \ - \smile$) that mesh with what in the present account is the movement's fundamental iambic meter. Beethoven is playing with rhythms, setting one against another, reversing them, reinterpreting dactyls as tribrachs or trochees, and iambics as amphibrachs, enlarging his rhythmic vocabulary but not allowing the pulsating underlying meter to falter until the opening section of the movement has run its course at measures 141–48; there the Presto's opening is evoked, but now as an ostinato, running in place for four measures that issue in an extended tonic chord, tutti, leading diminuendo into the trio, Assai meno presto (mm. 149–64).

At first glance, the meter of the trio, Assai meno presto, seems to be cretic,

EXAMPLE 6.8.   Presto, mm. 1–24.

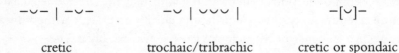

with a trochee and tribrach in place of the second long of the third foot
(ex. 6.9) (mm. 153–54, 161–62):

$$-\smile-\ |\ -\smile- \qquad\qquad -\smile\ |\ \smile\smile\smile\ | \qquad\qquad -[\smile]-$$

cretic   trochaic/tribrachic   cretic or spondaic

The appearance is deceptive. More persuasively, Thomas J. Mathiesen proposes that the rhythmic patterns of the trio are better suited to paeonic meter, especially to paeon primus $[-\smile\smile\smile]$, in which case the eight-measure
phrases (starting with mm. 149–56 and mm. 157–64) "would represent
paeonic tetrameter, which is precisely the common length for this meter."[22]
The cretic feet, then, could be interpreted, not as outlining the fundamental meter of the movement, but as rhythms articulated within a ruling paeonic
meter. One possible way of scanning the trio along these lines is to view

EXAMPLE 6.9.   Presto: Trio, assai meno presto, mm. 149–55.

each foot as consisting of a dotted half-note (thesis) and three quarter-notes (arsis), simplified as follows:

Paeonic Meter: $-[\smile\smile\smile]$ | $-[\smile\smile\smile]$ | $-\smile\smile\smile$ | $-[\smile\smile\smile]$ |
Cretic Rhythm: $-\smile-$ | $-\smile-$ | $-\smile$ $\smile\smile\smile$ | $-\smile-$ |

Mathiesen explores a still more complex and subtle possibility, finding that the opening rhythm of the trio is closest to the pattern known as paeon di-aguios, which consists of a long thesis, a short, and a long arsis ($-\smile$ | $-$): "the initial long is like a thesis not only in that it falls on a downbeat but also because it is sustained as it swells to the short eighth note; on the other hand, the final long is like an arsis, even though it too falls on a downbeat, because the diminuendo and following rests give it a sense of lifting rather than positioning."[23] He also observes that the length of the thesis and arsis vary as the phrase develops and that the strings provide a "metric echo" at the end of each metric line.

Cretic and paeonic rhythms usually suggest a slow march, often of a solemn martial or festive character, but Beethoven grasped their potential for sounds both *piano* and dolce. It may also be worth noting that the basic foot of the trio ($-\smile-$) is an inversion of the amphibrach foot ($\smile-\smile$) that opened the Presto itself.

In the contrasting section of the trio (mm. 181ff), where we reach the symphony's innermost recess, the winds give voice to a Viennese classical-style, long-phrased, yearning melody (ex. 6.10). But even here the paeonic-cretic pattern survives in the horns, at first throbbing quietly in the background, and then, crescendo and with urgently shortened note values, ultimately

EXAMPLE 6.10.   Presto: Trio, mm. 181–94.

EXAMPLE 6.11.   Presto: Trio, mm. 223–36.

emerging into dominance at measures 207ff. The horns reassert the main figure (−⏑−) against a sustained "curtain" in the strings, sempre diminuendo and decrescendo, until at the end it passes to the lowest strings, *ppp*, and the Presto resumes (ex. 6.11).

FOURTH MOVEMENT: ALLEGRO CON BRIO

The finale displays a whirling kaleidoscope of rhythms. It opens with two explosive choriambic strokes (−⏑⏑− | −⏑⏑−) (ex. 6.12). The choriambic rhythm, a close relative of cretic, sets the finale in motion; it is treated as though it were a thematic motif, a figure to be developed, a highly condensed point of departure which, like the opening strokes of the *Eroica* Symphony, initiates the action by unleashing bound energy.

The strings then take up the "turning" figure that dominates the movement (−⏑⏑ ⏑⏑⏑⏑ | −⏑⏑ ⏑⏑⏑⏑ | −⏑⏑ ⏑⏑⏑⏑ | −⏑− |) (ex. 6.13). Again, with due allowance for alternative readings, the passage may be scanned as three dactylic-proceleusmatic feet (−⏑⏑ + ⏑⏑⏑⏑) followed by a cretic (−⏑−). But, as we saw above, Czerny keenly interpreted the underlying meter of the passage as solidly marked spondaic feet of equal duration (−⏑́ | −⏑́ |), with a sforzando accent on the second beat of each spondee, an arsis-thesis pattern like the lifting and striking of a sledgehammer.[24] This appears to be the ruling meter of the finale. Czerny did not point out that in the opening four bars of the movement these spondaic accents are reversed, the strings trading *fortissimos* with the rest of the orchestra—timpani, brass, and winds—in call and response style, but with greater emphasis on the first beat (thesis-arsis). Thus, the turning figure at measure 5 is both an arrival and a reinterpretation of the spondaic accent, creating a disequilibrium that will be settled only in the finale's closing measures.

To an even greater extent than in the earlier movements, Beethoven here spins a web of related, interlocking rhythms, which are experienced simultaneously in their differentiation and fusion. The choriambics of measures 1–4 (−⏑⏑−) seem to be perpetuated in the turning figure as well, with beats 1 and 3 of each measure providing the two longs and the two sixteenths on beat 2 providing the two shorts. And with a slight shift at climactic junctures of the action (mm. 52–62, 263–73) choriambics are transmuted into dotted-rhythm trochees or ditrochees with strongly cretic implications (ex. 6.14).

EXAMPLE 6.12.   Allegro con brio, mm. 1–4.

EXAMPLE 6.13.   Allegro con brio, mm. 5–8.

EXAMPLE 6.14.   Allegro con brio, mm. 52–62.

III

A highly diversified and imaginative use of the ancient poetic meters thus extends to all the movements of the Seventh Symphony. It is true, of course, that an ingenious analyst can profitably apply principles of prosodic scansion to many compositions, and particularly to music with the regular time-signatures characteristic of Beethoven's era. Beethoven himself not infrequently developed an entire movement from rhythmic materials analogous to readily identifiable Greek meters (e.g., the iambic Menuetto of the First Symphony; the dactylic scherzos of the Fifth and Ninth symphonies). In no other extended work by Beethoven, however, do the poetic meters serve so plainly and pervasively as the generative source of the whole, and this weighs in favor of the proposition that the Seventh Symphony was conceived as a conscious development of classical meters. Perhaps weighing even more heavily is the fact that the Seventh Symphony seems uniquely accessible to what we might term "double scansion"—that is, scansion both of the pulse that rises from the time-signatures and of the complementary pulses that are implicit in the thematic or rhetorically expressive materials. For, in Mathiesen's words, "it is the interplay of the arsis and thesis, the various durationally based rhythmic patterns, and the ways in which they are organized in the longer metric patterns"—an interplay prominent in Beethoven's Seventh—that are unique to classical meter.[25]

The Seventh Symphony's fundamental character derives from its pronounced metrical dimension, with its highly streamlined rhythmic palette of obsessively repeated patterns, employed singly and in combination. As a consequence, the symphony offers a relatively limited range of melodic types and structural possibilities. Each of its five large sections (counting the Poco sostenuto separately) features a virtually continuous flow of rhythmic action: there are no fermatas, ritards, accelerandos, or other dislocations or discontinuities of tempo; and there are no tempo changes within the movements except for the conventional scherzo-trio contrasts in the Presto. Even the major-mode section of the Allegretto does not break that movement's stride. Rhythmic regularity sometimes bordering on invariance is throughout a compositional given. The inevitable result is the avoidance of significant pauses or other interruptions; also absent are fantasia, rhapsodic, highly ornamented, or recitative styles. It is self-evident that principles of classical prosody aren't easily applied to music featuring melismatic passages, rapidly shifting tempos, uneven phrase lengths, or themes composed from heterogeneous materials or without clearly defined accents.[26] Compositional strategies involving multiple motifs of dramatically divergent lengths and shapes are also out of the question, as are techniques like the Fifth Symphony's elaboration of the ways in which a thematic-rhythmic figure can be varied, condensed, fragmented, and amplified.

Without minimizing the importance of its melodic dimension or of its harmonic and structural complexity, it can be said that the rhythmic-metrical sphere is more crucial in the Seventh Symphony than in any other of Beethoven's symphonies, even allowing for individual movements like the corner movements of the Fifth and Eighth symphonies and several of the scherzos, and despite the accuracy of Adorno's more general observation that in many or even most of the symphonies, "the detail work, the latent wealth of interior forms and figures, is eclipsed by the rhythmic-metrical impact."[27] The Seventh Symphony is a linked sequence of expansive structural layouts of a powerfully rudimentary type; in the words of Adolph Bernhard Marx, the Romantic critic admired by Beethoven, "everything in the A-major Symphony is definitely formed, clearly and unambiguously designed."[28] Greater subtlety of structure would have been at odds with the symphony's rhythmic austerity and its stark range of bold dynamic effects.

In summary, this symphony exhibits a streamlining, even a one-sidedness, that seeks only minimal accommodation with the late-Haydn or Mozartian models of symphonic decorum and symmetrical closure. It is the climax of a process begun in the opening measures of the *Eroica* Symphony, sweeping away the residues of the classical-style symphony while retaining its outer shell and replacing its mirthful, Apollonian rationalism with a rhetoric that more effectively projects conceptions of motion pushed to the limits, even to excess, abandon, and extravagance.

IV

Beethoven left no commentary on the Seventh Symphony, either written or spoken, detailed or aphoristic, no explanation of its deployment of Greek meters. Unlike several other of his symphonies and orchestral overtures, which have referentially suggestive titles, subtitles, performance indications, or literary texts, or which utilize clearly identifiable characteristic styles or topics, there are no denotative leads here. In their absence, it is tempting to retreat to a formalist position, to view the mobilization of metrical power in the Seventh Symphony as driven in the main by a desire to maximize the rhythmic constituents of the work, thereby to achieve a host of striking effects, sonorities, and inflections. Beethoven's dotted-rhythm meters, propelled by the disparity in length between the first and second longs, are surely in the first place his idiosyncratic invention of a form of unstoppable motion. But the process need not have been solely a formal tactic devoid of rhetorical significance; and here the symphony's extensive use of Greek meters may itself be suggestive, for it is doubtful that Beethoven was simply enamored of poetic scansion for its own sake.[29] Czerny was not the only musician who took it for granted that the rhetoric of the symphony itself was bonded in some way to the meters that were its point of departure, and perhaps even to the cultural and historical contexts in which those meters originated. Some nineteenth-century commentators thought Beethoven's conspicuous use of Greek poetic meters in the symphony implied connections between it and Greek music or poetry, and with ceremonies and celebratory events of the antique world.

Writing in 1829, Henri de Castil-Blaze discerned in the Allegretto "an antique physiognomy," and suggested that the movement "is based on the music of the ancient Greeks," remindful of the verse of Anacreon and Sappho, and of the Roman Horace.[30] Even earlier, in 1824, A. B. Marx sensed in the Poco sostenuto "the kind of invocation with which we are particularly familiar in epic poets,"[31] and in 1859 he heard the finale as a "Bacchic ecstasy."[32] Ludwig Nohl, another eminent Beethoven biographer of the Romantic era, was skeptical of such ideas, pointing out that one can imagine countless exotic scenarios: "if one wishes to go further and to abandon the boundaries of pure concrete reality," he wrote, "one can perceive a victory celebration or even a feast of Bacchus . . . and indeed of Walpurgisnacht and the annual fairs and festivals [Jahrmarktsfest von Plundersweilern]."[33] Despite the soundness of such objections, several writers, including Richard Wagner, were led to write about the finale's "orgiastic" or "dithyrambic" character;[34] and in 1888 Wasielewski—who was not unacquainted with the writings of Marx and Wagner—extended this to the entire work: "In view of the fiery and wildly rapturous character of its main movements, one could name [the Seventh Symphony] 'The Dithyrambic,'" a characterization that others also found attractive, including Riemann, Jean Chantavoine ("le sentiment dionysiaque, dont s'inspire la symphonie en *la*"), and Donald Francis Tovey (the finale "remains unapproached in music as a triumph of Bacchic fury").[35] This trend, which obviously owed more than a little to Nietzsche's *The Birth of Tragedy Out of the Spirit of Music* (1872), was capped in the late nineteenth century by Liszt's pupil Otto Neitzel, who attached to the symphony a fatuous mythological program that proceeds from the awakening of Terpsichore to the "wild pulsations" of a Bacchanalia.[36] (Arnold Schering somehow overlooked the Homeric and Bacchic possibilities, opting instead for a narrative closely tracking scenes from Goethe's *Wilhelm Meisters Lehrjahre*.)[37]

A modern critic may aspire to draw more precise—or less fanciful—conclusions from demonstrable associations between the specific meters and the ancient poetic genres in which those meters are customarily found, as well as the ritual occasions which gave rise to those genres. At first glance, such an approach might seem promising: the stately spondaic meter with which the Poco sostenuto opens reminds us that *spondee* (σπονδεῖος) means "libatio" and that solemn libation hymns customarily opened ceremonial events at Delphi and elsewhere.[38] But the auspiciousness of this approach begins to fade with the first measures of the Vivace, whose metrical ambiguity makes identification of any equivalent poetic genres highly improbable, and whose putative rhythmic components are so commonplace that they resist assignment to particular literary genres or ceremonial occasions.[39]

Similar difficulties pertain to the Allegretto. Heroic (Homeric, epic) verse, the oldest of Greek verse forms, which provided the model for most subsequent epic poetry and a host of other poetic genres, is in dactylic-spondaic hexameter, with a free interchange of dactyls and spondees in any foot within the line except the last, which almost always calls for a spondee. Beethoven, of course, understood hexameters well enough and even left a few samples of his scansion and settings of several lines from Homer;[40] so it is meaningful that the Allegretto's sequences of dactyls and spondees fall into eight-foot periods that diverge sharply from the Homeric model in both the number of their feet and the invariance of their pattern. This drastic simplification has little to do with Homer's flexible heroic line, presenting an unbroken metrical structure that achieves its quasi-hypnotic effect by repetitive incantatory and rhythmic means, crafting something closer to a musical equivalent of symbols of eternity such as the meander or the perfect circle. Moreover, heroic verse is only one genre in which dactyl/spondee combinations are to be found; the Allegretto's metrical pattern is more characteristic of Homer's Alexandrian imitators and their Latin successors, especially Catullus.

It is tempting to join Wagner and Tovey in hearing the choriambic pulse that animates the finale as strongly suggestive of modalities that might be dubbed dithyrambic or Bacchic. To Beethoven's contemporaries, the Bacchic festivals were, as Friedrich Schlegel put it in his Vienna lectures of early 1812, "the consecrated ceremonial of the season," where the poet was granted "a Saturnalian license for the play of his fancy" and the imagination was momentarily set free from all the "fetters of law, custom, and propriety."[41] The dithyramb, however, whether as dance or as a genre of Greek choral poetry, was performed at a wide variety of Dionysian rites—vintage, fertility, sacrificial, and harvest—and accordingly had no single fixed character; it could be joyful or somber, euphoric or lamenting, "now in laughter now in tears," depending on the season.[42]

Thus, however appealing connections of this kind may momentarily seem to some listeners, it will always remain a matter of contention whether Beethoven's choices of particular meters in the Seventh Symphony also imply an attempt to represent the genres, moods, and ceremonies with which those meters traditionally were, or were thought to be, associated. There seem to be at least two insuperable difficulties: first, that multiple potential models exist for each poetic meter or metrical sequence; second, that any attempt to denote musical equivalents of poetic meters is vulnerable to charges of subjectivity or arbitrariness, for the meters of music and poetry are comparable only on a metaphoric level.

Nevertheless, there are signs that Beethoven himself was far from hostile to the idea of representing Bacchic states—perhaps understood in their most commonplace way as ecstatic, orgiastic, vehement, or Saturnalian—in his music.[43] In 1801, he composed ballet music to accompany a "Dance of Bacchus" in the ballet master Salvatore Viganò's *Die Geschöpfe des Prometheus* (The creatures of Prometheus).[44] Although in that essentially pastoral-style work he merely succeeded in sounding Haydnesque, he was so taken by the concept that he pursued the festive and celebratory implications of the same "heroic . . . dance of Bacchus" in the finale of the *Eroica* Symphony. His continuing interest in representing Dionysian states in his orchestral music is evidenced by a striking prose notation on a leaf of sketches, set down around 1818, when he was mulling over imaginative conceptions for one or more new symphonies. "Adagio Cantique—Pious song in a symphony in the ancient modes—Lord God, we praise Thee, alleluia!—either alone or as introduction to a fugue," he wrote, and went on to elaborate his idea of a choral symphony: "the vocal parts would enter in the last movement or already in the Adagio. The violins, etc., of the orchestra to be increased tenfold in the last movement, in which case the vocal parts would enter gradually—in the text of the Adagio Greek myth, *Cantique Eclesiastique*—in the Allegro, celebration of Bacchus."[45] Thus, leaving aside in the present context his allusions to the Christian deity and to medieval ecclesiastical liturgy, Beethoven was thinking about symphonic projects that utilized the ancient modes, were associated with Greek myth, and were descriptive of Bacchic celebration. The "Adagio Cantique" project was never realized as such; but soon after, the Ninth Symphony offered an implied cosmogonic narrative that closed with a setting of a text by Schiller saturated with imagery drawn from Greek and Roman mythology and featuring an oration evocative of the classical rhetorical tradition as well as a chorus of Aeschylean purposes and proportions.

V

It may well be that, starting even as early as the *Eroica* Symphony, Beethoven was thinking of the symphonic genre in connection with or as a vehicle to evoke the Antique. One does not want to restrict the potential implications of Beethoven's title—*Sinfonia eroica*—which are scarcely transparent, complicated as they are by his original intention to dedicate that same symphony to Napoleon Bonaparte. An equation of heroism and the ancients may not exhaust the meaning of the title, but it surely has a claim to consideration, if only because of Beethoven's deep attachment to Plutarch's *Lives* of the heroes and because Greece, in Ernst Bücken's phrase, was universally perceived as "the Ur-Heimat of the hero."[46]

To those among his contemporaries who shared Beethoven's cultural assumptions, the designation "eroica" itself could readily have been understood as a plain reference to Greek or Roman classical subjects. This is so, not only because the word *heroic* signifies the heroic age, chivalrous and valiant deeds, epic poetry, and the meters of Homeric verse, but because large-scale artistic productions of the period were dubbed "heroic" almost exclusively when they dealt with subjects from classical mythology. For example, of the seventeen major ballets staged in Vienna between 1792 and 1807 that were called *heroisches, heroisch-tragisches, heroisch-allegorisches,* or *heroisch-pantomimisches* on their printed programs, all but two were retellings of mythological stories.[47] These works continued the tradition of the *ballet héroïque* of the earlier eighteenth century, a genre that culminated in five works by Rameau, and which the librettist Fuzelier called "a completely new type of Ballet . . . that brought together all the best known Festivals of Antiquity."[48]

Similarly, a survey of opera premieres at the Theater-an-der-Wien between 1801 and 1810 turns up seventeen operas described wholly or partly as *heroisch*.[49] Here, the designations are somewhat looser, for even several of Schikaneder's fairy-tale productions like *Raoul, der Blaubart* and *Der Stein der Weisen* are identified as *heroisches;* nevertheless, once again, all but a handful of those called heroic are drawn from ancient mythology or history. And this usage perpetuates an older stage tradition, one that associated "heroic" with classical subjects, including operas and other theater works by such composers as Rameau, Gluck, Piccini, Salieri, and Paer.

In this context, *Sinfonia eroica* was a daring hybrid title, applying the designation "heroic" not to opera, oratorio, melodrama, or ballet, but to an orchestral symphony of unprecedented length and rhetorical grandeur. Of course, the "Marcia funebre" Adagio and the subtitle "Composta per festeggiare il sovvenire di un grand' uomo" are also strongly reminiscent of the French Revolution's public memorials to its leaders; but this avenue, too, leads to the ancients: the revolution draped itself in the mantles of the Caesars, staging imagined Greek and Roman celebrations and festivities, exalting especially Rome's tribunes and leaders as its own, and emulating the presumed traditions of the Roman republic. Thus, it can be argued that Beethoven's documented absorption and transformation of French Revolutionary musical rhetoric and imagery already was imprinted with the stamp of antiquity. At the very least, large-scale, multimovement symphonies, when performed in their entirety without interruption, had the potential to transform the large-scale orchestral concert into an occasion for something like communal ritual or celebration.[50]

These observations about the Third Symphony suggest that the Seventh Symphony may have marked a culminating stage of Beethoven's classicizing symphonic project, elaborating a highly imaginative idea—to represent or evoke the ancient pagan world via a fantasy reconstruction of its music.

In recent decades musicology has come ever closer to accurate reconstructions of ancient Greek music from its surviving vestiges (archeological remains and notated musical fragments), iconographical representations, or written accounts.[51] But in Beethoven's time nobody could have known what Greek music actually sounded like. This obscurity, however, may have presented more of an opportunity than an obstacle, providing an opening for the creation of an imaginary sound-world that might convey an idea of the mysterious and exotic music of antiquity—and even of antiquity itself. A historically informed attempt to reconstruct real Greek music was not Beethoven's purpose; nor would it have suited his audiences at Vienna's University Hall at the celebratory premiere performances on 8 and 12 December 1813. Closer to his apparent purposes was to employ some identifiable feature or singularity resonant of the Antique or evocative of it in a distinctive way. And such a feature was readily at hand in the meters of classical poetry, which were familiar to all who had received a classical education as well as to musicians and music lovers who read the discussions of Greek and Roman verse, its scansion and its musical analogues, that were widely available in manuals on prosody, composition textbooks, music dictionaries, and music journals of the time.[52] In this way, Beethoven's appropriation of an array of antique poetic meters as the formative substance of the A-major Symphony opened pathways between his world and the presumed world of antiquity, its music, its ideals, and its belief systems.

VI

What might be called a Renaissance impulse animates some of the great creative events and intellectually productive eras of the last two millennia. It is an impulse to preserve, reaffirm, and renew the cultural forms, conceptions, and ideals of the ancient world. Even the period that we conventionally label the Renaissance was preceded by a series of earlier classical revivals in the Middle Ages, including a Carolingian *renovatio*, Ottonian and Anglo-Saxon revivals at the beginning of the second millennium C.E., and a Mediterranean revival in the twelfth century.[53] And there have been any number of post-Renaissance renaissances as well. A historian might well hazard that, starting with the Romans who perpetuated and recreated the arts of Phidias and Sophocles, there has been a constant, though fluctuating, process of renaissance, renovation, and appropriation of the Antique. In the Italian Renaissance the process extended beyond literature and the visual arts to music; as Claude Palisca put it, "the revival of ancient learning and of certain ancient artistic and musical practices that it revealed was a potent force in the development of music in the Renaissance."[54] One of the earliest attempts at a revival of ancient music is also among the most far-reaching: the circle of late sixteenth-century Florentine intellectuals, musicians, and connoisseurs (known as the Camerata) investigated the surviving vestiges and descriptions of Greek music and urged the imitation of the ancient songs with a view to a revival in modern staged music of the union of poetry and music that was thought to have characterized Greek drama.[55] These ideas, circulated in writings by Giovanni Bardi, Vincenzo Galilei's *Dialogo della musica antica et della moderna* (1581), and Jacopo Peri's preface to Corsi's *Eurydice* (1600), helped shape the Florentine *stile rappresentativo,* and were not without their impact on Venetian opera, beginning with the premiere of Monteverdi's *Orfeo* at Mantua in 1607.

Examples of efforts to recreate ancient music (often along highly fanciful lines) could be multiplied—for example, Debussy and Ravel's simulation of a neo-Pagan harmonic language and modal rhetoric evocative of Greek and Roman mythology.[56] Analogous retrospective trends appeared in numerous countries at the onset of twentieth-century modernism, fusing aesthetic and nationalist aspirations by invoking the sense of a dawn-of-time culture indigenous to a composer's own national or ethnic identity—the Magyar for Bartók and Kodály, the Scythian for Prokofiev, the Russian atavistic legacy for Stravinsky, the epoch described in the Kalevala for Sibelius. Closer to Beethoven's project in time and purpose, however, is the French composer Jean-François Le Sueur's treatise, *Exposé d'une musique* (1787), which advocated that France's composers seek to recapture Greek ideals by utilizing the meters of Greek prosody in their own sacred music.[57] It was Le Sueur's belief that "la Musique pourroit acquérir un nouveau moyen d'imitation, en empruntant dans le corps de ses mesures les divers Rhythmes des Grecs."[58] And such views converged with the belief of the Romantic poets that the ancient and even primeval remained locked within—and therefore accessible through—the component rhythms of language: "Syllables are words of the primal language *[Sylben sind Worte der Ursprache]*" was Achim von Arnim's striking formulation of this resonant idea.[59]

An important wave of Antique, especially Hellenic, revival had been well under way in the eighteenth century under the aegis of neoclassicism. The impulse was very much in evidence among those German thinkers and poets—Herder, Lessing, Schiller, and Goethe—whose ideas constituted the inexhaustible quarry from which German Romanticism was mined, and subsequently among the exponents of early Romanticism, all of whom saw themselves as the protectors and inheritors of classicism even as they redefined the classic in accordance with their own emergent sensibility.

Johann Joachim Winckelmann famously perceived in the Antique "a noble simplicity and quiet grandeur *[eine edle Einfalt und eine stille Grösse]*."[60] And this perception was in line with classical doctrines of symmetry, harmony, proportion, and the Olympian blending of grace, decorum, and dignity that was long believed to be the essence of the Greek idea. Some of the Romantics, however, felt the need to take account of Dionysian and Laocoönian strains in Greek culture, and this Romanticist revisionism uncovered veins of frenzy, supreme exertion, ecstasy, euphoria, agony, and what might be called a neobarbaric current at the very center of Hellenism. Those are some of the qualities which, translated into sound, transformed the Viennese classical style with shattering force in Beethoven's *Eroica,* Fifth, and Seventh symphonies. Beethoven broke with the dominant Olympian and Apollonian models of the Antique (and thereby reconfigured his own era's musical Classicism), giving voice in his symphonies to a Dionysian rhetoric capable of representing not only extreme states of being but virtually every form of division in nature, in society, and in human consciousness itself. From this standpoint, the Seventh Symphony may be understood as marking a decisive stage in an ongoing mythopoeic reconception of the symphony that started with the *Eroica* Symphony, and which perhaps was continued with the tone-painting of "Creation" in the introduction to the Fourth Symphony, the multiple evocations of communal or ceremonial modalities in the Fifth Symphony, and the programmatic representation of wholeness, disruption, and recovery of a Rousseauist Arcadia in the *Pastoral* Symphony.

With the A-major Symphony, a fully realized neo-Antique style came into being—muscular, powerful, restless, imbued with unstoppable energy, saturated with ritual and ecstatic implications. Although its predicate may have been the reconstruction of an ancient musical language, it was a newly imagined one, a tongue that had never previously been heard. Redolent of the Antique, it was also supremely modern and innovative, a key work in the formation of Beethoven's late style. One might say of it what Pietro Aretino wrote about the classicizing paintings of the Italian Renaissance painter Giulio Romano, that they are "Antiquely modern and modernly antique [Anticamente moderni e modernamente antichi]."[61] In 1794, Friedrich Schlegel advocated an almost identical fusion, writing to his brother August Wilhelm, "To me, the problem of our poetry appears to be the unification of the essentially Modern with the essentially Antique [Vereinigung des Wesentlich-Modernen mit dem Wesentlich-Antiken]."[62] This was a fusion consciously sought by Beethoven's greatest contemporaries—by Schiller in his "Naive and Sentimental Poetry" and the preface to Die Braut von Messina, and by Goethe in his surreal image of a time-eradicating union between Faust and Helen. And by Beethoven himself, perhaps, in the Seventh Symphony and, later on, in his ultramodernist blending of Greek mythology and Christian medievalism in the Ninth Symphony and its unrealized prototype, the "Adagio Cantique."

Viewed from these admittedly metaphorical perspectives, Beethoven might be described as a Renaissance composer in the age of early Romanticism, likened to those artists and thinkers of the Renaissance such as Mantegna, who, in Panofsky's words, "aspired to a comprehensive restoration of the classical world from its visible and tangible remnants."[63] The Seventh Symphony, then, can be seen as a unique outcome of a Renaissance impulse that was abroad among Beethoven's contemporaries, whose ambition was to align themselves with and to revalidate the cultural, ethical, and aesthetic premises of Antiquity.

Indeed, many hoped to discover a portal, not only to the Hellenic, but to grand and mysterious conceptions of the holy, even to fulfill a quest for the Uralt—the fabled primeval world that gave birth to the most ancient forms of worship and belief. For the revival of Antiquity is often accompanied by a special interest in theological issues, especially in the so-called pagan mysteries that were the carriers of ancient religious doctrines and practices.[64] In the late eighteenth and early nineteenth centuries, the revival of classicism was not only a project for Romanticists but for Deists and Freemasons seeking to confirm the ubiquitous existence of the idea of one supreme god, even as their imaginations were fired by descriptions of the polytheistic pantheons of the ancient nations. And this may have some bearing on the circumstance that the composition of the Seventh Symphony in 1811–12 coincided with an unexpected turn, during Beethoven's fifth decade, to the mythologies and deities of the ancient world.

VII

Whatever else it may be, Romanticism is a metaphysics of longing, a striving for all potential objects of desire, both those that have been lost and those that have yet to be achieved. The very attempt to define Romanticism, whose definitions are so notoriously diverse, becomes one more confirmation of its inherent elusiveness. Romanticism's primary affective mode is yearning *(Sehnsucht)*—for every possible goal, for each glimpse of felicity, for restoration of every conceivable loss. And among these, perhaps the most deeply mourned of losses, one that becomes emblematic of every other, is the idea of a primordial harmony that was thought to have existed in the Greco-Roman world, uniting humanity, nature, and the gods. Virtually every major German philosopher, aesthetician, and thinker from the 1790s to the early twentieth century—from poets such as Schiller, Herder, Schelling, Jean-Paul Richter, and Novalis, to thinkers such as Kant, Hegel, Marx, Nietzsche, and Freud—valorized the Hellenic spirit, viewed the *griechische Jugendzeit* as a lost paradise or Golden Age. The superiority of the Hellenic is tacitly assumed, as Frances Yates has shown:

> The great forward movements of the Renaissance all derive their vigour, their emotional impulse, from looking backwards. . . . [T]he search for truth was thus of necessity a search for the early, the ancient, the original gold from which the baser metals of the present and the immediate past were corrupt degenerations. Man's history was not an evolution from primitive animal origins through ever growing complexity and progress; the past was always better than the present, and progress was revival, rebirth, renaissance of antiquity.[65]

For many of the most eminent thinkers and poets of Beethoven's time, Hellenic classicism was interwoven with conceptions of the fragmentary and the unfinished; with the windswept, weathered, roughened, broken, and maimed sculptures and temples of the ancients; with aphoristic fragments

of pre-Socratic philosophy and snatches from lost writings or mute hieroglyphics. From the very instant of their excavation, those artworks, places
of worship, cities, and even civilizations that represented the classical ideal
were seen as already ravaged by the destructive forces of time, war, and mutability. It seemed to follow that the calm reflectiveness *(Besonnenheit,
sophrosyne)* that these works once personified was forever beyond recovery.
And that was one conclusion of Schiller's "sentimental" (i.e., modern or
Romantic) poet, who realized that the harmonious and naive Greek *Jugendzeit*
cannot be restored, and accordingly that we are condemned to a constant
state of hovering, striving, falling short. In a famous passage in the first of
his Vienna lectures, A. W. Schlegel elaborated on Schiller's conception:

> the poetry of the ancients was the poetry of enjoyment, and ours is that of
> desire: the former had its foundation in the scene which is present, while the
> latter hovers betwixt recollection and hope. . . . The Grecian ideal of human
> nature was perfect unison and proportion between all the powers—a natural
> harmony. The moderns, on the contrary, have arrived at the consciousness of
> an internal discord which renders such an ideal impossible; and hence the en-
> deavour of their poetry is to reconcile these two worlds between which we
> find ourselves divided, and to blend them indissolubly together.[66]

Thus, Romanticism longs for the classical as the quintessential embodiment
of all those ideals that are no longer available to the modern world, a world
in need of renewal and regeneration. And at the same time it regards classicism as always beyond our grasp.[67]

Beethoven surely came under the influence of pre-Romantic and Romantic
ideas. But if he was a Romantic, his was a sui generis form of Romanticism,
one that achieved the unachievable, mapped the infinite, synthesized chaos
and order, and recovered the classic. Beethoven never settled for mere striving, perpetual longing, incompletion. Rather, he insisted on the possibility
of achieving classical reconciliation and wholeness, despite all. In defiance
of Romantic logic and intuition, and even as he participated in a project that
privileged the unattainable, he reached what in principle cannot be reached.
He accepted only one aspect of the Romantic premise—what is lost or unachieved is longed for—but he never accepted the corollary, that what is
longed for cannot be recovered. In all but the merest handful of his endings, whether instrumental or vocal, he cleaves to the principle of expecta-

tion, to faith in the possibility of a good ending, as in the closing lines of *An die ferne Geliebte:*

> Dann vor diesen Liedern weichet,
> Was geschieden uns so weit,
> Und ein liebend Herz erreichet,
> Was ein liebend Herz geweiht.

> Then, what has separated us until now
> Succumbs to these songs,
> And a loving heart attains
> That to which a loving heart is consecrated.[68]

For Beethoven, evidently, the classical had never been altogether lost but remained in a state of dormancy, awaiting only the force of an imaginative act to reawaken it and to set its transformational powers in motion. He was no stranger to melancholia and nostalgia, but these were rarely the defining modalities of Beethoven's Romanticism. To him, it may be, the classical actually signified that which had resisted the ravages of time, managed to survive after having been buried, sunk, demolished, melted down, reduced to ashes, and scattered broadcast. Every artifact and graven image rescued from the windswept sands, the cellars of dead cities, and the tombs of ancient eminences is to be regarded as one more confirmation that the classical is an image of survival as well as an image of loss.

VIII

In the end, Beethoven's Seventh Symphony needs to be approached from an array of endlessly ramifying perspectives. As a Renaissance undertaking, it exalts the Hellenic along with its conceptions of order, morality, and virtue; it aims to resurrect the music of the ancient world, thereby to gain access to the presumed childhood of civilization. As a modernist symphony it bears what may be the hallmarks of a dynamic era of revolution and war—a rhythm-dominated musical language, rhetoric, and grammar. As a critique of neoclassicism, it undermines the precepts of a calm and symmetrical classicism, preferring those dynamic polarities of tranquillity and terror, con-

THE RHYTHMS OF ANTIQUITY   133

tainment and abandon, and dream and intoxication that Nietzsche later identified as "the Apollonian-Dionysiac duality."[69] It taps into an undercurrent of restlessness within classicism, what M. H. Abrams described as "a controlled violence . . . , a self-ordering impetus of passion . . . , a sovereign order in rage."[70] I have argued here that Beethoven's Seventh exemplifies Romanticism's yearning for the classical. But one can readily reverse the formulation, as Mario Praz did when he suggested that Classicism itself, "inasmuch as it strives longingly towards a fantastic pagan world, rather than sharing in the state of serene equilibrium proper to so-called classical works of art . . . , shares in the same spiritual travail which is usually defined as characteristically and *par excellence* 'romantic.'"[71]

We will, of course, always retain the option of hearing the Seventh Symphony without regard to its disclosure of sonic pathways to the antique world: of hearing it for its embodiment of ecstatic and heightened states; for its evidence of the varieties of religious experience; for its musical manifestations of the sacred, ritual, and ceremonial; and as the apotheosis of every kind of organized motion of the human body, acting individually or in concert. In the Seventh Symphony Beethoven harnessed some of the simplest and most ancient forms of rhythm, set them in motion, showed them evolving from monorhythmic cells into polyrhythmic networks, harnessed them to harmony, melody, and rhetoric, attached them to emotional affects, and made them capable of approximately rendering complex states of being. Rhythm here remains a signifier for all the regularities of natural events, whether the recurrent motions of the heavens, tides, and climates, or those of play, dance, and the endless interaction of human beings with nature through the processes of labor and play. If we add to these the inevitable cycles of birth and death, the turning of the generations as well as of the seasons, rhythm is eminently useful as an emblem of creation, of life coming into being— stirring, moving, awakening, emerging from the depths, finding its voice, becoming sentient, combining into ever larger entities.

And here a caveat may be in order: the rhythmic dimension of the Seventh Symphony privileges archetypes of force, the hierarchical, and the communal rather than celebrating inwardness or individual sensibility. Nietzsche, who saw this quality of Beethoven's music as a way of bringing human beings into a "higher, more ideal community," nevertheless observed that, in Dionysian states of intoxication, including those brought on or enhanced by music, "the *principium individuationis* is disrupted, subjectivity disappears entirely before the erupting force of the general element in human life."[72] Many today may be more skeptical of the Seventh Symphony's pull to ecstatic conformity (foreshadowing the "Ode to Joy" with its collectivist injunction—"Seid umschlungen, Millionen!"—to submit to a superior will) that is exerted by the hegemonic power of rhythm, but they may well find its gravitational force difficult to withstand.

CHAPTER SEVEN

THE MASONIC THREAD

Beethoven's name does not appear on the surviving membership lists of any Masonic or other fraternal society; nor has it ever been claimed that he belonged to a specific lodge or order. Nevertheless, the young violinist Karl Holz, who served him as a personal assistant between 1824 and 1826, and who had Beethoven's written authorization to write his biography, flatly asserted, "Beethoven was a Freemason, but not active in later years."[1] Thayer took it as a "fact" that the composer entered the Masonic order early on and continued to visit the lodges until "after the loss of his hearing."[2] But Thayer did not provide any documentary support for his statement. Accordingly, Theodor Frimmel was right to conclude that Beethoven's actual membership in any Masonic or similar organization remains improbable, at best.[3] But this doesn't rule out Paul Nettl's belief that Beethoven was "the incarnation of Masonic ethics and philosophy, a 'Mason without badge.'"[4]

Beethoven's early intellectual and political outlook crystallized at a time when Freemasonry was already under siege in the Habsburg world, when emperors and princes had decided that their earlier toleration of or even sympathy for Freemasonry no longer suited their purpose of enlisting outstanding individuals in imperial reform projects. Whereas in the 1770s Elector Maximilian Friedrich had authorized the founding of Masonic lodges in Bonn and Cologne, and both he and his successor Maximilian Franz numbered prominent Freemasons and members of the quasi-Masonic anticlerical Order of Illuminati among their most trusted advisors, Freemasonry was heavily restricted starting in the mid-1780s, and its activities were essentially suspended by 1788.[5] Founded in 1781, the local lodge of the Order of Illuminati dissolved of its own accord in 1785 rather than await an official prohibition, inevitable in the wake of a ban already instituted in Munich, where the Order's founder and chief, Adam Weishaupt, had his headquarters.[6] Beethoven was closely associated with but—perhaps because by statute students were "excluded, for their own benefit"[7]—was not a formal member of the Bonn *Lesegesellschaft* (reading society), a successor organization founded in December 1787 and devoted to the dissemination of enlightened thought and literature. Erstwhile Masons and Illuminists flocked into the *Lesegesellschaft,* which became the center of Bonn's intellectual life and which commissioned Beethoven's cantatas of 1790–91 on the death of Emperor Joseph II, WoO 87, and on the elevation of Leopold II, WoO 88.[8]

When Beethoven arrived in Vienna in late 1792, it was a highly inopportune time to be a Freemason. In the wake of the French Revolution, fraternal societies came to be regarded as intrinsically conspiratorial and were put under ever tighter surveillance; the lodges were disbanded early in the reign of Emperor Franz II.[9] Freemasonry was effectively outlawed by December 1793, and members of the Order and any other so-called secret societies were subject to the *Kriminalpatent* of 2 January 1795. It appears that some remnants of the movement went into secret resistance, but most retired into unspoken opposition rather than risk the fate of those Habsburg Jacobins who were imprisoned and even executed during those years.[10] Still, police suspicions of ongoing Masonic activity were not entirely groundless. During the French occupations of Vienna in 1805 and 1809 there were several short-lived attempts to revive Freemasonry there. A secret lodge, founded around 1810 and reportedly named "Zu den drei blauen Himmeln," held meetings in Vienna as well as at the summer palace of the court theater director Count Ferdinand Pálffy in the suburb of Hernals. The lodge survived until 1812, when it was uncovered and dissolved by the police; its members, including eminent theater personalities such as Pálffy, the tenor Giuseppe Siboni, and perhaps the dancer Louis Antoine Duport, were placed under close surveillance, arrested on 4 May 1812, interrogated, and charged; some were compelled to forswear future participation in secret societies; others were dismissed from the imperial service; still others were exonerated. Masonic historians mention another lodge, reportedly established in Vienna's Town Hall district under the direction of "Prince Dietrichstein," which also suspended operations in 1812, but this may have been the winter headquarters of the Hernals lodge.[11] There are also confirmed reports of thwarted attempts by some Prussian officers to set up a lodge in 1814–15.

Apart from these abortive endeavors, the only known Masonic lodges in Vienna during Beethoven's lifetime were the "official" or "patriotic" lodges—such as the "Wildensteiner Ritterschaft auf blauer Erde"—that were founded with the approval of the state.[12]

There is no evidence to support speculation that Beethoven might have been a member of a clandestine Masonic lodge or other prohibited organization, as his early biographer Anton Schindler broadly hinted when he wrote that in 1815 he frequently met with Beethoven at a "rather remote room in the beer-house 'Zum Rosenstock' in the Ballgässchen . . . and came to know the place as a quasi-crypt [Quasi-Krypta] of a number of Josephinians of the truest dye, to whom our master presented no discordant note."[13] Nevertheless, there are substantial indications that Beethoven was favorably disposed toward Freemasonry, was familiar with its language, shared some of its main intellectual interests, and, on occasion, seemed to have identified himself as a Masonic sympathizer. Certainly many of his closest friends, teachers, patrons, and associates were connected with the Masonic movement, and many had formerly been actual members of Masonic organizations and especially of the Order of Illuminati. By 1784, the "Stagira" lodge to which Bonn Illuminists belonged was headed by the court organist Christian Gottlob Neefe and numbered among its members the court musicians Nikolaus Simrock and Franz Anton Ries—all three individuals of vital importance in Beethoven's early life. Other members included Beethoven's friends, the brothers Johann Peter Eichhoff and Johann Joseph Eichhoff.[14] In a famous letter to Simrock, the hornist who later became his Bonn publisher, Beethoven wrote frankly about political repression in Vienna; in other letters, he called Simrock (born 1752) "my dear old papa" and described him as "much beloved by your comrades."[15] Ries (born 1755), Bonn's best violinist, provided vital support to the family survivors after the death of Frau van Beethoven in 1787, and Beethoven repaid him by taking Ries's son, Ferdinand, under his wing in Vienna after 1800.[16] Neefe was Beethoven's main composition teacher at Bonn, mainly in the years 1780 or 1781 to 1784; he was also his immediate superior in the court chapel, and presumably his mentor in other ways. It is conceivable that as a committed Illuminist—and earlier a member of the Masonic lodge "Karoline zu den drei Pfauen" in Neuwied—Neefe might have attempted to influence the young musician, but Beethoven was still only in his early teens when the Order was disbanded. Furthermore, by 1789 at the very latest, Neefe had renounced his Illuminist views. In that year, in the final revision of his autobiography *(Lebenslauf),* he described his induction into the Order of Illuminati in June of 1781 and his later disillusionment: "I had the honor and the good fortune of being admitted into a society *[Gesellschaft]* that was meant to consist of the most virtuous and wisest men, who were united in desiring to work according to a grand plan for the happiness of mankind. The original plan was truly grand and excellent. In the course of time, however, I uncovered many deficiencies, many human weaknesses, and indeed even worse things, so that I decided once more to distance myself."[17]

Those who were of Beethoven's own generation came along too late to have joined the Freemasons or the Order of Illuminati in Bonn, but it is amply clear from their letters and album entries that many of his intimate friends, including the Breuning brothers and Franz Gerhard Wegeler, shared the Masonic commitments to virtue, service, and brotherhood and, beyond these, were passionately opposed to tyranny in every form.[18] As a medical student and later as Professor of Obstetrics at the University of Bonn, Wegeler (born 1765) was a disciple of Dr. Franz Wilhelm Kauhlen (1750–93), an "outspoken *Aufklärer*" who was initiated into the Order of Illuminati in Bonn on 12 July 1782 under the code name Tasso; Wegeler's writings on science and medicine are said to reflect his mentor's beliefs.[19] After the reestablishment of Masonic lodges in the Rhine region under the French occupation and thereafter, Wegeler became a prominent Freemason. He wrote the text of a well-known Masonic song, "Brüder, reicht die Hand zum Bunde," as well as new texts for two of Beethoven's lieder, "Der freie Mann," WoO 117, and "Opferlied," WoO 126, for use in initiation ceremonies in the lodges; and these were published by Simrock in 1806 and 1808 respectively. In a letter of 2 May 1810, Beethoven wrote to Wegeler, "I am told that in your Masonic Lodges you sing a song composed by me, presumably in *E major,* which I myself do not possess. Do send it to me."[20] It is worth noting that Beethoven took it as a matter of course—and made no objection— that his songs had been adapted for Masonic purposes. Beethoven's correspondence with Wegeler is marked not only by deep personal affection but by mutual trust and a frankness that seems to bespeak shared beliefs as well. To Wegeler he stressed his commitment to use his art in the service of the poor and of humanity at large. A letter to Wegeler of the mid-1790s perhaps evokes imagery of a Masonic sort: "I guarantee that the new temple of sacred friendship which you will erect upon these qualities, will stand firmly and for ever, and that no misfortune, no tempest will be able to shake its foundations."[21] As for Ferdinand Ries, who later collaborated with Wegeler on the *Biographische Notizen über Ludwig van Beethoven,* he too was a Freemason, and he wrote a considerable amount of Masonic music, including a cantata for tenor, male chorus, and orchestra (1805); "Das Fest der Maurer," for tenor, male chorus, and piano; and "Bei Eröffnung der Tafellogen," for solo, male chorus, and string quartet (1810). Several of his Masonic compositions were published by Simrock.[22]

On 14 May 1789, Beethoven and his friends Karl Kügelgen and Anton Reicha matriculated at the University in Bonn as candidates in philosophy under the rectorate of the Illuminist Professor Kauhlen.[23] Other professors who backed the young Beethoven adhered to a variety of positions on the political spectrum and ought not to be viewed primarily in terms of their connection to Freemasonry. For example, the poet and subsequent Jacobin Eulogius Schneider, who participated in and later fell victim to the Terror, was the leading force in the *Lesegesellschaft* behind the commission of Beethoven's funeral cantata for Emperor Joseph II; and Beethoven was a subscriber to his *Gedichte* (1790). (Later, from 1791 to 1794, Schneider did belong to a Masonic lodge in Krefeld.) The Kantian philosopher Bartholomäus Fischenich, who brought one of Beethoven's early lieder to the attention of Friedrich Schiller's wife and reported to her the young composer's ambition to set "An die Freude"—widely used in Masonic circles—in its entirety, was an independent thinker, sharply critical not only of court and church, but also of radicals who advocated violence.[24]

Regardless of their political differences and affiliations, Beethoven's friends, teachers, colleagues, and patrons were united by their belief in the *Aufklärung,* and particularly by their faith that an enlightened aristocracy might advance the goals of fraternity, justice, service, virtue, and freedom of thought. Thus, there was no insuperable ideological barrier between Illuminists like Neefe or Mozart's beloved friend Count August Clemens Hatzfeld and an *Aufklärer* like Count Ferdinand Waldstein, for all of them were dedicated to working for what the latter called his "favorite chimera"— the "Glück der Menschheit."[25]

As is well known, many of the leading Viennese supporters and patrons of music in the 1780s and 1790s were Freemasons or sympathetic to Masonic ideals. Among the aristocratic patrons of Mozart, Haydn, and Beethoven in Vienna were Masons like Prince Nikolaus I Esterházy (1741–1809); Count

Johann Nepomuk Esterházy; Count (later Prince) Johann Baptist Dietrich-stein-Proskau; Count Anton Georg Apponyi; and Prince Karl Lichnowsky. Members of the Thun-Hohenstein, Pálffy, and Erdödy families were active in Masonic circles.[26] Gottfried van Swieten's formal membership in any lodge is undocumented, but there is much evidence of his Masonic leanings.[27] Alberto Basso proposes, but does not prove, that Swieten's influential Society of Associated Cavaliers (Gesellschaft der associierten Kavaliere)—a consortium consisting of Swieten, the Princes Schwarzenberg, Lobkowitz, Dietrichstein, and counts Apponyi, Batthiany, and Johann Esterházy, devoted to the promotion of "ancient" and new music—was of Masonic orientation and membership.[28] Lichnowsky was by far the most important of Beethoven's Viennese patrons from late 1792 to 1806 or 1807 and his friend until the Prince's death in 1813. He was a lodge brother of Mozart's and has also been identified as a member of the Order of Illuminati.[29] Under his aegis Beethoven toured Prague, Dresden, Leipzig, and Berlin, thereby tracking Mozart's almost identical tour of those cities in Lichnowsky's company five years earlier; but although Beethoven and Mozart may have enjoyed the hospitality of Free-masons in those cities, it is not demonstrated that the tours were somehow substantially Masonic in nature.[30] At the Prussian court Beethoven played for Friedrich Wilhelm II and dedicated to him the Sonatas for Cello and Piano, op. 5. Unlike his uncle Frederick the Great, who was a thirty-third-degree Freemason, Friedrich Wilhelm II was not a Mason, but he tolerated Freemasonry during its most difficult days, issuing an order protective of the National-Mutterloge in 1796; his son and successor Friedrich Wilhelm III, eventual dedicatee of the Ninth Symphony, was a "generous patron of the Order" who in 1798 exempted Masonic lodges from an edict of 20 October 1798 otherwise banning secret societies.[31]

An important conduit between Beethoven and his patrons was Nikolaus Zmeskall von Domanovecz, who, soon after the composer's arrival in the capital, became his abiding Viennese friend and confidant. According to the Fischhof Manuscript, which includes documents and memoirs intended for an early, projected biography of Beethoven, "Through the influence of Z. [Zmeskall], who was a passionate friend of the arts and sciences, and himself a cello virtuoso, he entered the houses of Baron van Swieten, Prince Lichnowsky, Herr Streicher and others who were subsequently of great importance for his career."[32] Zmeskall himself can now be identified as a Freemason, for his name appears as a "visiting Brother" (perhaps from a Budapest lodge as yet unidentified) on the registers of the Vienna lodge "Zur wahren Eintracht" for 1783.[33] On the whole there seems reason to think that Beethoven was initially welcomed in Vienna (and perhaps later on in Prague) by members of a loose network of individuals who were closely allied with Freemasonry or the Order of Illuminati.

In 1808, Beethoven was invited to become chief kapellmeister at the Westphalian court of Napoleon's younger brother Jérôme Bonaparte (1784–1860), and he utilized this offer to obtain in 1809 an annuity from the Archduke Rudolph and the princes Lobkowitz and Kinsky that guaranteed him a substantial income on condition that he remain on Habsburg soil. The details of the terms and negotiations of the Westphalian offer remain obscure; no court documents relative to it have as yet been unearthed. Jérôme Bonaparte, king of Westphalia from 1807 to 1813, was a Freemason, inducted in February 1801 into the Toulon lodge "La Paix," where he was identified as the son of a Freemason. There is no evidence, however, that the king's Masonic affiliations influenced the offer to Beethoven. Still, Beethoven was invited to take a post just vacated by Johann Friedrich Reichardt, partisan of the French Revolution and editor of a notable early collection of Masonic songs (1776).[34]

Perhaps one ought not to make too much of the Masonic orientation of Beethoven's patrons. Emperor Joseph II encouraged Freemasonry in the early 1780s as part of his successful effort to enlist Austria's most influential individuals, including its best minds, in his program of reform and curtailment of entrenched privilege; for a while it was in vogue to be a Freemason, and many individuals joined lodges enthusiastically but without lasting conviction. Among them, however, were many (Mozart, for example) for whom affiliation with Freemasonry remained a decisive, defining feature of their lives.

In the earliest years of the nineteenth century, Beethoven, perhaps seeking to renovate his political beliefs after almost a decade of relative quiescence, dedicated a series of uncommissioned major works to leading proponents of enlightened rule—Swieten, Joseph von Sonnenfels, Czar Alexander I— a series that was to have culminated in the planned dedication of the *Eroica* Symphony to Napoleon Bonaparte.[35] In the present context, it is noteworthy that they all, with the possible exception of Czar Alexander, were regarded as Freemasons, that Sonnenfels was one of the most prominent Viennese leaders of the Order of Illuminati, and that Swieten was listed on police documents as a clandestine leader, or at least a supporter, of that same Order. The Violin Sonata, op. 47, dedicated to the Freemason Rodolphe Kreutzer in 1805—in accordance with an intention first announced in October 1803—may well be considered part of this series.[36] Other dedicatees of Beethoven's works who were known Masons or Illuminists include Goethe, Friedrich von Matthisson, Zmeskall, and Haydn. If we add Prince Lichnowsky and his family, to whom several major works were dedicated, including the Piano Trios, op. 1, the Sonata in C minor, op. 13, the Second Symphony, op. 36, the Sonata in A-flat, op. 26, the Fifteen Variations and Fugue in E-flat, op. 35, and *Die Geschöpfe des Prometheus,* op. 43,[37] it becomes legitimate to wonder if these dedications may have been motivated at least partially by Masonic considerations.

Masons readily gravitated to the bookselling and publishing trade; Mozart's publishers included the Masons Rudolf Gräffer, Franz Anton Hoffmeister, Pasquale Artaria, Christoph Torricella, and Johann Anton André. Several of them or their successors became Beethoven's publishers as well, and to judge from his letters he apparently felt comfortable with publishers like Hoffmeister, Gottfried Christoph Härtel, and Nikolaus Simrock, Masons all, with whom he could freely express nonconformist attitudes. Indeed, the frankest and most telling expressions of his political views are in letters to these three men.[38]

A considerable number of the poets most admired by Beethoven or whose poems he set to music were Masons, Illuminists, or—here, the classic example is Schiller—closely linked to Freemasonry by their writings, associations, or ideological affinity. Such luminaries as Goethe, Herder, Wieland, Klopstock, and Lessing are known to have been Masons or Illuminists, as were such lesser but nevertheless celebrated figures as Matthisson, Ludwig Hölty, Matthias Claudius, and Gottfried August Bürger.[39] In 1800, Beethoven wrote a unique, laudatory letter to Matthisson, an active Freemason whose "Adelaide," op. 46, "Opferlied," WoO 126 and op. 121b, "Andenken," WoO 136, and "An Laura," WoO 112, inspired several of the composer's finest lieder.[40] He dedicated "Adelaide" to Matthisson, the only poet other than Goethe to be honored with a Beethoven dedication. Of course, one hesitates to draw firm conclusions from the preponderance of Masons among Beethoven's lieder collaborators; these poets came to maturity at the high tide of the secret societies, and one informed historian has estimated that "at some point in time most writers belonged" to one or another of them.[41]

In contrast, writers who came to maturity after the death of Emperor Joseph II had no such option; thus, after 1790, poets in the Habsburg realm had no visible organizational ties to Freemasonry. And it is important to remember that a sizable number of lapsed Freemasons and Illuminists renounced their earlier associations and in a few instances even actively supported repressive measures against the secret societies during the period when conspiracy theories were rampant.[42]

II

In addition to these abundant indications of Beethoven's close associations with Freemasons and Illuminists, there are a variety of remarks and allusions in Beethoven's letters and other writings that may have Masonic overtones. Conspicuous among these are numerous references to "fraternity" and its cognates; in Beethoven's time these often carried a potentially Masonic significance in addition to their resonance as part of the political vocabulary of the Enlightenment and the French Revolution. Masons regarded their community as a brotherhood, called each other "brother," and preached brotherly love as a cardinal virtue. In their rituals of fraternization *(Verbrüderung)*, successful candidates achieved the right to be called "brother," thereby signifying their acceptance into the order. As a standard Masonic encyclopedia puts it, "The name of brother is the most universal and highest honorary title in every mystery cult and belongs to the essence of every religious alliance."[43] Thus, it may be meaningful that Beethoven used the salutation "Dear Brother" or some variant of it in letters to Franz Anton Hoffmeister, Franz Brunsvik, Ignaz von Seyfried, Georg Friedrich von Treitschke, and Heinrich Joseph von Collin. His earliest preserved letter to Hoffmeister repeats the phrases, "beloved and worthy brother" or "worthy brother" five times, as though to underscore their significance, and adds "your brother L. v. Beethoven" at the close.[44] Since Hoffmeister was a well-known Freemason, and Beethoven expressed dissident political views in letters to him, these are almost certainly Masonic allusions. But Beethoven's designations of Collin and Treitschke as his "brother[s] in Apollo" are arguably intended to signify that he regarded these writers as his collaborators in art, as members of the fraternity of artists.[45] A similar reference to the composer Ignaz von Seyfried as "My dear and beloved Brother in Apollo"

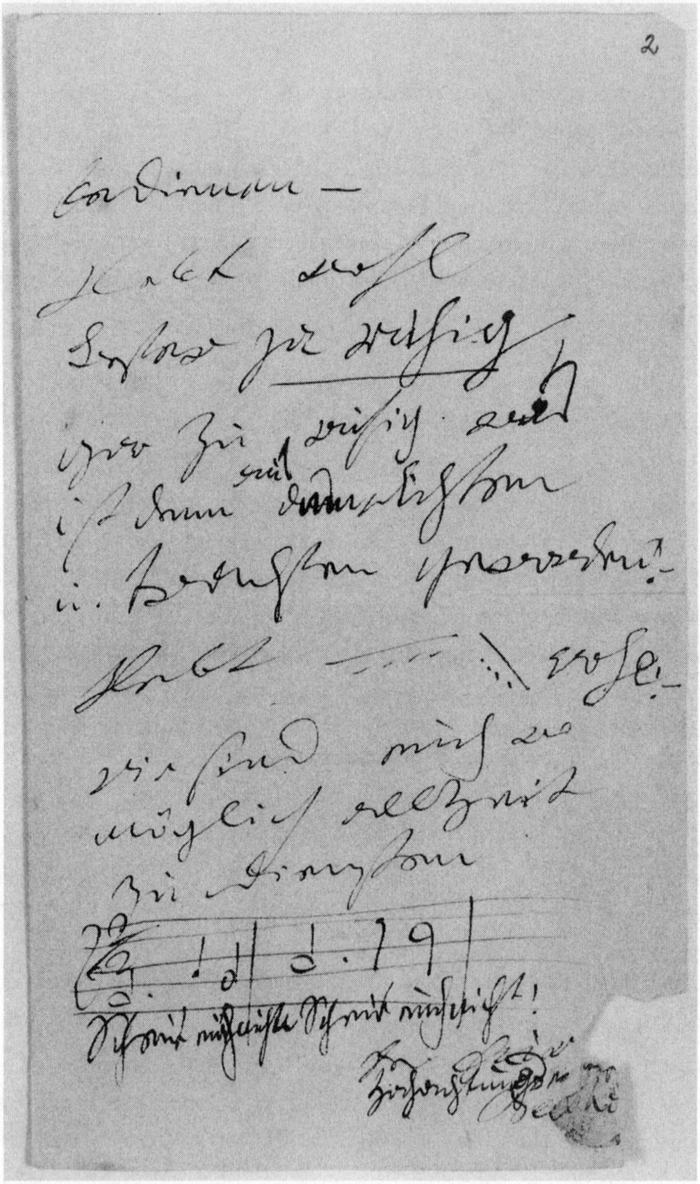

FIGURE 7.1. Beethoven, p. 2 of an undated letter to Georg Friedrich Treitschke. By permission of the Beethoven-Haus Bonn. Collection of H. C. Bodmer.

is less clear, because Seyfried's early career was closely intertwined with the Freemasons Mozart and Emanuel Schikaneder, and he furnished (as it happens, inaccurate and secondhand) information to Treitschke about Mozart's Masonic activities.[46]

I do not know if Treitschke, who was Beethoven's librettist for the 1814 revision of *Fidelio,* had Masonic leanings or connections. Toward the close of an undated letter to the poet, Beethoven bids him farewell with the words "Lebt wohl"—a standard way of signing off.[47] But between the two words he has interpolated a drawing of an ascending line followed by a descending one, with dots or dashes under each line (fig. 7.1). The sketchiness of the drawing makes a definitive reading impossible, but the figure may represent a try square, a tool used to lay out or test right angles, which is also a universal emblem of Freemasonry, symbolizing morality, truthfulness, and honesty. When Masonic brothers part from one another they are said to do so "on the square."[48] To embed a representation of the square in the phrase "Lebt wohl" might signify bidding farewell "on the square," or, perhaps, be read as an injunction to live an upstanding life.[49]

In October 1811 Beethoven wrote to the Berlin poet Christoph August Tiedge, whom he had met at Teplitz during the summer, expressing his deep appreciation at Tiedge's agreement to use the intimate form of address between them. "You welcomed me, my Tiedge, with the password *[Bundes-Wort] Du,* and I accept it."[50] Kaznelson concluded that "The *Bundeswort* can only be the "Thou" of the Freemasons."[51] This seems reasonable enough, inasmuch as the reference books indicate that "*Bund* is the general designation for the organization of Freemasons" and "*Wort* is disseminated everywhere as a recognition sign" of the Masons.[52] To receive and give the *Du,* therefore, and to designate it as the *BundesWort* is to use it in consciousness of a Masonic implication, and very likely as a reference that takes a mutual Masonic background of the two men as a given.[53]

In a letter of around 1824, Beethoven wrote to the music dealer Max Joseph Leidesdorf:

> Give Herr Ries, the bearer of this note, some easy compositions for pianoforte duet [at a good price], or, even better, free of charge—Behave according to the purified doctrine *[betragt euch nach der gereinigten Lehre]*—All good wishes
>
> > Beethoven
> > Minimus[54]

As Frimmel noted, this sounds very much like a reference to Masonic doctrine.[55] Beethoven appears to be signaling Leidesdorf that the bearer, Ferdinand Ries's younger brother Franz Joseph (1792–1860), who resided in Vienna after 1819, was a Mason and therefore deserving of a discount or gift. "Minimus," then, could be taken as Beethoven's jesting allusion to the mystifying profusion of Masonic code names or grades, in which he facetiously placed himself at the lowest level.[56]

On the last leaf of the sketches for the Adagio of the "Razumovsky" Quartet, op. 59, no. 1, Beethoven wrote, "A weeping willow or acacia tree on my brother's grave [Einen Trauerweiden oder Akazien-Baum aufs Grab meines Bruders]."[57] This has been interpreted in various ways, particularly as expressive of Beethoven's feelings about one or another of his brothers, but to those versed in Masonic lore there seems no doubt that it has Masonic significance, for the acacia is widely "considered the symbolic plant of Freemasonry," standing variously for innocence, incorruptibility, immortality, resurrection, and mourning; at funerals of Freemasons twigs of acacia are thrown into the grave.[58] Viewed from a Masonic perspective, Beethoven's notation is to be read as a reference, literal or allegorical, to the death of a fellow-Mason.[59] The acacia is also venerated as a sacred tree in non-Masonic contexts—among the ancient Egyptians, in Arabic traditions, and in biblical texts—but such references are fairly esoteric, certainly more so than references to the acacia as a Masonic burial symbol. Allusions to the willow are extremely rare though not completely unknown in Freemasonry; in particular one finds them in rites of the thirty-second-degree of the Ancient and Accepted Scottish Rite, initially founded in the eighteenth century, and, later on, in the Ordre des Noachites Français (known as Maçonnerie napoléonienne), established by followers of Napoleon Bonaparte in 1816, clearly too late to have affected Beethoven's formulation.[60] Thus, the Masonic interpretation doesn't fully account for the "weeping willow" reference or for the fact that Beethoven's phrase continues to remain open to fruitful biographical interpretation in connection with his brothers.

Also lending themselves to multiple interpretations are the three Egyptian and Orphic inscriptions that Beethoven copied out from Schiller's essay, "Die Sendung Moses" (The mission of Moses) and kept under glass upon his writing desk during his later years. The first two are Saitic inscriptions about the veiled goddess Isis, one allegedly taken from a statue of her and the other said to have been inscribed on either a temple or a pyramid at Sais;

the third is from an Orphic hymn used in initiation rites of the Eleusinian Mysteries.

Ich bin, was da ist.
Ich bin alles, was ist, was war, und was seyn wird, kein sterblicher Mensch
   hat meinen Schleier aufgehoben.
Er ist einzig von ihm selbst, u. diesem Einzigen sind alle Dinge ihr Daseyn
   schuldig.

I am that which is.
I am everything that is, that was, and that shall be. No mortal man has
   lifted my veil.
He is unique unto himself, and it is to this singularity that all things owe
   their existence.[61]

We have already examined "the veil of Isis" image as a widespread Romantic trope with erotic and metaphysical overtones (see chapter 4); now we turn to its Masonic implications. The Saitic lines were frequently quoted during Beethoven's lifetime, for example in Voltaire's essay "Des Rites Égyptiens" and Kant's *Critique of Judgment*.[62] It was, after all, the time of Bonaparte's voyage down the Nile, and it was the age of Mozart's *Die Zauberflöte,* with its images of a quasi-Masonic mystery cult flourishing within a pyramidal Heliopolis; in Paris in 1801, a travesty of *Die Zauberflöte* was presented under the title *Les Mystères d'Isis.* The French Revolution gave impetus to a remarkable vogue for Egyptian culture;[63] Egyptomania gripped the educated classes, so it is evident that Freemasonry, whatever its claim on the Egyptian mysteries and whatever its appropriation, as one of its sacred texts, of Plutarch's *Isis and Osiris,* where the lines about the veiled goddess first appeared (ch. 9, 354C), had no monopoly on these inscriptions. Nevertheless, a strong argument can be made that for many people in Beethoven's time they would resonate with Masonic implications. As the Beethoven scholars Arnold Schmitz and Albert Leitzmann pointed out, the Masonic lodges of the Josephinian period "were much occupied with the Mystery Cults of the Egyptians,"[64] evidenced by writings that were not without their impact on *Die Zauberflöte.*[65] Indeed, the exploration of the ancient mysteries was *the* crucial intellectual enterprise for Freemasons of the Josephinian decade, a far-ranging attempt to establish that the rituals and doctrines of Freemasonry not only closely paralleled the secret doctrines of the ancients, but were continuous with them, having been handed down through the centuries to successive generations of the elect by those who were chosen to be the carriers of redemptive knowledge. Thus, almost every issue of the weighty Viennese *Journal für Freymaurer* featured an extended article or monograph on one of the mystery religions—Pythagorean, Eleusinian, Etruscan, Osiric, Hebraic, Mithraic and Zoroastrian, Cabirian, Brahman, and Dionysian.

With negligible textual variations, the Isis passages migrated from the Freemason Voltaire's "Des Rites Égyptiens" and the Orphic text from Bishop Warburton's *Divine Legation of Moses* to a monograph on the origins of Freemasonry among the ancients written by "Bruder Decius," the Masonic pseudonym for the Jena philosopher and Illuminist Karl Leonhard Reinhold, and published in two parts in the *Journal für Freymaurer* (1786) and in revised and expanded form as a separate book (1788). From the latter, the inscriptions soon found their way into Schiller's essay (1791), where Beethoven encountered them.[66]

Apart from its Masonic pedigree, Schiller's essay is thoroughly steeped in the Masonic view of the ancient mysteries and admittedly leans heavily on Reinhold, whom he credits in a closing footnote; in particular, Schiller stresses the ritual essence of the inscriptions, which have to do with the hierophant's renaming of candidates in the course of their initiation. He notes that the Egyptian priests did not name the divinity, whose uniqueness required no further specification: "A name, said they, is only a need for pointing a difference; he who is unique *[einzig]*, has no need of a name, for there is no one with whom he could be confounded." After quoting the first two of the three passages, Schiller goes on, tracking his source almost word for word: "In the hymn which the hierophant, or guardian of the sanctuary, sang to the candidate for initiation, this was the first instruction given concerning the nature of the divinity." The third inscription, on the singularity of the divinity, follows.[67] Schiller's emphasis on the ceremonial function of the quotations is a matter of some importance, inasmuch as the Masons and Illuminati were not merely interested in the Egyptian inscriptions as the fascinating residuum of an ancient cultic religion but actually used them in their own rituals. A catechism drawn from an initiation ritual for applicants to the grade of Illuminatus Major of the Order of Illuminati reads, in part:

FRAGE: Wo kamen Sie her?

ANTWORT: Aus der Welt der ersten Auserwählten.

FRAGE: Wohin wollen Sie?

ANTWORT: In das Allerheiligste.

FRAGE: Wen suchen Sie da?

ANTWORT: Den, der da ist, der da war, und der da ewig seyn wird.

FRAGE: Was erleuchtet Sie?

ANTWORT: Das Licht, das in mir wohnt, und nun angezündet ist.

QUESTION: Where have you come from?

ANSWER: From the world of the first chosen.

QUESTION: Whither do you want to go?

ANSWER: To the innermost sanctum.

QUESTION: Whom do you seek there?

ANSWER: The one who is, who was, and who always shall be.

QUESTION: What inspires you?

ANSWER: The light, which lives in me and is now ablaze in me.[68]

The probability that Beethoven was mindful of the Masonic implications of the Isis inscriptions is heightened by the fact that in his already cited letter of consolation to Countess Erdödy of 19 September 1815, he refers to the Temple of Isis as the goal of a purifying initiatory process along Masonic lines:

> We finite beings, who are the embodiment of an infinite spirit, are born to suffer both pain and joy; and one might almost say that the best of us obtain *joy through suffering*— . . . . May God grant you greater strength to enable you to reach your *Temple of Isis,* where the purified fire *[geläuterte Feuer]* may swallow up all your troubles and you may awake like a new phoenix.[69]

A conversation between Beethoven and Karl Holz at the beginning of March 1826 similarly suggests a ready familiarity with conventionally Masonic aspects of the Egyptian mystery rites. Holz wrote in the conversation book:

Dear fellow! If you leave behind nothing but your sketchbooks, they won't lead to any such quarrel, because they are hieroglyphics, from which no man will derive wisdom!
—
These are the Mysteries of Isis and Osiris.[70]

Another of Beethoven's cryptic characterizations is of Anton Schindler as a "Samothracian" and "Samothracian R[asca]l *(Samotrazischer L[umpenker]l)*."[71] Schindler, who was gratified by what he took to be an affectionate phrase and even asked Beethoven to write "a *canon* on the theme 'Lumpenkerl von Samotr[azien],'"[72] himself interpreted it as an allusion to ancient ritual ceremonies of Samothrace: "By the word 'Samothracian' Beethoven is here referring . . . to the Samothracian mysteries (of the mythical heroic age, 2000 B.C.), which were based partly on music. He designated me thus as a sharer in the Beethoven mysteries."[73] And here one may want to recall how Schindler described that he exchanged a meaningful—implying Masonic—special handshake with Beethoven on their first meeting: "A handshake implied even more *[Ein Händedruck besagte noch weiteres],*" he wrote.[74] Frimmel had little doubt that Beethoven's use of the word "Samothracian" is Masonic, signifying "one who was initiated" into the ancient mystery cult.[75] On the other hand, Beethoven may have been aware that the Cabirian rituals featured phallic worship, and that the Samothracian deities were a male couple, Cabeiros and the youth who was his cup-bearer.[76] In that case it is conceivable that Beethoven coined the phrase "Samothracian *L[umpenker]l*" as a euphemism for what he may have perceived, rightly or not, to be Schindler's sexual orientation.[77] In another letter, Beethoven continued to associate Schindler with the ancient world, addressing him as "Most excellent *L[umpenker]l* of Epirus and not less of Brundusium and so forth!"[78] Of course, in still others, Beethoven dubs Schindler "Papageno," but this may have a non-Masonic significance despite the evident connection to Mozart's Masonic opera. In the end, many will want to attribute the whole matter to Beethoven's lifelong penchant for using quirky names for members of his retinue, a penchant which was at its peak around this time with such names as "Falstaff" (Ignaz Schuppanzigh), "Diabolus" (Diabelli) and "Dominus Bernardus" (Joseph Karl Bernard); a variety of names for members of Countess Erdödy's retinue ("Chief Steward" for Sperl, "Violoncello" for

Josef Linke, "Magister" for Brauchle); and a cluster of military grades for the publisher Steiner and his associates, with "Generalissimo" reserved for Beethoven himself.[79]

III

Setting aside the lieder that Wegeler adapted for Masonic purposes, Beethoven wrote only a few works that were arguably intended for actual use in the lodges. One such is his setting of Goethe's "Bundeslied," for solo voices, chorus, and winds, op. 122 (1797–1824), a poem that is identified as Masonic in the editions of Goethe's collected works and heads the list of his Masonic writings in the encyclopedias of Freemasonry.[80] Indeed, one authority asserted that the "Bundeslied" is included in almost all Masonic songbooks and sung in virtually every German-speaking lodge.[81] It opens:

> In allen guten Stunden,
> erhöht von Lieb' und Wein,
> soll dieses Lied verbunden
> von uns gesungen sein!

> Whene'er the hour is good,
> Inspired by love and wine,
> Shall we, united,
> Sing this song!

Beethoven designated it on the autograph "to be sung in companionable circles." Other songs possibly written with the lodges in mind are Beethoven's two settings (one with chorus and orchestra accompaniment) of Matthisson's "Opferlied," op. 121b and WoO 126, with its evocation of ritual, and that of G. C. Pfeffel's "Der freie Mann," WoO 117, for solo and chorus, with its account of the hallmarks of a free man, including the Masonic-sounding verse:

> Wer ist ein freier Mann?
> Dem nicht Geburt noch Titel,
> Nicht Sammtrock oder Kittel

Den Bruder bergen kann;
Der ist ein freier Mann![82]

Who is a free man?
He from whom neither birth nor title,
Neither velvet jacket nor smock
Can conceal the brother,
He is a free man!

Whether specific musical patterns or motifs in Beethoven's instrumental music can be interpreted as characteristic-style topics or tropes drawn from an available vocabulary of Masonic musical symbolism remains an open question.[83] It is true, for example, that almost all music written for use in Masonic rituals is in the key of E-flat major (the three flats being of especial symbolic import) and the sequences of three detached chords that open *Die Zauberflöte* are clearly emblematic there of the rapping motifs that signify urgent requests for admittance at the climax of Masonic rituals of advancement. But E-flat is not inevitably a Masonic key, and the three choral entries and responses that open the Kyrie of Beethoven's *Missa solemnis,* for example, are not necessarily Masonic but are, because of their occurrence in the context of a genre of Catholic religious music, even more likely intended to represent the Holy Trinity or the triune nature of the sacred in general. Context drives interpretation in such instances; we readily accept that such musical tropes express a Masonic symbolism when they occur in Mozart's patently Masonic opera, while we are far from certain that the rapping motif in variation 13 of the "Diabelli" Variations is specifically Masonic.

If we take context into account, and if we consider that Freemasonry's main symbols are derived from architecture, Beethoven might conceivably have woven Masonic motifs into an overture such as "The Consecration of the House *[Die Weihe des Hauses],*" op. 124, celebrating the opening in 1822 of the Josephstadt Theater in Vienna. To those in the know, the inclusion of Masonic touches in this work, with its Masonic-sounding title, would have seemed extremely apt, especially since in such a context Masonic musical rhetoric is bound to evoke not only Freemasonry but the sacred, the sublime, and ideas of God as the supreme architect. It may be that Donald Francis Tovey had some such conception in mind when he wrote rather opaquely about the "Consecration of the House" Overture that he had "some reason to believe that the thrice three quaver chords" that accompany the opening of the double fugue "are a Masonic symbol, like the *Dreimaliger Akkord* in Mozart's *Zauberflöte*."[84]

Several other works have been or could be interpreted as expressions of one or another salient feature of Masonic doctrine. For example, in light of the centrality of ideas of brotherhood in Freemasonry, some might want to offer a Masonic reading of Don Fernando's ringing declaration, as the prisoners gather in the light of day:

Es sucht der Bruder seine Brüder
Und kann er helfen, hilft er gern.

The brother seeks his brethren;
and if he can help them he gladly does so.

These lines are not in Bouilly's or Sonnleithner's librettos, nor in the 1806 revision, but were added by Treitschke and Beethoven for the final version of 1814. With these words, the prisoners who had been entombed for no apparent reason are identified as an allegorical band of suffering brethren, freed from tyranny by a noble prince. It is not hard to imagine that Freemasons could have viewed *Fidelio* in the context of the abolition of their Order in the wake of the French Revolution, expressive of their own sense of a suffocating imprisonment and imposed silence.[85] Moreover, Freemasons could have regarded *Fidelio* as in some sense a latterday representative of the *Zauberflöte* tradition rather than primarily as a celebration of conjugal love and an allegory of the triumph of enlightened rule over arbitrary despotism. (It may be that Beethoven scholarship has overemphasized the characterization of *Fidelio* as a didactic "rescue opera" along French lines.) The opera certainly has the trappings of Masonic initiatory ritual that Viennese audiences were familiar with from Mozart's *Die Zauberflöte*: the movement from darkness to light, the multiplicity of deprivations and tests of endurance, the passage through death to resurrection, the reunion and apotheosis of the bridal couple. Edward J. Dent fully understood this when he wrote, "Florestan and Leonore . . . are Tamino and Pamina grown up and facing the fire and water of our own world."[86]

Of course, the ascent from the dark nether regions to an illuminated higher realm is a central Enlightenment and *Aufklärung* image as well as a Masonic one. Nevertheless, the latter perception may not be trivial or peripheral, especially when we bear in mind that a prominent Freemason, Prince Lichnowsky, was the motive force behind *Fidelio* and its first revisions. On no other occasion in Beethoven's life did a patron follow every stage of a work's composition, revision, and production in such detail and with such unlimited concern. Moreover, the opera was produced by another of Mozart's Masonic brothers, Emanuel Schikaneder, the librettist of *Die Zauberflöte,* who resumed the directorship of the Theater-an-der-Wien in September 1804 and guided *Fidelio* onto the stage a year later.

In the Choral Fantasia, op. 80, Dent saw "the mystical spirit of eighteenth-century Freemasonry, the new religion of liberty, equality and fraternity."[87] It isn't altogether clear that these conceptions are implicit in the text of what Tovey so persuasively identified as Beethoven's latter-day ode for St. Cecilia.[88] Dent is surely right, however, to see in the Choral Fantasia "an improvisation and a vision," deeply indebted in its form, instrumentation, and ideological stance to the choruses of Egyptian priests in *Die Zauberflöte.*[89] And Beethoven followed Mozart's example in wanting to represent the quest for illumination, so fundamental to Masonic imagery:

Wenn der Töne Zauber walten
Und des Wortes Weihe spricht,
Muss sich Herrliches gestalten,
Nacht und Stürme werden Licht.

Auss're Ruhe, inn're Wonne
Herrschen für den Glücklichen.
Doch der Künste Frühlingssonne
Lässt aus beiden Licht entstehn.

When the magic of sound holds sway
And the consecrated word speaks,
Then shall magnificence take form,
Night and storms become light.

Outward calm, inner rapture
Reign over those fortunate ones

While the vernal sun of art
Lets light arise from both.

The first treatment of the passage from darkness to light in Beethoven's
oeuvre may already be found in his Funeral Cantata on the Death of Emperor Joseph II, WoO 87, of 1790. Its text, closely mirrored in the musical
setting, contrasts night and illumination:

Ein Ungeheuer, sein Name Fanatismus,
stieg aus den Tiefen der Hölle,
dehnte sich zwischen Erd' und Sonne,
und es ward Nacht!

A monstrous creature, its name Fanaticism,
Arose from the depths of Hell,
Extended itself between earth and sun
And it was Night!

And its primary image, whose setting marks the first appearance of Beethoven's so-called "Humanitätsmelodie," is of the ascent to the light:

Da stiegen die Menschen, die Menschen an's Licht,
da drehte sich glücklicher die Erd' um die Sonne,
und die Sonne wärmte mit Strahlen der Gottheit.

Then mankind ascended unto the light,
Then the earth revolved with increased happiness around the sun
And the sun warmed it with divine radiance.

In the choral finale of the Ninth Symphony, as with the prisoners in *Fidelio,* another band of brethren searches for illumination, spanning the heavens in quest of the deity and of joy:

Laufet, Brüder, eure Bahn,
Freudig, wie ein Held zum Siegen.

Brothers, run your course,
Joyfully, like a hero to the victory!

Beethoven's setting of Schiller's "An die Freude" is famous for its representation of a universal fraternity realized within a harmonious holy family, shielded by protective maternal and paternal images.

Alle Menschen werden Brüder
wo dein sanfter Flügel weilt. . . .
Brüder! überm Sternenzelt
muss ein lieber Vater wohnen.

All mankind become brothers
Where thy gentle wings tarry. . . .
Brothers! above the vault of the stars
There surely dwells a loving Father.

Schiller wrote "An die Freude" at a time when he was closely linked to Masonic circles in Leipzig, especially through his intimate friend, the Mason and Illuminist Christian Gottfried Körner, but he himself apparently was not actually a lodge member.[90] That the poem is a celebration of Masonic brotherhood is quite apparent, however, from the large number of the musical settings of it that were composed and published in Masonic collections and widely used in the lodges.[91] Moreover, it has been convincingly interpreted as a Masonic poem, and Otto Baensch has suggested that Beethoven's choral finale may even have been intended to represent a quasi-Masonic ceremony, albeit a thoroughly unorthodox one.[92] Surely the "Ode to Joy" finale of Beethoven's Ninth is an unqualified affirmation of Freemasonry's universal and most stringent value—brotherhood. If that is so, the symphony's implied narrative may be one wherein the melody that embodies the idea of fraternity overwhelms and supersedes those flawed values that Beethoven took to be represented in the first three movements, namely, "despair" in the Allegro ma non troppo; frivolity ("nur Possen") in the scherzo; "tenderness" in the Adagio molto e cantabile (see below, pp. 204, 218–21). In this sense the work could be regarded as moving through a set of initiatory experiences that are fulfilled by a climactic arrival on Freemasonry's highest plane of virtue. There is no need to specify more closely the geography of these moves, which may be pictured in various ways; for example as devotional journeys refusing the seductions of doubt, diversion, and inwardness in single-minded pursuit of unalloyed faith; or as ventures through darkness into an ecstatic state of illumination wherein mankind and the divine are merged.

Nevertheless, the poem's polytheistic fusion of classical, Christian, and Eastern motifs; its utopian overtones; its celestial, Arcadian, and Elysian imagery; and its antityrannical posture, while appropriate to certain segments of Freemasonry, might have been inimical to others. This is perhaps especially true of several revolutionary lines in Schiller's first version of the poem, which so appealed to Beethoven that he copied them into his sketches and *Albumblätter,* but which, perhaps for reasons of discretion, did not find their way into the Ninth Symphony's final text:

Bettler werden Fürstenbrüder

Beggars become brothers of princes[93]

Männerstolz vor Königsthronen,—
. . . Untergang der Lügenbrut.

Manly pride before the throne of kings,
. . . The downfall of the liars' breed![94]

Ernst Wangermann has argued that taken as a whole, "An die Freude" is best understood as an expression of the outlook of the Order of Illuminati:

> Whereas pre-Illuminist Freemasonry had been no more than a kind of inner emigration, an oasis in which it was possible to escape from the prejudices and divisions of society at large, the Illuminati aspired to project their moral principles into society and thereby to transform it. At the end of the process there was the intoxicating vision of the universal brotherhood of man, transcending existing religious and national division, which has received its classical expression in the words of Schiller's "Ode to Joy": *Seid umschlungen, Millionen!*[95]

Despite the eminent tenability of this and similar positions, however, it remains prudent to emphasize that Freemasonry is rooted in an ancient set of traditions, which are the seedbed for a host of disparate creeds. The quasi-Masonic ideas and symbols in the texts of works like *Fidelio,* the Ninth Symphony, and Haydn's *Creation* predate Freemasonry (which came into being as an organized movement no earlier than the seventeenth century) and are traceable to alternative sources.[96] Thus, much leeway must be allowed—and much uncertainty will remain—for such ideas and symbols are almost never exclusive to Freemasonry, deriving, as they do, from a vast range of conventional and esoteric sources, drawing upon classical mythology, world religions, ritual practices, occult knowledge, Enlightenment thought and philosophy, utopian literature, Rosicrucianism, Romanticism, magic, cosmogony, and natural science. Moreover, each of the main contending factions within Freemasonry had its distinct ideological orientation, and among them they covered a broad spectrum of ideas from rationalism to mysticism, and, politically, the entire spectrum from radical opposition to the established social order to zealous support of repressive regimes.[97]

Viennese censors were expert in spotting potentially subversive ideas, yet they often chose to allow the expression of Masonic or quasi-Masonic viewpoints—such as those that may be found in *The Creation, Fidelio,* and the Ninth Symphony—and to permit countless performances of *Die Zauberflöte* despite its frankly Masonic text, imagery, and social perspectives. Quick to prohibit clandestine organizations that might harbor potential enemies of the state, the police were often tolerant of the expression of rationalist ideas and Masonic symbols, for these could serve as an escape valve for a discontented populace. Open dissent was not permitted, but images of illumination, justice, moral uplift, and fraternity were authorized so long as they were expressed in the vocabulary of benevolent kingship.

CHAPTER EIGHT

THE MASONIC IMAGINATION

A fresh examination of a crucial personal document from Beethoven's fifth decade may permit us to expand the range of his Masonic references and to enlarge the scope of future investigations of this subject. The document is Beethoven's Tagebuch, which he kept from 1812 to 1818.[1] It contains several explicit Masonic references and a large number of other entries that arguably have Masonic significance.

"Our world history has now lasted for 5816 years," wrote Beethoven in the Tagebuch at the beginning of 1816 (no. 71). And two years later, in another entry written at the turn of a new year, but now couched in faintly astrological language, he wrote, "Our consciousness on our planet is calculated as 5818 years" (no. 145). The dates "5816" and "5818" in Beethoven's Tagebuch—representing the Christian calendar date plus 4000—are not slips of the pen. They are frankly Masonic datings, for many Masonic groups habitually placed the creation of the world (Anno Lucis) at 4000 B.C. and dated their events and records accordingly. Some Masonic documents employ other dating systems, sometimes with a 3000-year differential, but the 4000-year differential is the one almost universally encountered in the lodges of France and Germany and in the records of Habsburg Freemasonry.[2]

Equally striking are Beethoven's lengthy extracts from Zacharias Werner's drama *Die Söhne des Thals. Ein dramatischen Gedicht. Erster Theil: Die Templer auf Cypern* (The sons of the valley: A dramatic poem, part 1, The Templars in Cyprus), published at Berlin in 1802 and reprinted in Vienna in 1813, for this is a drama steeped in legends of the origins and martyrology of Freemasonry, which, according to several spurious but widely circulated accounts, was considered to have originated in the medieval period among the Knights Templars. Werner's play is based on the most prevalent myth—the "First Legend of Perpetuation," which was floated in 1754—of the chivalric genesis of Freemasonry in the aftermath of the suppression and spoliation of the Order in A.D. 1307 and the immolation of its leader, Jacques de Molay.[3] The action is laid in Cyprus, prior to the destruction of the Order. Beethoven copied into the Tagebuch the text of several exchanges between Molay and Robert d'Heredon, who eventually helped to found an international brotherhood to carry out the ideals of the martyred leader. In the extracts, Robert affirms his fealty to Molay:

> ROBERT: In holy consciousness of duty,
> He has taught me abstinence and renunciation,
> And left his heaven to me!

Molay in turn urges "resignation and renunciation" upon Robert, dubs him a hero, and anoints him his successor:

> MOLAY: You are a hero—you are what is ten times more,
> *a real man!* . . .
> ROBERT: Blushing, I bow before your greatness!
> MOLAY: You shall surpass me . . .
> Be a lord of men!

I propose to take these patently Masonic references, not merely as curious remnants of Beethoven's earlier contacts with ideas and practices of Freemasonry, but as indications of a Masonic thread in the Tagebuch or, at the least, as sufficient authorization to examine other entries in the Tagebuch for their potential Masonic implications. Without any expectation of settling the issue, I will make a case for reading the Tagebuch as a diary analogous to those that were required to be maintained by candidates in the Order of Illuminati. It is not my purpose to assert, nor do I believe it possible to demonstrate, that Beethoven was actually associated with, or a member of, an as-yet-unidentified clandestine fraternal society; nor do I wish to use evidence of his links to Freemasonry as a rationale for esoteric readings of his works.[4] (I do not, however, exclude the possibility that he belonged to a latter-day *Lesegesellschaft* or informal reading group with strong Masonic or Illuminist leanings.) Rather, I want to explore whether it is possible to locate in Beethoven's Tagebuch the influence of Masonic conceptions and symbols, the traces of what Frances Yates in a similar connection called "a certain style of thinking which is historically recognizable," thereby, perhaps, enabling us better to understand what he believed and how his mind worked.[5]

Modeling itself on the rigorous training in scholastic and spiritual matters required by the Society of Jesus, the Order of Illuminati aspired to be "a learned society *[eine gelehrte Gesellschaft],* in which, through example and instruction, the understanding is guided and the heart improved." It called upon its candidates "To read the ancients, to show diligently what you read, to think things over. . . . To make oneself familiar with the ancient and modern doctrines of ethics [and] philosophy, such as the Stoic, Epicurean, etc., [and] to search out examples of these in ancient and recent history."[6] In its statutes, and in a document entitled *Instructio pro recipientibus,* it furnished reading lists drawn from the ancients and from eighteenth-century moralists and philosophers, urging candidates and members to read books "that serve for the cultivation of the heart . . . and all others that are rich in the cultivation of moral and political maxims."[7]

A candidate for the first degree of the Order (Apprentice or Novice) was required to furnish to his leader a monthly written report (the so-called *quibus licet*) of his progress and diligence. And those who had reached the second (Minerval) grade were instructed to prepare a diary and other written materials. The opening section of the *Instructio insinuatorum, seu potius receptorum* states that "Everyone must maintain a diary, wherein he notes down precisely and accurately everything that he receives from or sends to the Order." Furthermore, he is to have in readiness folios of paper on which

a) Characters, deeds, ways of thinking of learned men of repute of ancient and recent times should be recorded and collected.

b) The same goes for elevated thoughts, especially sentiments, moral aphorisms and systematic ideas of such people as well as for books that are recommended or required by the Order. These collections shall, upon request, be shown and also submitted as an indication of diligence.[8]

Initiates were to be instructed in how to maintain these written documents:

> each will be given an easy cipher of the Order and will be shown how to no-
> tate it, and how to prepare the diary and the *quibus licet*. He will be given
> copies of these instructions; if necessary he will also be loaned good books,
> and permitted to and shown how to make excerpts from them and to strive
> above all to prepare himself and to find clarity.[9]

In Vienna in the 1780s, Ignaz von Born, the outstanding Masonic theorist who was also a prominent leader of the Order of Illuminati, took steps
to create an academy of science *(Akademie der Wissenschaft)* at the center of
Viennese Freemasonry, and to this end established two learned journals,
Physikalische Arbeiten der einträchtigen Freunde in Wien (1783–88) and the *Journal für Freymaurer* (1784–86), and several Masonic lodges—"Zur wahren Eintracht" and Mozart's "Zur Wohlthätigkeit"—into which flocked writers,
artists, and scholars, along with enlightened aristocrats and other citizens.
More than a score of special membership meetings (called *Übungslogen*) were
held between November 1782 and December 1785 "at each of which three
or four members gave prose or verse readings of their choice, on subjects
from history, ethics, and philosophy, and usually dealing with the Ancient
and recent Mysteries and secret societies."[10] Thus, the emphasis of the Order of Illuminati on scholarship and the written word entered and transformed the Masonic tradition, creating, so to speak, a rationalist left wing
in Habsburg Freemasonry. It is this trend within Freemasonry, particularly
as it emanated from Bonn and Vienna during the 1780s, that seems to have
left indelible traces on Beethoven's sensibility.

For six years Beethoven used the Tagebuch to help him take stock of his
situation, to regain his equilibrium, to give him insight into his conflicts,
and to externalize his pain and confusion over life's mounting vicissitudes.
He filled the diary with personal outcries, with notes on trivia of daily life,
and with words of wisdom drawn from a variety of sources—from proverbs,
poetry, drama, philosophy, and theology. The Tagebuch records Beethoven's
struggle to withstand adversity, his willingness—indeed determination—to
sacrifice his desires for personal gratification, his decision to devote himself
wholly to his art, to God, and to humanity, even if to do these things meant
isolating himself from the world. It shows him seeking a new start, weigh-

ing alternatives, trying to discover what he believes in, sorting out what is necessary to achieve illumination and wisdom. And, in the end, it shows him groping for an answer to a fundamental question: how, in the face of encroaching mortality and doubt, is he to live a good life?

In embarking on so momentous an exploration Beethoven perhaps recalled what he had heard about diaries kept by his mentors, friends, and colleagues among the Bonn Illuminists, who were enjoined to create similar documents as aids to clarification and as proof that they were worthy of advancing to the higher degrees of the Order, such advancement being a prerequisite for access to the most consecrated forms of knowledge. There is no compelling reason to suppose that Beethoven prepared the Tagebuch in connection with an actual process of initiation or promotion. It does, however, bear some of the hallmarks of such a document: extracts from approved writings on morality, religion, and philosophy; self-observation, with emphasis on the acknowledgment of personal shortcomings; affirmations of adherence to precepts of virtue and duty. It is instructive to compare the Tagebuch with another presumed Illuminist document, Neefe's "Lebenslauf," which analogously enumerates books that shaped his thinking; describes his inner feelings, moral dilemmas, hypochondria, and conflicted attitudes about sex; underscores his love of family and devotion to a "grand plan" to achieve "human happiness"; and concludes with a revealing section headed "Result of My Self-Observation."[11] It may be that at this juncture in his life Beethoven half-automatically turned back to his intellectual origins, to his formative years, when he was part of a vital group, sharing its ideals, attitudes, and enthusiasms, taking as his models those whom he admired for their dedication to the good, the true, and the beautiful. The Tagebuch, then, can be seen as his halting, fragmented attempt to formulate principles for living a creative and praiseworthy life in accordance with what he perceived to be the sacrificial and altruistic precepts of the advanced fraternal orders during the decade of the Josephinian *Aufklärung*. And that may be why there are in his Tagebuch numerous ideas that closely parallel, and may well be drawn from, Masonic and Illuminist doctrine.

The opening entry of Beethoven's Tagebuch contains what may be an evocation of a symbolic journey, the acceptance of a ritual death involving separation from the world and the flesh, and a call for resurrection into a new life:

Submission, deepest submission to your fate, only this can give you the sacrifices — — — for this matter of service. O hard struggle! — Do everything that still has to be done to arrange what is necessary for the long journey *[zu der weiten Reise]*. You must — — find everything that your most cherished wish can grant, yet you must bend it to your will. — Maintain an absolutely steady attitude.

You must not be a *human being, not for yourself, but only for others:* for you there is no longer any happiness except within yourself, in your art. O God! give me strength to conquer myself, nothing at all must fetter me to life.

No satisfactory explanation has been offered for the reference to the "long journey": the context strongly suggests that it has to do, not with a literal journey by Beethoven to or from the Bohemian spas or to Linz, but with ideas of submission, sacrifice, and service in an unspecified, sacred cause. A potential clarification emerges if we consider the "journey" in the Masonic sense, as a wandering through darkness in quest of illumination, as a departure from the quotidian in search of the supernal, as a venture into painful realms of experience in exchange for access to arcane knowledge, and as a necessary stage in finding internal peace and achieving maturity.

Later entries confirm Beethoven's sense of the journey as a metaphor for a rite of passage or a quest for a transcendent goal. "Show me the course where at the distant goal stands the Palm!" he writes in 1813 (no. 17). A cluster of entries, all written down in 1815, show him seeking the right path in pursuit of virtue and a felicitous existence: "In thy passage over this earth," he quotes from the Indian poet Kalidasa, "where the paths are now high, now low, and the true path seldom distinguished, the traces of thy feet must needs be unequal; but *virtue* will press thee right onward" (no. 63c).[12] And from Hesiod's *Works and Days:* "For vice walks many paths full of present sinful desires and thereby induces many to follow it. But virtue leads on to a steep path and cannot attract men as easily and swiftly, especially if elsewhere there are those who call them to a sloping and pleasant road" (no. 68). Beethoven accepts that it will be a long and hard journey, a *via dolorosa,* requiring moral fortitude and the capacity to resist temptation: "You take the hardships as signposts *[Wegweiserinnen]* toward an agreeable life" (no. 67). These entries may also be viewed in the context of Beethoven's already cited letter of that same year to Countess Erdödy after the death of her son, assuring her that she will find purification through fire as she makes her way to the Temple of Isis.[13]

"There are no sedentary heroes" asserts one Masonic authority.[14] Just as the journey is central to myths of the hero, Masonic rituals of initiation take their point of departure in ancient cultic practices, in the Eleusinian and Pythagorean processions, in the trajectories of the heavenly bodies, in Neoplatonic conceptions of the soul's peregrinations. The Masonic journey retains overlapping meanings of a symbolic "holy wandering" as well as of its reenactment in a literal "rite of circumambulation," consisting of a "formal procession around the altar or other holy and consecrated object."[15] In typical induction and promotion ceremonies, the initiate makes three such "journeys"; as the ceremony draws to a conclusion with the third circumambulation, one of the Overseers intones: "the journey toward death is a journey toward the goal of our perfection."[16] The initiate must "conquer" himself, "nothing at all must fetter [him] to life" (no. 1).

During rituals of circumambulation, the candidate travels first from West to East and eventually returns "from East to West by way of the South."[17] The lodge and the altar are oriented toward the East (on an East–West axis), with the Master of the Lodge positioned at the easternmost point. Orientation is of the utmost importance, because each direction has a particular set of rich symbolic associations attached to it, with East signifying the source of light and wisdom as well as the ultimate goal of life; West representing variously the close of day, death, a place of "darkness and ignorance," but also the place where one must "seek the thing which has been lost"; South, of course, is light, warmth, beauty, the place of midday and refreshment; and the Masons call North a "Place of Darkness," emblematic of "the profane and unregenerated world."[18] "East morning—West evening—South noon—North midnight" (no. 14). When Beethoven wrote those words in 1813 near the beginning of his Tagebuch, he expressed *in nuce* the Masonic symbolic interpretations of the cardinal points of the compass.

Beethoven's Tagebuch is itself oriented toward the East, with multiple quotations from a variety of writings on Eastern—especially Hindu and Brahman—religious divinities and beliefs; it contains as well aphoristic poetry by the Persian thirteenth-century poet Sa'di in Herder's free translations, most of which were published in Herder's *Blumen aus morgenländischen Dichtern gesammlet* (Flowers Gathered from Eastern Poets) in 1792 (nos. 5–6, 55–58). Apart from the Herder collection and the Georg Forster translation of the Indian drama *Sakuntala,* which were widely read, Beethoven here displayed an unusual erudition; his Tagebuch contains extracts from Charles

Wilkins's translation of the *Bhagavad-Gita* and Forster's translation of William Robertson's *An Historical Disquisition Concerning the Knowledge which the Ancients Had of India,* and writings by Sir William Jones and Paulinus a Sancto Bartholomaeo as translated by the scholar of Zoroastrian and Brahman religion Johann Friedrich Kleuker (nos. 61–65, 93–94).[19] This attention to Eastern ways of thought is strongly suggestive of Masonic preoccupations, for intellectuals of the period came to Eastern thought in all its manifestations through the Masonic literature and by way of the supposedly oriental rites practiced by the Freemasons in their exotic temples. (Individual lodges in various European countries, including Austria, were organized under supreme bodies designated as the Grand Orient; thus, Mozart's lodges were called "Beneficence" and "New-Crowned Hope" in "the Orient of Vienna.")[20] Eastern religion and literature was a special preserve of the Freemasons: Kleuker was both a Freemason and an Illuminist; Forster was a prominent Mason and possibly an Illuminist;[21] Herder and Goethe, who stimulated the German vogue for *Sakuntala* and Orientalism in general, had both been recruited into the Order of Illuminati in Weimar.

Masonic initiation is conceived of as a passage through darkness to an illuminated state of being. In a typical ceremony, the candidate is blindfolded until a climactic moment, when he is at last permitted to see the light.[22] As in the Masonic "journey," a symbolic meaning is embodied in the ritual as a dramatic representation of the transition from blindness to sight. Thus, it is suggestive that in several Tagebuch entries the divinity is portrayed as the personification of light; these descriptions of the attributes of the Godhead are copied from a variety of sources, ancient and Eastern. First, from a hymn in praise of Parabrahma: "O God . . . You are the true, eternally blessed, unchangeable light of all times and spaces" (no. 61b). Two such passages are taken from Sir William Jones's "Hymn to Narayena":

What glorious light
Thy pow'r directed? Wisdom without bound.

(no. 62)

Wrapt in eternal solitary shade,
Th' impenetrable gloom of light intense,
Impervious, inaccessible, immense.

(no. 65)

From Kant's *Allgemeine Naturgeschichte und Theorie des Himmels* Beethoven took the incantatory phrase, "When in the state of the world order and beauty shine forth, there is a God" (no. 105b). Finally, Homer's *Odyssey* provided the composer with a classic image of the bringing of illumination to the world:

> And the rosy dawn arose from the noble bed of Tithonus
> And brought light to the gods and mortal men.
>
> (no. 74)

A state of illumination is reached only after a transition out of darkness, from which it is inseparable. Mackey writes, "Darkness is the symbol of initiation. It is intended to remind the candidate of his ignorance, which Freemasonry is to enlighten; of his evil nature, which Freemasonry is to purify; of the world, in whose obscurity he has been wandering, and from which Freemasonry is to rescue him."[23]

All initiatory processes take the form of a series of trials, symbolic or actual. In the Tagebuch, Beethoven underscores his acceptance of the need to undergo arduous tests of fidelity, diligence, devotion, and obedience—to determine if he is capable of perfecting his moral character, worthy of admission to the ranks of the purified. Can he endure the trials? Beethoven enlists the gods, fate, and his musical forebears to fortify his capacity for endurance, which he describes as the "chief characteristic of a distinguished man: endurance *[Beharrlichkeit]* in adverse and harsh circumstances" (no. 93). From Homer he copies the motto, "For Fate gave Man the courage to endure *[ausduldenden Muth]* to the end" (no. 26); from the depths of his own experience he writes, "Endurance *[Ertragung]*. Resignation. Resignation. Thus we profit even by the deepest misery and make ourselves worthy" (no. 78). And he draws strength from the images of his great predecessors: "Portraits of Handel, Bach, Gluck, Mozart, and Haydn in my room — They can promote my capacity for endurance *[Duldung]*" (no. 43).

Stoical acquiescence in the designs of fate is thus a central topic of the Tagebuch: indeed, the diary opens with the injunction, "Submission, deepest submission to your fate" (no. 1) and contains numerous other references to fate and related subjects. Among these is a cluster of allusions to the influential contemporary dramatic genre known as *Schicksalstragödie* (fate tragedy), in which, typically, an oracular fatal prediction of the downfall of a hero, a family, or a larger entity is inexorably fulfilled. Dramas of crime, guilt, and punishment modeled on Greek and Roman examples, their action is characterized by a "suffocating atmosphere that paralyzes all volition."[24] Such precursors of this genre as Calderón's *La banda y la flor* and plays by Carlo Gozzi are mentioned in the diary (nos. 13, 21), which also contains extracts from Schiller's *Die Braut von Messina,* the *Trauerspiel* that initiated the genre in 1803, and from works by two of its leading exponents— Zacharias Werner and Adolph Müllner (nos. 7, 8, 60, and 118).

As Tamino and Papageno well knew, the command of silence is one of the main tests of endurance required of those who aspire to membership or, when already initiated, to a higher degree. To undergo a trial of silence is a universal Masonic ordeal and token of fidelity, inculcated in Freemasons by oath and enforced by threats of punishment ranging from censure to expulsion.[25] "Its secret doctrines are the precious jewels of the Order," write Mackey and Clegg; secrecy and silence "constitute the very essence of all Masonic character."[26] And silence is one of the salient and recurrent themes of Beethoven's Tagebuch, with four separate entries extolling its virtues. Two of them are taken from Herder's *Blumen aus morgenländischen Dichtern gesammlet:* "Learn to keep silent, O friend. Speech is like silver, but to be silent at the right moment is pure gold" (no. 5, "Silence *[Das Schweigen]*"), and "Spare even the closest friend your secrets; how can you ask fidelity of him, when you deny it to yourself?" (no. 59, "Silence *[Verschwiegenheit]*"). Beethoven also copies out a Latin proverb, *Audi multa, loquere pauca,* "Listen to much, but speak little" (no. 115), which sums up one of the attributes of a dutiful Freemason.[27]

In a confessional diary like Beethoven's one might well expect to find evidence of a tension between disclosure and secrecy, revelation and concealment. Indeed, in one entry Beethoven observes that evil is "easier to endure" when it is shared with others (no. 136). Of unmistakably Masonic cast, however, is another entry, which explicitly refers to silence as a condition for the initiation of novices into one of the mystery religions, Brahmanism. "Five years of silence is required of future Brahmans," notes Beethoven (no. 94c), thereby evincing his lively interest in the initiation practices of the Hindus and Brahmans, practices that preoccupied serious Freemasons of the time.[28] Similar lengthy periods of enforced silence were required of novitiates in other religions and students of ancient and esoteric mysteries—from the school of Pythagoras to cabalism—as well as in every variety of Freemasonry.[29] The statutes of the Order of Illuminati required that every apprentice give his recruiter "a written pledge of silence *[einen Revers de silentio],*" and described "Silence and secrecy" as "the soul of our Order *[Stillschweigen und Geheimnis sind die Seele unsers Ordens].*"[30] A section of the statutes personally signed by Adam Weishaupt emphasizes: "Silence is the greatest law, that is why [a candidate] is not permitted to speak about his acceptance by the Order, even to presumed Brothers of the Order."[31] The Illuminists never expected that their statutes and their members' private writings would be made public, as they were in 1787 after their seizure by the Bavarian authorities.[32] In this connection it may also be noteworthy that the multiple endorsements in the Tagebuch of the command of silence were written during the period of Masonic prohibition and of ubiquitous police surveillance, of which Beethoven was well aware, as we know from his conversation books. In considering Masonic or quasi-Masonic references in the Tagebuch, one needs to bear in mind the widespread and virulent conspiracy theories of the post-1789 period, which regarded the Order of Illuminati, the Jacobins, the Knights Templars, the Carbonari, and the Freemasons as indivisible segments of a vast clandestine organization whose aim was the overthrow of organized authority, religious and secular.

Closely related to the trials of silence and secrecy is the trial of seclusion, which here takes the form of a shamanistic or monastic withdrawal into a self-imposed isolation. In the Tagebuch, the peasant hut is a symbol of tranquil retreat—a place of worship and of healing. "A farm, then you escape your misery!" (no. 66); "And then a cowl to end this unhappy life" (no. 84); "And a small peasant house [if *Hof* means *Bauernhof*] —— a small chapel —— in it the hymn written by me, performed for the glory of the Almighty, the Eternal, the Infinite. Thus may my last days flow by —— and those of future Mankind. —" (nos. 41–42). Like an anchorite of a religious order, Beethoven accepts the need for abnegation and withdrawal, hopes to find a simple haven where he can occupy himself in creative service, prayer, and sacrifice, seeking thereby to renounce a profane existence and to become, as it were, "holy by initiation," to adapt a phrase from Clement of Alexandria.[33]

Thus, Beethoven's Tagebuch is in many ways a dissertation on the sacrificial and renunciatory paths to blessedness. It constitutes a record of his ordeals, through which he is tested and tempered, and gives evidence that he has dedicated himself to service. The goals of his journey may be fulfilled only by sacrifice and purification. That is why the opening words of the Tagebuch—its exordium, which appears to express Beethoven's initiatory purposes—speak of "submission," "sacrifices," "service," and call upon God to give him "strength to conquer [him]self." It is only through renunciation of the self that he may enter service. As we have already seen in the Prologue to this book, Beethoven chose a sacrificial path to redemption, one that he also saw as essential to further the development of his art. "I must not continue my present everyday life; art demands this sacrifice too" (no. 25; see also nos. 40 and 169). He took as his models the martyrs of the Knights Templars: "Sacrifice yourself without fame and reward" (no. 60a), and of Sparta: "These Lacedaemonians died ready to risk death or life for honor;—rather, they crowned death and life with honor" (no. 100). "*Socrates and Jesus were my models* [Socrates *u.* Jesus *waren mir Muster*]": those words entered in a conversation book for May 1820 show Beethoven's identification with those who sacrificed their lives for truth and salvation.[34] A letter of 1816 to Countess Erdödy reveals his understanding that perfection can only be achieved by way of extreme suffering: "It cannot be otherwise for man; and *in this respect his strength must stand the test,* that is to say, he must *endure without complaining and feel his worthlessness* and *then again* achieve *his perfection,* that perfection which the Almighty will then bestow upon him—."[35]

The Knight Templar Robert d'Heredon learned the lesson of "abstinence and renunciation" from his master and shouldered those burdens because he knew that though he "sinks down into the dust" he will inevitably rise again, and go forth "cleansed of the calamity" (no. 60d). Beethoven sought that same cleansing, aspired to the chief attribute of Brahma: *"Free from all passion and desire, that is the Mighty One"* (no. 61a). He adopted the *Bhagavad-Gita's* definition of a "blessed" man, as one "who, having subdued all his passions, performeth with his active faculties all the functions of life" (no. 64a). He knew that he was tempted to sin but trusted in divine forbearance; that is the transparent meaning of an eloquent passage: "If afterwards I become darkened through passion for evil *[durch Leidenschaft zum Bösen verdunkelt]*, I returned, after manifold repentance and purification, to the elevated and pure source, to the Godhead — And to your art" (no. 63a).

Initiation, we have seen, is a rite of purification. In all initiation ceremonies of the ancient mysteries, writes Mackey, "the first step taken by the candidate was a lustration or purification. The aspirant was not permitted to enter the sacred vestibule, or take part in the secret formula of initiation, until by water or by fire he was emblematically purified from the corruption of the world which he was about to leave behind."[36] Renunciation of desire also inevitably includes sexual renunciation; the candidate must be abstinent, free of impure thoughts. "O God! give me strength to conquer myself. . . . [W]ith A [presumably the initial of a beloved woman] everything goes to ruin" (no. 1); "O terrible circumstances, which do not suppress my longing for domesticity, but [prevent] its realization" (no. 3). Beethoven condemns in himself those impulses that prevent him from climbing the hill of virtue.

There is a continuity between primitive initiation rites and the rituals of the secret fraternal societies, ancient and modern, in that they all serve to establish male identity while enforcing a separation from the feminine, a turning away from interests perceived as unmanly. Initiation and promotion ceremonies are widely understood as strategies to detach young males from dependence on women.[37] Accordingly, Spartan, heroic, and patriarchal images are valorized, as are ideals of friendship, fraternity, and masculinity. But detachment from the feminine may not be without its price: in this sense, too, rituals are ordeals of suffering, ceremonies of humiliation. Beethoven fully accepts the need for the suppression of his libidinal interest in the world, and finds a model for that suppression in Brahman and Stoic thought, which he has now reached by way of the metaphysical mode of thought called Speculative Freemasonry. It is not beyond possibility that he was drawn to Freemasonry and Illuminism in part because they offered the brotherhood of man as compensation for his abandoned marriage project, thereby diminishing the pain of that renunciation, transforming a private hurt into a sacred obligation.

The withdrawal from women, already hinted at in Beethoven's letter of 6–7 July 1812 to the "Immortal Beloved," is written large in his Tagebuch, which privileges an exalted, mystical state of self-denial modeled on the exotic deities. ("No man hath lifted my veil," reads the inscription of Isis.) And soon after commencing the Tagebuch, in moving to "rescue" his nephew from the boy's mother, Beethoven stages a ritual of masculine purification; he will raise a boy to manhood, become both his father and mother, remove him from a perceived baleful feminine presence and its attendant temptations. Viewing his nephew's mother, Johanna van Beethoven, as the Queen of Night and himself as Sarastro,[38] he enacts in real life a Masonic ceremonial drama in which the paternal-priestly embodiment of wisdom successfully staves off the dangers of a mother's influence. "I too could well have produced the second part of *Die Zauberflöte*," Beethoven writes.[39] Still, we should not exaggerate Beethoven's late-period renunciation of the feminine. His invocations of Isis, Minerva, and Schiller's Freude, daughter of Elysium, indicate that he prominently numbered the feminine deities in his pantheon. Clearly at stake in the Tagebuch is an unresolved conflict over the feminine in which desire and renunciation remain in perpetual contention.

The Order of Illuminati required that a candidate furnish an "account of his own conduct on occasions where he doubted of its propriety."[40] Throughout the Tagebuch, Beethoven offers such accounts, revealing his feelings of contempt or disdain for others (nos. 34, 137), sounding a self-critical note particularly in regard to his sexual urges. "From today on never go into that house — — without shame at craving something from such a person" (no. 28); "With regard to T . . . , never go there where one could do wrong out of weakness" (no. 104). In a much-quoted passage he perceives a moral gulf between love and the mere release of sexual tension: "Sensual gratification without a spiritual union is and remains bestial, afterwards one has no trace of noble feeling but rather remorse" (no. 122). Occasionally he softens somewhat the harshness of his self-condemnation: "The frailties of nature are given by nature herself and sovereign Reason shall seek to guide and diminish them through her strength" (no. 138). But his main tendency is to condemn ethical lapses or failures, in part because they arouse in him painful feelings of guilt. From Schiller's *Die Braut von Messina* he took the lines: "This one thing I feel and clearly perceive: / Life is not the sovereign good, / But the greatest evil is guilt" (no. 118).

He was stricken with guilt over his harshness toward his sister-in-law Johanna van Beethoven: "It would have been possible without hurting the widow's feelings, but it was not to be. . . . I have disregarded my own welfare for my dear Karl's sake, bless my work, bless the widow, why cannot I entirely follow my heart and henceforth — — the widow — —" (no. 159). Conscious that he had breached the boundaries of honor and right conduct, he prays for forgiveness: "God, God, my refuge, my rock, O my all, Thou seest my innermost heart and knowest how it pains me to have to make somebody suffer through my good works for my dear Karl!!! O hear, ever ineffable One, hear me, your unhappy, most unhappy of all mortals" (no. 160), and eventually he confesses his inability to cure his sin; he is tormented by the question his conscience poses to Johanna: "Lamentable Fate, why can I not help you?" (no. 164).

We have by no means exhausted the Masonic implications of the Tagebuch. The many proverbs, aphorisms, and other wise sayings that appear in it are arguably consistent with instructions to members and initiates of the Order of Illuminati to record edifying and moral passages in their diaries. Clearly, however, numerous other entries in the Tagebuch—observations on the price of music paper, references to household or family concerns, listings of letters sent and money owed, remarks on planned compositions or performances, aides-mémoire for creative ideas, and random jottings of all kinds—have no apparent connection to Freemasonry. The Tagebuch also contains a fair number of references that may be interpreted in a variety of ways but that are consistent with or may be interpreted as signs of his interest in Masonic lore, symbolism, and ritual practice. For example, in a series of connected entries that Beethoven seems to have excerpted from a single source, perhaps a Masonic article or monograph on the Brahman Mysteries, and that he describes as having been drawn "from Indian literature" (no. 94), he writes of the great antiquity of "the pagodas from unhewn stone mountains in India" (no. 94a); Masonic tradition has it that the Brahman rock temples within which the hierophants explained the mysteries to the worshipers of Brahma and his fellow divinities were the most ancient prototypes of the Masonic temples.[41] The rock temples were conspicuously decorated with phallic representations, so it is not surprising that an adjoining entry refers to "the idea of the lingam" as an example of divine purpose in Brahmanism (no. 94e); Masonic texts often note that the phallus "was universally venerated among the ancients, and that too as a religious rite, without the slightest reference to any impure or lascivious application."[42] "Hunting and agriculture make the body agile and strong" (no. 95) may be another of Beethoven's approving references to the rigorous training required of Brahman novitiates.

Equivocal meanings abound here and in other entries: after referring to his guardianship of nephew Karl as "this holy cause," Beethoven writes, cryptically, "In any event, the token *[Kennzeichen]* has been accepted" (no. 81). In Freemasonry, the "token" signifies brotherly recognition, "an outward act as evidencing an inward pledge."[43] Elsewhere (no. 17), we have seen that Beethoven evokes the palm tree, a classical and Christian emblem of triumph over adversity and sin, and one often found in Masonic contexts, including its adoption as a popular lodge name. And several of the Tagebuch's entries about the idea of friendship (see nos. 57, 59, 103, and 127) may have Masonic implications or can be read as references to fraternity, to which it is inseparably linked in Masonic thinking.[44] Masonic writers took over from ancient cosmology ideas about the universe as a single organism, in which the planets and heavenly bodies were continually influencing one another and determining the makeup and intelligence of the life forms that inhabited them. Thus, when Beethoven copied into his Tagebuch (no. 106) a quasi-astrological passage of this kind from Kant's *Allgemeine Naturgeschichte und Theorie des Himmels,* he may have been participating in a conception that had been absorbed by the Masons from their readings in the mystery religions.

These same materials are, we must reemphasize, also consistent with a knowledge of the sources from which Masonic tropes, rituals, symbolism, systems, practices, and doctrine are drawn—and especially from every form of organized ritual, ranging from primitive rites and ancient cults to their modern counterparts. Thus, the possibility that Beethoven came to these subjects by a route other than Freemasonry cannot be excluded, for there was a considerable contemporary literature by such mythologists, orientalists, and philosophers as Schelling, Creuzer, Majer, Görres, and Hammer-Purgstall.[45] But this is a less likely alternative, considering that the voluminous literature produced by the Freemasons and their adherents was the primary vehicle through which individuals of intellect and sensibility learned of these wayward, intriguing, and hermetic topics, which otherwise were available primarily to scholars and connoisseurs of esoterica.

The Tagebuch's Masonic entries ought not to be viewed as indications that Beethoven necessarily endorsed Freemasonry as a movement or cause. In them, he not only transmitted approved thoughts from Masonic sources, but was able to give voice to his own feelings and creed through Masonic language, imagery, and symbols. Freemasonry provided him with an exalted rhetoric to express ideas about things he held sacred. Within the Masonic dimension, he could undertake his own initiation through purification, acknowledge and transcend his own weaknesses, partake of communal experience, revisit his youth, renovate an endangered idealism, and rediscover and revalidate his capacity for belief.

In all likelihood, then, Freemasonry was an important stimulus to Beethoven's way of thinking about issues of being and morality, aspects of its doctrines and ritual contributing to the mental framework within which, in his fifth decade, he strove to reformulate his understanding of the self, the deity, and the world. At least partly through the mediation of Freemasonry, which ecumenically promoted the study of comparative religion and mythology, he gained entry to ideas of the holy, to rich conceptions of divinity founded in ancient, esoteric, and especially Eastern attitudes. Freemasonry offered a vocabulary for the formulation of ideas of service, purification, and transcendence. It embodied an initiatory way of regarding the world, a dualistic view of life as a transition from a lesser to a higher state of being, a passage from the nether regions to the celestial, from body to spirit, death to resurrection, darkness to light. Its dualisms of course embrace the converse of these symbolic passages as well, those running from East to West, life to death.

Some of the conceptions to be found in the Tagebuch are a continuation of Beethoven's earlier ideas and preoccupations: for example, the younger Beethoven frequently expressed Stoic attitudes of resignation and Christian notions of service. In his Heiligenstadt Testament of 1802, Beethoven described his crisis of melancholia as a kind of initiatory illness, in the course of which he journeyed to the Underworld, touched death, and reemerged in a holy state. The Tagebuch extends and deepens lifelong tenets of belief. There is, however, a vast gulf between the Tagebuch's ecstatic assent to doctrines of purification by arduous trial and Beethoven's earlier Plutarchian remarks, such as the Testament's "*Patience,* they say, is what I must now choose for my guide, and I have done so" or his outcry to Wegeler in 1801, "*Resignation,* what a wretched resource! Yet it is all that is left to me."[46] The Freemasonry we encounter in the Tagebuch is not simply an extension of Beethoven's earlier Masonic outlook, which was by contrast a rationalist and altruistic conception not clearly differentiated from Josephinian ideas about brotherhood, justice, humanity, and an enlightened social order, with a fairly conventional admixture of radical platitudes from Enlightenment sources, Stoicism, and Schiller's version of Kantian philosophy. The younger Beethoven's thought had been characterized by an unquestioning reliance upon reason and a corresponding antipathy to what he regarded as mysticism, fanaticism, and superstition, as we have seen from his letter to Heinrich von Collin in 1808 inveighing against frivolous or obscurantist opera texts (see chapter 5, p. 95).[47] In the Tagebuch in 1816–18, he continued to appeal to reason, approvingly citing Kant's words on "wisest Reason" (no. 105) and adding his own reference to "sovereign Reason" (no. 138). But by then Beethoven was no longer hobbled by a somewhat inflexible, rationalist mode of thought. Now, through his greater openness to Freemasonry's symbolic and initiatory dimension, he permitted himself to enter an ineffable, inscrutable, unfathomable world, redolent of mystery, the unknown, the infinite, the unreachable. That this is also an inexhaustible realm for the free exercise of an artist's imagination goes without saying.

Freemasonry was thus uniquely capable of helping to reconcile Beethoven's hunger for the imaginative with his reliance on reason. In the patchwork of ideas that constitute the Masonic systems, rationality is constantly invoked, while superstitions are cloaked in the language of pseudoscience. One door of Freemasonry leads to the house of reason, another to the alchemical laboratory.

Masons who took the symbolic system seriously were empowered to follow Isis and Brahma, Mohammed and Zoroaster, but without renouncing Jehovah or Jesus Christ. On the evidence of his Tagebuch and his framed copy of the inscriptions of Isis, it is clear that Beethoven was fascinated by descriptions of the attributes of divinity taken from Indian, Egyptian, and Greco-Roman sources. What is especially striking is that however multifarious the descriptions and whatever their origins in a welter of polytheistic sources, they all derive from the premise that there is always one supreme God. From Brahman sources: "He is eternal, omnipotent, knowing all things [and] present everywhere" (no. 93a). From the *Bhagavad-Gita:* "You alone are the true [Bhagavan]—the blessed one, the essence of all laws, the image of all wisdom of the whole present world—" (no. 61b); and from Jones's vedic Hymn to Narayena:

Before Heaven was, Thou art:
Ere spheres beneath us roll'd or spheres above,

Ere earth in firmamental ether hung,
Thou sat'st alone.

(no. 62)

This deity has no source other than himself: according to the Orphic hymn, "He is unique unto himself, and it is to this singularity that all things owe their existence"; and from a commentary on the *Rig-Veda*, "He, the Mighty One, is present in every part of space. His omniscience is self-inspired and His conception comprehends every other" (61a). In another Veda-like effusion transcribed by Beethoven, God is said to be invisible and beyond conception, from which "we may conclude that He is eternal, omnipotent, knowing all things, and present everywhere" (93b). And, according to Warburton, even Isis "was represented by the later Egyptians to be the Governor of the universe."[48]

Beethoven had entered, via mythic thinking, a dialectic between what Schelling called "a monotheism of rationality" and "a polytheism of the imagination."[49] Certainly, the polytheistic aspect of Beethoven's thought, manifested in his powerful attraction to oriental theology and the Eastern myths, came to the fore during the years of the Tagebuch; but *Vielgötterei* did not supplant his attraction to Christian imagery, as we know from invocations of the Mosaic and Christian God in his Tagebuch and of the "loving Father" in the Ninth Symphony's "Ode to Joy." The Egyptian and Orphic inscriptions and the excerpts from Brahman and other texts in the Tagebuch also coincide with Beethoven's readings and copious underlinings in an 1811 edition of the Protestant Christoph Christian Sturm's *Betrachtungen über die Werke Gottes im Reiche der Natur und der Vorsehung auf alle Tage des Jahres.* And it is with a passage from Sturm's devoutly Christian book that the Tagebuch closes:

Therefore, calmly will I submit myself to all inconstancy and will place all my trust in Thy unchangeable goodness, O God! My soul shall rejoice in Thee, immutable Being. Be my rock, God, be my light, my trust for ever!

(no. 171)

It is a fusion or unification of the world's diverse imagery of divinity that fired Beethoven's imagination and creative intellect. Beethoven was not an atheist, as Haydn reportedly once called him in a fit of anger. Nor was he an adherent of any established religion or church. Rather, in the course of a stormy intellectual journey that reached a double bar with the quotation from Sturm in 1818, he revealed his close kinship to those Deists, free-thinkers, and Freemasons who managed to locate in every polytheistic pantheon one supreme, omnipotent, ultimately unnamable deity.

CHAPTER NINE

THE SHAPE OF A JOURNEY:
THE "DIABELLI" VARIATIONS

We have already touched on some of the things that Diabelli's waltz may metaphorically represent or call to mind: the homelike and comfortable, simple joys and merriments, innocence and not-knowing. The theme is contented, unaware of tragedy, let alone of oblivion or extinction. As a beginning, it is also a symbol of beginnings, embodying, therefore, the universe of significances that attach to beginnings. Thus, it may evoke ideas of birth, origins, creation, the vernacular, the earthly, the familiar, the commonplace, the humble, the national, and home. As a simple product of plain human creativity it bespeaks the transparent value of ordinary experience, implies the interchangeability of firstness and lastness, and stands as a sign for the earthly stuff out of which the celestial is spun.[1] As soon as it is appropriated as the theme of a set of variations it is no longer a creative artifact complete in itself but, most importantly for Beethoven's purposes, provides the exordium of an essay on metamorphosis. A symbol that both encourages and defies decoding, it is crammed with potentialities.

The Alla marcia, maestoso designation of variation 1 says that we have resolutely embarked on a journey, taken the first stride in an unfolding trajectory, turned away from dance and the play impulse. The march was added to the plan of the "Diabelli" Variations only in 1822–23, in the work's final stages, and this may suggest that Beethoven wanted to make some such implication explicit. In departing from Diabelli's theme, it also sets out from every state of unawareness implied by the theme, but as yet without any hint of its own purposes. Indeed, the march may itself be unaware of anything except the need—or determination—to commence. If that is so, then the Alla marcia is a recommencement, a beginning beyond the beginning, the first, supremely confident (maestoso) stride into an as-yet-unknown spiritual cosmos, taking an unfaltering stance in favor of new directions.[2] The reason for this confidence is unclear, suggesting that it may rest, not on knowledge or logical precedent, but on faith.[3]

One way to understand the highly differentiated character of many of the individual variations is to view them as radically different modes of motion toward an unspecified objective—marching, striding, running, racing, dancing, along with others for which we have no descriptive words—always overcoming obstacles, sometimes easily, sometimes only by great exertion or adroit maneuvers. They are analogous to the études in pedagogical keyboard methods, often appropriately bearing such allegorical titles as *Gradus ad Parnassum,* that exhibit, at progressing levels of difficulty, the paths to improvement and mastery. Following the squarely self-reliant 4/4 time signature of the opening march, the time signature of the next seven variations reverts to 3/4. They are contrasted in tempo, proceeding from Poco allegro of variations 2 and 3 to Un poco più vivace, Allegro vivace, Allegro ma non troppo, and Un poco più allegro in variations 4–7, respectively. Rhythmic variation is Beethoven's predominant technique here, each of the variations elaborating one or more strikingly different rhythmic figures. Those figures perhaps are also designed to illustrate some of the varieties of classical poetic meters, and this enhances their individuality just as it situates them in an ancient and learned tradition (see ex. 9.1).

Variation 2 features an easy, regular alternation of chords between the left and right hands, played *leggiermente,* with a subtle rhythmic digression at measures 25–28 that avoids any sense of invariance while underscoring the uniformity of the syncopations. In variation 3, a rhythmic and melodic pattern is established and then, before we can take it for granted, subverted at measures 20–24 by an unprepared, opaque shift to a *pianissimo* running-eighth-note ostinato in the bass against a sustained diminished seventh chord in the treble (ex. 9.2). It is as though the variation has declined the rosalia, momentarily choosing stasis as a preferable option; and then, after being seemingly stuck in this mode for four measures, resuming its assigned route without explanation and floating easily toward a celestial cadence, *piano.*

By contrast, variation 4 pursues a more strenuous route to the upper registers, a long crescendo leading to a staccato cadence, *forte.* Variation 5 is the first variation to feature an ascending figure in its early measures;

EXAMPLE 9.1.   "Diabelli" Variations, incipits, variations 1–33.

Alla Marcia maestoso

Var. 1

Poco allegro

Var. 2

L'istesso tempo

Var. 3

Un poco più vivace

Var. 4

Allegro vivace

Var. 5

Allegro ma non troppo e serioso

Var. 6

Un poco più allegro

Var. 7

EXAMPLE 9.1 *(continued)*

Poco vivace

Var. 8

dolce e teneramente

sempre legato

Allegro pesante e risoluto

Var. 9

Presto

Var. 10

sempre staccato ma leggiermente

Allegretto

Var. 11

Un poco più moto

Var. 12

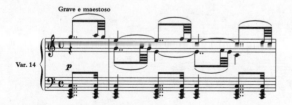

Vivace

Var. 13

Grave e maestoso

Var. 14

EXAMPLE 9.1 *(continued)*

Presto scherzando

Var. 15

Allegro

Var. 16

Var. 17

Poco moderato

Var. 18

Presto

Var. 19

Andante

Var. 20

Allegro con brio

Var. 21

EXAMPLE 9.1 *(continued)*

Var. 22

Allegro molto *alla "Notte e giorno faticar" di Mozart*

Var. 23

Allegro assai

Var. 24

Fughetta
Andante

Var. 25

Allegro

Var. 26

Var. 27

Vivace

EXAMPLE 9.1 *(continued)*

Var. 28

Var. 29

Var. 30

Var. 31

Var. 32

Var. 33

EXAMPLE 9.2.   Variation 3, part 2, mm. 20–24.

clambering upward, it finds securely accented footholds, celebrating its sure forward movement in a flurry of anapests and sforzando accents at the end of each section, thereby to underscore the decisiveness of this navigational choice.

Several of these early variations contain a calculated irregularity or a surprising or anomalous feature; thus, part one of variation 4 is a measure short (fifteen measures), providing an elliptical jolt that opens a momentary space of indeterminacy until part two reverts to its full quota of measures; elsewhere there are touches of capriciousness and whimsy, a jesting spirit, asymmetries, strange progressions, or jagged inversions. We don't know what Beethoven intended by these touches; they are unlike the deliberate flecks of strangeness by which an artist sometimes articulates a sense of beauty's indefinable but necessary individuality. Perhaps they are only asymmetries for their own sake, or a provisional defeat of Gestalt-like expectations in order subsequently to restore a magnified sense of wholeness. But these touches of weirdness may also be read as emblems of difficulty on an implied narrative route, of obstacles on the path to virtue, salvation, or a safe resting-place. Ironically, a composer who, because of his departures from a presumed (and ill-defined) classical model, had, often unfairly, been charged with bizarrerie by uncomprehending listeners, hidebound critics, and classicizing competitors, has now chosen actually to represent the bizarre, the grotesque, the undecorous, the unbeautiful, the incomplete, finding these essential to his larger purposes.

As the variations enter increasingly unfamiliar terrain, we seem to be passing through the early stages of a process of detachment from the theme. There is little time to linger, no attempt thoroughly to map the landscape through which the Virgilian composer-performer-guide is escorting us. Rather, there is a sense of increasing urgency, of the need to maintain for-

EXAMPLE 9.3.   Variation 7, part 2, mm. 29–32.

ward motion at all costs. Variation 6, Allegro ma non troppo e serioso, marked *fortissimo* and punctuated with sforzandos, intensifies the sense of hastening, but it seems as yet too early to think about an eventual outcome. Instead, there is a casting about in search of an orientation, suggested by the use of polarities of height and depth and by techniques of mirror-imaging: the variation commences in the upper registers and repeatedly plunges downward, only to reverse its direction with equal force in part two. By contrast, the leaping dotted-rhythm figure and running triplets of variation 7, with its *all'ottava* rise into the stratosphere at the end, tell not only of an overriding upward inclination but of an emergent sense of excitement at the prospect of an ultimate harbor, however distant (ex. 9.3).

With variation 8, Poco vivace, marked *dolce e teneramente,* we reach a provisional resting place within which a moment of thoughtful, songful meditation offers relief from the exertions of the first seven variations. It exemplifies the first appearance in the "Diabelli" Variations of a crucial expressive quality of Beethoven's late style that Kerman named "the vocal impulse,"[4] a songfulness, overflowing with longing and often conveying a touch of the spectral, found in its most heightened form in *An die ferne Geliebte,* in the Arioso dolente of Opus 110 and the Cavatina of Opus 130, and in all the great adagios and largos of the late sonatas, the late string quartets, and the Ninth Symphony.[5] Dreamlike, ghostly, poetic, this variation quietly presses upward, its ascending tendency emphasized by a *sempre legato* rising figure in the left hand.

EXAMPLE 9.4.   Variation 9, part 2, mm. 17–20.

The wide separation of bass and treble lines is a sign for the spaciousness of this haven.

After this moment of repose, onward motion resumes with variation 9, Allegro pesante e risoluto. In 4/4, it is a sibling of the Alla marcia, equally purposeful, stalwart, imbued with energy. Up to this point, Beethoven has written highly intricate variations using a limited harmonic and rhythmic palette. He has been tone-painting in black and white, an austerity of means perhaps standing for a singleness of purpose or immutability of faith. But now we have his first departure from 3/4 time since the Alla marcia. Also with this variation, written in C minor—then modulating into A-flat, D-flat, with an enharmonic change into C-sharp, before returning to the tonic—he deviates for the first time from Diabelli's key, C major.

At the same time, in part two of variation 9, Beethoven introduces a striking trope of motion, climbing the rungs of the scale as though it were a ladder, and then starting over again, each time from a higher position (ex. 9.4). Thus, one third of the way through the "Diabelli" Variations, he temporarily settles the primary direction of the course that the variations are to pursue. In the presto variation 10, marked *sempre staccato ma leggiermente,* once again in C major and 3/4 time, the ascents have a scherzoso, joyous, other-worldly rapidity, starting repeatedly in the lowest bass to provide contrast with the highest points reached by the right hand, and ending with a chord that spans six full octaves. Variations 11 and 12 explore linear, flowing textures and modes of activity. The former withdraws from striving for a moment, sensing the possibility of contentment; perhaps we have here been granted an anticipatory glimpse of the set's closing Menuetto, a quick prophecy of the ending.

Stepping back for a moment, we seem to be witnessing the musical embodiment of a journey in progress, one that moves from familiar ground to an altered, increasingly rarefied sphere in which there is also access to an ever-expanding range of sensations and feelings. By now, two processes are simultaneously in play, one describing modes of detachment from a known beginning and another offering a series of partial disclosures of an as yet indistinct ending. Detachment is rendered in the audibly disjunct stages of a metaphorical ascent from lower to higher as well as in the contrasts of acceleration and deceleration that speak to the fitful, even capricious, progress of human endeavor. Even as the variations unfold the theme's implications, they distance themselves from the vernacular, tradition, the familiar, the already known, and move into unplumbed regions jam-packed with novel affects, events, and adventures.

Upward motion is present in virtually every variation, not surprisingly, because an upward direction governs the opening measures of the theme and is implicit in the very idea of the "cobbler's patch" itself. The descending fourth that opens the theme, the falling fifths at measures 5–8, and the rosalias are crucial counterpoises to the rising seconds that in measures 25–30 eventually assert their independence of ordinary boundaries. Upward and downward tendencies remain in perpetual contention, but in the theme, as in many of the variations, the downward pull is not given the last word. Diabelli has provided a rock-solid *Sehnsucht* (yearning) figure that yields to the rosalia in a stroke of comic transcendence. The rosalia finds it easy to climb, it avoids necessity (breaks the rules; it is a trickster-musician's prank), it shows how to dodge fate by a simple maneuver. The point of the rosalia—and its utility to Beethoven—is that it is both an emblem of ascent and a shortcut technique for achieving it.

The "Diabelli" Variations thus seems to outline a trajectory not merely from here to there but from here to higher, featuring those spatial images of ascent and descent fundamental in literature, religion, and myth. Some of these have been inventoried and interpreted by Northrop Frye:

> for poets, the physical world has usually been not only a cyclical world but a "middle earth," situated between an upper and a lower world. . . . The upper world is reached by some form of ascent and is a world of gods or happy souls. The most frequent images of ascent are the mountain, the tower, the winding staircase or ladder, or a tree of cosmological dimensions. The upper world is often symbolized by the heavenly bodies. . . . The lower world,

reached by descent through a cave or under water, is more oracular and sinister, and as a rule is or includes a place of torment and punishment.[6]

Beethoven fleshes out his own wordless narratives by inventing or en-
larging an imaginative vocabulary of musical equivalents for the varieties of
upward movement—climbing passages, rising scales, leaps, and modulations;
exploitation of the uppermost registers of the keyboard, and emphasizing
the distance between high and low by great registral contrasts between bass
and treble. Frye rightly reminds us that the Latin word for ladder is *scala,*
from which derive "the techniques of measurement on which all the sciences depend, and which inform the arts as well, notably music."[7] It ought
to be stressed, however, that in addition to their sacred, mythological, and
celestial implications, the higher regions may stand for any exalted or inaccessible goal, including such objects of longing as the beloved, perfection,
the blessed, wisdom, and virtue. An end point is not meant to be so defini-
tively identified that it would lose its capacity to touch us in unexpected ways,
to awaken individual responses to its endless implied purposes. Archetypes of
ascent are populous and inclusive; a pilgrim may find respite in a humble
lodging as well as in the starry firmament or on the mountain top. Not necessarily in quest of ecstasy or utter purification, the traveler may be in search
of ordinary contentment.

Elsewhere in this book, I have called attention to passages copied by
Beethoven into his Tagebuch that refer to ascending pathways as metaphors
of laborious quests for virtue and other affirmative goals. Two of them are
worth repeating here. The first is from Kalidasa's *Sakuntala:* "In thy passage
over this earth, where the paths are now high, now low, and the true path
seldom distinguished, the traces of thy feet must needs be unequal; but *virtue*
will press thee right onward" (no. 63c);[8] the second, from Hesiod's *Works
and Days:* "For vice walks many paths full of present sinful desires and thereby
induces many to follow it. But virtue leads on to a steep path and cannot
attract men as easily and swiftly, especially if elsewhere there are those who
call them to a sloping and pleasant road" (no. 68b). The upward trajectory
of the "Diabelli" Variations, too, traverses a road to a longed-for site of deep
spiritual import. And like Kalidasa's and Hesiod's, it is a difficult journey,
steering a hard course, rejecting the easy, downward path in favor of the
high road to virtue. Alternately Herculean and effortless, painful and rap-

turous, Beethoven's variations advance now by small degrees and now by immense leaps, but always ultimately upwards, seeking entry to an unplumbed universe that is the locus of unfulfilled longings.

Some listeners hear variation 13, with its dramatic, dotted-rhythm rapping motif, as "great comic buffoonery," or as "a comic little piece . . . a kind of loud postman's knock."[9] But others may prefer to hear the *forte* rapping figure as an insistent call to attention, and the soft two-note tapping figure that follows as its quiet pendant, either echoing or responding. In Freemasonry, rhythmic figures of this type were used to convene members of a guild or lodge.[10] And one might well be reminded of the rapping for admittance by candidates that climaxed rituals for elevation to higher degrees in the various Masonic orders.[11] But there are wider implications in this cretic-spondaic metrical figure ($-\smile-$ | $--$): rapping motifs of this kind may be requests for admittance, calls to action, signals for awakening, or summonses to assembly, all of which may have something to do with the sacred aura that attaches to the "Diabelli" Variations. Perhaps, then, the figure can profitably be considered both as an urgent signal from without and as an interior sign of spiritual quickening, enjoining the devout voyager to vigilance as he or she approaches holy ground or arrives at a consecrated portal, demanding entrance (see ex. 9.1, variation 13).

Such a portal may have been reached in variation 14, which, setting aside variation 8, exhibits the first serious break in what has been a succession of quick- or moderate-tempo variations. It is a slow march, Grave e maestoso, its double-dotted rhythm and the modulation from C major to E minor at measure 8 conveying more than a hint of the funereal; no trace remains here of the optimistic sense of setting out that marked the opening Alla marcia. It is now clear that the journey has uncovered a tragic seam. The heavy downward movement in part one is followed by a Sisyphean, upward striving that emerges from the lowest registers of the keyboard. There is a sense of working against great odds; but although progress is slowed it is not altogether blocked; indeed, there is an even greater effort required at the end, leading to a renewal of motion, which is continued and intensified in the following three variations (nos. 15, 16, and 17). In them, Beethoven details new modes of upward motion: now unfettered, the dominant character is once again all about jubilation and energetic hastening.

Pervaded by a pre-Brahmsian, wistful melancholia, variation 18, to be played *dolce,* could be thought of as yet another expansion of the range of musical signs for motion even as it suggests a temporary retreat into sadness and reflection. Or perhaps it is a study in the representation of questions and answers, alternating between dialogic and hortatory modes of expression. Variation 19, a Presto, resumes the race at breakneck speed; but with the andante variation 20, in 6/4, marked *espressivo,* there is a radical change in mood and a pause in the sequence of modes of activity. Brooding, expressive, past comprehension, it is, in Blom's words, music evoking "beauty of an unearthly and unfathomable kind."[12] The unharmonized descending fourth in the low bass that opens this variation is scarcely making its first appearance, but here, by its andante tempo and dotted half-notes, are elaborated some of the expressive implications of that portentous interval that Beethoven explored, first in the Adagio of the "Hammerklavier" Sonata in B-flat, op. 106, and then in the Arietta of the C-minor Sonata, op. 111.

Pausing once again, perhaps we can offer one or two thoughts about the structure of the "Diabelli" Variations. Some have sought to locate sonata-form features in this set, to group the variations into movement-like sections, to impose concepts of organic connectedness on the work that are more likely to be characteristic of classical sonatas, symphonies, and chamber music genres than of discursive forms like sets of variations. It may be preferable, however, to view the structure of Opus 120 instead as clusters of variations representing forward and upward motion of every conceivable kind, character, and speed, leading to and eventuating in slower, songful, affect-laden variations. These strategically placed plateaus, as they might be called, provide spacious havens for spiritual and physical renewal in the wake of the exertions that have preceded each of them. After variations 8 and 14, variation 20 is the set's third such plateau, offering a protected enclosure within which to deliberate upon the cost of such endless striving and sacrifice, perhaps to determine whether the implied protagonist has the will to continue and the capacity to endure. The plateaus now will come more frequently, and by their increased amplitude and affective intensity they will begin to dominate the discourse as the lineaments of an approaching destination assume more definite form. Each plateau explores different degrees and aspects of slowness, sharply contrasting with the sharply profiled, motion-filled variations that experiment with degrees and kinds of quickness, until, as we will see, arriving at the edge of motionlessness in the Poco adagio that precedes the final variation. The image of an achieved ending is close at hand.

The next three variations in the sequence are again all about motion, rhythmic diversity, and incongruous juxtapositions. Variations 21 and 22 revert to comic modes, thereby restoring a human scale and sense of proportion. They also return to the knockabout spirit of Diabelli's theme, suggesting, perhaps, that this arduous pilgrim's journey has not been altogether in the service of an as yet unachieved future but has also gathered its share of tangible compensations in the here and now. Concerning the parody quotation from *Don Giovanni* in variation 22, Jürgen Uhde asks whether it is "A caprice—or a deeper allusion?" and he concludes that the question "can no longer be decided."[13] On the comic side, the variation teases Diabelli: "I know where you got your theme from!" But that does not prevent "Notte e giorno faticar"—"To work day and night"—from also being read as a literal statement or complaint about the human condition (see ex. 9.1, variation 22). As in the question and admonition "Muß es sein? Es muß sein!" of Beethoven's String Quartet in F, op. 135, it is not always easy to distinguish between a jest and a profound existential comment.

Diabelli's German dance is not Beethoven's only sign for the vernacular, the topical equivalent of Dante's use of Italian in the *Divine Comedy;* the Alla marcia, too, stands for the mother tongue, as does this high-wire take-off of Leporello's aria. Each of them provides a denotational baseline from which to distinguish high and low, to calculate distances between the commonplace and its incorporeal metamorphoses, to locate the heavens from an earthly vantage point, to know the sacred by having experience of the profane. On a simpler level, we can view this variation as another of Beethoven's commedia dell'arte essays in musical ascent—dashing upward, climbing, falling, beginning again, triumphing, exiting laughing. This may be clearest in measures 6–8, where Beethoven ignored Mozart's cadential falling fifth in favor of an upward sprint to the tonic (ex. 9.5).

Beethoven furnished fairly elaborate performance directions for variation 24, a Fughetta andante, marked *una corda, sempre legato.* This variation, the fourth of Beethoven's essays in slowness, investigates tender yearning in a devotional mode, expressed in a voice that owes much to Bach's Goldberg Variations.[14] Indeed, a striking feature of some of the set's later variations

EXAMPLE 9.5.   Variation 22, mm. 6–8.

is their adoption of style characteristics associated with or derived from several of Beethoven's great predecessors. The series is inaugurated with the quotation from *Don Giovanni* in variation 22, continues with variation 23 (a keyboard étude in the tradition of Johann Baptist Cramer or Carl Czerny)[15] and variation 24 (J.S. Bach), and closes in variations 31, 32, and 33 with evocations respectively of a central aspect of Bach's keyboard manner, a quasi-Handelian double-fugue allegro, and an other-worldly minuet that is Mozartian in its austerely ornamented beauty. Hans von Bülow was the first to call attention to these allusions, though he surely went too far in dubbing them a "compendium of the history of music."[16] Their significance is far from clear, but one possibility is that the vast scope of the issues raised in the "Diabelli" Variations required a corresponding battery of powerful responses, which Beethoven located in the combined wisdom of several of his predecessors, who now joined him as collaborators in a mighty endeavor.

"Andante" has a special meaning in the "Diabelli" Variations, being reserved for three of the variations—nos. 20, 24, and 30—that can be seen as examples of those structured and highly differentiated plateaus that mark the successive stages of consolidated achievement in an arc of mythopoeic experience. In variation 24, "Andante" is at once a tempo designation, a sign for an affective or psychological quality, and an indication of a specific mode of motion. This Andante has the character of a pilgrim's walk, steady, devout, confident; it has no need to hurry, for its goal is constant and its faith secure. On the other hand, it knows that it cannot linger here; there is still more ground to cover. To dispel any thought that we have reached a terminus, we are quickly reminded that this is only one stage in the ascent. Variations 25 to 28 are all about continuation, joyous hastening, and anticipation. We have the impression of a marked lessening of resistance; we are no longer on an obstacle course. Additional modes of motion are brought into play—

in variation 25 an allegro skipping motif in the right hand against an evenly flowing pattern of sixteenth-notes, *leggiermente;* triplets, *piacevole,* in no. 26, and more triplets, running at top speed, *vivace,* in no. 27; with variation 28, a sudden shift to 2/4 inaugurates a series of emphatic staccato sforzandos on the strong beats. A retreat to *piano* and an unexpected quarter-note rest leaves us at a threshold.

With variations 29 through 31, we reach a last, enormously extended plateau from which to view the no longer concealed destination and to reflect upon the path that has brought us to it. Three successive slow variations, all in C minor (the first such shift into C minor since variation 9), disclose Beethoven's audacious conception—perhaps remindful of the twinned adagios of Mozart's G-minor String Quintet, K. 516, and Beethoven's own juxtaposition in the "Hammerklavier" Sonata, op. 106, of a colossally extended Adagio sostenuto and a miraculously condensed Largo *introduzione* to the Fugue—namely, that it requires multiple perspectives of inwardness to capture the turbulent and exalted feelings that have been awakened as the long journey nears its end. Ideas of death and perfection, achievement and loss, ecstasy and annihilation contend with one another in these linked studies in the varieties of musical slowness.

Variation 29, headed Adagio ma non troppo, opens the sequence. Marked *piano* except for two gently swelling crescendo-decrescendos, it is a *mezza voce* renewal of longing, an essay in slow motion where memory is transmuted into song. Kinderman tellingly describes it as "a kind of baroque lament, which could easily be imagined in a setting for a solo melody instrument and figured bass."[17] The lament carries us to variation 30, which is another devotional walk, in 4/4 time, Andante, sempre cantabile, to be played *sempre legato, una corda,* with overlapping, flowing, ascending phrases in free imitation. As the music traverses these hushed regions, there is a mingled sense of acceptance and sorrow attendant on the crossing of a boundary, of achieving a state that now appears to be beyond strife.

Variation 31, too, is laden with expressive indications: titled Largo, molto espressivo, it is marked *sotto voce,* with several *espressivo, ritardando,* and *dolce* passages as well. Whereas flutes and a solo violin in the Benedictus of the *Missa solemnis* depict a fluttering descent of an invisible emanation from the divinity to the altar, Beethoven here seems to be describing the trembling, ecstatic ascent of a soul as it drifts toward heaven, likening the stirrings of the heart to rising sequences of shimmering trills and copiously ornamented

EXAMPLE 9.6.   Variation 31, part 2, mm. 6–9.

EXAMPLE 9.7.   Variation 32, Poco adagio, mm. 161–66.

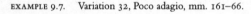

mini-cadenzas reminiscent of some of Mozart's later sonata adagios, but especially like the Arietta of Beethoven's own C-minor Piano Sonata, op. 111.
The 9/8 time signature and the extremely slow tempo open up a wide clear-
ing for chromatic embellishment (ex. 9.6).

Once again, the voice is J. S. Bach's, the variation showing a special affinity
with the twenty-fifth of the Goldberg Variations, but there is no need to
search for a precise model; rather, Bach's tone, sound, and voice have been
thoroughly assimilated into Beethoven's own late-style persona. In these

reflections on an impending arrival in a new world, ecstasy collides with sorrow as the long journey's end is thoroughly suffused with lamentation, perhaps because to come to an ending is to exhaust the prospect of continued striving, which has become a way of life. Having reached the innermost core of feeling, the music overflows with songful melancholia, but without any trace of despondency. A dominant-seventh chord leaves the variation suspended, unresolved, identifies it retrospectively as the last stage of a three-part slow introduction to a fugue. Surely, an ending is now imminent, for fugue is traditionally employed in learned and sacred musical genres to represent inexorable motion toward—and symbolic achievement of—vaunted goals such as wisdom or faith, best suited also to convey feelings of triumph and elation that accompany momentous achievements. But the path to this ending is repeatedly blocked—the fugue abruptly breaks off at measure 117, resuming only to give up the ghost at measure 160 in a *fortissimo* chord and a harplike arpeggiated flourish, a curtain that at measure 161 unveils a Poco adagio that introduces a wholly unexpected idea of an ending.[18] Thus, after several shifts in direction, its efforts at summation running into impermeable barriers, the Fuga has finally abandoned what had turned into a frantic search for an exit rather than for an ending, and it has surrendered its pretensions to finality.

Instead of a contrapuntal, giocoso affirmation, the Poco adagio reveals the persistence of unbounded yearning even at the end of the journey. Action slows to the point of immobility, but not of apathy. Barriers and labyrinths, now transformed into welcoming thresholds and open portals, succumb to awe, faith, and the affective power of slowness. In measures 161–66 we learn what it feels like to move blindfolded through an invisible barrier located in a darkened space (ex. 9.7).

The initiatory journey has been completed. The "Diabelli" Variations can now end by passing through a liminal sphere to its final plateau—the Tempo di menuetto.

CHAPTER TEN

INTIMATIONS OF THE SACRED

Evocations or representations of the sacred in Beethoven's late works were observed from early on. In 1828, his collegial acquaintance, the Viennese composer Ignaz Seyfried, suggested that the flute's slow trill on the words "de Spiritu Sancto" in the Incarnatus of the *Missa solemnis* (m. 134) is to be taken as a sign for the fluttering dove, heaven's messenger, as it pursues its hovering descent to the Virgin in the Annunciation.[1] Seyfried's suggestion is recalled in Warren Kirkendale's exemplary paper, "New Roads to Old Ideas in Beethoven's *Missa Solemnis*," which demonstrated beyond dispute what had once been taken for granted but was later partially forgotten, namely, that the *Missa solemnis* draws from a reservoir of expressive musical topics or characteristic-style features and gestures that had accumulated over time in the genres of European music for the Catholic church. Mostly the symbolic topoi have to do with discrete text-music associations, especially those connecting the gestures of the liturgy to their "counterparts in the rhetorical figures of the music" (p. 667).[2] Among many such traditional topics inventoried by Kirkendale are the use of trombones for the "judicare" of the Credo "to symbolize divine power" (p. 669); the practice of beginning the Gloria "with a rapidly rising melody, the rhetorical figure of the *anabasis*" (p. 668); and the deployment of tremolos in the Gloria to simulate the quaking trepidation of those awaiting judgment or, in the Credo, "for the invocation of Christ enthroned in heaven" (p. 671). Beethoven drew on traditional practices in other ways as well, using "declamation on a quasi monotone" for "affirmative statements which reject contradiction" (p. 682); and in the final fugue, "Et vitam venturi saeculi" (mm. 309ff), invoking the major triad so that it "retains its old symbolism of perfection and fulfillment, now for the life after death" (p. 684). While Kirkendale emphasizes the ways in which Beethoven's ideas of the sacred originated in traditional musical and theological tropes, he does not altogether neglect Beethoven's late-style innovations, such as the "sudden entry of the high, bright solo violin (g''') into the very dark, low orchestral background" in the last measure of the Praeludium, thus creating in music an effect analogous to the concept of *lux in tenebris* (p. 688); and in the Benedictus, "the initial long, slow *katabasis* in the flutes and solo violin as the descent of Christ upon the altar" (p. 689).

Kirkendale had both predecessors and successors; he himself continued and amplified the work of Erich Schenk, who wrote a lengthy paper on Beethoven's use of Baroque theme types in his late-period instrumental music to represent states of deprivation, suffering, and death, and argued that the piano sonatas, opp. 110 and 111, the string quartets, opp. 131 and 132, and the Grosse Fuge, op. 133, were in part constructed from allegorical motifs of the Baroque translated by Beethoven with "epigrammatic brevity into his own musical symbolic language."[3] In an illuminating paper, William Kinderman elaborates some of the rhetorical implications of height and depth in Beethoven's music, seeing descending and ascending figures as expressive of the contours of Christ's life; reading the "sudden plunge in register" accompanied by a sudden transformation of the musical texture in the Incarnatus as signifying the descent from heaven; and interpreting a certain high E-flat sonority in the *Missa solemnis* and the Ninth Symphony as a conjuring of the celestial and its promise of transcendence.[4]

Wilfrid Mellers, in a set of wide-ranging and often eloquent interpretations, seeks to displace the *Missa solemnis* from an exclusively Catholic context: "Though this music has Christian connotations, in that it quotes plainsong and flows in imitative polyphony, its atmosphere is . . . more Hellenistic than Christian."[5] Mainly, however, he maintains that significant events in the *Missa solemnis* are actually drawn from an extensive lexicon of Masonic musical tropes. Thus, symmetrical structures are seen as Masonic because they are "architecturally . . . balanced" (p. 299); the Kyrie's "three entries of the chorus, and three soloistic answers" are said to be transparent references to "the threefold knocking by the candidate for initiation on the door of the Lodge" (p. 300); parallel thirds are identified as a Masonic "symbol for harmonious relationship" or "brotherhood" and especially so when scored for clarinets and bassoons "which were by this time established as Masonic instruments" (p. 300); orchestrations for winds and strings are interpreted as

"Masonically interlocked" (p. 301). The key of E-flat major is accurately identified as the "Masonic ritual key" (p. 295), but the keys of G minor, C, F, D minor, and B-flat also are said to project significant aspects of Masonic doctrine. In the Kyrie, D major is held to signify an association "with the Godhead" (p. 298). Mellers thus attributes "direct Masonic symbolism" to a variety of musical commonplaces, but without pausing to establish what might compel a Masonic interpretation rather than a conventional one. For example, he asserts that the use of dotted rhythms on repeated notes "signifies Masonic resolution and fortitude," even though he himself recognizes that this ubiquitous figure "tends to have something of that implication in most European music" (p. 300).

Not everyone will be fully convinced by all of these interpretations, but it is evident from these examples that Beethoven's late oeuvre greatly expands the variety of topics and musical-rhetorical figures expressive or symbolic of religious experience, the totality of which surely add up to a sacred style to place alongside the pastoral, heroic, serioso, military, and other so-called characteristic styles available to composers of the classical era—one that goes well beyond the churchly style employed in earlier or more conventional examples of the religious musical genres. Whether derived from preexistent compositional materials accumulated in the course of musical evolution or invented by Beethoven himself, these have to do primarily with associations between musical and/or textual events and religious concepts, ideas, and figures. But the identification of these kinds of musical-rhetorical figures or metaphors scarcely exhausts the sphere of the sacred in late Beethoven, which also includes invocations of religious feeling and explicit allusions to the deity in the *Missa solemnis,* the finale of the Ninth Symphony, and the "Heiliger Dankgesang . . . an die Gottheit" of the A-minor String Quartet. In these, and in the hymns and hymnlike melodies that are so frequently encountered in late Beethoven sonatas and string quartets that they become a signature feature of his last works, the intention to denote aspects of the sacred is apparent. Similarly, there are several striking uses in late Beethoven of the ancient ecclesiastical modes—in the Et Incarnatus of the *Missa solemnis* and the "Seid umschlungen, Millionen" of the Ninth Symphony finale; and in the "Heiliger Dankgesang," which is written "in the Lydian mode." And there are ideas for never-composed works like the "Pious song in a symphony in the ancient modes" (1818) and the "choruses in the ancient modes," including one in the Lydian mode, projected for an oratorio on Saul (1826).[6] All of these carry powerful religious or mythic associations.

Beethoven created more than his share of conceptual topoi symbolic of the sacred. Allusions to the sacred in his late music, however, are not necessarily limited to more or less literal, descriptive text-music analogies within religious genres and their associated repertoire of conventionally denotative signs. His more interesting contributions to the musical symbolization of the sacred may consist in shaping musical form and rhetoric in ways suggesting an initiatory view of existence. For example, we earlier imagined that we could glimpse the outline of a devotional journey in the very structure of the "Diabelli" Variations, and we paid attention to the goal-directed strategies and varied forms of motion by which such a pilgrimage might pursue its arduous goal, including the resolute march of variation 1 and the andante pilgrim's walk of variation 24. Another such walk—on a melody reminiscent of a Bachian or Lutheran-style chorale—materializes in the closing pages of the Allegro risoluto finale of the "Hammerklavier" Sonata, providing a temporary respite from the furious action and instilling the action with a devout character (ex. 10.1).

The individual as a member of an indissoluble community is thereby represented by a fusion of musical signs, for if a measured walk brings to mind the steadfastness required of a solitary pilgrim in his unremitting quest, chorale-like melody may be emblematic of a congregation bound together in faith. After the episode concludes, ritardando, subsiding into the B-flat tonic, the pilgrim's walk melody is seamlessly but briefly subsumed into the fugue, which then resumes its flight (mm. 269–84). Of course, musical allegories of journeys—usually by a series of tonal tableaux that engage issues of departure and return—are already implicit in some of Beethoven's earlier works, for example, in the Piano Variations, op. 34, the *Pastoral* Symphony, and so patently in the "Lebewohl" Sonata, op. 81a. But in late Beethoven such implied circuitous narratives tend to convey weighty spiritual implications, for they appear to be imbued with a purposeful and moral character in the service of an exalted principle.

Beethoven also greatly expanded the metaphoric powers of musical ascents and descents, although he left open for Schubert and the later Romantic composers the exploration of unfathomable descents, often carrying overtones

EXAMPLE 10.1.   "Hammerklavier" Sonata in B-flat, op. 106, Allegro risoluto, mm. 249–77.

of the subterrestrial and demonic, as in the opening movement of the "Unfinished" Symphony and in a variety of ambitious works by composers from Liszt to Mahler. Without making any claim that Beethoven's late works are inspired by or written in emulation of the great cosmological ladders of the world's sacred books and myths, or, more specifically, of such images of world-shaping ascents as "the laborious climb" in Dante's *Purgatorio* or the ascent through the planetary spheres in the *Paradiso,* it seems possible to think of some of them as Beethoven's contribution to—really, construction of— a related resonant tradition.[7] The mythopoeic arc of Beethoven's Ninth Symphony, for example, appears to inscribe a trajectory that runs from a shattering downward-thrusting moment of Creation upward through a series of fleeting Arcadian moments to Elysium; and prominent among the mul-

EXAMPLE 10.2.   "Hammerklavier" Sonata in B-flat, op. 106, Adagio sostenuto, mm. 1–5.

tiple images of desire that find fulfillment in its Ode to Joy is that of a loving father-God who dwells beyond the firmament's uppermost boundary.
On a contrasting microcosmic level, and setting aside its vaunted function
as a rising third to counterbalance the falling thirds of the main theme, the
two-note "afterthought" opening of the Adagio sostenuto of the "Hammerklavier" Sonata in B-flat, op. 106, may be likened to a sublimely simple
ascent to something like a sacred shrine or altar, at the least a solemn approach to a place of utmost significance. Compressed into the smallest space
possible for inscribing a forward and upward movement—two notes and no
more, A–C♯ sounded in unison octaves—it generates power to intensify the
Sehnsucht-drenched Adagio, in which lament is fused with prayer, worship
with awe, activating feelings associated with the most sanctified experiences,
for this rising figure is potentially a referent for every imaginable passage
from a lower to a higher place (ex. 10.2).

   In our examination of the Violin Sonata in G, op. 96, we saw that detours
and unpredictable surprises blocked the finale's path to a smooth landing,
and we took this as an example of Beethoven's multiple late-style strategies
to find an appropriate ending. The finale encountered several dislocations
and interruptions, a return to tempo primo only after unsuccessful tries, and
even then the music had to pass through a final and unexpected Poco adagio
before becoming fully entitled to an ending. We might see in this a strategy of what could be called "labyrinthian form," perhaps analogous to the
convoluted narrative strategies of myth and ritual. Unexpected events and
tests of endurance mark an unpredictable journey that must overcome
obstacles before eventually finding a safe haven or resting-place. In this strategy of complicating the ending Beethoven seems to have found possibilities
for rendering solutions commensurate with profound questions. A worth-
while ending deserves to be postponed, kept in abeyance until the right

moment. Beethoven decides to extend the narrative, thereby to enrich its substance. This strategy became a serious topic in his late music: the construction of barriers as a necessary precondition to locating a portal, following a thread leading out of a labyrinth, finding corridors that emerge into the light.

We encountered similar labyrinthian modalities in the vicissitudes of variation 32 of the "Diabelli" Variations, and they exist on the most expansive scale in the Ninth Symphony, each of whose earlier movements are retrospectively described by the baritone as unsatisfactory quests to locate a theme and a tonality that could serve as perfect emblems of fraternity and faith, of the deity, and of a hallowed region called Elysium. In the end, Beethoven's oracular spokesman reveals that we have been following the wrong road and suggests that there is another, a right way—"Ha dieses ist es. Es ist nun gefunden," the composer wrote on the sketches for the unveiling of the "Freude" theme—that we ought to pursue together.[8]

The Largo of the "Hammerklavier" Sonata, op. 106, is not a self-contained slow movement but, like the 35-measure Molto adagio of the "Waldstein" Sonata and the 16-measure Adagio of the Cello Sonata in C, op. 102, no. 1, a condensed introduction to a finale—here, the fugue that Beethoven designated "Allegro risoluto." Without calling on descriptive texts or other denotational aids, it too considers and rejects a series of possible avenues of continuation before settling on the fugue as an appropriate ending. In this respect it also has an affinity with the Overtura to the Grosse Fuge, which launches a succession of apparently discontinuous gestures, darting in various directions and abruptly breaking off to try another way.[9] Tovey describes how the Largo of Opus 106 proceeds via a succession of descending thirds until "the right key for the finale" is discovered: "Halts are called at 4 significant places," he writes, "and the situation debated at each" (ex. 10.3).[10]

Eventually, in these works, the search for an ending enters an ambiguous, liminal domain, a threshold that by straddling the profane and the sacred permits passage from the former to the latter. Separated from the world and inoculated by faith against temptation, the traveler reaches the final stage of an exacting pilgrimage and achieves a state of holiness. Barrier and portal are merged in late Beethoven's simulacra of the liminal; arrived at a threshold, action is slowed to the point of immobility. We earlier encountered this same process as it played out in the transition from the fugue to the closing minuet of the "Diabelli" Variations: after the fugue abandoned its multiple efforts

(continued)

EXAMPLE 10.3 *(continued)*

at summation, a Poco adagio materialized, forming a final barrier, which turned out to be permeable precisely because it hovers on the edge of utter stillness, withdrawing from action into the interiority of pure thought.

The implications of motionlessness for the representation of the sacred have not gone unnoticed. Calling attention to Beethoven's reliance upon extremely slow tempos combined with an "avoidance of melodic and harmonic movement" to represent motionlessness, Kirkendale connected this topos to "the ancient conception of God as the one who possesses *apatheia,* is free from all passions and, as the first cause of being, is himself immovable."[11] Emphasizing Catholic interpretations of Beethoven's setting of the *Missa solemnis,* Kirkendale did not pursue potential links to the very similar descriptions of divinities of the ancient and Eastern religions that Beethoven transcribed into his Tagebuch and elsewhere. But it is instructive to consider the aphorism, "For God, Time absolutely does not exist *[Zeit findet durchaus bey Gott nicht statt]"* that Beethoven took from a writing on Indian religious practices and copied into his Tagebuch in 1816 (no. 94d).[12] And it is worth considering the potential connection between Eastern ideas about time or motionlessness and Beethoven's emotional calls for the suppression of his personal passions except those directed toward art and the deity. We have already observed that Beethoven repeatedly privileged the suppression of his longings for sensual gratification and even for ordinary happiness, as a way of demonstrating his worthiness, defining the "blessed" person as one who, like the deity, has transcended the pulls of desire (nos. 61a, 64a).

An aura of the holy surrounds the time-stopping moments in many of the late works, including the "Diabelli" Variations, the Adagio and finale of the Ninth Symphony, the Benedictus of the *Missa solemnis,* the slow movements of the string quartets, and the Sonata in C minor, op. 111. Those moments are located in unspecifiable regions, seemingly outside space and time, beyond the frontiers of ordinary experience. Perhaps that is why the Adagio molto semplice e cantabile movement of Opus 111, the Arietta, projects an archaic character, though it may also be because, as Schenker pointed out, "the variations display the simplest type of that oldest technique . . . which mounts from variation to variation by means of an augmented rhythmic movement."[13] In any case, the sense of an exalted ceremonial progression is nearby, enhanced by Beethoven's exploitation of what Tovey calls "an infinite variety of quivering ornament."[14] In the fourth variation, unbroken sequences of thirty-second-note triplets, without accents or phrase markings,

EXAMPLE 10.4.   Sonata in C minor, op. 111, Arietta, mm. 106–32.

EXAMPLE 10.4 *(continued)*

metamorphose from shakes at the interval of the fifth into oscillating octaves (mm. 80–81), at which point they condense into a shimmering sonic barrier that blurs any distinction between rapid movement and the depths of stasis. The idea of motionlessness is brought to mind by accelerated motion, rhythmic diminution, and minimal harmonic action. At measure 89, the tempo speeds up slightly and the triplets are displaced to the upper registers, while the octaves in the bass give way to repeated dotted sixteenths in the treble register, marked *pianissimo* and *leggiermente.* The action appears to cast about for a direction, preparing for a climactic, revelatory event, which materializes in the cadenza following variation 4, when an extended trill gives way to a triple trill on the dominant seventh of E-flat, rising in chromatic steps until it has reached its uppermost limit, prying the lines apart until at last (at mm. 117–18) they simultaneously find the most remote upper and lower registers, suggesting that a way through the barrier is now clear. A tranquil, rarefied passage heralds entrance to a celestial place or an otherwise transfigured state of being, and with the full restatement of the opening theme, in C major (mm. 130–31), we experience a piercing sense of arrival comparable to hearing the first notes of the "Diabelli" Variations Menuetto (ex. 10.4).

As we have come to expect in late Beethoven, however, finalities are seldom expeditiously achieved. Here, emergence into a radiant world occurs in stages rather than all at once. In the coda at measures 160–61 a trumpet-like trill vaults to a high G, sforzando, inaugurating another extended trill

EXAMPLE 10.5.   Sonata in C minor, op. 111, Arietta, mm. 172–77.

which, against a pattern of thirty-second-note triplets, rings rejoicingly in the upper registers until a series of runs, arabesques, flourishes, and rushing descending scales in parallel motion return to the beginning and to three closing measures that recapitulate the sonata's descent to the depths and its now untrammeled ascent to a place where discrepancies of height and depth are no longer an issue (mm. 172–77; ex. 10.5).

Many of Beethoven's close observers have always heard intimations of the sacred in the Sonata in C minor, op. 111—"a visionary aura that had never been known in music before" (Kerman); "a magic alternation of darkness and ethereal lightness" (Matthews); "a continuous striving to the heights . . .

like a silver thread . . . woven between earth and heaven" (Bekker); "an ethe-real atmosphere, as if the music has entered a transfigured realm" (Kinder-man).[15] Rolland referred to it as "This white on white, this immobile lake," and he was reminded of the "almost impassive smile of Buddha."[16] Others have sensed that the sonata pursues a path that runs between the nether and the celestial regions, a path that eventually reaches a long-sought, ineffable place. Uhde, for example, sees an unspecified "theological meaning," especially in the implied contrast between "the dark world of the first movement and the radiant world of the second movement"; translating this meaning into Ernst Bloch's utopian vocabulary, Uhde finds in the sonata "the anticipa-tory resplendent brilliance of the new [voranleuchtende Glanz des Neuen]."[17] Perhaps, however, there is a deep melancholy that goes hand in hand with the prospect of leaving the earth behind, despite all compensating promises of perfection, beauty, and eternal life. Adorno may have had this in mind when he called attention to the nostalgic sadness at the core of the Arietta's transfiguring journey: "The close of the Arietta variations has such a force of backward-looking, of leavetaking, that, as if over-illuminated by this departure, what has gone before is immeasurably enlarged. . . . Utopia is heard only as what has already been."[18] Adorno thus captures the sense of exhaustion, depletion, and suppressed homesickness that accompanies every pilgrim on his journey; but his closing sentence probably poses an unnec-essary dichotomy, for more often than not the utopian reflex aims to re-store an archaic harmony enshrined in memory, seeks reentry to a real or imagined paradise lost. In any event, utopia always needs its models; it can-not wholly invent images of transcendence without summoning the effigies of "what has already been," which, however thoroughly misplaced or overpowered, still retain the potential to be sought for and even, perhaps, recovered.

Beethoven's late-style experiments in the rhetoric and structure of musical liminality are not to be taken solely as representations or evocations of the sacred. His construction of metaphorical labyrinths, barriers, thresholds, journeys, ascents, and descents surely have something to do with mystical and other states associated with the extreme varieties of religious experi-ence; but imagery of worship and initiation is also discoverable in every fun-damental process of universal being—creation and dissolution, growth and maturity, leave-taking and homecoming. Furthermore, the keen sentiments that are usually labeled religious or sacred are drawn from what William James called "a common storehouse of emotions," derivatives of fear, sexual life, and biological states of dependency.[19] Thus, feelings of ecstasy and awe, or apprehensions of the sublime and supernatural, may attend the vicissitudes of an ordinary human life as well as those of a devotional journey.

Accordingly, we would do well to remain open to the expansive resonance of Beethoven's liminal imagery, which overflows the borders of the sacred, potentially attaching to a wealth of other phenomena, including the ordinary objects of desire and the artifacts of sublimation. Schiller defined "the Holy in human beings [as] the moral law *[das Heilige im Menschen, das Moralgesetz]*."[20] In the end, distinctions between secular and sacred may not matter, for there is an authentic sense of the holy that attaches to the tides of human experience and natural occurrence in all their variety.

CHAPTER ELEVEN

THE SENSE OF AN ENDING:
THE NINTH SYMPHONY

I want to bring together several anomalous events from Beethoven's last period, involving three of his most consequential works. In March 1819, Beethoven authorized the publication in England of his four-movement "Hammerklavier" Sonata in B-flat, op. 106, in a variety of abridged or altered forms. "Should the sonata not be suitable for London," he wrote to his former student, Ferdinand Ries, who was acting as Beethoven's advocate, "I could send another one"; but, inasmuch as that would be "most inconvenient," he had no objection if the first two movements or the fugal finale were to be published as separate works. As an alternative, he suggested that the sonata might be converted into a three-movement work, omitting the closing Largo and Fugue and altering the order of the remaining movements. He apologized to Ries for the sonata's deficiencies, explaining, without a hint of irony: "The sonata was written in distressful circumstances, for it is hard to compose almost entirely for the sake of earning one's daily bread; and that is *all* that I have been able *to achieve.*"[1] In the course of time, the sonata actually appeared in London as two separate works—a "Grand Sonata" consisting of the first three movements in the order 1–3–2; and an "Introduction and Fugue," made up of the Largo and Allegro risoluto.

No musical analyst has ever studied the "Hammerklavier" Sonata in these curiously altered forms, but much ink has been spilled over the issue of our second, more famous, example—Beethoven's relatively untroubled acceptance of the publisher Matthias Artaria's request that he compose a more accessible finale for the String Quartet in B-flat, op. 130, to replace the difficult Grosse Fuge, which would be published as a separate work, numbered Opus 133. Beethoven's friend Karl Holz, who had been delegated by

Artaria to plead his case with the composer, anticipated great resistance, for he knew that Beethoven "set great store" by the Fugue, but he achieved his goal rather easily. "Beethoven told me he would reflect on it, but by the next day I received a letter giving his agreement."[2]

Of course, Beethoven had often drastically revised his works. He had set aside completed sections of larger works, such as the *Leonore* overtures or the "Andante favori," WoO 57, originally written for the Sonata in C, op. 53 ("Waldstein"). He had even incorporated movements written for one work into another; for example, the discarded finale of the Violin Sonata in A, op. 30, no. 1, in the Sonata in A, op. 47 ("Kreutzer"). But the "Hammer-klavier" Sonata's rearrangement and the deletion of the Grosse Fuge are of a different order; they are beyond ordinary conceptions of revision and recomposition, such as of the string quartets, op. 18, nos. 1 and 2, or the "Waldstein" Sonata, "An die Hoffnung," or even *Fidelio*.[3] In those works, he had yet to find a final or good enough form for his creative idea; in the later works he has himself broken up or authorized the deconstruction of already completed masterpieces and recast them in radically different, and even seemingly aberrant, structures, showing an utter disregard for the clear indications that the existing finales contain culminating cross-references to germinal materials in the earlier movements.

With the exception of the inconclusive debate over which of the two finales for the B-flat Quartet is the "correct" one, these anomalies have never attracted serious critical attention; indeed, they have been brushed aside, at-tributed to Beethoven's frailty or eccentricity, his preoccupation with fam-ily matters, his sensitivity to criticism of his modernist experiments, or his pragmatic willingness to compromise principle for some extra cash.[4] For to take Beethoven seriously would suggest that he may have held a different view from our own concerning the formal integrity of his music. We might want to investigate whether the "Hammerklavier" Sonata revisions some-how anticipate the rearrangements of sonata-cycle structure that emerge in the last sonatas, with their displacements of the expected order of events, or even whether these recastings might have been the expression of some unfamiliar creative principle. We might begin to wonder if there is some larger significance, beyond evading the Imperial Censor's regulations, to Beethoven's truncated performance of the *Missa solemnis* (reduced to the Kyrie, Credo, and Agnus Dei) and its retitling as "Three Grand Hymns with Solo and Chorus Voices" at the Vienna concert of 7 May 1824. We would want to ask uncomfortable questions: Can an aesthetic object like the "Hammerklavier" Sonata or the *Missa solemnis* be subdivided or rearranged and still survive as a work of art? Can a perfected cyclic work like the B-flat Quartet be recreated as an alternative work of equivalent perfection? Does its remodeling force us to conclude that the original is in some way aesthetically inadequate?

Certainly these revisions—if that is what they ought to be called—undermine notions of the organic perfection of Beethoven's greater works. After all, the replacement of the Grosse Fuge may be circumstantial evidence of the noninevitability of Beethoven's structures; the reconstituted quartet with its rondo finale may even exemplify some unstated principle of alternative narrativity. A reading along these lines might propose that Beethoven agreed to replace the finale, not because of dissatisfaction or commercial compromise (though these may have helped to set the process in motion) but because he grasped the possibility of working out a different solution to the narrative line, one in which the quartet finds closure on Biedermeier terrain rather than in an exotic, metaphysical zone. Beethoven discovered two strategies that would complete his conception: one is a powerful and multivalent structure adequate to serve as an arena for the triumph of will over mortality (or some such metaphor); the other is the simplest of rondos, steeped in the play-impulse, concerned with present well-being rather than anticipation.

These examples—to which, in a moment, I will add one more—imply that for certain of Beethoven's late works there may exist a plurality of potential alternatives, which may be actualized or remain dormant, depending on intuition, contingency, and whim. The question of what constitutes a finished work is thrown open, reminding us that in certain of his completed autographs Beethoven continued the process that he normally reserved for the earlier stages of composition, setting out further possibilities, including radical alterations in goal as well as style or detail. In particular, the revision of movement endings was one of his long-standing preoccupations. In works of his middle period, Emil Platen observed, Beethoven continued to make essential alterations in the closing sections of movements after the works had already taken concrete notational form; for example, in the scores of the "Razumovsky" String Quartets, op. 59, nos. 1 and 2, "out of a total of seven movement endings, six were altered after the fact, four in essential ways."[5] Indeed the relationship between sketches and compositional goals has always been more problematical than some scholars were willing to allow. As Lewis Lockwood showed, the closer one looks at the sketches the less one can continue to accept as an article of faith that "as a work progresses from first inklings to final realization it should pass through successive phases of growth and clarification of structure, and of complication of detail in relation to that structure, becoming progressively more definite en route to its goal."[6] To further thicken the issue, Janet Levy has pointed out that one "cannot assume that the goals of a completed work are necessarily the same as the goals of the sketches for it," inasmuch as the composer's intentions may well have changed or become clarified during the course of the work.[7] Composition is not always a process in which the composer eventually finds a lapidary form for a predetermined idea. With Beethoven, not only is there no prospective inevitability, there may even be no inevitability after the fact. His sketches and autographs may well be a series of rough maps to a multiplicity of universes, to a jammed network of paths taken and not taken.

Nineteenth-century music critics could not have accepted such concepts of perpetual openness and mutability of purpose. Otto Jahn, for instance, though initially bewildered by the proliferation of Beethoven's sketches, ultimately reassured himself of their place in an evolutionary order. Despite Beethoven's apparent "uncertainty and groping," he wrote, "I have found no instance in which one was compelled to recognize that the material chosen was not the best, or in which one could deplore that the material which he rejected had not been used."[8] In reality, however, Beethoven's recompositional enterprises embody some strange mixture of free will and chance. His unpredictable imagination constantly takes him (and us) unawares; at every stage of the compositional process the composer calculates directions and ways of continuing. Above all, he asks how he is to end, for a late-Beethoven ending is often in some sense a surprise ending, one that must be discovered—even, paradoxically, when it was conceived of in advance.

It is against this backdrop that we can now bring into play Carl Czerny's startling assertion, which he related separately to Jahn and Gustav Nottebohm, that Beethoven had contemplated replacing the choral finale of the Ninth Symphony.[9] When Beethoven's biographer Anton Schindler questioned this report, the esteemed jurist Leopold Sonnleithner sent a letter to the editor of the *Allgemeine musikalische Zeitung* in 1864 confirming that Czerny had more than once told him the same thing: "Some time after the first performance of the Ninth Symphony, Beethoven, within a small circle of his most devoted friends, among whom was Czerny, said that he realized he had committed a blunder *[Mißgriff]* with the last movement of the symphony; he wanted, therefore, to discard it and in its place write an instrumental movement without voices; he already had an idea in mind for it."[10] Although Beethoven's comment postdated the May 1824 premiere, his misgivings actually preceded the symphony's completion as well, because ideas for an instrumental finale to the Ninth Symphony—later used in the A-minor String Quartet, op. 132, where it is ushered in by a stormy recitative, a "palpitating cry" in which Kerman detects affinities with the Ninth's finale strategy—appeared in sketches of late 1822 or early 1823 and were revived in sketches of perhaps a year later as well, that is, after the choral finale was close to completion.[11] However, even if Beethoven never converted his misgivings into action—for we know that on 16 January 1825 he sent the symphony, with the choral finale intact, to Schott's Sons for publication— the proposed replacement of the "Ode to Joy" takes its place squarely in the center of our sequence: all three examples express Beethoven's intention, either by truncation or by substitution, to separate a colossal finale with powerful metaphysical implications from the main body of a major cyclic composition and to seek an alternative and more conventional way of bringing it to a conclusion. At issue is Beethoven's sense of an ending.

Of course, we ought not to overlook Beethoven's uncertainties about these alternatives; not only was no new finale ever written for the Ninth Symphony, but the "Hammerklavier" Sonata remained intact in its Viennese publication. Of the three, only the B-flat String Quartet finale was unambiguously removed, and even that decision, as recent trends in the performance of the late quartets suggest, may be reversible. Nevertheless, the evidence for Beethoven's discontent with these finales—no matter how momentary and ambivalent—is fairly clear. Less clear is why he was unwilling or unable irrevocably to vouch for these monumental and affirmative last-period finales.

II

There are endings and endings. *Fidelio,* the "Lebewohl" Sonata, *Wellington's Victory,* and dozens of animated rondos show that Beethoven was quite capable of writing comic, mock-epic, optimistic endings of the kind Henry

James once described as "a distribution at the last of prizes, pensions, husbands, wives, babies, millions, appended paragraphs, and cheerful remarks."[12] Beethoven was scarcely a stranger to reunions and rescues, betrothals and marriages, reconciliations, rejoicings, and rewards—all the paraphernalia of ultimate celebration ubiquitous in the comedy of manners, in classical sonata style, and in every variety of opera, whether *buffa, seria,* or of the French "rescue" genre. Even his turn-of-the-century experiments in finale form— in such works as the "Malinconia" String Quartet, op. 18, no. 6, the Opus 27 piano sonatas, the Opus 34 and Opus 35 variations, and the Second and Third symphonies—continued to operate within these traditional modes of dénouement.[13] But his late finales are located well beyond the perimeters of normal—classical, if you will—experience, in regions of cataclysms, apocalypses, and resurrections. It is as though he were elaborating, in a dizzying display of his creative powers, the limitless variety of endings that his imagination could conjure up.

Traditional endings are not abandoned, but they are achieved only after painful postponements; order is discovered or restored, but without permanently assuaging the fear of disintegration. Late Beethoven has no penchant for *couleur de rose.* He wants to achieve order, but not by pretending that disorder does not exist; he will not settle for merely representing "the complacent delight in an idyllic reality" of which Nietzsche once wrote.[14] "It is not that we are connoisseurs of chaos," Frank Kermode explained, in a book whose title I have borrowed, "but that we are surrounded by it, and equipped for coexistence with it only by our fictive powers."[15]

Chaos is the natural, teeming matrix of creativity; Beethoven's art is carved from it and retains its impress. Elysium can be gained only by overcoming terrifying obstacles: the road to immortality leads through death; the baritone's proposed search for something "more pleasant and filled with joy" must cross the barrier of the terror fanfare *(Schreckensfanfare)* with which the finale opens, a satanic eruption in which, as the novelist Alejo Carpentier observed, the "broken, maimed, twisted" materials of the fanfare are "merged into a chaos that [is] a gestation of the future."[16] The terror fanfare and the rehearsal of the themes, proclaiming the need to dismantle the first three movements, are a return to the deepest reaches of disorder as a precondition for one last attempt to get things right.

For the masters of the Classical style in its floodtide—including the young Beethoven—all happy endings were more or less alike; for late-period

Beethoven, all happy endings are dissimilar, because they are uncertain renderings of an impermanent felicity, elaborating novel solutions to the problem of the ending. It is this sense of impermanence that may have undermined Beethoven's faith in his most powerful late-period affirmations. An ineluctable skepticism warred with his will to affirm and transcend; doubt survived every symbolic affirmation. Perhaps Beethoven was concerned that, by their crushing affirmations, his colossal endings tended to overwhelm the works they were intended to crown, skewed their proportions, intruding upon issues customarily reserved to earlier movements of a sonata cycle. (It is a variant of the problem of the *Leonore* overtures, which could not serve as beginnings because they preempted the action of the opera.) Perhaps, after all, considering the Grosse Fuge after the heat of its creation had subsided, Beethoven was uncomfortable with so disjunctive a contrast to the inwardness of the penultimate Cavatina. Perhaps, reflecting on the Ninth Symphony, he found his recapitulation of the themes to be too drastic a rejection of the realms of experience that the Allegro ma non troppo, Molto vivace, and Adagio molto e cantabile movements had traversed.

The "Ode to Joy" is, of course, unique even among Beethoven's most unpredictable late-period finales. In it, he invoked every conceivable strategy for the realization of his prophetic and apocalyptic purposes, bringing to bear mythic scenarios, descriptive materials, programmatic indications, unifying patterns, characteristic styles, and the entire repertory of tonal allegory and other musical symbolism at his command.[17] Thereby he sought to magnify music's power to control inchoate forces. Inevitably, however, such attempts to make music denotative tend to reduce the sphere of music's sovereignty by yielding up territory to other forms of expression—to narrative, myth, and language. For referential materials—by virtue of their essential externality—undermine the symmetries and coherences of musical form; and language (here, Schiller's text), because it owes its primary allegiance to verbal and philosophical ideas, dilutes the power of sound, narrows the range of music's potential meanings. By introducing a choral finale into his symphony Beethoven even appeared to sanction in advance Wagner's assertion of the inferiority of music: "'Where music can go no farther, there comes the word' (the word stands higher than the tone)."[18]

Moreover, with the rejection of the themes, we are suddenly asked to consider the earlier movements of the symphony as ideological constructs rather than as music: Beethoven's sketchbook memoranda inventory their perceived limitations—"This reminds us of our despair . . . ; this is a mere farce . . . ; this is too tender"—and suggest that we ought to "seek something more pleasing, more cheerful, more animated."[19] Music moves from the sensuous sphere of sound into the ascetic sphere of thought. The programmatic in music has its own purposes—to strive to capture the denotative abilities of other arts, to disguise a deficiency of structure, to expound rhetorical points of view. But not least among its purposes is to place limits on music, to pretend that music is merely another language, reducible to the rational and verbal, to an expressible idea, image, or scenario.

Some critics may want to free the Ninth Symphony from its own referential baggage, to open up a wider range of the work's symbolic resonances, which lie beyond the implications of its text and of Beethoven's own intentionality. When he proposed to cancel the "Ode to Joy" as the finale of the Ninth Symphony, Beethoven himself was tempted to play the critic's role. Indeed, in the finale of the Ninth Symphony, the composer had already become his own critic: "O Freunde, nicht diese Töne." In effect, the baritone tells us, "What you have heard is insufficient. I reject it, as you should. Let me show you another way." And when he revealed to Czerny that he was thinking about an instrumental finale, Beethoven momentarily judged the choral finale inadequate as well. Suddenly, the entire structure was on the brink of condemnation.

III

Not all endings take their composers unawares. Like the *Eroica* Symphony, the "Kreutzer" Sonata, and possibly the Opus 130 String Quartet, the Ninth Symphony appears to have been composed from the perspective of an ending that was already in Beethoven's compositional plan or, at least, was already in view.[20] In so doing, however, he ran the risk of finding that the preconceived ending was no longer adequate to the material that preceded it, or even that the finale no longer bound what had gone before into a retrospective coherence. Prospectively, it may have seemed a brilliant notion to write three movements to represent, severally, "despair," "farce," and "excessive tenderness," and thus to qualify them for supersession by the "Ode to Joy." After the fact, Beethoven may well have found the designations restrictive and his scenario of rejection and transcendence unsatisfyingly schematic.

There may have been a miscalculation in the conception of the finale; or, perhaps, by its very extravagance the idea may have taken control of the compositional process, with the unintended consequence that Beethoven's strategies for making music denotative might have been purchased at too high a price. Reflecting on his finale, Beethoven may have become uneasy about its potential for crushing a skeptical temper, unpersuaded by the effortlessness of his D-major victories of enthusiasm over uncertainty. The mature Schiller had repudiated "An die Freude" as naive and outdated (he then reversed himself, rewrote the poem, tried to salvage it);[21] now Beethoven, too, seems to have questioned his setting of that poem in his choral finale, perhaps even asked himself just how far he continued to believe in the sentiments expressed in "An die Freude."

The contemplated instrumental finale would have taken leave of the ideological dimension, set aside the *Gesamtkunstwerk* conception along with its denotational vocabulary, and instead privileged music's unique expressive powers. Constructed from the tenderly urgent yearning motif in triple meter that he had inscribed in his sketchbooks, it would have represented a return from the abstractness of the frozen firmament to the warmth of the earth, a reversion from a mythic to a human scale (ex. 11.1).

Eventually, however, Beethoven seems to have concluded that he had underestimated his own achievement. At any rate, his Ninth Symphony remained intact, unfolding endless implications, continuing to frustrate every attempt—including his own—permanently to fix or limit its meanings. The symphony's drive for denotation is in fact far from being merely reductive; it is itself a prime symbol of the impulse to enlarge meaning. It is so by virtue of the imagery embedded in its formal structure, which stands for a multiplicity of questing structures in nature, life, myth, and art. And it is even so by reason of its inevitable failure to achieve pure denotation, its inability to circumscribe musical meaning, texts and allegorical signposts notwithstanding. For what Beethoven achieved by encoding referential materials into his music is the sense of the untranslatable striving for—and even reaching—an intelligibility unachievable in principle.

Given this potential for deadlock, Beethoven elected to let his choral finale stand. But there was another urgent reason to let it stand. Much as he may have wanted to continue the processes of revision, Beethoven needed to go

EXAMPLE 11.1.   Ninth Symphony, sketches for an instrumental finale (Nottebohm, *Zweite Beethoveniana*, pp. 181–82).

a. Around June–July 1823. Aut. 8/2, fol. 8r.

b. Around June–July 1823. Aut. 8/2, fol. 36v.

EXAMPLE 11.1 *(continued)*
c. Fall 1823. A 50.

forward. Doubtless he was impatient to have done with the last of the three time-consuming projects—the others being the *Missa solemnis* and the "Diabelli" Variations—that had inhabited his mind for almost six years. Eventually, he had to call a halt to an ongoing project, even one, like the setting of the "Ode to Joy," which had been incubating for almost a third of a century and whose working-out had occupied him, on and off, for years. In the Ninth Symphony and the *Missa solemnis* Beethoven had explored a broad spectrum of musical symbolism and of music-text equivalents. Having pushed these possibilities to their outer limits, he never again tackled a vocal project; plans for a requiem and one or two more masses were abandoned, as were thoughts of a setting of Goethe's *Faust* and ideas for several operas, including Grillparzer's *Melusine*. Immediately after the concerts of May 1824, he began writing the series of string quartets that he had been thinking about since mid-1822 and that were to absorb his creative energies until the onset of his final illness in late 1826.

There may well be something in Beethoven's creative personality that impelled him to the revising of finales. The capacity for endless metamorphosis is at the heart of his imaginative gift, but it itself runs the danger of yielding to the chaotic; it defeats form, and it makes endings improbable, for it will not accept any ultimate resting place, or any other implication of finality. That may be why Beethoven needed not only to devise new endings but to revise old ones. By changing finales he casts uncertainty on his story's outcome; like Scheherazade, he keeps fate at bay by perpetual narrative. "Enough, it's time it ended," says Beckett's Hamm, but, like Beethoven, he is reluctant to call it a day: "Yes, there it is, it's time it ended and yet I hesitate to — to end."[22]

IV

Those like Beethoven who are drawn to utopian solutions are condemned to uncertainty or disappointment. Early on, when what Beethoven called the "revolutionary fever [Revolutionsfieber]" had burned out,[23] he tried to turn disillusion to heroic ends: his *Eroica* Symphony is the exemplary musical text on post-Thermidor disillusionment, even if its disenchantment was grafted onto an affirmation of Bonapartism, complete with its own imperial implications and Roman vestments. Later on, however, when others had fallen silent, Beethoven continued to pursue an interior, supernal revolution, undeterred by the knowledge that affirmations may eventually turn out to be flawed.

Unlike the *Eroica* Symphony—so patently a product of the aftermath of the French Revolution—the Ninth Symphony finds its ideological orientation in the prerevolutionary decade, returning to an undifferentiated idealism saturated with a searing sense of unrealized possibilities, possibilities that could be represented only by an unprecedentedly modernist style and rhetoric. "Alle Menschen werden Brüder" summons up an archaic battle-cry, in which both revolution and utopia are yet to come. Though the revolution, the Josephinian *Aufklärung,* and the high tide of the fraternal societies now belonged to history, there were residues—the memory of shared altruistic fervor, the glimpse of a harmonious and just social order, the overthrow of convention. For the Beethoven of 1824, the sense of the failure of an idealistic project was no longer an issue; rather, it had given way to a determination to recapture these well-remembered felicities in which utopia—past, not future—had been actualized.

However, the summoning up of the spirit of utopia inevitably disinters its dystopian underside as well. By its unremitting embrace of fraternity Schiller's thrilling slogan suggests a suppression of individuality reminiscent of the coercive tendencies that have characterized utopian blueprints from Lycurgus and More to Babeuf, Fourier, and Marx. That may be why the implications of Schiller's text include not only a tender sigh for a better world but an authoritarian insistence on conformity as a precondition of salvation.[24]

> Gladly, as His suns fly
> Across heaven's mighty path,
> Hasten, Brothers, on your way,
> Joyfully, like a hero on to victory.[25]

The heroic tone conceals a celebration of thralldom. "An die Freude" may be read as an oath of loyalty, a willing declaration of subservience. The brothers rejoice to be part of the clockwork of God's universe ("Wie seine Sonnen fliegen"); their orbits are fixed, their task is to glorify and obey the Father who, in return, will grant His love and withhold His vengeance. Dissenters and deviants, however, are not welcome in this compliant fraternity:

> He who has had the great fortune
> To be a friend to a friend,
> He who has won a gracious wife
> Let him mingle his jubilation with ours!
> Yes, and he who has even one kindred soul
> On this globe to call his own!
> But he who has never known these, let him
> Steal away, weeping, from this band.

"All men become brothers" has imperceptibly shifted into the subjunctive, and even the imperative—"All men must be brothers!" Fraternity is intolerant of difference. Ecstatic brotherhood is bound by fear—of the creator, of lovelessness, of isolation, of expulsion. That is why—for us, if not for Schiller and Beethoven—the hidden hero of "An die Freude" may be precisely that weeping heretic who rejects joyful conformity and accepts exile. Those who choose Elysium yield up their individuality to the group, receiving, in return, promises of eternal youth and of love ("ein holdes Weib"). But these may be empty promises, conditional on blind obedience. The psychoanalyst Otto Fenichel understood this well: "The participation in power is permitted—but in a restricted sense, *on conditions,* and the subjects and children, because they are in need of this participation, are ready to pay the price of this limitation."[26] It is a Faustian bargain without a Faust.

We are swept into an irreconcilable dialectic between strivings for individual autonomy and powerful regressive pulls toward fusion and oblivion, a dialectic that Hans Loewald has thrown into high relief: against the traditional view that "the emergence of a relatively autonomous individual is the culmination of human development," he observes, is "a growing awareness of the force and validity of another striving, that for unity, symbiosis, fusion, merging, or identification—whatever name we wish to give to this sense of and longing for nonseparateness and undifferentiation."[27] It is into this matrix of undifferentiated communality that the Ninth Symphony draws us. No longer does Beethoven write a symphony to "celebrate the memory of a great man"; the programmatic purposes of the *Eroica* Symphony have given way to the boundless collectivity of the Ninth Symphony; history has been transmuted into myth beyond heaven's starry vault. The underside of Romanticism's consecration of the individual is a mosaic of its oceanic longings— variously for love, for death, for the infinite, for immersion in nature, for the *Ewig-Weibliche,* for universal brotherhood, and, most fatefully, for merging with groups—national, religious, or political. Whether we can participate in such blissfully passive and ultimately irresponsible states without losing our capacity for free will and without opening the way to regressive social tendencies, remains a disconcerting question.

By the unprecedented intensity of the finale's rhetoric, by the multitheism of its symbolism—the Greek mythic signposts, the Christian-medieval gestures embedded in the Andante maestoso, and the orientalism of the Alla marcia's "Turkish Music"—and by the convergence of thematic, harmonic, and rhythmic patterns contending for closure, Beethoven achieved a sense of fusion so complete that it stands as the model of rapturous surrender to collectivity.[28] Its fusion of styles and procedures is matched by the multivalence of its forms, which constitute a palimpsest of superimposed hybrid structures—a set of variations; one or another sonata form; a four-movement cycle superimposed on a sonata-allegro concerto form with double exposition (Rosen); a cantata; a through-composed text-derived form; a suite; a divertimento; an operatic finale; and even a free fantasy.[29]

With blinding simultaneity, Beethoven's music and Schiller's text promise a variety of extreme states, states that cloak regressive longings in feelings of magical omnipotence: blissful symbiosis with a nurturing preoedipal mother ("All creatures drink joy from Nature's breasts"); oedipal capitulation to a forgiving (or punishing) father who must be both sought ("Brothers, above the vault of the stars, there surely dwells a loving Father!") and placated ("Prostrate yourselves, ye multitudes"); a thrusting drive for physical union ("Drunk with rapture we enter thy sanctuary"); a Spartan, warlike eroticism ("Hasten, Brothers, on your way, joyfully, like a hero on to victory"); and an undifferentiated, polymorphous love that precipitously erases all distinctions of gender.

> Embrace, ye multitudes!
> Let this kiss be for all the world!

Beethoven's and Schiller's ecstatic communality here finds its most profoundly compressed image: the band of brothers, God, Elysium's daughter Freude, and the nameless multitudes are all dissolved in a single embrace, a wholesale coalescence. Individuality appears to be at serious risk of annihilation.

Although this vision of a harmonious society-to-come is obviously vulnerable to absorption by the prevailing order, which naturally would choose to view Beethoven's symphony as a mythologized imperial portrait set against a benevolent Habsburg landscape or subsequent equivalent,[30] the Ninth Symphony cannot be read in the main as a symbol of submission to authority or of engulfment in the mass. Its fraternal slogan, its unprecedentedly radical musical procedures and styles, its quest for new meanings, all echo resistance to the given. That is why it begins with open fifths, tonal indeterminacy, a sense of the void. Well before Bertolt Brecht, Beethoven knew that "something is missing [etwas fehlt],"[31] and it is the search for what is missing—the "Freude" melody, brotherhood, a benevolent God-father, Elysium, the multiple objects of converging quests—that impels Beethoven's symphony forward to its culmination.

Ultimately, the coercive and subversive implications of the Ninth Symphony may be inseparable, perhaps because Beethoven's futuristic impulse— to create things that had never before existed—warred with his yearning to belong to tradition. "If only one wanted to separate oneself from the past," he mused in his Tagebuch, "still the past has created the present" (no. 44). The whole point of Beethoven's finale, however, was to discover a melody, a major key, and an Elysian haven that would permit the momentary setting aside of all questions and uncertainties. The "Ode to Joy" celebrates and rekindles the revolutionary flame, that explosive historical moment that promises to transform society and social relations in a single consuming instant, one of such utter power and clarity that it cannot be devalued by later events, for it distils humanity's accumulated strivings and hopes into an essence as yet unsullied by doubt or disillusion. True, utopia as "not yet" constantly contends with utopia as "no more." Everything ends. Beethoven knew that. But he also demonstrated that something remains. And though we may not share his confidence, we will be hard put to ignore his apocalyptic call for the suppression of doubt.

CHAPTER TWELVE

THE HEALING POWER OF MUSIC

For Edward W. Said

There are documented reports telling of occasions when Beethoven and Schubert used their music for a singular purpose. The first was set down by the nineteenth-century biographer Otto Jahn, who over the years had been gathering materials for a full-length life of Beethoven along the lines of his great *W. A. Mozarts Leben,* and had "assembled letters, . . . documents, authentic memoranda and traditions" for that purpose.[1] Among those whom he personally interviewed was the composer's intimate friend Antonie Brentano née Birkenstock, when she was in her eighties. Jahn printed a brief account of the interview in an article published in 1867, which included the following recollection:

> During her sojourn in Vienna in the years 1809 to 1812 Frau Antonie Brentano was often ailing for weeks at a time, suffering to such an extent that she withdrew to her room, where she remained by herself, unfit to see anybody. On such occasions Beethoven was regularly in attendance; he came in, seated himself without any further ado at a piano in her antechamber and improvised; when he had "said everything and given solace" to the sufferer in his own language, he left as he had come, without taking notice of anybody else.[2]

The passing of half a century had not affected Frau Brentano's memory. A letter to her sister-in-law Bettina, written in early 1811, described these same events at the very time that they were taking place:

> *Beethoven* has become for me one of the dearest *[liebsten]* human beings. . . . His whole nature is simple, noble, good-natured, and his tender-heartedness

would grace the most delicate woman. It speaks in his favor that few know him, and even fewer understand him. He visits me often, almost daily, and then he plays spontaneously because he has an urgent need to alleviate suffering, and he feels that he is able to do so with his heavenly sounds. . . . That there is such power in music I hadn't yet known until *Beethoven* informed me of it.[3]

A related and in some ways even more poignant story is told in connection with Beethoven's former student, the pianist Dorothea von Ertmann née Graumann, who was one of the leading exponents of his keyboard music, and to whom he dedicated the Piano Sonata in A, op. 101, written in 1816 and published the following year. After the death of her three-year-old son, in 1804, she found herself unable to weep—and she was additionally troubled by Beethoven's failure to offer his condolences in person. Some years afterward she told her niece, "I could not understand at all why he did not visit me after the death of my beloved only child."[4] Apparently he had some reluctance to come to her house, and finally—reportedly at her husband's urging—he invited her to his own home. According to Felix Mendelssohn's account, when Beethoven sat down at the keyboard, his only words to his bereaved friend were "We will now talk to each other in tones." He played for more than an hour until, as she said, "he told me everything, and in the end even brought me comfort *[Er sagte mir alles, und gab mir auch zuletzt den Trost]*."[5] According to another account of the incident, recalled by the noted actress Antonie Adamberger, he uttered not a single word of greeting, but sat down at the piano and played for Ertmann until at last "she began to sob and thus her grief found both expression and relief."[6] "I felt as if I were listening to choirs of angels celebrating the entrance of my poor child into the world of light," Ertmann told her niece. "When he had finished, he pressed my hand sadly and went away as silently as he had come."[7]

A parallel anecdote from the life of Franz Schubert indicates that Beethoven was not the only composer who invested his music with such unusual powers. In March 1825 Schubert participated in a psychotherapeutic treatment of a young woman, Louise Mora, while she was being treated under hypnotism by the painter Ludwig Schnorr von Carolsfeld, who moonlighted as a mesmerist healer, sometimes in collaboration with Romantic writer Friedrich Schlegel.[8] Schubert was called in because the patient persisted in awakening from a sleep induced by hypnosis.

EXAMPLE 12.1.   Schubert, Deutscher Tanz in B-flat, op. 33, no. 7, D783, mm. 1–4.

Schnorr kept detailed minutes of the treatment; the entry for 20 March 1825 reads:

> In the evening at 7:30 the patient was hypnotized. She fell asleep, was placed in her armchair, and awoke soon thereafter. After the sounding *[Berührung]* of several chords from no. 7 of Schubert's German Dances she fell asleep [see ex. 12.1]. At a quarter to eight, after again [hearing] the above mentioned Deutscher Tanz, she again fell asleep.

Four days later, the treatment continued, as recorded in the minutes for 24 March:

> In the evening at 7:25 the s[omnambulist] fell into a trance when Herr Schubert played the same German Dance that regularly produced that effect upon her. She was awakened in a clairvoyant state, rubbed her eyes etc., when, at 7:45, Herr S[chubert] sang and accompanied himself in a lied that was in the same key [B-flat] as that German Dance; then the patient fell into a trance and then a sleep that lasted until the lied ended, at which point she was mesmerized (magnetized). Around 8:00 a renewed trance, because Herr S[chubert] played that familiar German Dance once again and said, "Don't wake up! *[Nicht wecken!]*" As she continued sleeping, he played still other things that she said she found pleasing. She was so taken with one of the German dances that the m[esmerist] once had to awaken her through stroking and found it necessary to stay with her.
>
> Among other pieces that were played was also "Der Wanderer," composed by himself, which similarly made a deep impression on her. She wanted to be awakened, which was done in the usual way by stroking. . . . On this musical occasion it was still very striking to remark the various ways in which the tones and chords could affect a s[omnambulist]. Several, which were very moving, produced the most wonderful motions and contortions of her body.[9]

Though it is uncertain which Schubert work titled "Der Wanderer" was designated, it seems to me most likely that it is Schubert's 1819 setting of a poem by that name by Schnorr's collaborator in Mesmerism, Friedrich Schlegel (ex. 12.2).[10] The music, in slow march time and marked *Langsam,* has a lulling character; and the imagery of the wanderer in the moonlight suggests a somnambulistic or clairvoyant state of being. "How clearly the moon's light speaks to me, encouraging me on my journey . . . gentle ebb, high tide, low in spirits, I wander on in the darkness, climb courageously, sing joyfully, and the world seems to be so good."

By participating in this curious venture into a byway of early nineteenth-century psychotherapy, Schubert not only encountered extreme and disabling mental states (as Lisa Feurzeig suggests) but expressed and acted on a desire to help cure them—and to do so by his music. He was a willing recruit in an effort to provide solace and aid to a suffering creature. In a quite literal sense, both he and Beethoven used music as an instrument of healing—in Antonie Brentano's words as a means "to alleviate suffering."

It is one thing for us to speak generally and imprecisely about the "healing power of music," and to invoke examples of it in the Orpheus or other myths and claims about the efficacy of that power by Plato, Aristotle, Pythagoras, Boethius, Luther, and Calvin. It is quite another to find plain signs that Beethoven and Schubert shared a matter-of-fact belief that music indeed has healing powers. More, they both *used* their music for healing purposes.

Of course, these anecdotes describe different kinds of attempts at healing—and different degrees of success. Schubert wanted to help a troubled young woman, evidently a stranger to him, whose Mesmerist therapists were successful in treating her minor physical complaints, such as hiccoughs, but were helpless to cope with her emotional needs. They were not gifted or empathic counselors; as Feurzeig shows, they attributed Louise Mora's episodes of self-destructiveness and frenzied raving to "anger and intransigence *[Zorn und Unversöhnlichkeit],*" for which their prescribed remedies were to bind her hands, to counsel her to maintain "a firm moral attitude," and to require her priest-confessor's attendance at the sessions.[11] They did not consider the possibility that their treatment might have activated in the patient a variety of concealed anxieties, morbid states, or forbidden desires. One is reminded of similar experiences and reactions by the eminent psychiatrists Charcot, Breuer, and Freud, who later in the century also found,

EXAMPLE 12.2.   Schubert, "Der Wanderer," D649 (1819), mm. 1–5.

to their dismay, that a regular byproduct of hypnotic or other intimate ther-apy was the inadvertent stimulation of such unsuspected fears and longings.

In contrast to Schubert's, Beethoven's efforts centered on countering the effects of depression, grief, and mourning in people whom he deeply cared about; and he effectively provided them with consolation that words could not achieve. His music enabled Dorothea Ertmann at last to find cathartic tears for her dead child. Through his music he reached the core of Antonie Brentano's desolation, established a bond compounded of sympathy, un-derstanding, and love, provided reasons for her to return to the world from the edge of despair.

Prominent in all three instances is that music is placed in the service of healing a suffering woman—from depression, heartbreak, rejection, pain, or unfulfilled longing. Also noteworthy is the essential wordlessness of the efforts: Beethoven deliberately remained mute, making no effort to put his sympathy into words; Schubert's only words, apart from the poetic texts of his lieder, were the urgently whispered command, "Don't wake up!" Music was able to say that which language could not express, could make a direct appeal to the emotions, could speak from the heart to the heart. Furthermore, in each case, it is a composer-performer who employs his music as an instrument of healing. The composer's presence, his actual participation as a musician in these rituals of healing, may suggest that it is the performance as much as the music that is essential to the recuperative process. Beethoven's playing signified that he understood what Antonie Brentano and Dorothea Ertmann felt, that he too had experienced despair and grief and thus could help them to mourn. In turn, Schubert acted as a personal agent; but in his case he was part of a team, providing music to aid in the trance- and sleep-inducing stage of the treatment. Often, then, healing may be in the physical act of making music—which can signify the bestowal of a gift upon one who is in need. Without the need, there can be no healing. More, without a reciprocal belief in the power of music, there can be no such healing. For this kind of healing involves a relationship between two people, of whom, in the psychoanalyst Phyllis Greenacre's telling phrase, "one is troubled and one is versed in the ways of trouble," mediated by a method whose effectiveness they both are willing to take for granted.[12] By contrast, when Mozart offered his C-minor Mass to his father as a token of his desire to heal the terrible breach between them, Leopold Mozart refused to accept the fiction that a musical work—even one of such magnitude—could make his family whole again. With that refusal, music reverted to being mere marks on a ruled page instead of the hieroglyphics of the heart's language.

II

These unusual episodes from the lives of Beethoven and Schubert are testimony to some of the ways in which music can heal, or, more exactly, can be put in the service of healing. But healing in music is not always individual, personal, reducible to a telling anecdote; often it touches on more wide-reaching issues of human suffering, injustice, and loss. Thus, for example, the closing chorales of many Bach cantatas crown narratives of sin or suffering, reaffirming shared beliefs, restoring sinners to grace, enfolding worshipers in the embrace of the congregation. Similarly, the peripatetic chorale melody in the St. Matthew Passion is a leitmotif of healing by way of reassurance, always keeping in sight the resurrection that follows Christ's crucifixion.[13]

EXAMPLE 12.3.   String Quartet in A minor, op. 132, Molto adagio: "Heiliger Dankgesang," mm. 1–6.

There seem to be numberless conditions to be healed through music and countless ways that music can heal. Indeed, it may be inherent in music's structural and rhetorical properties that it can serve as a metaphor for many forms of recovery and restoration, renewal and resurrection. It might be said that the episodes involving Beethoven and Schubert started with therapy, but our subject is not therapy. It is the power of music to set things right.

Beethoven's late works in particular may illustrate several aspects of this power. Perhaps the most transparent example flows from the inscription at the head of the String Quartet in A minor, op. 132, which reads, "Holy Song of Thanks by a Convalescent to the Divinity, in the Lydian Mode." By these words, Beethoven stipulates that music can be considered a representation of healing and convalescence, a barrier against death (ex. 12.3). Such ideas have an ancient lineage:

> The sons of Autolycus, working over Odysseus,
> skillfully binding up his open wound . . .
> chanted an old spell that stanched the blood
> and quickly bore him to their father's palace.
>
>   (*Odyssey*, 19.513–19, Fagles trans.)

The biblical echoes of Beethoven's heading, with its appeal to the Deity, are not far from the surface; the most famous of these is the account of David's healing of Saul's melancholia:[14]

And it came to pass, when the *evil* spirit from God was upon Saul, that David took an harp, and played with his hand; so Saul was refreshed and was well, and the evil spirit departed from him.

(1 Samuel 16.23)

Many have seen Beethoven's movement title as an autobiographical allusion, expressing his own feelings of gratitude upon recovery from an illness. But biographical interpretations of the inscription are surely not the whole story. The "Heiliger Dankgesang" is not simply a composer's musical offering in return for a lessening of physical pain and a prolongation of his own life; it is also a prayer for healing of the soul, offered by those who need to have their sins forgiven, who are struggling for emergence from melancholia or loss of faith. As Kirkendale has shown, Beethoven's choice of mode revives an ancient tradition, recorded by Cassiodorus and communicated by the sixteenth-century Italian theorist Gioseffe Zarlino, "that the Lydian mode is a remedy for fatigue of the soul, and similarly for that of the body."[15] In the A-minor string quartet, prayer is rewarded by an imperceptible quickening, by revival through contact with the Godhead, and finally by a rebirth, which the composer designates in the score as "Feeling new strength *[Neue Kraft fühlend]*" (ex. 12.4).[16] The Lydian mode has served Beethoven's purpose; now in D major and 3/8 time he can return to life from a realm of suffering and meditation. In this vision of restoration, prayer magnified by music in a sacred mode achieves an irresistible power, not only to stave off personal illness and death, but to cleanse the soul of its doubts, sins, and imperfections.

The idea of healing through prayer occupies only a minor and fairly conventional place in earlier Beethoven; for example, in the "Gellert" Songs, op. 48—"Bitten" (Prayer) and "Bußlied" (Song of atonement)—and the *Pastoral* Symphony finale, with its closing "Gott wir danken Dir." The topic of an answered prayer is given greater weight in the closing sections of Beethoven's *Missa solemnis*. The Agnus Dei is a lengthy plea for mercy, a plea to be relieved of the sins of the world. The desolate feelings aroused by the somber, even despairing Adagio cannot be relieved easily or organically; they require a deus ex machina, the sound of trumpets and fanfares heralding miraculous transformations, disjunctive shifts from the timelessness of the church into historical time, from inner to outer. The prayer for divine mercy

EXAMPLE 12.4.   String Quartet in A minor, op. 132, Molto adagio: "Neue Kraft fühlend," mm.
31–34.

accomplishes its work—or reaches its nethermost depth—and then, in the Dona nobis pacem, it is transformed into a plea for peace rather than mercy; on the score of the ensuing Allegretto vivace Beethoven wrote the words, "Prayer for inner and outer peace."

Music's healing powers are conspicuous in the sheer multiplicity of classical-style endings that crown every kind of achievement: a return to community or to a pastoral-Arcadian state of nature, an ascent to a sacred region or the discovery of a loving deity beyond the outermost vault of the heavens, the removal of impediments to the union of lovers (as in *An die ferne Geliebte* or *Fidelio*). Celebrations are the order of the day in Beethoven: of exalted marriage, of brotherhood, or of the freeing of prisoners from bondage, in every kind of emergence into the light, or in any other fulfillment of an arduous quest. In the Ninth Symphony this takes the form of anticipating, withholding, and then discovering a melody of surpassing beauty and simplicity, one from which every trace of dissonance, conflict, or anxiety has been excluded (ex. 12.5).

The purpose of the "Ode to Joy" is reconciliation—within the band of brothers, between God and his creatures, of the millions and the solitary individual. But this melody and the text with which it is forever intertwined opens on the endless varieties of utopia: not only love, brotherhood, familial reconciliation, and religious devotion, but images of beauty, social harmony, and every possible symbol of perfection. Remember, this is a moment of reassembly following the violent rejection of everything that had gone be-

EXAMPLE 12.5.   Symphony No. 9 in D minor, op. 125, finale, mm. 92–101.

fore, a rejection heightened by the strident blast of discordant sound—which Wagner aptly named a "Terror Fanfare *[Schreckensfanfare]*"—that opens the movement. This is healing with a vengeance: the restoration of a unity that had been lost when the established world had been found wanting by Beethoven, its creator, and then taken apart.

The trumpet call in act 2 of *Fidelio* demonstrates the metaphoric sweep of a single, unaccompanied instrument, a simple tonic arpeggiated chord, which awakens, rouses to action, and signals salvation all at once. The climactic call announces the arrival of Fernando, an individual of conscience, the messenger of a good prince; it also proclaims the imminence of liberation, including the literal emergence of Florestan and the prisoners from confinement in darkness. Above all, it offers testimony to the immense power of sound. This, too, was known to the ancients; Joshua was instructed to have his priests circle the city of Jericho bearing seven trumpets: "And it shall come to pass that when they make a long blast with the ram's horn, and when ye hear the sound of the trumpet, all the people shall shout with a great shout; and the wall of the city shall fall down flat, and the people shall ascend up every man straight before him" (Joshua 6.4–5).

III

Examples could readily be multiplied. Still, music is not simply an agency of healing; and not all music has healing powers. Sometimes—as in the "Terror Fanfare"—it tears the lid off humanity's destructive impulses, or it reveals an abyss, spins nightmares about the void, the end of things. But when it lays bare such a psychic wound it thereby opens up the possibility of healing it. "Ermattet, klagend"—weary, lamenting—is one of late Beethoven's

EXAMPLE 12.6.   Piano Sonata in A-flat, op. 110, Fuga: Allegro ma non troppo, mm. 116–118.

EXAMPLE 12.7.   Piano Sonata in A-flat, op. 110, Fuga: Allegro ma non troppo, mm. 136/37–43.

eloquent expressive instructions in his native language, used in the fugal finale of the Sonata in A-flat, op. 110, to signal the rematerialization of the Adagio's grief-ridden "Klagende Lied" ("Arioso dolente," "Song of Lament"; ex. 12.6). It takes all of Beethoven's imaginative powers to overcome this grief. The sonata's culminating Fugue returns, headed "Little by little reviving to life *[Nach und nach wieder auflebend]*," marking an emergence from deep confinement, a resumption of existence (ex. 12.7).

Finally, the Cavatina of the String Quartet in B-flat, op. 130, speaks of grief but also of consolation. It was perhaps the only work about which Beethoven confessed that it brought him to tears: "He really wrote it with tears of sadness in his eyes," reported Karl Holz, "and admitted to me that no other work of his own had ever made such an impression on him, and that even the remembered feelings aroused by this piece always cost him new tears."[17] This represents a notable softening of Beethoven's customary stoicism, for he almost always avoided an appeal to tearful sentiments in his music, preferring, like the French Revolution's composers, to convert grief into public display and exhortation, as in the Andante of the Fifth Symphony, or into ceremonial ritual, as in the Marcia funebre of the *Eroica* Symphony and the Allegretto of the Seventh Symphony. In the finale of the Ninth Symphony, the Adagio is explicitly rejected as "too tender" *(zu zärtl[ich])*,

EXAMPLE 12.8.   String Quartet in B-flat, op. 130, Cavatina ("Beklemmt"), mm. 40–44.

in the words Beethoven used in his sketches to describe its first theme.[18] Here, however, in the penultimate movement of the B-flat String Quartet, he openly permitted himself to acknowledge music's power to represent depths of suffering and of fear. The contrasting section of the Cavatina, marked *Beklemmt,* plunges into darkness, melancholia, and dread. And by that unprecedented expression indication, taken from his mother tongue and carrying an almost tangibly oppressive physicality, Beethoven poses the most difficult questions—how to endure pain of this intensity, how to awaken from a burdensome nightmare, how to breathe freely again (ex. 12.8). And the fact is that Beethoven found two satisfactory answers to those questions in the alternative closing movements of the B-flat String Quartet that he left for posterity to puzzle over.

The opening of the Grosse Fuge appropriately is called "Overtura" because it is a prefiguration of the action, a pot-pourri of working materials, and thus literally a reversion to a state prior to the commencement of action. It presents itself as a labyrinthian process, a set of apparent dead ends, with each segment apparently in search of a beginning, a path to the fugue. One by one, disparate motifs burst into view and abruptly break off; it is, in Kerman's description, as though the composer were hurling "all the thematic versions at the listener's head like a handful of rocks" (mm. 1–30).[19] Though the overture's primary image is of a chaoticized state of being, order will eventually emerge from this splintered chaos, the fragments coalescing into a gigantic three-part fugue, as a coherent universe is assembled from improbable ingredients. Thus, the Overtura is a return to beginnings, a representation of creation, of fracture and assembly, and thereby an emblem of art's supreme restorative power.

In the substitute finale Beethoven moves directly from the torment-ridden Cavatina to a pastoral celebration of life's simple gifts. The return to nature is achieved without much struggle. Paradise is gained (or regained) by a quick stroke. In this alternative version of healing, we need to act swiftly, without thinking too much; a simple change of perspective permits us to hurdle the barrier that separates affliction from affirmation. Whereas the Grosse Fuge is learned and encyclopedic, the rondo is a Haydnesque romp, illustrating that healing can be effected either by way of wisdom or by way of innocence. Both endings are authentic versions of the dialectic of suffering and healing that is central to Beethoven's creative project.

ABBREVIATIONS

AmZ	*Allgemeine musikalische Zeitung.*
Briefe	*Ludwig van Beethoven Briefwechsel Gesamtausgabe.* Edited by Sieghard Brandenburg. Beethovenhaus edition. 8 vols. Munich: Henle, 1996–.
Frimmel, *Handbuch*	Theodor von Frimmel. *Beethoven-Handbuch.* 2 vols. Leipzig: Breitkopf & Härtel, 1926.
Kerst	Friedrich Kerst, ed. *Die Erinnerungen an Beethoven.* 2 vols. Stuttgart: Julius Hoffman, 1913.
Kinsky-Halm	Georg Kinsky. *Das Werk Beethovens. Thematisch-bibliographisches Verzeichnis seiner sämtlichen vollendeten Kompositionen.* Completed and edited by Hans Halm. Munich: Henle, 1955.
Konversationshefte	*Ludwig van Beethovens Konversationshefte.* Edited by Karl-Heinz Köhler, Grita Herre, Dagmar Beck, et al. 11 vols. Leipzig: VEB Deutscher Verlag für Musik, 1968–2001.
Kunze	Stefan Kunze et al., eds. *Ludwig van Beethoven: Die Werke im Spiegel seiner Zeit. Gesammelte Konzertberichte und Rezensionen bis 1830.* Laaber: Laaber-Verlag, 1987.
Letters	*The Letters of Beethoven.* Edited by Emily Anderson. 3 vols. London: Macmillan, 1961.
New Grove	*The New Grove Dictionary of Music and Musicians.* 6th ed. Edited by Stanley Sadie. 20 vols. London: Macmillan, 1980.
Nottebohm, *Beethoveniana*	Gustav Nottebohm. *Beethoveniana.* Leipzig: Peters, 1872.
Nottebohm, *Zweite Beethoveniana*	Gustav Nottebohm. *Zweite Beethoveniana. Nachgelassene Aufsätze.* Leipzig: Rieter Biedermann, 1887.

Schindler-MacArdle	Anton Schindler. *Beethoven As I Knew Him.* Edited by Donald W. MacArdle, trans. Constance Jolly. London and Chapel Hill: University of North Carolina Press, 1966. Translation of 3rd ed. of Schindler, *Biographie von Ludwig van Beethoven.* Münster: Aschendorff, 1860.
Schindler-Moscheles	Anton Schindler. *The Life of Beethoven.* Edited by Ignaz Moscheles. Boston: Oliver Ditson, n.d. [1841]. Translation of 1st ed. of Schindler, *Biographie von Ludwig van Beethoven.* Münster: Aschendorff, 1840.
Solomon, *Beethoven*	Maynard Solomon. *Beethoven.* 2nd, rev. ed. New York: Schirmer, 1998.
Solomon, *Beethoven Essays*	Maynard Solomon. *Beethoven Essays.* Cambridge, Mass.: Harvard University Press, 1988.
Tagebuch	Maynard Solomon. "Beethoven's Tagebuch of 1812–1818." *Beethoven Studies* 3 (1982): 193–288. Also in Solomon, *Beethoven Essays (q.v.),* pp. 233–95. Translated into German as *Beethovens Tagebuch* (Mainz: Hase & Koehler, 1990); into Italian as *Il Diario di Beethoven* (Turin: Mursia Editore, 1992); and into Japanese (Tokyo: Iwanami Shoten, 2001). In the text and notes, each entry is identified by the number assigned to it in the foregoing editions.
Thayer-Deiters-Riemann	Alexander Wheelock Thayer. *Ludwig van Beethovens Leben.* Edited and enlarged by Hermann Deiters and Hugo Riemann. 5 vols. Leipzig: Breitkopf & Härtel, 1907–17; reissued 1922–23.
Thayer-Forbes	*Thayer's Life of Beethoven.* Edited by Elliot Forbes. 2 vols. Princeton: Princeton University Press, 1964; rev. ed., 1967.
Thayer-Krehbiel	A. W. Thayer, *The Life of Ludwig van Beethoven.* Edited and completed by Henry E. Krehbiel. 3 vols. New York: Beethoven Association, 1921.
WoO	Werke ohne Opuszahl (works without opus number). Numbers assigned by Kinsky-Halm *(q.v.)* to works not given opus numbers by Beethoven or his publishers.

NOTES

Prologue

1. For details of the published editions, see Tagebuch in the list of abbreviations, above. Parenthetical references in the text are to Tagebuch entries, identified by the numbers assigned in those editions.

2. Letter to Schotts Söhne, 17 September 1824, *Briefe,* vol. 5, p. 368 (no. 1881), *Letters,* vol. 3, p. 1141 (no. 1308).

3. Letter to Hans Georg Nägeli, 9 September 1824, *Briefe,* vol. 5, p. 362 (no. 1873), *Letters,* vol. 3, p. 1139 (no. 1306).

4. In an earlier discussion of strategies of prolongation I speculated that Beethoven's creativity "may have served . . . to provide an imaginative counterbalance to the forces of disintegration," thereby to achieve a "nullification of death through its transfiguration into bliss." Maynard Solomon, "The Ninth Symphony: A Search for Order," in *Beethoven Essays,* pp. 27–30.

5. See William James, *The Varieties of Religious Experience: A Study in Human Nature* (New York: Longmans, Green, 1902; reprint, New York: Modern Library, n.d.), pp. 186, 193, 205.

Chapter 1. The End of a Beginning

1. Walter Riezler, *Beethoven,* trans. G. D. H. Pidcock (London: M. C. Forrester, 1938), p. 233.

2. William Kinderman, "The Evolution and Structure of Beethoven's 'Diabelli' Variations," *Journal of the American Musicological Society* 35 (1982): 310; Kinderman, *Beethoven's Diabelli Variations* (Oxford: Clarendon Press, 1989), p. 71. In the latter, Kinderman characterizes the theme as a "beer hall waltz" (p. 67). For similar remarks, see Eric Blom, *Classics: Major and Minor* (London: Dent and Sons, 1958), p. 56; Karl Geiringer, "The Structure of Beethoven's *Diabelli Variations,*" *Musical Quarterly* 50 (1964): 497. In a distinction without much of a difference, another noted scholar, August Halm, granted

that the theme may be "trivial, but is not—or hardly—banal, and in no way base, like the Blue Danube Waltz," and he was unsure whether the publisher Antonio Diabelli's theme "is more trivial than, for example, the theme of the 'Eroica' Variations [op. 35]." August Halm, *Beethoven* (Berlin: Max Hesse, 1927), p. 180. In a more subtle formulation of the basic idea, Kurt von Fischer writes, "Beethoven's prodigious variation work . . . is to be understood as a dialogic critique of Diabelli's primitive theme." See Kurt von Fischer, "Beethoven—Klassiker oder Romantiker," in *Beethoven-Symposion Wien 1970*, ed. Erich Schenk (Vienna: Böhlaus, 1971), p. 94.

3.   *Berliner Allgemeine musikalische Zeitung* 7 (1830): 370–71, quoted in Kunze, p. 417.

4.   Cappi and Diabelli's announcement, *Wiener Zeitung*, 16 June 1823, reprinted in Alexander Wheelock Thayer, ed., *Chronologisches Verzeichniss der Werke Ludwig van Beethovens* (Berlin: Schneider, 1865), p. 151; English trans., Donald Francis Tovey, *Essays in Musical Analysis: Chamber Music* (London: Oxford University Press, 1944), pp. 124–25 (translation amended).

5.   Schindler-MacArdle, p. 252.

6.   Ibid., pp. 252–53.

7.   "The fee for the Variat. would be 40 ducats at most," wrote Beethoven to Antonio Diabelli, early November 1822. *Briefe*, vol. 4, p. 545 (no. 1507), *Letters*, vol. 2, p. 975 (no. 1105, translation amended).

8.   Schindler placed the initiation of the plan in the winter of 1822–23 instead of before the summer of 1819; the beginning of the composition in May 1823; and the intended number of variations at only "six or seven." See Schindler-MacArdle, pp. 252–53, and Schindler-Moscheles, p. 89.

9.   Janus a Costa, review of the "Diabelli" Variations, in *Journal für Literatur, Kunst, Luxus und Mode* 38 (1823): 635–37, quoted by Kunze, p. 415.

10.   Heinrich Rietsch, "Fünfundachtzig Variationen über Diabellis Walzer," *Beethovenjahrbuch*, ed. Theodor von Frimmel, vol. 1 (Munich and Leipzig: Georg Müller, 1908), p. 38. "It is well known that Beethoven loved a drastically simple variation theme," observed Joseph Kerman, citing, *inter alia*, the "Appassionata" Sonata in F minor, op. 57, the Violin Concerto, and the "Diabelli" Variations. Joseph Kerman, *The Beethoven Quartets* (New York: Knopf, 1967), p. 61.

11.   Donald Francis Tovey, *Essays in Musical Analysis: Chamber Music* (London: Oxford University Press, 1944), pp. 126–27; Tovey, *Beethoven* (London: Oxford University Press, 1944, reprint, 1965), p. 127. Uhde, unaware that Beethoven conceived the set and wrote two-thirds of the variations in 1819, suggested that the theme initially drew Beethoven's interest because of its "remarkable similarity" to the Arietta of the Sonata in C minor, op. 111, of 1821–22. Jürgen Uhde, *Beethovens Klaviermusik I: Klavierstücke und Variationen* (Stuttgart: Reclam, 1980), pp. 504–5.

12.   Pianists as a rule do not take the theme's "vivace" tempo marking seriously, with most performers setting a pace of about 88 to 90 beats to the dotted half-note. A faster tempo—of, say, 100 to 108 per dotted half-note—would significantly affect our per-

ception of the theme, giving it a keener, more bracing, scherzo-like character. Vivace is a highly unusual tempo or expression indication for waltzes and *Ländler* of the period. It is worth noting that the marking appears both in the published score and in Beethoven's autograph, but not in the sketches, suggesting that it may have originated with Beethoven rather than Diabelli.

13. Noting Gustav Theodor Fechner's formulation, "the idea that *the scene of action of dreams is different from that of waking ideational life,*" Freud concluded: "What is presented to us in these words is the idea of *psychical locality.*" Sigmund Freud, *The Interpretation of Dreams,* vol. 5 of *Standard Edition of the Complete Psychological Works of Sigmund Freud,* ed. and trans. James Strachey et al., 24 vols. (London: Hogarth Press, 1953–74), p. 536.

14. Percy Bysshe Shelley, "A Defence of Poetry," in *Essays and Letters,* ed. Ernest Rhys (London: Walter Scott, 1887), pp. 36–37.

15. Shelley, "A Defence of Poetry," in *Essays and Letters,* p. 12.

16. Preface to the second edition of *Lyrical Ballads,* in *The Poetical Works of William Wordsworth,* ed. Thomas Hutchinson (London: Henry Frowde, 1906), p. 935.

17. Novalis, *Henry von Ofterdingen,* trans. Palmer Hilty (New York: Ungar, 1964), pp. 114, 116. Writing in a journal with which Beethoven was very familiar, the Kantian critic C. F. Michaelis saw variation form as a process from which "the soul of the listener obtains pleasure, in that it can automatically look through the veil, finding the known in the unknown, and can see it develop without effort." C. F. Michaelis, "Ueber die musikalische Wiederholung und Veränderung," *AmZ* 6 (1803–4), col. 200, trans. Elaine Sisman, *Haydn and the Classical Variation* (Cambridge, Mass.: Harvard University Press, 1993), p. 236. Of course, Michaelis could not anticipate Beethoven's late variation style; he is still bound here to neoclassic precepts of order, which is why he regards the goal of variation as the achievement of "attractive diversity" and warns of the danger of "creating a quixotic *[abentheuerliche]* mixture of heterogeneous figures" (translation amended). For a preliminary discussion of Romanticism and defamiliarization, see Solomon, *Beethoven Essays,* p. 26.

18. Cited in René Wellek, *A History of Modern Criticism, 1750–1950,* vol. 1 (New Haven: Yale University Press, 1955), p. 192, from Herder, "Von Ähnlichkeit der mittleren englischen und deutschen Dichtkunst" (1777), in vol. 9 of *Sämtliche Werke,* ed. Bernhard Suphan et al., 33 vols. (Berlin: Weidmann, 1877–1913), pp. 529–30.

19. *Wiener Zeitung,* 9 June 1824, reprinted in *Schubert: Die Dokumente seines Lebens,* ed. Otto Erich Deutsch (Kassel: Bärenreiter, 1964), p. 241, translated by Eric Blom in *Schubert: A Documentary Biography,* ed. Otto Erich Deutsch (London: Dent, 1946), pp. 348–49 (translation amended). For further details, see Rietsch, "Fünfundachtzig Variationen," pp. 28–50.

20. Letter to Peter Joseph Simrock, 10 February 1820, in *Briefe,* vol. 4, p. 363 (no. 1365), *Letters,* vol. 2, p. 872 (no. 1005, translation amended).

21. Letter to Breitkopf & Härtel, 9 August 1812, in *Briefe,* vol. 2, p. 287 (no. 591), *Letters,* vol. 1, p. 384 (no. 380).

22. Beethoven used the title "Lied mit Veränderungen" for his set of variations on Goethe's "Ich denke dein," WoO 74, written for Josephine Deym and Therese Brunsvik and published in January 1805; *Veränderungen* is also used on the first page of the music of the autograph of the "Kakadu" Variations for piano trio, op. 121a, initially composed circa 1803: "Veränderungen mit einer Einleitung u. Anhang. von L. v. Beethoven." See Kinsky-Halm, p. 353. For Beethoven's use of German for expression and tempo markings, see Richard Gottschalk, "Beethovens deutsche Kunstausdrücke," *Muttersprache* 42 (1927), cols. 65–69; see also Schindler-MacArdle, p. 512 n. 380.

23. Furthermore, there is no hint of such an intention in Diabelli's original publication notice of 1823 announcing Beethoven's set, a notice which indeed may have been written or drafted by Beethoven—or at least was subject to his approval.

24. Erich Auerbach, *Mimesis: The Representation of Reality in Western Literature* (Garden City, N.Y.: Doubleday Anchor, 1957), p. 174.

25. Beethoven wrote to Diabelli, ca. 20 July 1825, with heavy sarcasm: "Why, then, do you still want a sonata from me?! You have a whole army of composers who can do it much better than I can. Give each of them a measure—what marvelous work may be expected from it? Here's to your Austrian Verein, which knows how to bring a cobbler's patch to perfection!" *Briefe*, vol. 6, p. 115 (no. 2017), *Letters to Beethoven and Other Correspondence*, ed. Theodore Albrecht, 3 vols. (Lincoln: University of Nebraska Press, 1996), vol. 3, p. 73 (no. 392, translation amended).

26. Kenneth Burke, "Exceptional Improvisation," review of *Some Versions of Pastoral* by William Empson, in *Poetry: A Magazine of Verse* 49 (1937): 347–50, at p. 348. See Empson, *Some Versions of Pastoral* (Norfolk, Conn.: New Directions, 1960), esp. pp. 84, 186–87, 239–40.

27. For stimulating remarks on cognate issues, see Edward W. Said, *Beginnings: Intention and Method* (New York: Columbia University Press, 1975, reprint 1985), pp. 29–42, 72–76; and Edward T. Cone, *Musical Form and Musical Performance* (New York: Norton, 1968), pp. 15–19.

28. Ernst Bloch, *Das Prinzip Hoffnung*, vol. 1 (Berlin: Aufbau-Verlag, 1954), p. 32.

29. See Solomon, *Beethoven*, p. 398.

Chapter 2. Beyond Classicism

1. Hugo Riemann, *Dictionnaire de musique* (Paris: Payot, 1931), p. 1132.

2. C. Hubert H. Parry, *Style in Musical Art* (London: Macmillan, 1911), p. 326.

3. Arnold Schmitz, *Das romantische Beethovenbild* (Berlin and Bonn: Dümmler, 1927); Ludwig Schiedermair, *Der junge Beethoven* (Leipzig: Quelle & Mayer, 1925); Jean Boyer, *Le 'Romantisme' de Beethoven* (Paris: Didier, 1938). See also William S. Newman, "The Beethoven Mystique in Romantic Art, Literature, and Music," *Musical Quarterly* 69 (1983): 354–87.

4. Tagebuch, in Solomon, *Beethoven Essays*, p. 258 (no. 43).

5. Friedrich Schlegel, *Lyceum* fragment no. 104, trans. Peter Firchow, *Friedrich Schlegel's Lucinde and the Fragments* (Minneapolis: University of Minnesota Press, 1971), p. 155.

6. Walter Riezler, *Beethoven* (London: Forrester, 1938), p. 106.

7. Paul Henry Lang, *Music in Western Civilization* (New York: Norton, 1940), p. 752.

8. Charles Rosen, *The Classical Style* (New York: Viking, 1971), pp. 380, 381, 384, 389, 393, 350.

9. Ibid., pp. 403, 379, 445, 384.

10. Ibid., p. 385; see also p. 379.

11. Rosen, *Sonata Forms*, rev. ed. (New York: Norton, 1980), p. 354.

12. For a related critique of exclusively formalist or technical criticism (the so-called *rein Musikalische*) see Hans Heinrich Eggebrecht, "Beethoven und der Begriff der Klassik," in *Beethoven-Symposion Wien 1970: Bericht,* ed. Erich Schenk (Vienna: Böhlaus, 1971), p. 59.

13. Joseph Kerman, "Theme and Variations," review of *Sonata Forms,* by Charles Rosen, *New York Review of Books,* 23 October 1980, p. 51.

14. Rosen, *Sonata Forms,* p. 354.

15. Kerman, "Theme and Variations," p. 53. Here Kerman may (or may not) be surprised to find himself allied to Richard Wagner, who also emphasized that sonata form is scarcely identical with, let alone exhausted by, the Classical style. Wagner perceived that the "same structure" could be found in Beethoven's last works as in his first: "But let us compare these works with each other," he exclaimed, "and wonder at the entirely new world which meets us there, almost in precisely the same form!" Wagner, *Beethoven,* trans. A. R. Parsons (New York: Schirmer, 1872), p. 52.

16. Rosen, *The Classical Style,* pp. 83, 82; see also pp. 74–75.

17. Ibid., p. 83.

18. Erwin Panofsky, "Artist, Scientist, Genius: Notes on the 'Renaissance-Dämmerung,'" in *The Renaissance: A Symposium, February 8–10 1952* (New York: Metropolitan Museum of Art, 1953), p. 78.

19. Friedrich Blume, entry, "Romantik," *Die Musik in Geschichte und Gegenwart,* 17 vols. (Kassel: Bärenreiter, 1949–86), vol. 11, col. 892; Blume, *Classic and Romantic Music: A Comprehensive Survey,* trans. M. D. Herter Norton (New York: Norton, 1970), p. 124. Dahlhaus similarly remarks upon "the simultaneity of the Classical and Romantic." Carl Dahlhaus, "Musik und Romantik," in *Musik-Edition-Interpretation: Gedenkschrift Günter Henle,* ed. Martin Bente (Munich: Henle, 1980), p. 136.

20. Blume, *Classic and Romantic Music,* p. 129.

21. Ibid., p. 127.

22. Baensch claims that such polarities as Classic and Romantic, Apollonian and Dionysian, tragic and comic are "basically nothing but vague collective terms for feelings we find qualitatively related, though we cannot further demonstrate this relationship by anything in the feelings themselves, and cannot reduce it to distinct character-

istics." Otto Baensch, "Art and Feeling," in *Reflections on Art*, ed. Susanne K. Langer (New York: Oxford University Press, 1961), p. 33.

23. Schmitz, *Das romantische Beethovenbild*, p. 178. Similar views are found in Paul Bekker, *Beethoven* (Munich: Schuster & Loeffler, 1911), p. 61, trans. M. M. Bozman as *Beethoven* (London: Dent, 1925), p. 61.

24. Wagner, *Beethoven*, p. 52 (translation amended).

25. In the following, I cite reviews in *AmZ* as typical of Beethoven criticism up to ca. 1815. After 1815, Romanticist devotees of Beethoven were in charge of such publications as *Wiener AmZ*, Schott's *Cäcilia*, and Schlesinger's *Berliner AmZ* (hereafter *BamZ*). For Haydn's reported reactions to Beethoven's music, see Solomon, *Beethoven*, chap. 8, pp. 98–103.

26. *AmZ* 1 (1798–99), col. 571.

27. *AmZ* 7 (1804–5), col. 321.

28. *AmZ* 7 (1804–5), col. 501. A later review withdrew the critique, finding the "greatest unity, with clarity and purity alongside the greatest complexity." *AmZ* 9 (1806–7), col. 497.

29. *AmZ* 9 (1806–7), col. 433.

30. *AmZ* 20 (1818), col. 792.

31. *AmZ* 3 (1800–1801), col. 800.

32. *AmZ* 9 (1806–7), col. 400.

33. *AmZ* 13 (1811), col. 349.

34. *AmZ* 13 (1811), cols. 349–51.

35. *AmZ* 28 (1826), cols. 310–11.

36. Ludwig Spohr, *Autobiography*, 2 vols. (London: Longmans, Green, 1865; reprint, New York: Da Capo, 1969), vol. 1, p. 213.

37. Carl Maria von Weber, letter of 1 May 1810 to Hans Georg Nägeli, in *Letters of Distinguished Musicians*, ed. Ludwig Nohl, trans. Lady Wallace (London: Longmans, Green, 1867), p. 209.

38. Letter of 25 May 1830 to Fanny Mendelssohn-Hensel, in Felix Mendelssohn-Bartholdy, *Reisebriefe aus den Jahren 1830 bis 1832*, 4th ed., edited by Paul Mendelssohn-Bartholdy (Leipzig: H. Mendelssohn, 1862), p. 8; quoted in Romain Rolland, *Goethe and Beethoven*, trans. G. A. Pfister and E. S. Kemp (New York and London: Harper, 1931), p. 69.

39. Franz Schubert, diary entry of 16 June 1816, in *Schubert: A Documentary Biography*, ed. Otto Erich Deutsch (London: Dent, 1946), p. 64.

40. Georg Wilhelm Friedrich Hegel, *The Philosophy of Fine Art*, trans. F. P. B. Osmaston, 4 vols. (London: Bell, 1920), vol. 3, p. 406. See also vol. 3, pp. 353, 417.

41. *Grillparzer's Werke*, ed. August Sauer, part 2, *Tagebücher und literarische Skizzenhefte*, vol. 3 (Vienna and Leipzig: Gerlach & Wiedling, 1916), pp. 171–72 (no. 2174); trans.

Gustav Pollak, *Franz Grillparzer and the Austrian Drama* (New York: Dodd, Mead, 1907), pp. 427–28. For additional classicizing rejections of Beethoven's music, see Solomon, *Beethoven*, pp. 353–54.

42. Schindler-Moscheles, pp. vii–viii.

43. Carl Czerny, *On the Proper Performance of All of Beethoven's Works for the Piano* (Vienna: Universal, 1970), p. 16.

44. *BamZ* 2 (1825): 166.

45. *BamZ* 5 (1828): 467.

46. *Revue musicale* 4 (1930): 279–86, 345–51, quoted by Kunze, p. 581.

47. René Wellek, *A History of Modern Criticism, 1750–1950*, 7 vols. (New Haven and London: Yale University Press, 1955–91), vol. 2, p. 1.

48. *Athenaeum* 1 (1798); in *Friedrich Schlegel 1794–1802: seine prosaischen Jugendschriften*, ed. Jakob Minor, 2 vols. in 1 (Vienna: C. Konegen, 1882), vol. 2, p. 220; trans. Firchow, *Schlegel's* Lucinde *and the Fragments*, p. 175.

49. E. T. A. Hoffmann, review of Beethoven's Fifth Symphony, *AmZ* 12 (1809–10), col. 633, in *E. T. A. Hoffmann's Musical Writings: "Kreisleriana," "The Poet and the Composer," Music Criticism*, ed. David Charlton, trans. Martyn Clarke (Cambridge: Cambridge University Press, 1989), p. 238. For an overview of Hoffmann's Beethoven criticism, see Peter Schnaus, *E. T. A. Hoffmann als Beethoven-Rezensent der Allgemeinen musikalischen Zeitung* (Munich and Salzburg: Katzbichler, 1977).

50. Extending Hoffmann's position, A. B. Marx proposed that Beethoven composed each of his works according to a "specific conception" or "fundamental idea *[Grundidee]*" that was the foundation of "the connectedness, unity, and harmony of its apparently discordant features." *BamZ* 6 (1829): 169–70; quoted by Kunze, p. 594.

51. Hoffmann, review of Beethoven's Fifth Symphony, *AmZ* 12 (1809–10), col. 633, trans. in *Hoffmann's Musical Writings*, p. 238.

52. Arthur Schopenhauer, *The World as Will and Representation*, trans. E. F. J. Payne, 2 vols. (1958; reprint, New York: Dover, 1966), vol. 2, p. 450.

53. August Wilhelm Schlegel, *Ueber dramatische Kunst und Litteratur*, 2nd ed., 3 vols. (Heidelberg: Mohr und Winter, 1817), vol. 3, pp. 14–15 (lecture 22), *A Course of Lectures on Dramatic Art and Literature*, trans. John Black, revised by Rev. A. J. W. Morrison (London: Bohn, 1846), p. 343.

54. Friedrich Schiller, "On Naive and Sentimental Poetry," in *The Works of Friedrich Schiller: Aesthetical and Philosophical Essays*, ed. Nathan Haskell Dole (New York: Bigelow, Brown, 1902), unnumbered vol. [2], p. 44.

55. Heiligenstadt Testament, 6–10 October 1802, *Briefe*, vol. 1, p. 123 (no. 106), *Letters*, vol. 3, pp. 1353–54 (appendix A).

56. "Zusammengestohlen aus Verschiedenem diesem u. jenem." Written on the autograph copy provided to the publisher, Schotts Söhne. Kinsky-Halm, p. 397.

57. Schiller, "On Naive and Sentimental Poetry," vol. 2, p. 52.

Chapter 3. Some Romantic Images

1.   Letter to Franz Gerhard Wegeler, ca. 1794–96, *Briefe*, vol. 1, p. 27 (no. 19), *Letters*, vol. 1, p. 21 (no. 15). See facsimile in *Beethoven als Freund der Familie Wegeler–v. Breuning*, ed. Stephan Ley (Bonn: F. Cohen, 1927), following p. 40. Several other "mistakes" in Beethoven's letters and autograph scores are noted by Alan Tyson in "Prolegomena to a Future Edition of Beethoven's Letters," *Beethoven Studies*, ed. Alan Tyson, vol. 2 (London: Oxford University Press, 1977), pp. 6–7.

2.   Sigmund Freud, *The Psychopathology of Everyday Life*, vol. 6 of *The Standard Edition of the Complete Psychological Works of Sigmund Freud*, ed. James Strachey in collaboration with Anna Freud and assisted by Alix Strachey and Alan Tyson, 24 vols. (London, 1953–75), p. 191.

3.   Quoted in *Beethovens Sämtliche Briefe*, ed. A. C. Kalischer, rev. Theodor v. Frimmel, 5 vols. (Berlin and Leipzig: Schuster & Loeffler, 1908–11), vol. 2, p. 291 n. (formerly in the Joseph Joachim collection). See also Hans Boettcher, *Beethoven als Liederkomponist* (Augsburg: Benno Filser, 1928), p. 48 n. 62.

4.   Letter to Therese Malfatti, May 1810, *Briefe*, vol. 2, p. 122 (no. 442), *Letters*, vol. 1, p. 273 (no. 258).

5.   On a folio sheet, alongside Beethoven's inscription of Herder's poem "Macht des Gesanges," at present on loan from the heirs of Stefan Zweig to the British Library, Department of Manuscripts, Loan 95 15. First published in Ludwig Nohl, *Beethoven's Brevier* (Leipzig: Günther, 1870), p. 104 n. See also *Führer durch die Beethoven Zentenar-Ausstellung der Stadt Wien 1927* (Vienna: Selbstverlag der Gemeinde Wien, 1927), no. 529.

6.   Therese von Brunsvik, memoirs, in La Mara, *Beethovens unsterbliche Geliebte: Das Geheimnis der Gräfin Brunsvik und ihre Memoiren* (Leipzig: Breitkopf & Härtel, 1909), p. 64; *Beethoven: Impressions of Contemporaries,* trans. O. G. Sonneck (New York: Schirmer, 1926), pp. 34–35.

7.   La Mara, *Beethovens unsterbliche Geliebte,* p. 58.

8.   Novalis, *Henry von Ofterdingen,* trans. Palmer Hilty (New York: Ungar, 1964), p. 15.

9.   Ibid., p. 33.

10.   Hölderlin, "Unter den Alpen gesungen," verses 10–12, in *Sämtliche Werke,* ed. Friedrich Beißner, 7 vols. in 12 (Stuttgart: Cotta; Kohlhammer, 1946–72), vol. 2, part 1, p. 44.

11.   Schiller, "Die Götter Griechenlands," in *Schillers Werke: Nationalausgabe,* ed. Julius Petersen and Gerhard Fricke, 42 vols. (Weimar: H. Böhlaus Nachfolger, 1943–84), vol. 1, p. 194, *The Works of Friedrich Schiller: Poems,* ed. Nathan Haskell Dole, trans. E. P. Arnold Forster (New York: Bigelow and Brown, 1902), unnumbered vol. [3], p. 159.

12.   Walter D. Wetzels, "Aspects of Natural Science in German Romanticism," *Studies in Romanticism* 19 (1971): 58.

13.   Novalis, *Schriften: Die Werke Friedrich von Hardenbergs,* ed. Paul Kluckhohn, Richard Samuel, et al., 4 vols. (Stuttgart: W. Kohlhammer, 1960–75), vol. 3, p. 664.

14. Maynard Solomon, "The Ninth Symphony: A Search for Order," in *Beethoven Essays*, p. 10.

15. Novalis, *Gesammelte Werke*, ed. Carl Seelig, 5 vols. (Zürich: Bühl, 1945), vol. 3, p. 266. An extensive discussion of the Romantic interchangeability of the arts may be found in the sometimes unreliable monograph by Irving Babbitt, *The New Laokoon: An Essay on the Confusion of the Arts* (Boston and New York: Houghton Mifflin, 1910). Babbitt saw all this as contributing to the "eclipse of reason" (p. 82).

16. A. W. Schlegel, "Die Gemählde," *Athenaeum: Eine Zeitschrift* 2, no. 1 (1799): 49–50.

17. Letter to Carl Friedrich Kunz, 24 March 1814, *Selected Letters of E. T. A. Hoffmann*, ed. and trans. Johanna C. Sahlin (Chicago and London: University of Chicago Press, 1977), p. 225.

18. Tieck, *Phantasien*, quoted by Oskar Walzel, *German Romanticism*, 5th ed., trans. Alma Elise Lussky (New York: Ungar, 1965), p. 125.

19. Schiller, *Sämtliche Werke: Historisch-kritische Ausgabe*, ed. Otto Güntter and Georg Witkowski, 20 vols. (Leipzig: Hesse & Becker, 1909–11), vol. 18, p. 83; English trans. in René Wellek, *A History of Modern Criticism*, vol. 1 (New Haven: Yale University Press, 1955), p. 251.

20. *The Poetical Works of William Wordsworth*, ed. Thomas Hutchinson (London: Henry Frowde, 1906), p. 631.

21. E. T. A. Hoffmann, "Kreisleriana: Part II," in *E. T. A. Hoffmann's Musical Writings: "Kreisleriana," "The Poet and the Composer," Music Criticism*, ed. David Charlton, trans. Martyn Clarke (Cambridge: Cambridge University Press, 1989), p. 130; see also Ronald Taylor, *Hoffmann* (New York: Hillary House, 1963), p. 62.

22. Walter Pater, "The School of Giorgione," in *The Renaissance: Studies in Art and Poetry* (London: Macmillan, 1914), pp. 134–35, reprinted in *Selected Writings of Walter Pater*, ed. Harold Bloom (New York: New American Library, 1974), pp. 55, 54.

23. "[G]edichtet . . . von Lud. van Beethoven" on the title page of the "Namensfeier" Overture, op. 115 (quoted by Kinsky-Halm, p. 333); and "Aufgabe von Ludwig van Beethoven gedichtet" on the title-page of Archduke Rudolph's Forty Variations for Piano on a Theme ["O Hoffnung," WoO 200] by Beethoven (Vienna: Steiner, 1819).

24. Jorge Luis Borges, "The Thousand and One Nights," in *Seven Nights*, trans. Eliot Weinberger (New York: New Directions, 1984), p. 42; *Confessions of St. Augustine*, book 11, section 14.

25. M. H. Abrams, "The Correspondent Breeze," in *English Romantic Poets: Modern Essays in Criticism*, ed. Abrams (Oxford and New York: Oxford University Press, 1960), p. 44.

26. Ibid., pp. 49–50. Abrams felt that the potential for increased understanding outweighed these risks: "in the course of time, a new metaphor arises which demonstrates its revelatory power at the same time that it reveals the inadequacies of preceding metaphors, is exploited until it becomes the predominant metaphor of an era, and is in turn displaced from its central position, yet . . . keeps recurring persistently in later eras."

Abrams, "A Reply," in *High Romantic Argument: Essays for M. H. Abrams,* ed. Lawrence Lipking (Ithaca: Cornell University Press, 1981), p. 172.

27. See Alexander G. F. Gode–von Aesch, *Natural Science in German Romanticism* (New York: Columbia University Press, 1941), p. 94 n. 8.

28. Abrams, "The Correspondent Breeze," p. 51.

29. Ibid., pp. 37–38.

30. For the regenerative symbolism of the four winds—variously the tyrannous, good, roaring, and gentle—in Romantic poetry, see W. H. Auden, *The Enchafèd Flood: or, The Romantic Iconography of the Sea* (Charlottesville: University Press of Virginia, 1950; reprint, 1979), pp. 75–81; also, Geoffrey Grigson, *The Harp of Aeolus and other Essays on Art, Literature and Nature* (London: Routledge, 1947), pp. 24–46.

31. Shelley, "Ode to the West Wind"; Wordsworth, *The Prelude* (1805), opening lines.

32. Wetzels, "Aspects of Natural Science in German Romanticism," p. 58 (on Ritter).

33. Ibid., p. 59 (on Novalis).

34. Tagebuch, in Solomon, *Beethoven Essays,* pp. 279–80 (nos. 105, 106, 108).

35. Goethe to Schiller, 8 December 1798, in *Der Briefwechsel zwischen Schiller und Goethe,* ed. H. G. Gräf and A. Leitzmann, 3 vols. (Stuttgart: Insel, 1955), vol. 2, p. 174 (no. 546), quoted by Moriz Sondheim in "Shakespeare and the Astrology of His Time," *Journal of the Warburg Institute* 2 (1939): pp. 243–44.

36. Northrop Frye, "The Drunken Boat: The Revolutionary Element in Romanticism," in *The Stubborn Structure: Essays on Criticism and Society* (Ithaca: Cornell University Press, 1970), p. 209.

37. *Des Bonner Bäckermeisters Gottfried Fischer: Aufzeichnungen über Beethovens Jugend,* ed. Joseph Schmidt-Görg (Bonn: Beethovenhaus, 1971), p. 69.

38. Christoph Christian Sturm, *Betrachtungen über die Werke Gottes im Reich der Natur,* 3rd ed. (Halle, 1784), *Reflections on the Works of God in Nature and Providence, for Every Day in the Year,* trans. Adam Clarke (Baltimore: Armstrong and Plaskitt, 1822), p. 270, entry for 10 June, entitled "Immensity of the Firmament."

39. Letter to Franz Brunsvik, 13 February 1814, *Briefe,* vol. 3, p. 8 (no. 696), *Letters,* vol. 1, p. 445 (no. 462).

40. Carl Czerny, *On the Proper Performance of All of Beethoven's Works for the Piano* (Vienna: Universal, 1970), p. 9 (translation amended).

41. Quoted by Ludwig Nohl, *Beethoven, Liszt, Wagner: Ein Bild der Kunstbewegung unseres Jahrhunderts* (Vienna: Braumüller, 1874), p. 111; for a parallel report, see Karl Holz to Otto Jahn, quoted in Kerst, vol. 2, p. 185.

42. For a thorough survey, see Julius Petersen, "Das goldene Zeitalter bei den deutschen Romantikern," in *Die Ernte: Abhandlungen zur Literaturwissenschaft. Franz Muncker zu seinem 70. Geburtstage,* ed. Fritz Strich and Hans Heinrich Borcherdt (Halle: Max Niemeyer, 1926), pp. 119–75.

43. "Von den unterschiedenen Gegenständen des Gefühls vom Erhabenen und Schö-

nen," in *Immanuel Kants Werke*, ed. Ernst Cassirer et al., 11 vols. (Berlin: B. Cassirer, 1912–22), vol. 2, p. 247.

44. Tagebuch, in Solomon, *Beethoven Essays*, p. 265 (no. 61).

45. Edmund Burke, *Philosophical Enquiry into the Origin of Our Ideas of the Sublime and Beautiful* (London: R. and J. Dodsley, 1757), here quoted from Kant, *Critique of Aesthetic Judgement*, trans. James Creed Meredith (Oxford: Clarendon Press, 1911), p. 130.

46. Frye, *A Study of English Romanticism* (Chicago: University of Chicago Press, 1968; reprint, 1982), p. 9.

47. Tagebuch, in Solomon, *Beethoven Essays*, p. 266 (no. 62).

48. Opening words of the "Schlußwort" to Immanuel Kant, *Kritik der praktischen Vernunft*, in *Immanuel Kants Werke*, vol. 5, p. 174, trans. in *The Philosophy of Kant: Immanuel Kant's Moral and Political Writings*, ed. Carl J. Friedrich (New York: Modern Library, 1949), p. 261. The passage continues: "The first [the wonder of the starred heaven] begins with the place I occupy in the external world of sense, and expands the connection in which I find myself into the incalculable vastness of worlds upon worlds, of systems within systems, over endless ages of their periodic motion, their beginnings and perpetuation. The second [the wonder of the moral law within] starts from my invisible self, from my personality, and depicts me as in a world possessing true infinitude which can be sensed only by the intellect. . . . The first view of a numberless quantity of worlds destroys my importance. . . . The second view raises my value infinitely, as an *intelligence*, through my personality." *Werke*, vol. 5, p. 174, *The Philosophy of Kant*, pp. 261–62.

49. *Konversationshefte*, vol. 1, p. 235 (Heft 7, 17r).

50. Rudolf Unger, " 'Der bestirnte Himmel über mir . . . ': Zur geistesgeschichtlichen Deutung eines Kant-Wortes," *Gesammelte Studien, II: Aufsätze zur Literatur- und Geistesgeschichte* (Berlin: Junker und Dünnhaupt, 1929; reprint, Darmstadt: Wissenschaftliche Buchgesellschaft, 1966), p. 61.

51. Kant, *Critique of Aesthetic Judgement*, p. 90.

52. Alan Tyson, "Beethoven's Heroic Phase," *Musical Times* 110 (1969): 140.

53. Aileen Ward, "Romantic Castles and Real Prisons: Wordsworth, Blake, and Revolution," *The Wordsworth Circle* 30, no. 1 (Winter 1999): 4, 8.

54. Ward, "Romantic Castles," p. 12

55. Ward, "Romantic Castles," pp. 6, 11.

56. Victor Brombert, *The Romantic Prison: The French Tradition* (Princeton: Princeton University Press, 1978), p. 5. See also Lorenz Eitner, "Cages, Prisons, and Captives in Eighteenth-Century Art," in *Images of Romanticism: Verbal and Visual Affinities*, ed. Karl Kroeber and William Walling (New Haven: Yale University Press, 1978), pp. 13–38.

57. Brombert, *The Romantic Prison*, p. 58.

58. For the equation of "darkness" and "deafness," see Tyson, "Beethoven's Heroic Phase," p. 141.

59. Heiligenstadt Testament, 6–10 October 1802, *Briefe*, vol. 1, p. 122 (no. 106), *Letters*, vol. 3, pp. 1351–52 (appendix A). Cf. "In my present condition I must withdraw from everything," letter to Karl Amenda, 1 July 1801, *Briefe*, vol. 1, p. 85 (no. 67), *Letters*, vol. 1, p. 64, (no. 53); and "I am living—alone—alone! alone! alone!" Letter to Karl August Varnhagen von Ense, 14 July 1812, *Briefe*, vol. 2, p. 273 (no. 583), *Letters*, vol. 1, p. 377 (no. 374).

60. Letter to Franz Gerhard Wegeler, 16 November 1801, *Briefe*, vol. 1, p. 89 (no. 70), *Letters*, vol. 1, p. 67 (no. 54).

61. The words "Les derniers soupirs" are written by Beethoven on a sketch for the Adagio. Nottebohm, *Zweite Beethoveniana*, p. 485. Karl Amenda reported Beethoven's remark that the movement was intended to describe the scene in the burial vault of Shakespeare's "Romeo and Juliet." Wilhelm von Lenz, *Beethoven: Eine Kunststudie*, 6 vols. (Hamburg: Hoffman & Campe, 1855–60), vol. 4, part 3, p. 17; Thayer-Forbes, p. 261.

62. Beethoven took expression indications seriously, calling them "the words describing the character of the composition" and emphasizing that they *"certainly refer to the spirit of the composition."* Letter to Ignaz Franz Mosel, 1817, *Briefe*, vol. 4, p. 130 (no. 1196), *Letters*, vol. 2, p. 727 (no. 845).

63. Abrams, "Structure and Style in the Greater Romantic Lyric," in *Romanticism and Consciousness: Essays in Criticism*, ed. Harold Bloom (New York: Norton, 1970), p. 227.

64. Auden, *The Enchafèd Flood*, p. 21.

65. Letter to Wegeler, 29 June 1801, *Briefe*, vol. 1, p. 80 (no. 65), *Letters*, vol. 1, p. 60 (no. 51).

66. Tagebuch, p. 269 (no. 66); see also p. 258 (no. 41).

67. Quoted by Nohl, *Beethoven's Brevier*, p. 104 n. See note 5 above.

68. *Konversationshefte*, vol. 6, p. 363 (Heft 76, 20r–20v).

69. Joseph Schmidt-Görg, "Missa solemnis: Beethoven in seinem Werk," in *Bericht über den internationalen musikwissenschaftlichen Kongress Bonn 1970*, ed. Carl Dahlhaus et al. (Basel: Bärenreiter, 1971), p. 19. "Das Resultat des Friedens ist Ruhe, ist Lustigkeit" (Beethoven-Haus Bonn, BH. 109, S. 10); "auch der Sopran kann seine innere Ruhe und Freude als Friedenszeuge in hohen Tönen zeigen" (Grasnick 5 DStB Bl. 28r). In the autograph, Beethoven initially worded the heading, "Darstellend den innern und äussern Frieden" (Nottebohm, *Zweite Beethoveniana*, p. 151). Kirkendale argues that Beethoven's heading "is deeply rooted in ancient theological concepts." Warren Kirkendale, "New Roads to Old Ideas in Beethoven's *Missa Solemnis*," *Musical Quarterly* 56 (1970): 697.

70. Tagebuch, p. 284 (no. 126).

71. Heiligenstadt Testament, 6–10 October 1802, *Briefe*, vol. 1, p. 123 (no. 106), *Letters*, vol. 3, p. 1354 (appendix A).

72. Joseph Kerman, *"An die ferne Geliebte,"* in *Beethoven Studies*, ed. Alan Tyson (New York: Norton, 1973), [vol. 1,] p. 129.

73. Ibid.; see Paul Bekker, *Beethoven* (London: Dent, 1925), p. 256.

74. Letter to Therese Malfatti, May 1810, *Briefe*, vol. 2, p. 122 (no. 442), *Letters*, vol. 1, pp. 272–73 (no. 258).

75. Letter to Countess Deym, 20 September 1807, *Briefe*, vol. 1, p. 324 (no. 294), *Letters*, vol. 1, p. 175 (no. 151).

76. Letter to Marie and Paul Bigot de Morogues, shortly after 5 March 1807, *Briefe*, vol. 1, pp. 306–7 (no. 273), *Letters*, vol. 1, p. 165 (no. 139).

77. Letter to Joseph Wilhelm von Schaden, 15 September 1787, *Briefe*, vol. 1, p. 5 (no. 3), *Letters*, vol. 1, p. 3 (no. 1).

78. Letter to Therese Malfatti, May 1810, *Briefe*, vol. 2, p. 122 (no. 442), *Letters*, vol. 1, p. 272 (no. 258).

79. Letter to the "Immortal Beloved," 6–7 July 1812, *Briefe*, vol. 2, p. 271 (no. 582), *Letters*, vol. 1, p. 376 (no. 373).

80. Novalis, *Schriften*, vol. 2, p. 47; Gode–von Aesch, *Natural Science in German Romanticism*, p. 108.

81. Friedrich Schlegel, *Ideas*, no. 1, in *Friedrich Schlegel's* Lucinde *and the Fragments*, ed. and trans. Peter Firchow (Minneapolis: University of Minnesota Press, 1971), p. 241.

82. Novalis, *Schriften*, vol. 1, p. 14.

83. Friedrich Schlegel, *Ideas*, no. 128, in Firchow, p. 253.

84. For the dissemination of the Veil of Isis trope and the Masonic route by which it evidently came to Beethoven's attention, see below, chapter 7, pp. 146–50, and pp. 281–82, nn. 61–62. See also Jurgis Baltrusaitis, *La Quête d'Isis: Introduction à l'égyptomanie* (Paris: O. Perrin, 1967).

85. *The Works of Friedrich Schiller: Poems*, pp. 227–29.

86. *Herzensergießungen eines kunstliebenden Klosterbruders*, quoted by Gode–von Aesch, p. 99.

87. "Paralipomena zu 'Die Lehrlinge zu Sais,'" in Novalis, *Schriften*, vol. 1, p. 110. "Einem gelang es—er hob den Schleier der Göttin zu Sais / Aber was sah er? Er sah— Wunder des Wunders—sich selbst."

88. Wegeler Collection, Beethoven-Archiv, Bonn. Facsimile in Stephan Ley, ed., *Beethovens Leben in authentischen Bildern und Texten* (Berlin: Cassirer, 1925), p. 129.

89. Letter to Tobias Haslinger, 10 September 1821, *Briefe*, vol. 4, p. 447 (no. 1439), *Letters*, vol. 2, p. 922 (no. 1056).

90. Letter of 19 September 1815, *Briefe*, vol. 3, p. 162 (no. 829), *Letters*, vol. 2, pp. 527–28 (no. 563).

91. "Cassandra" (1802), in *The Works of Friedrich Schiller: Poems*, p. 209.

92. Henry David Thoreau, *Walden, or Life in the Woods* (Boston: Ticknor and Fields, 1854), reprinted in *The Norton Anthology of American Literature*, ed. Ronald Gottesman et al. (New York and London: Norton, 1979), vol. 1, p. 1593.

Chapter 4. Pastoral, Rhetoric, Structure

1.   Bion, Idyll 1, "The Lament for Adonis," in *Theocritus, Bion and Moschus Rendered into English Prose,* ed. and trans. Andrew Lang (London: Macmillan, 1901), pp. 172–73. Classical pastoral poetry was known in German translation during Beethoven's time, e.g., *Theokritos, Bion und Moschos,* trans. Johann Heinrich Voß (Tübingen: J. G. Cotta, 1808).

2.   See Wye Jamison Allanbrook, *Rhythmic Gesture in Mozart: "Le nozze di Figaro" and "Don Giovanni"* (Chicago and London: University of Chicago Press, 1983).

3.   Renato Poggioli, *The Oaten Flute: Essays on Pastoral Poetry and the Pastoral Ideal* (Cambridge: Harvard University Press, 1975), p. 9; see also pp. 135–36, 322. For an eloquent discussion and brief taxonomy of such interludes, which he terms "pastoral insets," see Andrew V. Ettin, *Literature and the Pastoral* (New Haven and London: Yale University Press, 1984), pp. 75–81.

4.   Allanbrook, *Rhythmic Gesture in Mozart,* pp. 131, 136, 173.

5.   Empson perceives "a natural connection between heroic and pastoral . . . they belong to the same play—they are the two stock halves of the double plot. It is felt that you cannot have a proper hero without a proper people." William Empson, *Some Versions of Pastoral* (London: Chatto & Windus, 1935; reprint, Norfolk, Conn.: New Directions, 1960), p. 186.

6.   See Leonard Ratner, *Classic Music: Expression, Form, and Style* (New York: Schirmer Books, 1980); Allanbrook, *Rhythmic Gesture in Mozart;* V. Kofi Agawu, *Playing with Signs: A Semiotic Interpretation of Classic Music* (Princeton: Princeton University Press, 1991); Adolf Sandberger, *Ausgewählte Aufsätze zur Musikgeschichte,* 2 vols. (Munich: Drei Masken, 1921–24), vol. 2, pp. 201–12; Willi Kahl, "Zu Beethovens Naturauffassung," in Arnold Schmitz, ed., *Beethoven und die Gegenwart: Festschrift [. . .] Ludwig Schiedermair* (Berlin and Bonn: Dümmler, 1937), pp. 220–65; F. E. Kirby, "Beethoven's Pastoral Symphony as a *Sinfonia caracteristica,*" *Musical Quarterly* 56 (1970): 605–23; Geoffrey Chew, "Pastorale," in *New Grove,* vol. 14, pp. 290–95; idem, "The Christmas Pastorella in Austria, Bohemia and Moravia" (Ph.D. diss., University of Manchester, 1968).

7.   Nottebohm, *Zweite Beethoveniana,* pp. 504, 378; see also Thayer-Deiters-Riemann, vol. 3, pp. 97–99, and Thayer-Forbes, p. 436. Influential eighteenth-century theorists tended to scorn naturalistic and imitative effects in music. See chapter 5, at n. 17.

8.   Early critics such as Wilhelm von Lenz and a reviewer writing in 1819 for the *Wiener Allgemeine musikalische Zeitung* readily spotted the sonata's pastoral style, as did such later writers as Herwegh, D'Indy, and Cobbett. See Wilhelm von Lenz, *Beethoven: Eine Kunst-Studie: Kritischer Katalog sämmtlicher Werke Ludwig van Beethovens mit Analysen derselben* (Hamburg: Hoffman & Campe, 1860), vol. 4, part 3, pp. 267–82; *Wiener Allgemeine musikalische Zeitung* 3 (1819), cols. 633–35, quoted by Kunze, pp. 324–25; Marcel Herwegh, *Technique d'interprétation . . . appliqué aux sonates pour piano et violon de Beethoven* (Paris: Magasin Musical, 1926), pp. 170–78; Vincent D'Indy, *Beethoven: A Critical Biography,* trans. Theodore Baker (Boston: Boston Music Co., 1912), p. 62; *Cobbett's Cyclo-*

pedic Survey of Chamber Music, ed. Walter Willson Cobbett, 2nd ed., rev. C. Mason (London: Oxford University Press, 1963), vol. 1, pp. 91–92.

9.   Approaching the significance of key choice from a practical perspective, Paul Bekker concluded that "Beethoven's choice of keys in his orchestral works derived from the tonal sphere of the dominant instruments." Paul Bekker, *The Orchestra* (New York: Norton, 1936, reprint, 1963), p. 112. He thinks that explains why trumpet-dominated orchestrations are in C and orchestrations featuring horns are in E-flat. "C is not more triumphant than C-sharp, but C is the tone most natural to the mechanism of the trumpets," and that is why works with "triumphal trumpet culminations" like the Fifth Symphony and the *Leonore* overtures are in C (p. 111). One implication is that E-flat major may be by association the key in which to evoke the sound of the horn, even when the music is written for other instruments.

10.   Joseph Kerman observes that the violin's move to G–E♭–B♭ and then to B♭–A♭–G (mm. 11–14) "seems to expand the horncall," transforming what could be seen as a half-expected cadential echo into a veritable "new beginning" (Kerman, personal communication).

11.   Denis Matthews, *Beethoven* (New York: Vintage, 1988), p. 120.

12.   *Wiener Allgemeine musikalische Zeitung* 3 (1819), cols. 633–35, quoted by Kunze, p. 325.

13.   Nottebohm was the first to observe similarities to "Der Knieriem bleibet, meiner Treu!" composed by J. C. Standfuss for the singspiel *Der lustige Schuster,* a sequel to *Die verwandelten Weiber oder Der Teufel ist los* (1766), which was well-known through later versions of *Der lustige Schuster* with music by Johann Adam Hiller. See Nottebohm, *Beethoveniana,* p. 30; see also Mary Rowen Obelkevich, "The Growth of a Musical Idea: Beethoven's Opus 96," *Current Musicology* 11 (1971): 91–114, at pp. 92–93. The singspiel source is itself reminiscent of a folk tune, "Ich bin nun wie ich bin."

14.   Lenz, *Kritischer Katalog,* vol. 4, part 3, p. 273.

15.   Joseph Kerman, *The Beethoven Quartets* (New York: Knopf, 1967), pp. 201–2.

16.   "Langsam" is apparently one of Beethoven's crucial afterthoughts, appearing in the published score but not in the original autograph.

17.   Lenz, *Kritischer Katalog,* vol. 4, part 3, p. 272. He described the cadenzas as projecting "a plain tonal rapture" unique in Beethoven's music.

18.   Frank Kermode, *The Sense of an Ending: Studies in the Theory of Fiction* (London: Oxford University Press, 1967), p. 18.

19.   "[T]he fugato subject, apparently unrelated to the rest of the movement, is none other than the first twelve notes of the variation theme played in the minor and in even eighth notes." Warren Kirkendale, *Fugue and Fugato in Rococo and Classical Chamber Music,* trans. Margaret Bent and the author (Durham: Duke University Press, 1979), pp. 242–43; Lenz observed the identity of the first seven notes, in *Kritischer Katalog,* vol. 4, part 3, p. 274 n.

Chapter 5. Reason and Imagination

1.   Letter to the directors of the Imperial and Royal theaters in Vienna, before 4 December 1807, *Briefe,* vol. 1, p. 333 (no. 302), *Letters,* vol. 3, p. 1444 (appendix I, no. 1).

2.   Letter to Franz Gerhard Wegeler, 29 June 1801, *Briefe,* vol. 1, p. 79 (no. 65), *Letters,* vol. 1, p. 58 (no. 51).

3.   Letter to Hans Georg Nägeli, 9 September 1824, *Briefe,* vol. 5, p. 362 (no. 1873), *Letters,* vol. 3, p. 1139 (no. 1306).

4.   Letter to Breitkopf & Härtel, 9 August 1812, *Briefe,* vol. 2, p. 287 (no. 591), *Letters,* vol. 1, p. 384 (no. 380).

5.   Letter to Bernhard Schotts Söhne, 17 September 1824, *Briefe,* vol. 5, p. 368 (no. 1881), *Letters,* vol. 3, p. 1141 (no. 1308); letter to Karl van Beethoven, 18 July 1825, *Briefe,* vol. 6, p. 109 (no. 2012), *Letters,* vol. 3, p. 1221 (no. 1402); letter to Emilie M., 17 July 1812, *Briefe,* vol. 2, p. 274 (no. 585), *Letters,* vol. 1, p. 381 (no. 376).

6.   Letter to Christian Gottlob Neefe, between the end of October 1792 and 26 October 1793, *Briefe,* vol. 1, p. 11 (no. 6), *Letters,* vol. 1, p. 9 (no. 6). Max Rudolf suggested that *meiner göttlichen Kunst* could also be rendered as "my God-given art" (personal communication, ca. 1978).

7.   Letter to Breitkopf & Härtel, 28 February 1812, *Briefe,* vol. 2, p. 246 (no. 555), *Letters,* vol. 1, p. 360 (no. 351). The original reads "meiner Himmlischen Kunst."

8.   Letter to Bernhard Schotts Söhne, 17 September 1824, *Briefe,* vol. 5, p. 368 (no. 1881), *Letters,* vol. 3, p. 1141 (no. 1308).

9.   Letter to Karl Amenda, 12 April 1815, *Briefe,* vol. 3, p. 137 (no. 803), *Letters,* vol. 2, p. 509 (no. 541).

10.   Letter to Archduke Rudolph, July–August 1821, *Briefe,* vol. 4, p. 446 (no. 1438), *Letters,* vol. 3, p. 1095 (no. 1248). This can be read as a reference to Rudolph rather than to Beethoven.

11.   Letter to Prince Nikolas Galitzin, ca. 6 July 1825, *Briefe,* vol. 6, p. 96 (no. 2003), *Letters,* vol. 3, p. 1225 (no. 1405, translation amended). Compare Wackenroder: "Alas! there can be no doubt that, stretch our spiritual wings as we may, we cannot escape the earth, for it pulls us back with brutal force and we fall again among the most vulgar of vulgar people." Wilhelm Heinrich Wackenroder and Ludwig Tieck, *Outpourings of an Art-Loving Friar,* trans. Edward Mornin (New York: Ungar, 1975), p. 118.

12.   Letter to Johann Nepomuk Kanka, autumn 1814, *Briefe,* vol. 3, p. 64 (no. 747), *Letters,* vol. 1, p. 474 (no. 502).

13.   Letter to Franz Brunsvik, 13 February 1814, *Briefe,* vol. 3, p. 8 (no. 696), *Letters,* vol. 1, p. 445 (no. 462, translation amended).

14.   Letter to Johann Nepomuk Kanka, autumn 1814, *Briefe,* vol. 3, p. 64 (no. 747), *Letters,* vol. 1, pp. 473–74 (no. 502).

15.   Letter to Nikolaus Zmeskall, 19 February 1812, *Briefe,* vol. 2, p. 244 (no. 553), *Letters,* vol. 1, p. 359 (no. 349). Compare Schiller's "Man raised on the wings of the

imagination leaves the narrow limits of the present, in which mere animality is enclosed, in order to strive on to an unlimited future." Schiller, *Letters on the Aesthetical Education of Man,* letter 24, quoted in *The Works of Friedrich Schiller: Aesthetical and Philosophical Essays,* ed. Nathan Haskell Dole (New York: Bigelow, Brown, 1902), vol. 1, pp. 87–88.

16. Letter to Wilhelm Gerhard, 15 July 1817, *Briefe,* vol. 4, p. 82 (no. 1141), *Letters,* vol. 2, p. 689 (no. 788).

17. Nottebohm, *Zweite Beethoveniana,* p. 375, Thayer-Forbes, p. 436 (translation amended). Beethoven's prescription, "More the expression of feeling than painting *[Mehr Ausdruck der Empfindung als Mahlerei]*" (Nottebohm, *Zweite Beethoveniana,* p. 378) closely parallels a formulation by the theorist Johann Jakob Engel, who wrote, "the composer should always paint feelings rather than objects of feeling." See *Über die musikalische Malerey* (Berlin, 1780), *J. J. Engel's Schriften: Reden und ästhetische Versuche,* vol. 4 (Berlin, 1844), p. 146, trans. Wye J. Allanbrook, "'Ear-Tickling Nonsense': A New Context for Musical Expression in Mozart's 'Haydn' Quartets," *St. John's Review* 38 (1988): 10. For indications that Beethoven may have read Engel, see Adolf Sandberger, "'Mehr Ausdruck der Empfindung als Malerei,'" in *Ausgewählte Aufsätze zur Musikgeschichte,* 2 vols. (Munich: Drei Masken Verlag, 1921–24), vol. 2, pp. 201–12. The influential theorist Johann Georg Sulzer also objected to naturalistic and imitative effects in music: "But such [tone-]painting violates the true spirit of music, which is to express the sentiments of feeling, not to convey images of inanimate objects." *Allgemeine Theorie der schönen Künste,* 2nd ed., 5 vols. (Leipzig: Weidmann, 1792–99), vol. 2, p. 357, quoted in *Aesthetics and the Art of Musical Composition in the German Enlightenment: Selected Writings of Johann Georg Sulzer and Heinrich Christoph Koch,* ed. Nancy Kovaleff Baker and Thomas Christensen (Cambridge: Cambridge University Press, 1995), p. 90.

18. Letter to Karl Wilhelm Henning, 1 January 1825, *Briefe,* vol. 6, p. 3 (no. 1920), *Letters,* vol. 3, p. 1165 (no. 1343).

19. "Hol der Henker das ökonomisch-Musikalische," letter to Breitkopf & Härtel, 21 August 1810, *Briefe,* vol. 2, p. 148 (no. 465), *Letters,* vol. 1, p. 284 (no. 272, translation amended).

20. Letter to Franz Anton Hoffmeister, ca. 15 January 1801, *Briefe,* vol. 1, p. 64 (no. 54, my translation), *Letters,* vol. 1, p. 48 (no. 44). See "Beethoven's *Magazin der Kunst,*" in Solomon, *Beethoven Essays,* pp. 193–204.

21. Draft Statement about a Complete Edition of His Works, undated [ca. 1822–25?], *Letters,* vol. 3, p. 1450 (appendix I, no. 6), *New Beethoven Letters,* ed. Donald W. MacArdle and Ludwig Misch (Norman: University of Oklahoma Press), pp. 395–96 (no. 344), *Ludwig van Beethovens sämtliche Briefe,* 2nd ed., edited by Emerich Kastner and Julius Kapp (Leipzig: Hesse & Becker, [1923]), pp. 631–32 (no. 1051), *Briefe,* vol. 8, as yet unpublished. My translation combines those in *Letters* and *New Beethoven Letters.*

22. Letter to Heinrich von Collin, autumn 1808, *Briefe,* vol. 2, p. 21 (no. 332), *Letters,* vol. 1, p. 197 (no. 175).

23. Letter to Franz Gerhard Wegeler, 16 November 1801, *Briefe,* vol. 1, p. 89 (no. 70), *Letters,* vol. 1, p. 68 (no. 54).

24. Letter to Emilie M., 17 July 1812, *Briefe,* vol. 2, pp. 274–75 (no. 585), *Letters,* vol. 1, p. 381 (no. 376). Lovejoy defined the Faustian aspect of Romanticism as a "demand for a perpetual transcendence of the already-attained, for unceasing expansion." Arthur O. Lovejoy, *The Great Chain of Being: A Study of the History of an Idea* (Cambridge: Harvard University Press, 1936; reprint, New York: Harper Torchbooks, 1960), p. 306.

25. Letter to Christine Gerhardi, 1797 or 1798, *Briefe,* vol. 1, p. 41 (no. 33), *Letters,* vol. 1, p. 29 (no. 23).

26. Immanuel Kant, *The Critique of Aesthetic Judgement,* trans. James Creed Meredith (Oxford: Clarendon Press, 1911), p. 119.

27. Edmund Burke, *Philosophical Enquiry into the Origin of Our Ideas of the Sublime and Beautiful* (London: F. C. and J. Rivington, 1812), pp. 104–5. He added, "a judicious obscurity in some things contributes to the effect of the picture," pp. 106–7. Compare Diderot's "Clarity is all right for convincing; it is of no use for moving. . . . Poets, speak incessantly of eternity, infinitude, immensity, time, space, divinity. . . . Be dark *[soyez ténébreux]!*" quoted by René Wellek, *A History of Modern Criticism: 1750–1950,* vol. 1 (New Haven: Yale University Press, 1955), p. 51.

28. Related ideas were widespread among followers of Schiller and the early Romantics. "In the creations of [the artist's] fantasy the dignity of human nature must be seen. From a lower sphere of dependence and limitation he must raise us up to himself and represent the infinite . . . in perceptible form." Christian Gottfried Körner, "Über Charakterdarstellung in der Musik," *Hören* 5 (1795), p. 148, quoted by Edward Lippman, *A History of Western Musical Aesthetics* (Lincoln: University of Nebraska Press, 1992), p. 135.

29. Letter to Breitkopf & Härtel, 18 October 1802, *Briefe,* vol. 1, p. 126 (no. 108), *Letters,* vol. 1, pp. 76–77 (no. 62); see also letter to Breitkopf & Härtel, ca. 18 December 1802, *Briefe,* vol. 1, p. 145 (no. 123), *Letters,* vol. 1, pp. 83–84 (no. 67).

30. Letter to Nikolaus Zmeskall, 9 February 1816, *Briefe,* vol. 3, p. 223 (no. 898), *Letters,* vol. 2, p. 559 (no. 608).

31. Thayer-Forbes, p. 982, Wilhelm von Lenz, *Beethoven: Eine Kunst-Studie* (Hamburg: Hoffmann & Campe, 1860), vol. 5, part 4, p. 217; Thayer-Deiters-Riemann, vol. 5, p. 318.

32. Franz Wegeler and Ferdinand Ries, *Biographische Notizen über Ludwig van Beethoven* (Coblenz: Bädeker, 1838), p. 87, Thayer-Forbes, p. 367.

33. Thayer-Forbes, p. 629, Thayer-Deiters-Riemann, vol. 3, p. 527.

34. *Konversationshefte,* vol. 4, p. 268, second half of November 1823 (Heft 46, 34r). A portrait of Weber by Carl Christian Vogel von Vogelstein was engraved in 1823 with the facsimile subscription, "Wie Gott will! Carl Maria von Weber," ibid., p. 379 n. 585.

35. Draft letter of 6 July 1825, in the De Roda sketchbook. *Briefe,* vol. 6, p. 98 (no. 2003); the passage does not appear in the variant version of the letter in *Letters,* vol. 3, pp. 1224–26 (no. 1405).

36. Letter to Nikolaus Zmeskall, 1798, *Briefe*, vol. 1, p. 43 (no. 35), *Letters*, vol. 1, p. 32 (no. 30).

37. Letter to Archduke Rudolph, 29 July 1819, *Briefe*, vol. 4, p. 298 (no. 1318), *Letters*, vol. 2, p. 822 (no. 955). Compare Schiller's "humanity cannot reach its final end except by *progress,* and . . . the man of nature cannot make progress save through culture, and consequently by passing himself through the way of civilisation." Friedrich Schiller, "Naive and Sentimental Poetry," in *The Works of Friedrich Schiller: Aesthetical and Philosophical Essays,* vol. 1, p. 307.

38. Letter to Johann Andreas Streicher, 1796, *Briefe*, vol. 1, p. 32 (no. 22), *Letters*, vol. 1, p. 25 (no. 18).

39. Ferdinand Hiller, in Kerst, vol. 2, p. 229.

40. Kerst, vol. 1, p. 51, Carl Czerny, *On the Proper Performance of All Beethoven's Works for the Piano,* ed. Paul Badura-Skoda (Vienna: Universal Edition, 1970), p. 8 (translation amended).

41. Letter to Sir George Smart, c. 11 October 1816, *Briefe*, vol. 3, p. 306 (no. 983), *Letters*, vol. 2, p. 606 (no. 664).

42. Letter to Sigmund Anton Steiner, shortly after 9 January 1817, *Briefe*, vol. 4, p. 8 (no. 1061), *Letters*, vol. 2, p. 661 (no. 749).

43. Letter to Alexander Macco, 1 November 1803, *Briefe*, vol. 1, p. 196 (no. 169), *Letters*, vol. 1, p. 100 (no. 85). Compare Beethoven's quotation from Pliny's *Epistulae* in his Tagebuch: "Nevertheless, what greater gift can be conferred on a man than fame and praise and eternal life?" Tagebuch no. 114.

44. The term *Ästhetik* or its cognates appears only once in Beethoven's letters; in his letter to Hoffmeister of 8 April 1802 he wrote, "The *lady* can have a sonata from me, and, moreover, from an *aesthetic* point of view I will in general adopt her plan." *Briefe*, vol. 1, p. 105 (no. 105), *Letters*, vol. 1, p. 73 (no. 57). The original reads: "die *dame* kann eine Sonate von mir haben, auch will ich *in Aesthetischer* hinsicht im allgemeinen ihren Plan befolgen."

45. Letter to Xaver Schnyder von Wartensee, 19 August 1817, *Briefe*, vol. 4, p. 99 (no. 1159), *Letters*, vol. 2, p. 700 (no. 803).

46. Schiller, *Letters on the Aesthetical Education of Man,* letter 10, reprinted in *The Works of Friedrich Schiller: Aesthetical and Philosophical Essays,* vol. 1, p. 38.

47. The main witnesses are the composer Ignaz von Seyfried and the poet Ludwig Rellstab. "*Don Giovanni* still has the complete Italian cut *[den italienischen Zuschnitt],*" reported Seyfried; "besides, our sacred art ought never to permit itself to be degraded to the foolery of so scandalous a subject." Ignaz von Seyfried, *Ludwig van Beethovens Studien* (Vienna: Haslinger, 1832), Anhang, p. 22. And Rellstab claimed that he heard Beethoven say, "I could not compose operas like *Don Giovanni* and *Figaro*. I have an aversion to that." See Ludwig Nohl, *Beethoven nach den Schilderungen seine Zeitgenossen* (Stuttgart: Cotta, 1877), p. 209. Against these is a wholly favorable remark in Beethoven's own letter to Gottfried Christoph Härtel, 23 August 1811: "The good reception of *Mozart's*

Don Juan gives me as much pleasure as if it were my own work." *Briefe,* vol. 2, p. 211 (no. 519), *Letters,* vol. 1, p. 334 (no. 323). Naturally, the letter should be given greater weight than the memoirs of acquaintances, but this would not be the only occasion on which Beethoven was able to hold opposing or even irreconcilable viewpoints.

48. Letter to Charles Neate, Thayer-Forbes, 620, Thayer-Deiters-Riemann, vol. 3, p. 506.

49. Letter to Georg Friedrich Treitschke, April 1814, *Briefe,* vol. 3, p. 20 (no. 707), *Letters,* vol. 1, p. 454 (no. 479, translation amended).

50. Letter to Breitkopf & Härtel, 23 August 1811, *Briefe,* vol. 2, p. 211 (no. 519), *Letters,* vol. 1, p. 334 (no. 323). Concerning his method of composition, Beethoven wrote, "Now that my health appears to be better, I merely jot down certain ideas as I used to do, and when I have completed the whole in my head, everything is written down, but only once—" Letter to Adolph Martin Schlesinger, 13 November 1821, *Briefe,* vol. 4, p. 455 (no. 1446), *Letters,* vol. 2, pp. 927–28 (no. 1060).

51. Kinsky-Halm, p. 397; Robert S. Winter, *Compositional Origins of Beethoven's Opus 131* (Ann Arbor: UMI, 1982), p. 109. Cf. Krehbiel's translation: "Put together from pilferings from one thing and another," Thayer-Forbes, p. 983.

52. In contrast to a "simple imagination" that apprehends "the whole object" all at once, Hobbes broached the idea of "a compound imagination" in which new images are formed from composites of existing ones. *Leviathan,* part 1, chapter 2.

53. Letter to Prince Nikolas Galitzin, ca. 6 July 1825, *Briefe,* vol. 6, p. 96 (no. 2003), *Letters,* vol. 3, p. 1224 (no. 1405).

54. According to Holz, quoted in Lenz, *Beethoven: Eine Kunst-Studie,* vol. 5, part 4, p. 219.

55. Letter to Archduke Rudolph, 1 July 1823, *Briefe,* vol. 5, p. 165 (no. 1686), *Letters,* vol. 3, p. 1056 (no. 1203).

56. Letter to Bernhard Schotts Söhne, 10 March 1824, *Briefe,* vol. 5, p. 278 (no. 1787), *Letters,* vol. 3, p. 1114 (no. 1270, translation amended). See also Thayer-Deiters-Riemann, vol. 5, p. 102.

57. See Tagebuch nos. 1, 40, 63, 88, 169.

58. Letter to Countess Marie Erdödy, 19 October 1815, *Briefe,* vol. 3, p. 161 (no. 827), *Letters,* vol. 2, p. 527 (no. 563).

59. Letter to Ignaz von Gleichenstein, February 1809, *Briefe,* vol. 2, p. 40 (no. 353), *Letters,* vol. 1, p. 214 (no. 195).

60. Letter to Hans Heinrich von Könneritz, 25 July 1823, *Briefe,* vol. 5, p. 198 (no. 1715), *Letters,* vol. 3, p. 1068 (no. 1212, italics omitted). This may be an allusion to a famous quotation from Virgil (*Aeneid* 7.312): "Flectere si nequeo superos, Acheronta movebo (If I cannot bend the high powers, I will move the infernal regions)." See Jean Starobinski, "Acheronta movebo," *Critical Inquiry* 13 (1987): 394–407.

61. Draft letter to Moritz Schlesinger, 15 July 1825, *Briefe,* vol. 6, p. 113 (footnote to no. 2015, my translation), abridged by A. C. Kalischer, *The Letters of Beethoven,* trans. J. S. Shedlock (London: Dent, 1909), vol. 2, pp. 390–91 (no. 1096).

62.   Letter to Nannette Streicher, August 1817, *Briefe,* vol. 4, pp. 103–4 (no. 1163), *Letters,* vol. 2, p. 705 (no. 810, translation amended).

63.   *Konversationshefte,* vol. 1, p. 326, 11 March 1820 (Heft no. 9, 111r). Thayer-Forbes, p. 747 (translation amended). Beethoven's source is Franz Maria von Nell's tragedy, *Herostratos* (Vienna: Gerold, 1821), extracts from which appeared in the *Conversationsblatt* in March 1820. See *Konversationshefte,* vol. 2, p. 452, following n. 788.

Chapter 6. The Seventh Symphony and the Rhythms of Antiquity

1.   Richard Wagner, *Das Kunstwerk der Zukunft* (1850), in vol. 2 of *Richard Wagner Sämtliche Schriften und Dichtungen,* 6th ed., 10 vols. (Leipzig: Breitkopf & Härtel, 1912), pp. 94–95.

2.   Paul Bekker, *Beethoven,* trans. M. M. Bozman (London: Dent, 1925), pp. 182–83.

3.   Walter Riezler, *Beethoven,* trans. G. D. H. Pidcock (London: Forrester, 1938), pp. 153–54, 157.

4.   Nottebohm, *Zweite Beethoveniana,* p. 102. Originally published in *Musikalisches Wochenblatt* 6 (1875): 245–49, 257–61. See Lewis Lockwood, "Nottebohm Revisited," *Current Thought in Musicology,* ed. John W. Grubbs et al. (Austin: University of Texas Press, 1976), pp. 139–91, esp. p. 165, for variants between the original publication and its republication in Nottebohm, *Zweite Beethoveniana.*

5.   Friedrich Mosengeil, quoted by Kunze, p. 310.

6.   See also, for example, W. J. v. Wasielewski, *Ludwig van Beethoven,* 2 vols. (Berlin: Brachvogel & Ranft, 1888), vol. 2, pp. 247–48; Riemann in Thayer-Deiters-Riemann, vol. 3, p. 402.

7.   Harry Goldschmidt, "Vers und Strophe in Beethovens Instrumentalmusik," in *Beethoven-Symposion Wien 1970: Bericht,* ed. Erich Schenk (Vienna: Böhlaus, 1971), pp. 97–120, at pp. 97–98, reprinted in somewhat different form in Goldschmidt, *Die Erscheinung Beethoven,* 2nd enlarged ed. (Leipzig: VEB Deutscher Verlag für Musik, 1985), pp. 153–73, at p. 153.

8.   My translation, from Anton Reicha, *Vollständiges Lehrbuch der musikalischen Composition,* German trans. Carl Czerny, 4 vols. (Vienna: Diabelli & Co., n.d. [1834]), vol. 2, p. 519. Czerny's edition draws from three treatises by Reicha: *Cours de composition musicale* (Paris, ca. 1816–18), *Traité de mélodie* (Paris, 1814), and *Traité de haute composition musicale* (Paris, 1824–26). Diabelli's half-title reads: *Reicha's Compositions-Lehre.* Goldschmidt's slightly variant transcription is taken from an unidentified secondary source.

9.   Riethmüller calls this dactyl "a seed, a cell, a figure or a motif in Rudolph Réti's sense," designed to play a key role "in the further fate of the symphony." *Beethoven: Interpretationen seiner Werke,* ed. Albrecht Riethmüller, Carl Dahlhaus, and Alexander L. Ringer, 2 vols. (Laaber: Laaber-Verlag, 1994), vol. 2, p. 55. The reference is to Rudolph Réti, *The Thematic Process in Music* (New York: Macmillan, 1951).

10.   Sir George Grove, *Beethoven and His Nine Symphonies,* 3rd. ed. (London: Novello, Ewer & Co., 1898; reprint, New York: Dover, 1962), p. 242.

11. Kinderman views the accented forte downbeat chords that occur at two-measure intervals as the largest rhythmic unit of the Poco sostenuto, and he persuasively proposes that the "power of this music derives in part from its synthesis of three rhythmic levels, which subdivide the basic slow pulse of the chords according to precise proportions." William Kinderman, *Beethoven* (Berkeley and Los Angeles: University of California Press, 1995), pp. 154–56.

12. "Many metrical forms, including most fifth-century ones, rest upon a combination of different types of rhythm." Paul Maas, *Greek Metre,* trans. Hugh Lloyd-Jones (Oxford: Clarendon Press, 1962), p. 42. "Increasingly, modern metrists have come to realize that it is unproductive to overemphasize the pattern at the highest level of generalization, thus treating m[eter] as a single, abstract, Platonic form. The idealized form is a mere set of unrealized possibilities, emptied of meaning, expressiveness, and effect." *The New Princeton Encyclopedia of Poetry and Poetics*, ed. Alex Preminger and T. V. F. Brogan (Princeton: Princeton University Press, 1993), p. 772. George Thomson writes, "[The poet] too is at liberty to invent phrases of his own if he pleases. At the same time, he possesses in common with his audience a large stock of phrases which have become stereotyped by constant usage; and it is out of these elements that he constructs the framework of most of his rhythmical designs." *Greek Lyric Metre* (Cambridge: Cambridge University Press, 1929; rev. ed. Cambridge: W. Heffer and Sons, 1961), pp. 6–7.

13. Literary theorists have observed that "[o]nce a pattern is recognized, even if unconsciously, it need be reproduced only often enough to reconfirm it, and even then not always wholly. . . . [T]he mind 'hears' the pattern as it 'hears' the line, simultaneously, continuously recording the fit." *New Princeton Encyclopedia of Poetry and Poetics,* pp. 771–72. C. S. Lewis has described this kind of phenomenon as "double audition," ibid., p. 772.

14. Riemann, giving as his example the rhythm of sixteenth–eighth–dotted-eighth, writes: "the first movement of the A-major Symphony presents a dominant anapestic rhythm, actually somewhat dithyrambic. (To hear dactyls here is naturally false.)" Thayer-Deiters-Riemann, vol. 3, p. 401. It isn't helpful that in his terminology "anapestic" and "dithyrambic" are taxonomically equivalent. For Nottebohm's analysis, see Nottebohm, *Zweite Beethoveniana,* pp. 102–5.

15. Still, Czerny elsewhere defines precisely this dotted-eighth–sixteenth–eighth sequence as what he calls the "light *[der leichte]*" form of dactyl found in 3/8 rhythms. See fig. 6.1, above.

16. Nottebohm, *Zweite Beethoveniana,* pp. 106–7.

17. Riemann thought that the 1806 sketch-bundle in the Gesellschaft der Musikfreunde known as A 36 contained materials possibly entered as late as 1815 and therefore that it ought not be used to date the Allegretto sketch. See Thayer-Deiters-Riemann, vol. 3, p. 400; see also Karl Nef, *Die neun Sinfonien Beethovens* (Leipzig: Breitkopf & Härtel, 1928), p. 217. Riemann and Nef may have been overly literal in ascribing Beethoven's phrase "Eine Trauerweide oder Akazienbaum aufs Grab meines Bruders," which

is to be found on a leaf of sketchbook A 36 (see Nottebohm, *Zweite Beethoveniana*, p. 83), to the year 1815. Tyson agrees with Nottebohm that the first sketch of the Opus 92 theme was probably intended for the slow movement of the String Quartet in C, op. 59, no. 3. See Alan Tyson, "The 'Razumovsky' Quartets: Some Aspects of the Sources," *Beethoven Studies,* ed. Alan Tyson (Cambridge: Cambridge University Press, 1983), vol. 3, pp. 126–27. And an examination of sketchbook A 36 by Sieghard Brandenburg confirms that the first sketch of the Allegretto theme was written at the same time as the surrounding Opus 59 sketches, even if, as seems to be the case, the "Trauerweide" entry actually was a later addition. (Brandenburg, personal communication.)

18. For an astute metrical analysis of the Allegretto along different lines, see Werner Bauer, "Antike Metren bei Beethoven," *Schweizerische Musikzeitung* 98 (1958): 249–52.

19. For these and related examples, see Nottebohm, *Zweite Beethoveniana*, pp. 108–9.

20. Riezler, *Beethoven,* p. 158.

21. Wasielewski, *Ludwig van Beethoven,* vol. 2, pp. 247–48.

22. Personal communication, March 25, 2001. Cretic and paeonic feet often occur in combination. Moreover, "[t]he first and the fourth paeons [−∪∪∪ and ∪∪∪−] are, in effect, cretics [−∪−] by resolution of their last and first syllables respectively." *New Princeton Encyclopedia of Poetry and Poetics,* p. 874.

23. Personal communication, 22 April 2001. The attributes of paeon diaguios are articulated by Aristides Quintilianus, *On Music, in Three Books,* trans. Thomas J. Mathiesen (New Haven: Yale University Press, 1983), p. 99 (sect. 1.16).

24. If it were not for the equal duration of the beats, the pattern could also be read as iambic.

25. Personal communication, 25 March 2001.

26. This was well understood by some eighteenth-century theorists, including Mattheson, who observed that there are many rhythms and other "materials in music of which the poetic art knows nothing." See Johann Georg Mattheson, *Der vollkommene Kapellmeister* (Hamburg: Herold, 1739), p. 170. Koch wrote that "music contains far more kinds of metrical feet than does poetry, which have neither been divided into particular classifications nor designated with specific names." Heinrich Christoph Koch, *Musikalisches Lexikon* (Frankfurt: Hermann, 1802; reprint, Hildesheim: Georg Olms, 1964), p. 958. Terminological differences and contradictory names for specific meters abound in the literature, heightening these disparities.

27. T. W. Adorno, *Introduction to the Sociology of Music,* trans. E. B. Ashton (New York: Continuum, 1976), p. 94, quoted in Theodor W. Adorno, *Beethoven: The Philosophy of Music. Fragments and Texts,* ed. Rolf Tiedemann, trans. Edmund Jephcott (Stanford: Stanford University Press, 1998), p. 118, translation amended.

28. Adolph Bernhard Marx, "Etwas über die Symphonie und Beethovens Leistungen in diesem Fach" (1824), quoted by Kunze, p. 640; trans. Wayne M. Senner, *The Critical Reception of Beethoven's Compositions by His German Contemporaries,* ed. Senner et al., vol. 1 (Lincoln, Nebraska: University of Nebraska Press, 1999), p. 71. The original reads: "so

tritt in der A-dur-Symphonie alles bestimmt geformt, klar und unzweideutig gezeichnet hervor."

29. On a later occasion, indeed, writing to publisher Adolph Martin Schlesinger, Beethoven referred disdainfully to critics who rely heavily on prosodic analysis, expressing his hope that Adolph Bernhard Marx would "continue to reveal more and more what is noble and true in the sphere of art. And surely that ought gradually to throw discredit upon the mere *counting of syllables.*" Letter to Adolph Martin Schlesinger, 15–19 July 1825, *Briefe,* vol. 6, p. 112 (no. 2015), *Letters,* vol. 3, p. 1222 (no. 1403).

30. Henri de Castil-Blaze, *Journal des débats politiques et littéraires,* 9 March 1829, quoted by Jacques-Gabriel Prod'homme, *Les Symphonies de Beethoven* (Paris: Delagrave, 1906), pp. 324–25.

31. Kunze, p. 640, trans. Senner, *Critical Reception of Beethoven's Compositions,* p. 71.

32. A. B. Marx, *Beethoven: Leben und Schaffen* (Berlin: Janke, 1859), vol. 2, p. 207. A skeptic might note that Marx was prone to discovering in Beethoven's compositions many highly imaginative programs; the symphony as a whole also reminded him of "the glorious age of the Moors," and the Allegretto brought to his mind a procession of "lamenting prisoners" pleading for their lives. See Kunze, pp. 641–42, trans. Senner, *Critical Reception of Beethoven's Compositions,* pp. 73–74.

33. Ludwig Nohl, *Beethoven's Leben,* vol. 2 (Leipzig: Günther, 1867), pp. 353–54.

34. Wagner, "Ueber das Dirigieren," in *Sämtliche Schriften und Dichtungen,* vol. 9, p. 179. For an informative survey of the reception of the Seventh Symphony, see Riethmüller et al., *Beethoven: Interpretationen seiner Werke,* vol. 2, pp. 45–62.

35. Wasielewski, *Ludwig van Beethoven,* vol. 2, p. 246; see also p. 249; Thayer-Deiters-Riemann, vol. 3, p. 401; Jean Chantavoine, *Les Symphonies de Beethoven* (Paris: Mellottée, n.d. [1932]), p. 223; Donald Francis Tovey, *Essays in Musical Analysis,* vol. 1, *Symphonies* (Oxford: Oxford University Press, 1935), p. 60.

36. Quoted by Riethmüller et al., *Beethoven: Interpretationen seiner Werke,* vol. 2, p. 60, from Otto Neitzel, *Beethovens Symphonien: nach ihrem Stimmungsgehalt erläutert* (Cologne: P. J. Tonger, [1891]), pp. 63–73. For an enthusiastic but diffuse attempt to connect certain specific rhythms used by Beethoven with Greek and Roman mythology and ancient poetic-musical forms, see Anna Gertrud Huber, *Ethos und Mythos der Rhythmen: Beiträge zu einer Renaissance der Werke von Johann Sebastian Bach und Ludwig van Beethoven* (Strasbourg and Zürich: Heitz, 1947); see also Huber, *Auf den Geisteswegen von Johann Sebastian Bach und Ludwig van Beethoven: Beiträge zu einer Renaissance ihrer Werke* (Leipzig, Strassburg, and Zürich: Heitz, 1938).

37. Arnold Schering, *Beethoven und die Dichtung; mit einer Einleitung zur Geschichte und Ästhetik der Beethovendeutung* (Berlin: Junker und Dunnhaupt, 1936), pp. 213–36.

38. See Mattheson, *Der vollkommene Kapellmeister,* p. 164; John Frederick Rowbotham, *A History of Music,* 3 vols. (London: Trübner, 1886), vol. 2, p. 48. Dispondaic sequences are almost always reserved by Beethoven for openings of movements, e.g., the Grosse Fuge, op. 130/133, and the Assai sostenuto of the String Quartet in A minor, op. 132.

According to Le Sueur, verse featuring "grave spondees" was "employed for hymns in honor of the gods, in the feasts and the sacrifices." See Jean-François Le Sueur, *Exposé d'une musique une, imitative, et particuliere à chaque solemnité; Où l'on donne les principes généraux sur lesquels on l'établit, & le Plan d'une Musique propre à la Fête de Noël* (Paris: Veuve Hérissant, 1787), p. 42.

39. Cretic, for example, can be associated with both comedy and tragedy; many lyric poems of the later classical and Hellenistic period also utilize cretic meter. Mattheson's notated musical equivalent, in 6/4 time, is half-note, quarter-note, half-note, and quarter-note rest, and he relates the meter to warfare and combat (see description of "Amphimacer" meter in *Der vollkommene Kapellmeister*, p. 168). In tragic drama cretic is often expressive of "intense or violent emotion, such as terror or religious fervour" (Thomson, *Greek Lyric Metre*, p. 67), emotional states which do not predominate in the Vivace.

40. Nottebohm, *Zweite Beethoveniana*, p. 328, Tagebuch no. 49, and Hans Boettcher, "Beethovens Homer-Studien," *Die Musik* 19 (1927): 478–85, esp. p. 482. See also Nottebohm, *Zweite Beethoveniana*, pp. 350, 474; Tagebuch no. 8; *Konversationshefte*, vol. 1, p. 374, vol. 3, p. 315, vol. 9, pp. 213–14; Boettcher, *Beethoven als Liederkomponist* (Augsburg: Benno Filser, 1928), p. 48. Beethoven marked the trochaic meter of the "Opferlied," op. 121b, on a sketch in 1824 (Nottebohm, *Zweite Beethoveniana*, p. 542). There are references—attributed to Beethoven—to metrical scansion in manuscript annotations of numerous études by J. B. Cramer, but I refrain from endorsing them because the annotations are exclusively in Schindler's hand and are almost certainly by Schindler rather than Beethoven. See J. S. Shedlock, ed., *Selection of Studies by J. B. Cramer, with Comments by L. van Beethoven* (London: Augener & Co. [1893]).

41. Friedrich Schlegel, *Lectures on the History of Literature, Ancient and Modern* [trans. J. G. Lockhart] (New York: Langley, 1844), pp. 34–35 (lecture 1).

42. Rowbotham, *History*, vol. 2, pp. 259–60.

43. Skeptics will rightly pass over Bettina Brentano's once widely cited letter to Goethe dated 28 May 1810, in which she reported Beethoven as saying: "Music is a higher revelation than all wisdom and philosophy, the wine which inspires one to new generative processes, and I am the Bacchus who presses out this glorious wine for mankind and makes them spiritually drunken." O. G. Sonneck, *Beethoven: Impressions of Contemporaries* (New York: Schirmer, 1926), p. 80. And it may also be noted that though several sketches dating from around 1815 may survive for an opera to a text by Rudolph von Berge, entitled *Bacchus: A Grand Lyric Opera in Three Acts*, Beethoven abandoned the libretto, which had been sent to him by his friend Karl Amenda. Thayer-Forbes, p. 618, Nottebohm, *Zweite Beethoveniana*, pp. 329–30, Thayer-Deiters-Riemann, vol. 3, p. 503.

44. André Levinson, "Le Ballet de Prométhée: Beethoven et Viganò," *Revue musicale* (1 April 1927): 87–97; Robert Lach, "Zur Geschichte der Beethovenschen 'Prometheus' Ballettmusik," *Zeitschrift für Musikwissenschaft* 3 (1920–21): 223–37.

45. Thayer-Forbes, p. 888 (translation amended), Nottebohm, *Zweite Beethoveniana*,

p. 163. Nottebohm writes that the notation was "later written down" on a "leaf that belongs to the second half of the year 1818." For a possible source of Beethoven's "Cantique ecclésiastique," see Mattheson's description of "Der Choral" as the first of the "Gattungen der Melodien und ihren besondern Abzeichen" (*Der vollkommene Kapellmeister*, pp. 210–11):

1. Der Choral, cantus choralis planus, gregorianus &c. demselben rechnet man zu Recitativum ecclesiasticum f. stilum ligatum z. E. die Collecten vor dem Altar &c.

   Antiphonam, den Wechsel-Gesang.

   Canticum, das Lied oder die Ode.

   Psalmum, den Psalm.

   Hymnum, den Lob-Gesang &c.

46. Ernst Bücken, *Der heroische Stil in der Oper* (Leipzig: Kistner and Siegel, 1924), p. 136.

47. Robert Haas, "Zur Wiener Ballettpantomime um den Prometheus," *Neues Beethoven-Jahrbuch* 2 (1925): 84–103. The exceptions dealt with chivalric-medieval subjects: *Die wiedergefundene Tochter Otto des II., Kaisers der Deutschen* and *Richard Löwenherz*. Other topical or characteristic names for ballets included *komisches, tragisches, allegorisches, fabelhaftes, ernsthaftes, romantisches,* and *orientalisches*. Not every classical subject is designated *heroisches;* for example, *Der Tod des Herkules* (4 October 1798); and *La morte di Cleopatra* (8 January 1800) are listed under the heading "tragisches Ballett"; and other ballets on classical subjects are simply called "Divertissements" or "pantomimisches Ballett."

48. James R. Anthony, "Opera," *New Grove,* vol. 13, p. 571.

49. Anton Bauer, *150. Jahre Theater an der Wien* (Zurich and Vienna: Amalthea, 1952), pp. 267–88.

50. See Mark Evan Bonds, "The Symphony as Pindaric Ode," in *Haydn and His World,* ed. Elaine Sisman (Princeton: Princeton University Press, 1997), p. 147. There may be insufficient reason to take the influential aesthetician Sulzer's remark, that the opening movement of a symphony "is like a Pindaric ode" in its "expression of grandeur, of the festive and of the elevated," as something more than an isolated analogy. See Johann Georg Sulzer, *Allgemeine Theorie der schönen Künste,* 5 vols., 2nd ed. (Leipzig: Weidmann, 1792–99), vol. 4, pp. 478–79, quoted by Bonds, "Symphony as Pindaric Ode," p. 133, and Michael Broyles, *The Emergence and Evolution of Beethoven's Heroic Style* (New York: Excelsior, 1987), p. 11.

51. For an indispensable account of the current state of the matter, see Thomas J. Mathiesen, *Apollo's Lyre: Greek Music and Music Theory in Antiquity and the Middle Ages* (Lincoln: University of Nebraska Press, 1999). See also *Riemann Musik Lexikon, Sachteil* (Mainz: Schotts Söhne, 1967), p. 351 and the relevant entries in *New Grove* and *Die Musik in Geschichte und Gegenwart.* For the types of music and their function in Greek life, see Mathiesen, *Apollo's Lyre,* pp. 23–157; for a compilation of early writings and treatises on Greek music, see section 1 (edited by Mathiesen) of Oliver Strunk, *Source Readings*

in Music History, rev. ed., edited Leo Treitler et al. (New York: Norton, 1998), pp. 3–109. Rowbotham's expansive discussion in his *History of Music* is useful for its representation of mid-nineteenth-century conceptions of Greek music; it also draws heavily on such eighteenth-century historians of Greek music as Friedrich Wilhelm Marpurg, *Kritische Einleitung in die Geschichte und Lehrsätze der alten und neuen Musik* (Berlin: Gottlieb August Lange, 1759).

52.   I have found it especially useful to consult descriptions of Greek poetic meters and their application to music in books and journals that were read by Beethoven, or at least available to him. These include Johann G. Sulzer, *Allgemeine Theorie der schönen Künste,* 2 vols. (Leipzig, 1771–74); Mattheson, *Der vollkommene Kapellmeister,* pp. 160–70; Heinrich Christoph Koch, *Musikalisches Lexikon* (Leipzig, 1802; reprint, Hildesheim: Georg Olms, 1964), cols. 953–63; and Johann Heinrich Voß, *Zeitmessung der deutschen Sprache* (Königsberg: Nikolovius, 1802). Voß's translation of the meters into musical notation was a topic of discussion between Beethoven and the poet Christoph Kuffner in April 1826; see *Konversationshefte,* vol. 9, pp. 213–14 (Heft 109, fols. 3r–4r). Several articles in the *AmZ,* a journal well-known to Beethoven, suggest extensive interest among musicians in the topic of Greek music, e.g., F. G. v. Dalberg, "Ueber griechische Instrumental-Musik und ihre Wirkung," *AmZ* 9 (1806–7), cols. 17–30, with an appended note by the editor, Friedrich Rochlitz; A. Apel, "Ueber Rhythmus und Metrum," *AmZ* 10 (1807–8), cols. 1–10, 17–26, 33–40, 49–62, 273–84, 289–98, 305–11, 321–31; Stollberg and Steuber, "Ueber die Erweiterung des Rhythmus in der Musik," *AmZ* 12 (1809–10), cols. 113–18. From contemporary theorists Ratner assembles a useful table of the poetic meters transposed into musical notation; see Leonard Ratner, *Classic Music: Expression, Form, and Style* (New York: Schirmer, 1980), pp. 71–72. Reicha's treatises may have been published too late to have affected the Seventh Symphony, but they are fully aligned with Reicha's earlier writings and those of the foregoing theorists. See Reicha, *Vollständiges Lehrbuch der musikalischen Composition,* vol. 2, pp. 471–77, 516–21. Beethoven did not use Greek modes in the Seventh Symphony, although, at first glance, that, too, might have been an effective way of simultaneously conveying the idea of the antique, the classic, the Greek, the exotic, and ritual. Perhaps the ancient modes could not adequately symbolize Greek music because they were so closely identified with music of the Catholic Church in the medieval period. The modes may have been too recognizable, whereas Beethoven needed a music of unspecific origin to simulate sounds associated with the Antique world.

53.   See, for example, Erwin Panofsky, *Renaissance and Renascences in Western Art* (1960; reprint, New York: Harper & Row, 1972), esp. pp. 8, 55.

54.   Claude Palisca, *Humanism in Italian Renaissance Musical Thought* (New Haven: Yale University Press, 1985), p. 6; see also p. 22.

55.   See Claude Palisca, "Camerata," *New Grove,* vol. 3, pp. 645–46, and *Humanism in Italian Renaissance Musical Thought,* passim; see also Thomas Walker, "Opera," *New Grove,* vol. 13, p. 550.

56.   Geoffrey Chew interprets the atmospheric and archaic rhetoric of such works as

Debussy's "L'Après-midi d'un faune," as intended "to suggest the pastoral music of Greek antiquity—in other words, to create a specifically Mediterranean pagan pastoral convention." Geoffrey Chew, "Pastorale," *New Grove*, vol. 14, p. 295.

57. Le Sueur, *Exposé d'une musique*, pp. 39–60. Le Sueur advocated the deployment in French music of certain antique meters "which the Greeks used for the expression of serious and tranquil subjects, for noble and heroic sentiments" (p. 51; see also p. 56). See also Jean Mogrédien, "Le Sueur, Jean-François," *New Grove*, vol. 10, p. 696. It may be significant that the exact metrical outline of the Allegretto's dactyl-spondee figure appears in a four-measure sequence in Le Sueur's book (p. 52).

58. Le Sueur, *Exposé d'une musique*, p. 39.

59. L. A. v. [Ludwig Achim von] Arnim, "Ueber deutsches Sylbenmaaß und griechische Deklamation," *Berlinische musikalische Zeitung* 1, no. 32 (1805): 125–26, at p. 125.

60. *Gedanken über die Nachahmung der griechischen Werke in der Malerei und Bildhauerkunst* (1755), quoted by René Wellek, *A History of Modern Criticism, 1750–1850*, vol. 1 (New Haven: Yale University Press, 1955), p. 299 n. 19.

61. Letter of June 1542, quoted in *Giulio Romano: Master Designer. An Exhibition of Drawings*, ed. Janet Cox-Rearick (Seattle: University of Washington Press, 1999), p. 17.

62. Friedrich Schlegel, letter to A. W. Schlegel, 27 February 1794, *Friedrich Schlegels Briefe an seinen Bruder August Wilhelm*, ed. Oskar Walzel (Berlin: Speyer and Peters, 1890), p. 170. For the early Romantic advocacy of a synthesis of ancient and modern poetic styles, see Walter Silz, *Early German Romanticism: Its Founders and Heinrich von Kleist* (Cambridge: Harvard University Press, 1929), pp. 213–19.

63. Panofsky, *Renaissance and Renascences*, p. 201.

64. A handful of exemplary books, in an extensive literature, includes Edgar Wind, *Pagan Mysteries in the Renaissance* (New Haven: Yale University Press, 1958); Aby Warburg, *The Renewal of Pagan Antiquity*, trans. David Britt (Los Angeles: Getty Research Institute, 1999); Erwin Panofsky, *Idea: A Concept in Art Theory*, trans. Joseph J. S. Peake (Columbia, University of South Carolina Press, 1968); Frances A. Yates, *Giordano Bruno and the Hermetic Tradition* (Chicago: University of Chicago Press, 1964).

65. Yates, *Giordano Bruno*, p. 1.

66. A. W. Schlegel, *A Course of Lectures on Dramatic Art and Literature*, trans. John Black, revised by Rev. A. J. W. Morrison from the "last German edition" (London: Henry G. Bohn, 1846), pp. 26–27 (lecture 1).

67. In his book on Beethoven, Wagner summed up the predicament: "the antique world stands before us an unattainable model." Richard Wagner, *Beethoven*, trans. Albert R. Parsons (New York: Schirmer, 1883), p. 111. Hegel, clearly having Schiller, Hölderlin, and Goethe in mind, observed that "a yearning towards Greek gods and heroes is not infrequently the theme of our poets"; and he did not always approve, for this "lamentation is expressed emphatically as in direct opposition to Christendom." G. W. F. Hegel, *The Philosophy of Fine Art*, trans. F. P. B. Osmaston, 4 vols. (London: G. Bell and Sons, 1920), vol. 2, p. 266.

68. Widespread mistranslations of the idiomatic *so weit* have deprived Anglo-American readers and listeners of the sense of imminent or inevitable reunion that the poem was intended to convey.

69. Friedrich Nietzsche, *The Birth of Tragedy out of the Spirit of Music,* in *"The Birth of Tragedy" and "The Genealogy of Morals,"* trans. Francis Golffing (Garden City, N.Y.: Anchor, 1956), p. 19.

70. M. H. Abrams, "The Correspondent Breeze," in *English Romantic Poets: Modern Essays in Criticism,* ed. M. H. Abrams (New York: Oxford University Press, 1960), pp. 37–54, at p. 52.

71. Mario Praz, *The Romantic Agony,* 2nd ed., trans. Angus Davidson (New York: Meridian, 1956), p. 11.

72. Nietzsche, "The Dionysiac World View" (1870), in *The Birth of Tragedy and Other Writings,* ed. Raymond Geuss and Ronald Speirs, trans. Ronald Speirs (Cambridge: Cambridge University Press, 1999), p. 120.

Chapter 7. The Masonic Thread

1. The original reads, "Beethoven war Freimaurer, aber in späteren Jahren nicht in Tätigkeit." Kerst, vol. 2, p. 187.

2. Alexander Wheelock Thayer, *Ludwig van Beethovens Leben,* 3 vols. (Berlin: Schneider, 1866; Berlin: Weber, 1872, 1879), vol. 3, p. 131, Thayer-Deiters-Riemann, vol. 3, p. 197; omitted from Thayer-Krehbiel and Thayer-Forbes.

3. See "Freimaurerei," in Frimmel, *Handbuch,* vol. 1, p. 152.

4. Paul Nettl, *Mozart and Masonry,* trans. Mrs. Robert Gold (New York: Philosophical Library, 1957), p. 127.

5. Winfried Dotzauer, "Freimaurergesellschaften im Rheingebiet: Die Anfänge der Freimaurerei im Westen des Alten Reiches," in *Freimaurer und Geheimbünde im 18. Jahrhundert in Mitteleuropa,* ed. Helmut Reinalter (Frankfurt: Suhrkamp Verlag, 1983; reprint, 1986), pp. 162–67; Dotzauer, "Bonner aufgeklärte Gesellschaften und geheime Sozietäten bis zum Jahre 1815 unter besonderer Berücksichtigung des Mitgliederbestands der Freimaurerloge 'Frères courageux' in der Napoleonischen Zeit," *Bonner Geschichtsblätter* 24 (1972): 78–142; Eugen Lennhoff and Oskar Posner, *Internationales Freimaurerlexikon* (Munich: Amalthea, and Graz: Akademische Druck- u. Verlagsanstalt, 1932), cols. 848–49. See also Joseph Hansen, *Quellen zur Geschichte des Rheinlandes im Zeitalter der französischen Revolution 1780–1801,* 4 vols. (Bonn: P. Hanstein, 1931–39), vol. 1, pp. 60–62; and Karl Hoede, "Die Aufklärungszeit im Rheinland," *Quatuor-Coronati-Hefte,* no. 6 (May 1969): 31–32.

6. An edict banning the Order of Illuminati was issued by Karl Theodor, the Elector of Bavaria, on 22 June 1784, and confirmed in subsequent edicts of March and August 1785. Albert G. Mackey, *Encyclopedia of Freemasonry,* revised and enlarged by Robert I. Clegg and H. L. Haywood, 3 vols. (Chicago: Masonic History Co., 1946), vol. 1, p. 475.

7.   Ludwig Schiedermair, *Der junge Beethoven* (Leipzig: Quelle & Mayer, 1925), p. 31.

8.   It is widely accepted by historians that former Illuminists "camouflaged" themselves in the *Lesegesellschaften* which they took the initiative in founding between 1782 and 1787 in Mainz, Coblenz, Trier, Bonn, Aachen, Cologne, and other cities. Max Braubach, "Eine Zeitschrift der Bonner Illuminaten," in Braubach, *Kurköln: Gestalten und Ereignisse aus zwei Jahrhunderten rheinischer Geschichte* (Münster: Aschendorff, 1949), p. 450, see also pp. 419–21; Hansen, *Quellen zur Geschichte des Rheinlandes,* vol. 1, pp. 16–18; Walther Ottendorf-Simrock, *Das Haus Simrock* (Ratingen: Aloys Henn, 1954), pp. 18–19.

9.   For the political context of the repression of Freemasonry after the death of Emperor Joseph II, see Ernst Wangermann, *From Joseph II to the Jacobin Trials* (London: Oxford University Press, 1959), esp. pp. 130–31, 175; Denis Silagi, *Jakobiner in der Habsburger-Monarchie: Ein Beitrag zur Geschichte des aufgeklärten Absolutismus in Österreich* (Vienna and Munich: Herold, 1962); John M. Roberts, *The Mythology of the Secret Societies* (London: Secker and Warburg, 1972).

10.   Wangermann, *From Joseph II to the Jacobin Trials,* pp. 157–91. For an informed synopsis of the presumed afterlife of the Order following its suppression and dissolution, see Ludwig Hammermayer, "Illuminaten in Bayern: Zu Geschichte, Fortwirken und Legende des Geheimbundes," in *Krone und Verfassung: König Max I. Joseph und der neue Staat: Beiträge zur Bayerischen Geschichte und Kunst 1799–1825,* ed. Hubert Glaser (Munich: Hirmer, 1980), p. 149. An overzealous police document in a Paris archive, datable to around 1810, entitled "Extrait d'un Mémoire sur les illuminés et l'Allemagne," lists many prominent literary, academic, and political figures—including more than a few known to Beethoven personally or through their writings and other activities—as "illuminés ou protecteurs de l'association." In search of surviving disciples of Weishaupt's Order of Illuminati, the document casts its net widely and indiscriminately, merging known or presumed former members of the Order (whom it calls "the true German Illuminists") and so-called *idéalistes,* the latter including followers of the mystic Jakob Boehme, among those who preach "moral and political regeneration." Brentano and von Arnim, the Romanticist editors of *Des knaben Wunderhorn,* are considered dangerous because their collection of German ballads and tales allegedly inflames the enthusiasm of the "basses classes de la Société, par les souvenirs, qu'il rappelle." The document is reprinted and discussed in Leopold Engel, *Geschichte des Illuminatenordens: Ein Beitrag zur Geschichte Bayerns* (Berlin: H. Bermuhler, 1906), pp. 447–61.

11.   The existence of the illicit Viennese lodges is recorded in Lennhoff and Posner, *Internationales Freimaurerlexikon,* cols. 1704–5; Eugen Lennhoff, *The Freemasons: The History, Nature, Development and Secret of the Royal Art,* trans. Einar Frame (London: Methuen, 1934), pp. 136–37; and *Allgemeines Handbuch der Freimaurerei,* ed. Verein deutscher Freimaurer (3rd revised ed. of Lenning's *Encyclopädie der Freimaurerei),* 2 vols. (Leipzig: Max Hesse, 1900–1901), vol. 2, p. 542. Police records concerning the Vienna-Hernals lodge have been located in the Österreichisches Staatsarchiv by Michael Lorenz, who provides valuable details, especially about Siboni's and Pálffy's involvement and the

disposition of charges against them; the records cited also list as members the court the-ater secretary Ignaz Freiherr von Pöck, a certain Muzarelli (perhaps Antonio Muzzarelli, the renowned choreographer), and a certain Quilicci or Guilicci. See Michael Lorenz, "'Viele glaubten und glauben noch, absichtlich'—Der Tod der Ludovica Siboni," *Schubert durch die Brille*, no. 23 (July 1999): 47–74, esp. pp. 51–53. "On 17 December 1812 the Emperor published a circular letter in which he expressly reminded all imperial officials that their oath of office forbade anyone to join this kind of secret society" (Lorenz, p. 53). A listing of thirty-two members and presumed members of the Vienna-Hernals Lodge is in Österreichischen Staatsarchiv, Allgemeines Verwaltungsarchiv (AVA) Polizeihofstelle (PHst), Ms. 1818/413cc. Although Beethoven of course knew Pállfy, Siboni, and Duport professionally, there is no indication that he had a closer, let alone a Masonic, connection to them. With these and one or two additional possible excep-tions there are no other names that can clearly be associated with Beethoven. "Prince Dietrichstein" has not been further identified; the prominent Freemason Prince Johann Baptist Carl Walther Dietrichstein-Proskau died in 1808; Count Moriz Joseph Johann von Dietrichstein-Proskau-Leslie (1775–1864) was well known to Beethoven as a friend, leader of the Gesellschaft der Musikfreunde, and director of the court theaters. (Thanks to Heinz Schuler for details on the Dietrichsteins.) The main link between Beetho-ven and Hernals seems to be that he visited the summer residence of Countess Erdödy there. A letter of 9 August 1809 from the countess to Gottfried Härtel of Breitkopf & Härtel mentions her Hernals residence: "Ich wohne zu Herrnhals bey Wien Nro. 18." Günther Haupt, "Gräfin Erdödy und J. X. Brauchle," *Der Bär: Jahrbuch von Breitkopf & Härtel* [1927], pp. 76–77. Beethoven's letter to the countess, ca. June or July 1810, seems to have been addressed to her there. *Briefe*, vol. 2, pp. 130–31 (no. 449), *Letters*, vol. 1, p. 282 (no. 270). Probably in early summer of 1810 (though Anderson dates the letter to around September 1812) he wrote to Gleichenstein: "Saturday or Sunday I shall perhaps invite you to Hernals." *Briefe*, vol. 2, p. 130 (no. 448), *Letters*, vol. 1, p. 391 (no. 391).

12. The "Wildensteiner Ritterschaft auf blauer Erde" lodge was founded in 1790 and numbered Archduke Johann among its members; it dissolved in 1823. See Rainer Hu-bert and Ferdinand Zörrer, "Die österreichischen Grenzlogen: Freimaurerei in Öster-reich 1869 bis 1918," *Quatuor Coronati Jahrbuch* 20 (1983): 144–45; Lennhoff and Pos-ner, *Internationales Freimaurerlexikon*, cols. 1706–07.

13. Anton Schindler, *Biographie von Ludwig van Beethoven* (Münster: Aschendorff, 1860), vol. 1, p. 231, as given in Thayer-Forbes, pp. 629–30; see also Schindler-MacArdle, p. 204 (translation amended). Apart from Schindler's own assertions, it cannot be established that he was in contact with Beethoven prior to 1822, let alone during the period in question.

14. For members of the "Stagira" lodge, see Alfred Becker, *Christian Gottlob Neefe und die Bonner Illuminaten* (Bonn: Bouvier, 1969), pp. 12–14, and Hansen, *Quellen zur Geschichte des Rheinlandes*, vol. 1, pp. 43–45. Johann Joseph Eichhoff, who addresses Beethoven in the intimate *Du* form, has an entry dated 25 October 1791 in Beetho-

ven's Bonn farewell souvenir album *(Stammbuch)*. See Theodore Albrecht, ed., *Letters to Beethoven and Other Correspondence,* 3 vols. (Lincoln: University of Nebraska Press, 1996), vol. 1, p. 20 (no. 13f).

15. Letters to Simrock, 2 August 1794, ca. 5 August 1820, and 4 October 1804, *Briefe,* vol. 1, pp. 25–26 (no. 17), vol. 4, p. 411 (no. 1403), vol. 1, p. 224 (no. 193); *Letters,* vol. 1, pp. 17–19 (no. 12), vol. 2, p. 898 (no. 1028), vol. 1, p. 120 (no. 99). Gustav R. Kuéss takes the words *"geliebt von ihren Kameraden"* to indicate a political or ideological bond, most likely among Illuminists. See Kuéss's perceptive historical essay "Beethoven— Freimaurer?" in *Quatuor-Coronati-Hefte,* no. 3 (January 1966): 35–42, at p. 40.

16. See Franz Wegeler and Ferdinand Ries, *Biographische Notizen über Ludwig van Beethoven* (Coblenz: Bädeker, 1838), p. 75, trans. Frederick Noonan as *Beethoven Remembered* (Arlington: Great Ocean Publishers, 1987), p. 65. Other Illuminist supporters of the young Beethoven were the theater director Gustav Friedrich Wilhelm Grossmann and, according to Irmen, the addressee of Beethoven's first surviving letter, Joseph Wilhelm von Schaden of Augsburg. See Hans-Josef Irmen, *Beethoven in seiner Zeit* (Zülpich: Prisca, 1998), pp. 66 and 440 n. 37, citing a telling reference to von Schaden in J.-J. Schings, *Die Brüder des Marquis Posa: Schiller und der Geheimbund der Illuminaten* (Tübingen, 1996), p. 40 n. 70. Even in his last decade, Beethoven was conversing with friends about Bonn's Freemasons and Illuminists. See, for example, the references to Grossman, Eulogius Schneider, and Heinrich Gottfried Wilhelm Daniels in *Konversationshefte,* vol. 1, p. 70, March–May 1819 (Heft 2, 78v–80r).

17. Walther Engelhardt, "Die Kieler Handschrift der Autobiographie Christian Gottlob Neefes 1748–1798," *Zeitschrift für Musikwissenschaft* 7 (1925): 470; also Engelhardt, ed., *Christian Gottlob Neefens Lebenslauf von ihm selbst beschrieben: Nebst beigefügtem Karackter, 1789* (Cologne: Arno Volk, 1957), pp. 20–21; Becker, *Neefe und die Bonner Illuminaten,* pp. 1–2; Irmen, *Beethoven,* pp. 64–65. For Neefe's earlier Masonic affiliations, including his publication in 1774 of a book of *Freimaurerlieder* under the anagrammatic pseudonym Fenee, see Paul Nettl, "Freimaurermusik," in *Die Musik in Geschichte und Gegenwart* (Kassel: Bärenreiter, 1955), vol. 4, cols. 891–92; Nettl, *Mozart and Masonry,* pp. 37–38.

18. See the entries in Max Braubach, ed., *Die Stammbücher Beethovens und der Babette Koch. Faksimile* (Bonn: Beethovenhaus, 1970; 2nd ed., 1995); see also letters to Theodora Johanna Vocke, 22 May 1793, and to Lorenz von Breuning, 1 October 1797, *Letters,* vol. 1, pp. 6, 27 (nos. 4, 21). Beethoven's Bonn friend the violinist and composer Andreas Romberg became a noted Freemason. See *Allgemeines Handbuch der Freimaurerei,* vol. 2, p. 255.

19. See Max Braubach, *Die erste Bonner Hochschule, Maxische Akademie und kurfürstliche Universität 1774/77 bis 1798* (Bonn: Bouvier and Röhrscheid, 1966), pp. 171, 181; for additional biographical details see Braubach, *Die erste Bonner Universität und ihre Professoren: Ein Beitrag zur rheinischen Geistesgeschichte im Zeitalter der Aufklärung* (Bonn: Universitäts-Verlag, 1947), pp. 172–76. Wegeler is named as an Illuminist in Hoede, "Die Aufklärungszeit im Rheinland," p. 33, but without further documentation. According

to Frimmel, Wegeler was "maliciously attacked" during the first French occupation as an opponent of the revolution. See Frimmel, *Handbuch,* vol. 2, p. 409.

20. Letter of 2 May 1810, *Briefe,* vol. 2, p. 119 (no. 439), *Letters,* vol. 1, p. 271 (no. 256). The titles of the new texts were "Bei der Aufnahme eines Maurers" and "Maurerfragen." The texts are reproduced in Wegeler-Ries, *Notizen,* pp. 67–69; *Beethoven Remembered,* pp. 61–62. Frimmel believes this shows that Beethoven "was somehow instructed concerning the Masonic lodges on the Rhine, whether it was by chance or through a brother of the Order. In [the latter] case Beethoven was therefore himself in the Order." Frimmel, *Handbuch,* vol. 1, p. 152. This is not necessarily so, for Simrock's published version may already have come to Beethoven's attention.

21. Letter of ca. 1795, *Briefe,* vol. 1, p. 28 (no. 19), *Letters,* vol. 1, p. 22 (no. 15).

22. Works as listed in *New Grove,* vol. 16, p. 10. See also Alberto Basso, *L'invenzione della gioia: Musica e massoneria nell'età dei Lumi* (Milan: Garzanti, 1994), p. 453.

23. For the political and organizational affiliations of the university professors see Braubach, *Die erste Bonner Hochschule.* But several professors not identified by Braubach as Illuminists appear on an extensive and perhaps overly inclusive listing of twenty-nine Bonn members of the Order in Hermann Schüttler, *Die Mitglieder des Illuminatenordens 1776–1787/93* (Munich: Ars Una, 1991), p. 199. Compare the membership lists in Richard van Dülmen, *Der Geheimbund der Illuminaten: Darstellung, Analyse, Dokumentation* (Stuttgart: F. Frommann, 1975), pp. 439–53. Bonifaz Anton Oberthür, a documented Illuminist from Würzburg, was the founding rector of the university in 1786. See Manfred Agethen, *Geheimbund und Utopie: Illuminaten, Freimaurer und deutsche Spätaufklärung* (Munich: Oldenbourg, 1984), p. 245 n. 103.

24. See Braubach, *Die erste Bonner Hochschule,* pp. 160–67. Fischenich was a trusted correspondent of Schiller and of the Mason and Illuminist Karl Leonhard Reinhold.

25. Waldstein, letter to Elector Maximilian Franz, October 1788, see Max Braubach, *Eine Jugendfreundin Beethovens: Babette Koch-Belderbusch und ihr Kreis* (Bonn: Röhrscheid, 1948), p. 62; for Waldstein, see also Josef Heer, *Der Graf von Waldstein und sein Verhältnis zu Beethoven* (Bonn: Beethovenhaus; Leipzig: Quelle & Meyer, 1933).

26. For further details, see Heinz Schuler, *Mozart und die Freimaurerei: Daten, Fakten, Biographien* (Wilhelmshaven: Noetzel, 1992). See also Basso, *L'invenzione della gioia,* p. 79 n.

27. See E. Wangermann, *Aufklärung und staatsbürgerliche Erziehung: Gottfried van Swieten als Reformator des österreichischen Unterrichtswesens 1781–1791* (Munich: Oldenbourg, 1978), pp. 12–16; H. C. Robbins Landon, *Mozart: The Golden Years, 1781–1791* (New York: Schirmer, 1989), p. 225; Joachim Hurwitz, "Haydn and the Freemasons," *Haydn Yearbook 1985,* vol. 16 (1986), pp. 78–79.

28. Basso, *L'invenzione della gioia,* pp. 512–20, with a list of members on p. 515. See also Otto Jahn, *Life of Mozart,* trans. Pauline Townsend (London: Novello, Ewer, 1882; reprint, New York: Kalmus, n.d.), vol. 3, pp. 218–19, and Reinhold Bernhardt, "Aus der Umwelt der Wiener Klassiker: Freiherr van Swieten," *Der Bär* (1929–30): 74–164. Several leaders or founding members of the London Philharmonic Society were Freema-

278   NOTES TO PAGES 140-42

sons, including Thomas Attwood, Ries, George Smart, and Giovanni Battista Viotti, from

sons, including Thomas Attwood, Ries, George Smart, and Giovanni Battista Viotti, from which Basso concludes that the society itself had "an unequivocal Masonic stamp." See Basso, *L'invenzione della gioia*, pp. 74, 439–41; see also Alberto Basso, "Origine e ispirazione massoniche della *Nona sinfonia:* Beethoven e la Philharmonic Society di Londra," in *Storia della massoneria: Testi e studi* (Turin: Editore MA, 1983), vol. 2, pp. 21–59, 235–37. Many of Beethoven's British admirers and supporters were Freemasons.

29. For Lichnowsky's Masonic affiliations in Vienna, see Schuler, *Mozart und die Freimaurerei*, pp. 114–15; Hans-Josef Irmen et al., eds., *Die Protokolle der Wiener Freimaurerloge "Zur wahren Eintracht" (1781–1785)* (Frankfurt: P. Lang, 1994), pp. 162, 165, 166, 170, 186, 201 (docs. 213, 219, 221, 225, 253, 276). For Lichnowsky's putative membership in the Order of Illuminati see Schüttler, *Die Mitglieder des Illuminatenordens*, pp. 94, 180, 227, citing two dependable archival sources. See also Irmen, *Beethoven*, pp. 163–64 and 447 n. 71.

30. See Irmen, *Beethoven*, pp. 167 and 448 n. 82.

31. Mackey, *Encyclopedia of Freemasonry*, vol. 1, p. 376; Lennhoff and Posner, *Internationales Freimaurerlexikon*, cols. 1244–45.

32. Clemens Brenneis, "Das Fischhof-Manuskript in der Deutschen Staatsbibliothek," *Zu Beethoven* 2 (1984): 45. The reference is to Andreas Streicher, piano manufacturer, music patron, and Schiller's trusted friend who aided the poet in his flight from Stuttgart.

33. Irmen et al., *Protokolle*, p. 162. Lichnowsky's name adjoins Zmeskall's on the registers as a visiting brother, suggesting an early association between the two men.

34. Daniel Ligou, ed., *Dictionnaire de la Franc-Maçonnerie*, 2nd ed. (Paris: Presses universitaires de France, 1987), p. 995; Lennhoff and Posner, *Internationales Freimaurerlexikon*, col. 1295. Reichardt's actual membership in a lodge is not documented; he served in Kassel from the winter of 1807 to autumn 1808 and may have nominated his own successor.

35. See Solomon, *Beethoven*, pp. 178 and 454 n. 17. Alexander I, Czar of Russia (1775–1825), although at first unfavorably inclined to Freemasonry, granted recognition to the lodges in 1810, and he himself later became a Mason. Lennhoff and Posner, *Internationales Freimaurerlexikon*, cols. 42–43. Tradition had it that Alexander reversed his father's ban on Freemasonry as early as 1803; see A. F. A. Woodford, ed., *Kenning's Masonic Cyclopaedia and Handbook of Masonic Archeology, History, and Biography* (London: George Kenning, 1878), p. 17. Although there is no proof that Napoleon Bonaparte was actually a Freemason, it was widely believed that he was initiated on the journey from Egypt to Malta and that he was enrolled in a lodge in Nancy in 1797. See Lennhoff and Posner, *Internationales Freimaurerlexikon*, cols. 1090–91; see also Ligou, *Dictionnaire*, p. 148.

36. See Ferdinand Ries, letter to Simrock, 22 October 1803, in Albrecht, *Letters to Beethoven*, vol. 1, p. 119 (no. 71). As early as 1785–86, Kreutzer belonged to the lodge "La Concorde," Orient, of the court of Versailles. Ligou, *Dictionnaire*, p. 665. It is possible that Kreutzer's (and perhaps Ambassador Bernadotte's) Masonic sympathies had some-

thing to do with Beethoven's warm reception at the French Embassy in Vienna in the early months of 1798. Bernadotte was in later years a prominent Swedish Freemason, but documentary evidence of his earlier initiation in France is not available. For Bernadotte's Masonic standing, see Ligou, *Dictionnaire*, pp. 128–29, 766; Lennhoff and Posner, *Internationales Freimaurerlexikon*, col. 168.

37. For a more complete list, see Solomon, *Beethoven*, p. 83, and Kinsky-Halm, pp. 775–76.

38. Härtel, whose firm published music for use in the Masonic lodges from as early as 1774 (see Georg Kloß, *Bibliographie der Freimaurerei* [Frankfurt: Sauerländer, 1844], nos. 1527, 1529, 1637), is identified as a Freemason in O. E. Deutsch, *Schubert: A Documentary Biography* (London: Dent, 1946), p. 77. Though Hoffmeister is assumed to have been a Freemason of long standing, his Viennese Masonic affiliations have not been established; in Germany he was a member and later music director of the Lodge "Balduin zur Leipzig" from 13 October 1799 (see *Allgemeines Handbuch der Freimaurerei*, vol. 1, p. 461); Simrock's "membership in the Order of Freemasonry is not established" (Hansen, *Quellen zur Geschichte des Rheinlandes*, vol. 1, p. 33), although he was a committed Illuminist (code name Jubal) and a leading publisher of Masonic music. The ideological standpoints of Beethoven's later publishers—Sigmund Anton Steiner, Tobias Haslinger, Anton Diabelli, C. F. Peters, Matthias Artaria, the Schlesingers, and Bernhard Schott's sons—have not been examined.

39. For details, see the relevant entries in Lennhoff and Posner, *Internationales Freimaurerlexikon;* Ligou, *Dictionnaire;* and Schüttler, *Die Mitglieder des Illuminatenordens*. For Herder's complicated associations with the secret societies and a list of his Masonic writings, see Wolfgang Kelsch, "Johann Gottfried Herder und die Freimaurerei," *Quatuor Coronati Jahrbuch* 18 (1981): 33–55, and Kelsch, *Licht—Liebe—Leben: Johann Gottfried Herder und die Freimaurerei* (Bayreuth: Loge Quatuor Coronati Nr. 808, 1994). For Goethe, see now W. Daniel Wilson, *Unterirdische Gänge: Goethe, Freimaurerei und Politik* (Göttingen: Wallstein, 1999).

40. Letter to Friedrich von Matthisson, 4 August 1800, *Briefe*, vol. 1, p. 52 (no. 47), *Letters*, vol. 1, pp. 41–42 (no. 40).

41. W. Daniel Wilson, *Geheimräte gegen Geheimbünde: Ein unbekanntes Kapitel der klassisch-romantischen Geschichte Weimars* (Stuttgart: Metzler, 1991), p. 17. Of some fifty individual books or multivolume sets in Beethoven's *Nachlaß*, six were by authors who had been members of the Order of Illuminati (Goethe, Feßler, Sailer, Meißner, Hufeland, and Bode); four were by noted Freemasons (Matthisson, Klopstock, Hölty, and Voß); and several others were by Masonic sympathizers (notably including Schiller) or were of Masonic interest. Beethoven's library is inventoried by Albert Leitzmann, *Beethoven: Berichte der Zeitgenossen, Briefe und persönliche Aufzeichnungen*, 2 vols. (Leipzig: Insel, 1921), vol. 2, pp. 379–83.

42. For an authoritative history of the conspiracy theories, see Roberts, *Mythology of the Secret Societies;* see also Ludwig Hammermayer, "Zur Geschichte der europäischen Freimaurerei und der Geheimgesellschaften im 18. Jahrhundert: Genese, Historiogra-

phie, Forschungsprobleme," in *Beförderer der Aufklärung in Mittel- und Osteuropa: Freimaurer, Gesellschaften, Clubs,* ed. Eva H. Balázs et al. (Berlin: Camen, 1979), pp. 9–68. See also Hammermayer, "Illuminaten in Bayern," pp. 146–73.

43. Lennhoff and Posner, *Internationales Freimaurerlexikon,* col. 1634; see also col. 225.

44. Letter to Franz Anton Hoffmeister, 5 December 1800, *Briefe,* vol. 1, p. 54 (no. 49), *Letters,* vol. 1, pp. 42–43 (no. 41).

45. In a draft letter to Moritz Schlesinger, 15 July 1825, Beethoven complains about the waste of his time in arranging for London publications: "The *correspondence* and the forwarding take too much of my time, and a priest of *Apollo* ought anyhow to be spared this." The context suggests that the reference to Apollo is a conventional reference to Apollo as the god of "All harmony of instrument or verse" (Shelley, "Hymn of Apollo"). *Briefe,* vol. 6, p. 113 (footnote to no. 2015), A. C. Kalischer, *The Letters of Beethoven,* trans. J. S. Shedlock (London: Dent, 1909), vol. 2, pp. 390–91 (no. 1096).

46. In addition, Hans-Werner Küthen hazards that the famous omitted name in the heading of the Heiligenstadt Testament, "für meine Brüder Carl und — — Beethoven," may have to do, not with his brother Nikolaus Johann, but with the "brothers of his (unknown) Vienna lodge." See Hans-Werner Küthen, *Ein unbekanntes Notierungsblatt Beethovens aus der Entstehungszeit der "Mondscheinsonate"* . . . (Prague: Resonus, 1996), pp. 27–28.

47. Letter to Georg Friedrich Treitschke, *Briefe,* vol. 4, p. 149 (no. 1216), *Letters,* vol. 2, p. 937 (no. 1068). Dated 1821 by Anderson, 1818–21 by Brandenburg; I would assign it to around 1814–17, the established period of the closest association between Beethoven and Treitschke.

48. "Masons are said to part on the square, because having met together, their conduct should be such that, when they part, no unkind expression or unfriendly action shall have deranged that nice adjustment of the feelings, which alone unites them in a band of brothers; an adjustment which can only be preserved by a constant application of the square of morality." Albert G. Mackey, *A Lexikon of Freemasonry* (new ed., New York: Maynard, Merrill, & Co., 1852; 14th printing, 1872), p. 453. See also Mackey, *Encyclopedia of Freemasonry,* vol. 1, pp. 80, 236, vol. 2, pp. 963, 1039, 1053–54.

49. Alternatively, the drawing can be read as one of several other related Masonic symbols: the triangle, compasses, or three equidistant points. But the dashes or dots underneath the lines are suggestive of the metric divisions inscribed on a builder's square.

50. Letter of 11 October 1811 to Christoph August Tiedge, *Briefe,* vol. 2, p. 220 (no. 525), *Letters,* vol. 1, p. 341 (no. 327).

51. Siegmund Kaznelson, *Beethovens ferne und unsterbliche Geliebte* (Zurich: Standard-Buch, 1954), pp. 59 and 373 n.

52. Lennhoff and Posner, *Internationales Freimaurerlexikon,* cols. 236 and 1722–23; *Allgemeines Handbuch der Freimaurerei,* vol. 2, p. 555.

53. There is no documentary confirmation of Tiedge's Masonic affiliations, but Varnhagen, who was another of the group of Berlin literary figures with whom Beethoven

associated that summer, and who had strong Masonic sympathies even before he joined a lodge in 1813, wrote that "the poet Tiedge . . . was in political respects one of our ardent confederates." K. A. Varnhagen von Ense, *Denkwürdigkeiten des eignen Lebens,* ed. Joachim Kühn (Berlin: Volksverband der Bücherfreunde / Wegweiser-Verlag, 1923), part 2, vol. 2, p. 109. See "Varnhagen," in Lennhoff and Posner, *Internationales Freimaurerlexikon,* col. 1630.

54.   *Briefe,* vol. 5, pp. 266–67 (no. 1777), *Letters,* vol. 1, pp. 139–40 (no. 120).

55.   Frimmel, *Handbuch,* vol. 1, pp. 334–35. See also Beethoven's references to ritual purification, in the Tagebuch (no. 63a) and in his letter to Countess Erdödy, 19 September 1815, *Briefe,* vol. 3, pp. 161–62 (no. 827), *Letters,* vol. 2, pp. 527–28 (no. 563).

56.   Because of its presumed reference to Ferdinand Ries, this letter has hitherto been thought to date from September 1805; Brandenburg cogently redates it to ca. January 1824 (see *Briefe,* vol. 5, pp. 266–67), but he unpersuasively reads *gereinigten Lehre* as a reference to Leidesdorf's conversion from Judaism to Catholicism.

57.   Nottebohm, *Zweite Beethoveniana,* p. 83.

58.   See "Akazie," in Lennhoff and Posner, *Internationales Freimaurerlexikon,* col. 35. See Albert G. Mackey, *Symbolism of Freemasonry: Its Science, Philosophy, Legends, Myths, and Symbolism* (1869), revised by Robert Ingham Clegg (Kila, Montana: Kessinger, n.d.), pp. 249–65; see also "Acacia" entries in Arthur Edward Waite, *A New Encyclopaedia of Freemasonry,* 2 vols. (London: W. Rider & Son, 1921; reprint, New York: University Books, 1970), vol. 1, pp. 1–4, and in Ligou, *Dictionnaire,* pp. 5–6.

59.   See, for example, Eduard Herriot, *The Life and Times of Beethoven,* trans. Adelheid I. Mitchell and William J. Mitchell (New York: Macmillan, 1935), p. 146; Jean and Brigitte Massin, *Ludwig van Beethoven* (Paris: Fayard, 1967), pp. 192 n. 4, and 651–52; Basso, *L'invenzione della gioia,* pp. 438–39; Jacques Henry, *Mozart frère maçon: La symbolique maçonnique dans l'oeuvre de Mozart* (Aix-en-Provence: Alinea, 1991), p. 38.

60.   See "Saule" and "Ordre," in Ligou, *Dictionnaire,* pp. 1086, 870; "Napoleons-Maurerei," in *Allgemeines Handbuch der Freimaurerei,* vol. 2, p. 76.

61.   The leaf containing Beethoven's copy of the inscriptions is in the Wegeler Collection, now on permanent loan to the Beethoven-Archiv, Bonn; facsimile in Stephan Ley, *Beethovens Leben in authentischen Bildern und Texten* (Berlin: Cassirer, 1925), p. 129 (Ley's transcription corrected). See also Schindler-MacArdle, p. 365. The Orphic provenance of the third inscription and its asserted use in rites of the Eleusinian Mysteries was first established by Jan Assmann, *Moses the Egyptian: The Memory of Egypt in Western Monotheism* (Cambridge, Mass.: Harvard University Press, 1997), pp. 98, 118–23, 239 n. 21, 246–47 n. 98, quoting William Warburton, *The Divine Legation of Moses Demonstrated on the Principles of a Religious Deist, from the Omission of the Doctrine of a Future State of Reward and Punishment in the Jewish Dispensation,* 2nd ed. (London, 1778), book 2, section 4, vol. 1, p. 202, reprinted in *The Works of the Right Reverend William Warburton, D.D., Lord Bishop of Gloucester,* 12 vols. (London: Cadell and Davies, 1811), vol. 2, pp. 45–46. Warburton's English rendering of the Orphic poem, which he located in works by Eusebius and Clement of Alexandria, reads:

I will declare a SECRET to the Initiated; but let the doors be shut against the profane. . . .
Go on, in the right way, and contemplate THE SOLE GOVERNOR OF THE WORLD: HE IS ONE,
AND OF HIMSELF ALONE; AND TO THAT ONE ALL THINGS OWE THEIR BEING. HE OPERATES
THROUGH ALL, WAS NEVER SEEN BY MORTAL EYES, BUT DOES HIMSELF SEE EVERY ONE.

The Eleusinian Mysteries are thought to have originated in Egypt. Beethoven added
the Orphic inscription, in smaller letters, perhaps as an afterthought. See Assmann,
p. 246 n. 98.

62. Voltaire, "Des Rites Égyptiens," *Oeuvres de Voltaire,* vol. 15, ed. M. Beuchot (Paris:
Lefèvre, 1829), pp. 102–6; the second of the three inscriptions is quoted in Immanuel
Kant, *The Critique of Aesthetic Judgement,* trans. James Creed Meredith (Oxford: Clarendon Press, 1911), p. 179 n., where Kant writes, "Perhaps there has never been a more
sublime utterance, or a thought more sublimely expressed, than the well-known inscription upon the Temple of *Isis.*"

63. See Ligou, *Dictionnaire,* pp. 624–25.

64. Arnold Schmitz, *Das romantische Beethovenbild* (Bonn: Dümmler, 1927), p. 88; Leitzmann, *Beethoven,* vol. 2, p. 374 (no. 182).

65. See especially Ignaz von Born's magisterial article, J. v. B. M. v. St. [Ignaz von Born,
Meister vom Stuhl], "Ueber die Mysterien der Egyptier," *Journal für Freymaurer. Als
Manuskript gedruckt für Brüder und Meister des Ordens. Herausgegeben von den Brüdern der
□ zur wahren Eintracht im Orient von Wien* 1, no. 1 (5784 [1784]): [17]–132. In its internal writings, the Order of Illuminati designated Austria as "Egypten." See *Einige Originalschriften des Illuminatenordens* (Munich: Anton Franz, 1787), as excerpted in *Die Illuminaten: Quellen und Texte zur Aufklärungsideologie des Illuminatenordens (1776–1785),* ed.
Jan Rachold (Berlin: Akademie-Verlag, 1984), p. 30.

66. Br.[uder] Decius [Karl Leonhard Reinhold], "Ueber die Mysterien der alten Hebräer," *Journal für Freymaurer* 3, no. 1 (5786 [1786]): 5–79, at 45–48; idem, "Ueber die
größern Mysterien der Hebräer," *Journal für Freymaurer* 3, no. 3 (5786 [1786]): 5–98;
idem, *Die hebräischen Mysterien oder die älteste religiöse Freymaurerey* (Leipzig: Georg Joachim
Göschen, 1788), with the inscriptions quoted at pp. 53–54. "Die Sendung Moses" was
initially published in Schiller's journal *Thalia* 10 ([1791]): 1–37, with the quotations at
pp. 17–18, reprinted in *Prosaische Schriften,* vol. 10 of *Schillers sämtliche Werke,* 12 vols.
(Stuttgart: Cotta, various dates), pp. 270–88, quotations at p. 278. For discussions, see
Leitzmann, *Beethoven,* vol. 2, p. 374; Frimmel, *Handbuch,* vol. 1, pp. 178–79, and Schmitz,
Das romantische Beethovenbild, pp. 85–88. Baensch showed that an edition of Schiller's
essay was Beethoven's immediate source, pointing out that the word order of the Saitic
lines as given in Reinhold's 1788 book is slightly different from that given by Schiller
and Beethoven. See Otto Baensch, *Aufbau und Sinn des Chorfinales in Beethovens neunter
Symphonie* (Berlin and Leipzig: Walter de Gruyter, 1930), p. 27 n. 3. The *Journal für Freymaurer* version of Reinhold's monograph, too, has trivial discrepancies from Beethoven's
text. For the widespread dissemination of the trope of the Veil of Isis, see Alexander
G. F. Gode–von Aesch, *Natural Science in German Romanticism* (New York: Columbia

University Press, 1941), pp. 97–113; see also Christine Harrauer, "'Ich bin was da ist . . .'
Die Göttin von Sais und ihre Deutung von Plutarch bis in die Goethezeit," *ΣΦΑΙΡΟΣ
Wiener Studien, Zeitschrift für Klassische Philologie und Patristik. Hans Schwabl zum 70.
Geburtstag gewidmet* (Vienna: Österreichischen Akademie der Wissenschaften, 1994–95),
vols. 107–8, part 1, pp. 337–355. For a discussion of non-Masonic implications of the
inscriptions, see pp. 67–70, above. The partial "doubling" of the first phrase of the Isis
inscription in Reinhold, Schiller, and Beethoven evidently originates with Voltaire.

67. Schiller, "Die Sendung Moses," *Prosaische Schriften*, p. 278, Thayer-Forbes, pp. 481–
82 (translation amended). Matthias Artaria asked in a conversation book of 1826, "Haben
Sie gelesen Über die Sendung *Moses* von *Schiller?* [Have you read Schiller's 'Die Sendung
Moses'?]." *Konversationshefte*, vol. 8, p. 282, 16–22 January 1826 (Heft 102, 23v). Beethoven's reply was not recorded.

68. [Johann Heinrich Faber,] *Der ächte Illuminat, oder die wahren, unverbesserten Rituale
der Illuminaten: Enthaltend 1) die Vorbereitung, 2) das Noviziat, 3) den Minervalgrad, 4) den
kleinen und 5) großen Illuminatengrad* (Edessa [Frankfurt]: Hermannische Buchhandlung,
1788), p. 142. The catechism is also used in Scottish Rite Freemasonry. The significance
of the passage was first observed by Irmen, *Beethoven*, p. 322.

69. *Briefe*, vol. 3, pp. 161–62 (no. 827), *Letters*, vol. 2, pp. 527–28 (no. 563). Beethoven's reference to ritual purification within the Temple of Isis is probably inspired by
the famous closing chapter of Apuleius, *The Golden Ass* (bk. 11). Aumont, successor to
the immolated Jacques De Molay as Grand Master of the Knights Templars, is said to
have taken for his seal the image of a phoenix brooding within the flames, bearing the
motto *Ardet ut vivat*, "She burns that she may live." Mackey, *Encyclopedia of Freemasonry*,
vol. 2, p. 771. Complicating this reference to the "Temple of Isis" is Schindler's invented
story that, "in the park of one of her seats in Hungary," Countess Erdödy "erected . . .
a handsome temple . . . expressing her homage to the great composer." Schindler, *Biographie von Ludwig van Beethoven* (Münster: Aschendorff, 1840), p. 69, trans. Schindler-
Moscheles, p. 43; reprinted in the second edition of the biography (Münster, 1845),
vol. 1, p. 69; omitted from the third edition (see Schindler-MacArdle, pp. 101, 212).

70. *Konversationshefte*, vol. 9, p. 97, first half of March 1826 (Heft 106, 6r).

71. Letters to Anton Schindler, 17 May 1823, end of February 1823, 21 April 1823,
and July–August 1823, *Briefe*, vol. 5, p. 125 (no. 1650), vol. 5, p. 67 (1587), vol. 5, p. 108
(1633), vol. 5, p. 204 (no. 1719); *Letters*, vol. 3, p. 1037 (no. 1180), vol. 3, p. 1072 (no.
1216), vol. 3, p. 1075 (no. 1223), vol. 3, p. 1079 (no. 1229).

72. *Konversationshefte*, vol. 2, p. 326, second half of January 1823 (Heft 20, 19a verso).

73. Schindler-MacArdle, p. 263.

74. Schindler, *Biographie* (1860), vol. 1, p. 231, Schindler-MacArdle, p. 204 (translation
amended).

75. Frimmel, *Handbuch*, vol. 1, p. 152. Descriptions of the religious ceremonies of the
Samothracians appear in F. W. J. Schelling, *Ueber die Gottheiten von Samotrace* (Stuttgart:
Cotta, 1815) and Br. R ** [Karl Leonhard Reinhold], "Ueber die kabirischen Myste-

rien," *Journal für Freymaurer* 2, no. 3 (5785 [1785]): 5–48. For Beethoven and Schelling, see Baensch, *Aufbau und Sinn des Chorfinales*, pp. 88–92; see also Irmen, *Beethoven*, pp. 421–22; Irmen et al., *Protokolle*, pp. 32, 270.

76. See "Mysterien von Samothrake," in Lennhoff and Posner, *Internationales Freimaurerlexikon*, col. 1087; Reinhold, "Ueber die kabirischen Mysterien," p. 47; "Samothrace," *Encyclopaedia Britannica*, 13th ed. (London, 1926), vol. 24, pp. 117–18.

77. Two Beethoven letters that may bear on such a perception are to Karl van Beethoven, 23 August 1823, *Briefe*, vol. 5, p. 219 (no. 1735), *Letters*, vol. 3, pp. 1083–84 (no. 1233), and to Schindler, 21 April 1823, *Briefe*, vol. 5, p. 109 (no. 1633), *Letters*, vol. 3, p. 1075 (no. 1223).

78. Letter to Schindler, 1 July 1823, *Briefe*, vol. 5, p. 67 (no. 1587), *Letters*, vol. 3, p. 1072 (no. 1216).

79. For code names in the Erdödy circle, see Countess Erdödy's poem to Beethoven, ca. 20 July 1815, *Briefe*, vol. 3, pp. 154–55 (no. 819), and Beethoven's letter to Countess Erdödy, after 20 July 1815, *Briefe*, vol. 3, p. 156 (no. 821), *Letters*, vol. 2, p. 518 (no. 549). For Steiner and associates, see Solomon, *Beethoven*, p. 335; for Schuppanzigh, see Paul Nettl, *Beethoven Handbook* (New York: Ungar, 1967), p. 230.

80. See *Allgemeines Handbuch der Freimaurerei*, vol. 1, p. 373; Lennhoff and Posner, *Internationales Freimaurerlexikon*, col. 618. Beethoven wrote two brief settings—the album composition WoO 151 and the canon WoO 185—of Goethe's "Edel sei der Mensch, hülfreich und gut," which is characterized as an "authentically Masonic proverb" in *Allgemeines Handbuch der Freimaurerei*, vol. 1, p. 374.

81. Heinrich Boos, *Geschichte der Freimaurerei: Ein Beitrag zur Kultur- und Literatur-Geschichte des 18. Jahrhunderts* (Arrau: Sauerländer, 1906), p. 350 and n.

82. WoO 117 and WoO 126 were published by Simrock in 1808 in *III Deutsche Lieder*.

83. Otto Jahn reached the skeptical conclusion that "A style of music specifically belonging to Freemasonry is of course inconceivable." Otto Jahn, *W. A. Mozart*, 4th ed., edited by Hermann Deiters (Leipzig: Breitkopf & Härtel, 1907), vol. 2, p. 117, trans. Jahn, *Life of Mozart* (London: Macmillan, 1882), vol. 2, p. 410. See also the caveat by Cecil Hill in "Masonic music," *New Grove*, vol. 11, p. 754.

84. Donald Francis Tovey, *Essays in Musical Analysis*, vol. 2, *Symphonies* (London: Oxford University Press, 1935), pp. 161–62; also p. 168. Basso sees the "Consecration of the House" as expressing the "Masonic ideal" (Basso, *L'invenzione della gioia*, p. 442).

85. To be sure, others would have had differing perceptions: the trials of Viennese Jacobins were only a few years in the past; and inasmuch as the Terror was also recent news, Bouilly's libretto may have been reckoned by some as a protest against revolutionary excess.

86. Edward J. Dent, "The Choral Fantasia," *Music & Letters* 8 (1927): 113; Dent, *Mozart's Operas: A Critical Study*, 2nd ed. (London: Oxford University Press, 1960), p. 259.

87. Dent, "The Choral Fantasia," pp. 116–17.

88. Tovey, *Essays in Musical Analysis*, vol. 2, p. 135. The authorship of the text, once

thought to have been by Christoph Kuffner, remains unsettled. Nottebohm found reasons to think that Treitschke might have been its author. See Nottebohm, *Zweite Beethoveniana*, p. 503 n; see also p. 264.

89. Dent, "The Choral Fantasia," pp. 114–15.

90. Schiller's precise relationship to the secret societies remains disputed. See Lennhoff and Posner, *Internationales Freimaurerlexikon*, cols. 1391–92; Irmen, *Beethoven*, p. 417. Schiller himself wrote in letter 10 of his *Briefe über Don Karlos,* "I am neither Illuminist nor Freemason, but . . ." See Schiller, *Prosaische Schriften*, p. 231. For Körner's Masonic and Illuminist affiliations, of which he informed Schiller, see Johann Joachim Christoph Bode, *Journal von einer Reise von Weimar nach Frankreich: im Jahr 1787*, ed. Hermann Schüttler (Munich: Ars Una, 1994), p. 32 n. 83.

91. See the lists of settings in Basso, *L'invenzione della gioia*, pp. 425–29, and Julius Blaschke, "Schillers Gedichte in der Musik," *Neue Zeitschrift für Musik* 72 (1905): 397–401. Possible Masonic sources of "An die Freude" are discussed in Gotthold Deile, *Freimaurerlieder als Quellen zu Schillers Lied "An die Freude"* (Leipzig: Adolf Weigel, 1907), and Hans Vaihinger, "Zwei Quellenfunde zu Schillers philosophischer Entwickelung," *Kant-Studien* 10 (1905): 386–89.

92. Baensch, *Aufbau und Sinn des Chorfinales*, p. 25 n. 2.

93. Nottebohm, *Beethoveniana*, pp. 41–42; ideas for a choral overture, noted among sketches for the Symphony in F, op. 93. In September 1824, Karl Joseph Bernard wrote in a conversation book: "Nowadays everything becomes debased and disapproved of. Instead of 'Bettler werden Fürsten Brüder,' your text now reads 'Alle Menschen werden Brüder.'" *Konversationshefte*, vol. 6, p. 362 (Heft 76, 16r).

94. Nohl, *Beethoven's Brevier* (Leipzig: Günther, 1870), p. 105, one of two quatrains from "An die Freude" reproduced from a tracing of Beethoven's handwriting with his name signed underneath. "They are surely Albumblätter," writes Nohl.

95. Ernst Wangermann, *The Austrian Achievement: 1700–1800* (London: Thames & Hudson, 1973), pp. 150–52.

96. As one Masonic scholar has pointed out in a discussion of Swieten's libretto for *The Creation*, "[T]he tradition of God as Architect was older than Freemasonry and is an idea on which we, as masons, hold no monopoly. Similarly the idea of the Brotherhood of Man is one by no means limited to masonic philosophy. The scenario provided by *The Creation*'s libretto, showing the ordered, reasoned and logical creation from original chaos to the appearance of man . . . is a perfect exemplification of the rationalist philosophy of the age of Enlightenment. . . . [T]hat masonic elements may exist is purely incidental, a happy accident for those who wish to identify them." J. M. Hamill, in response to John Webb, "Joseph Haydn: Freemason and Musician," in *Ars Quatuor Coronatorum*, vol. 94 of *Transactions of Quatuor Coronati Lodge No. 2076 for the Year 1981* (Letchworth: Garden City Press, Ltd., 1982), pp. 61–82, at p. 76. For further discussion, see Joachim Hurwitz, *Joseph Haydn und die Freimaurer* (Frankfurt: P. Lang, 1996), pp. 62–73.

97. There are numerous putatively Masonic images, tropes, and preoccupations in the

texts of several *Festspiele* celebrating the Habsburg regime for which Beethoven per-functorily provided music, including "Die Ruinen von Athen," op. 113; "König Stephan, oder Ungarns erster Wohltäter," op. 117; and "Die Weihe des Hauses," op. 114/WoO 98 (partly adapted from op. 113). Kotzebue, a convinced Freemason who was skilled at flattering the powerful, wrote the texts for "Die Ruinen von Athen" and "König Stephan."

Chapter 8. The Masonic Imagination

1.   For details of the published editions, see Tagebuch in the list of abbreviations, above. Parenthetical references in the text are to Tagebuch entries, identified by the numbers assigned in those editions. Beethoven's original manuscript of the Tagebuch has disap-peared, and the editions rely on Anton Gräffer's copy. In what follows, one must take into account clear evidence that the text was censored during the copying process to mask several references to Brahman religion, among them "Brahm," "dreyfache Zeit," "Bhagavan," and "Sonne, Aether, Brahma" (no. 61); "Yōg" (no. 64); and "Sah' Brahm nur seinen Geist" (no. 65).

2.   Some other Masonic groups started their calendars at different dates, e.g.: Scottish Rite Masons, 3760 B.C.; Knights Templars, A.D. 1118; Royal Arch Masons, 530 B.C.; and Royal and Select Master Masons, 1000 B.C. For a listing of the main Masonic cal-endars see "Calendar," in Albert G. Mackey, *Encyclopedia of Freemasonry,* revised and en-larged by Robert I. Clegg and H. L. Haywood, 3 vols. (Chicago: Masonic History Co., 1946), vol. 1, pp. 172–73; see also vol. 3, p. 1182. See also "Calendrier," in Ligou, *Dic-tionnaire,* pp. 185–86. The calendar of the Order of Illuminati used a modified Persian system with an origination point of 21 March 630 A.D. (see W. Daniel Wilson, *Geheim-räte gegen Geheimbünde: Ein unbekanntes Kapitel der klassisch-romantischen Geschichte Weimars* [Stuttgart: Metzler, 1991], p. 365); but Viennese Illuminists used the standard Habsburg Masonic calendar in their publications. The Masonic significance of the Tagebuch dat-ings was first noted, in 1990, in the paperback edition of Solomon, *Beethoven Essays,* pp. 270, 288.

3.   Divergent tendencies trace Freemasonry to Biblical origins, ancient mystery cults, chivalric traditions, the guilds of masons, and various esoteric sources. The first version of the Knights Templars legend of origin was introduced in about 1754, and banned by 1782; another version, the "Second Legend of Perpetuation," founded on a forgery called the Charter of Larmenius, surfaced in Paris around 1804. See Arthur Edward Waite, *A New Encyclopaedia of Freemasonry,* 2 vols. (London: W. Rider & Son, 1921; reprint, New York: University Books, 1970), vol. 2, pp. 213, 218–24.

4.   For representative Masonic readings, see Jacques Chailley, "Sur la signification du quatuor de Mozart K. 465, dit 'les dissonances,' et du 7ème quatuor de Beethoven," in *Natalica Musicologica: Knud Jeppeson septuagenario collegis oblata,* ed. Bjørn Hjelmborg and Søren Sørensen (Copenhagen: Wilhelm Hansen, 1962), pp. 283–92; Hans-Josef Irmen, *Beethoven in seiner Zeit* (Zülpich: Prisca, 1998); Alberto Basso, *L'invenzione della gioia:*

Musica e massoneria nell'età dei Lumi (Milan: Garzanti, 1994). For an extended Masonic interpretation of the *Missa solemnis,* see Wilfrid Mellers, *Beethoven and the Voice of God* (London: Faber and Faber, 1983), pp. 291–369 (see pp. 199–200, below).

5.   Frances A. Yates, *The Rosicrucian Enlightenment* (London: Routledge & Kegan Paul, 1972), p. 220.

6.   Statutes, in *Einige Originalschriften des Illuminatenordens* (Munich: Anton Franz, 1787), reprinted in *Die Illuminaten: Quellen und Texte zur Aufklärungsideologie des Illuminatenordens (1776–1785),* ed. Jan Rachold (Berlin: Akademie-Verlag, 1984), p. 36. The statutes were formulated in a *Lehrplan* to cover the Order's original tripartite grade system: Apprentice, Minerval, and Minerval illuminatus. See "Illuminaten," in Eugen Lennhoff and Oskar Posner, *Internationales Freimaurerlexikon* (Munich: Amalthea, and Graz: Akademische Druck- u. Verlagsanstalt, 1932), cols. 729–33. The Order's instructions, in essentially identical form, were circulated in the Bonn "Stagira" lodge; see Alfred Becker, *Christian Gottlob Neefe und die Bonner Illuminaten* (Bonn: Bouvier, 1969), pp. 40–47.

7.   Rachold, *Illuminaten,* pp. 45–46, 55.

8.   Rachold, *Illuminaten,* pp. 47, 64, 65.

9.   Becker, *Neefe und die Bonner Illuminaten,* p. 43; Rachold, *Illuminaten,* pp. 29, 59.

10.   Johann Pezzl, letter to Karl Leonhard Reinhold, quoted by Helmut Reinalter, "Ignaz von Born als Freimaurer und Illuminat," in *Die Aufklärung in Österreich: Ignaz von Born und seine Zeit,* ed. Helmut Reinalter (Frankfurt: P. Lang, 1991), p. 45. See also Edith Rosenstrauch-Königsberg, "Eine freimaurerische Akademie der Wissenschaften in Wien," in *Revolution und Demokratie in Geschichte und Literatur: Zum 60. Geburtstag von Walter Grab,* ed. Julius H. Schoeps and Imanuel Geiss (Duisburg: Braun, 1979), pp. 151–69.

11.   See Walther Engelhardt, "Die Kieler Handschrift der Autobiographie Christian Gottlob Neefes 1748–1798," *Zeitschrift für Musikwissenschaft* 7 (1925), and Engelhardt, ed., *Christian Gottlob Neefens Lebenslauf von ihm selbst beschrieben: Nebst beigefügtem Karackter, 1789* (Cologne: Arno Volk, 1957), esp. pp. 23–25. Earlier editions of the "Lebenslauf," beginning with its publication in the *AmZ* 1 (1798–99), cols. 241–45, 257–61, 273–78, 360–64, omit several of the passages crucial for such a reading. The idea of Neefe's "Lebenslauf" as an initiatory document is broached in Irmen, *Beethoven,* pp. 31–32.

12.   Kalidasa, *Sakontala,* trans. Georg Forster (Mainz and Leipzig, 1791), p. 123 (act 4).

13.   Letter of 19 September 1815, *Briefe,* vol. 3, pp. 161–62 (no. 827), *Letters,* vol. 2, pp. 527–28 (no. 563). See p. 149 above.

14.   Jean Mourgues, "Voyages," in Ligou, *Dictionnaire,* p. 1240; see "Reisen, Wanderungen...," in Lennhoff and Posner, *Internationales Freimaurerlexikon,* cols. 1296–98, and "Reisen" in G. Lenning [Friedrich Moßdorf], *Encyclopädie der Freimaurerei,* 3 vols. (Leipzig: Brockhaus, 1822–28), vol. 3, pp. 209–16, the last with extensive quotations from authentic rituals. "The Journey is one of the mystical trials undergone by applicants in various grades, and each has its particular symbolic meaning" (p. 209). The universality of the circuitous journey in Christian theology, world myth, quest litera-

ture, and Romanticism is illustrated and analyzed in M. H. Abrams, *Natural Supernaturalism: Tradition and Revolution in Romantic Literature* (New York: Norton, 1971; reprint, 1973).

15. Albert G. Mackey, *Symbolism of Freemasonry: Its Science, Philosophy, Legends, Myths, and Symbolism* (1869), revised by Robert Ingham Clegg (Kila, Montana: Kessinger, n.d.), p. 141.

16. Heinz Schuler, *Mozart und die Freimaurerei* (Wilhelmshaven: Noetzel, 1992), pp. 44–45. For additional examples of such journeys in several generic Masonic initiation rituals, see Hans-Josef Irmen, *Mozart: Mitglied geheimer Gesellschaften* (Zülpich: Prisca, 1988), pp. 101–7, 123–24, 135–36.

17. H. L. Haywood, *Symbolical Masonry: An Interpretation of the Three Degrees* (New York: George H. Doran, 1923), p. 98.

18. For the foregoing, I rely primarily on Mackey, *Encyclopedia of Freemasonry*, vol. 1, pp. 301–2, 336; vol. 2, pp. 717, 954, 1101; Mackey, *Symbolism of Freemasonry*, p. 336; Haywood, *Symbolical Freemasonry*, pp. 102–4, 152; William Preston, *Illustrations of Masonry* (London: printed for the author, 1772; numerous later editions), as referred to in Lennhoff and Posner, *Internationales Freimaurerlexikon*, col. 1297.

19. Beethoven's conception of the East, its sacred thought, and its deities is woven from a variety of authentic, spurious, and even fictional or imaginative materials. Thus, extracts from the *Bhagavad-Gita* (no. 64a) are found side by side with a spurious shastra from the Vedas that was recited to Alexander Dow (no. 93b) and an ode in Vedic style by Sir William Jones (nos. 62, 65). The Tagebuch also perpetuates several mistaken ideas about Brahman ritual practices. But historical accuracy is not an issue here; rather, Beethoven is to be regarded as a transmitter of materials that had become embedded in historical memory as an imaginary construction or idea of the East. For a discussion of history as the reception of memory ("mnemohistory") distinct from history as a factual record of past events, see chapter 1 of Jan Assmann, *Moses the Egyptian: The Memory of Egypt in Western Monotheism* (Cambridge, Mass.: Harvard University Press, 1997). Assmann writes: "Mnemohistory is concerned not with the past as such, but only with the past as it is remembered" (p. 9).

20. Otto Erich Deutsch, *Mozart: A Documentary Biography* (London: A. & C. Black, 1965), p. 287; Mackey, *Encyclopedia of Freemasonry*, vol. 2, p. 743; see also Heinz Schuler, "Die Mozart-Loge: 'Zur neugekrönten Hoffnung' im Orient von Wien. Eine Quellenstudie," *Mitteilungen der Internationalen Stiftung Mozarteum* 37 (1989): 1–44.

21. "[H]is membership in the Illuminati is disputed" (W. Daniel Wilson, *Geheimräte gegen Geheimbünde* [Stuttgart: Metzler, 1991], p. 385). For Forster's status as a Freemason, see *Allgemeines Handbuch der Freimaurerei*, ed. Verein deutscher Freimaurer (3rd revised ed. of Lenning, *Encyclopädie der Freimaurerei*), 2 vols. (Leipzig: Max Hesse, 1900–1901), vol. 1, pp. 292–93; he was the son of Johann Reinhold Forster, translator of Eastern writings and an active Mason. See Lenning, *Encyclopädie der Freimaurerei*, vol. 1, p. 243. To balance the scales somewhat, the dramatist Adolf Müllner, whose drama *Die Schuld* is excerpted in the Tagebuch (no. 7), became a bitter antagonist of Freemasonry. See *Allgemeines Handbuch der Freimaurerei*, vol. 2, p. 62.

22. In Irmen's reconstruction of one of Mozart's initiation ceremonies, the Master of the Lodge says, "Brother Overseer, let us permit the invalid to see the light!" See Irmen, *Mozart,* p. 105.

23. Mackey, *Symbolism of Freemasonry,* p. 155.

24. Oskar Walzel, *German Romanticism,* 5th ed., trans. Alma Elise Lussky (New York: Ungar, 1965), p. 264. See the critical essay by the poet who wrote "An die ferne Geliebte": Aloys Jeitteles, "Gegen die romantische Schicksalstragödie," *Wiener Moden-Zeitung und Zeitschrift für Kunst, schöne Literatur und Theater* 2, no. 24 (22 March 1817): 189–93.

25. Mackey, *Encyclopedia of Freemasonry,* vol. 2, p. 821.

26. Mackey, *Encyclopedia of Freemasonry,* vol. 2, pp. 739, 920.

27. "The duty of a Freemason . . . to say little, and to hear and think much." See "Duty," in Mackey, *Encyclopedia of Freemasonry,* vol. 1, p. 298.

28. In his article on the Indian Mysteries, Born refers to "Verschwiegenheit" as a crucial attribute of "the high Brahmans." See Br. B★★★ [Ignaz von Born], "Ueber die Mysterien der Indier," *Journal für Freymaurer* 1, no. 4 (1784): 50, 52.

29. See Mackey, *Encyclopedia of Freemasonry,* vol. 2, p. 920.

30. Rachold, *Illuminaten,* pp. 43, 38.

31. Rachold, *Illuminaten,* p. 50; see also Becker, *Neefe und die Bonner Illuminaten,* p. 47.

32. As Georg Simmel has observed in his study of pledges of secrecy in secret orders, the "purpose of secrecy is, above all, *protection.* Of all protective measures, the most radical is to make oneself invisible." See *The Sociology of Georg Simmel,* trans. and ed. Kurt H. Wolff (New York: Free Press, 1950), p. 345. It seems only natural that an easing of the strictures on secrecy should have occurred during the period of official toleration of Freemasonry in the Josephinian years, especially those preceding the restrictive *Freimaurerpatent* of 1785. Where self-protective measures are considered unnecessary, the injunction to silence may persist primarily as a ritual formality.

33. As given in Mircea Eliade, *Birth and Rebirth,* trans. Willard R. Trask (New York: Harper & Brothers, 1958), reprinted as *Rites and Symbols of Initiation: The Mysteries of Birth and Rebirth* (New York: Harper & Brothers, 1965), p. 120.

34. *Konversationshefte,* vol. 1, p. 211, January 1820 (Heft 6, 63r).

35. Letter of 13 May 1816, *Briefe,* vol. 3, p. 258 (no. 934), *Letters,* vol. 2, p. 578 (no. 633, translation amended). An analogous idea is expressed in a congratulatory letter of 1819 to Archduke Rudolph: "There is hardly any good thing which can be achieved—without a sacrifice; and it is precisely the nobler and better man who seems to be destined for this more than other human beings, no doubt in order that his virtue may be put to the test." Letter of 3 March 1819, *Briefe,* vol. 4, p. 245 (no. 1292), *Letters,* vol. 2, p. 813 (no. 948).

36. Mackey, *Symbolism of Freemasonry,* p. 94.

37. See, for example, Theodor Reik, *Ritual: Psycho-Analytic Studies,* trans. Douglas Bryan (New York: Farrar, Straus and Co., 1946), p. 146. Reik's views are based on observations by the anthropologist Leo Frobenius; see especially Frobenius, *Die Masken und Geheim-*

bünde Afrikas (Halle, E. Karras, 1898). Eliade, on the other hand, sees rituals primarily as avenues to sacredness. See *Birth and Rebirth*, pp. 73–74.

38. "I have replied to her this time not like a Sarastro but like a Sultan." Letter of 27 July 1816, *Briefe*, vol. 3, p. 278 (no. 955), *Letters*, vol. 2, p. 589 (no. 644). For references to Johanna van Beethoven as the Queen of Night, see *Briefe* nos. 904, 907, 1120, 955, 971, 906, 1193, 1326, *Letters* nos. 611, 612, 616, 644, 654, 719, 835, 967.

39. Letter to Kanka, 6 September 1816, *Briefe*, vol. 3, p. 295 (no. 971), *Letters*, vol. 2, p. 597 (no. 654).

40. John Robison, *Proofs of a Conspiracy Against all the Religions and Governments of Europe, Carried on in the Secret Meetings of Free Masons, Illuminati, and Reading Societies*, 2nd ed. (London: Cadell and Davies, 1797), p. 119.

41. Mackey, *Symbolism of Freemasonry*, pp. 106–8.

42. Mackey, *Symbolism of Freemasonry*, pp. 112–13; Mackey, *Encyclopedia of Freemasonry*, vol. 2, p. 769. Rosicrucian tracts accumulated extensive data on the phallus as a universal emblem of procreative power ("the male generative principle") among the world religions, especially those of the East. See, for example, Hargrave Jennings, *The Rosicrucians: Their Rites and Mysteries*, 5th ed. (London: Routledge, [1887]), pp. 45–47, 91, 189–91, 233–53, 391–93.

43. Mackey, *Symbolism of Freemasonry*, p. 135.

44. See "Friendship," in Mackey, *Encyclopedia of Freemasonry*, vol. 1, p. 383; "Freundschaft," in Lennhoff and Posner, *Internationales Freimaurerlexikon*, col. 540.

45. See, for example, Friedrich Creuzer, *Symbolik und Mythologie der alten Völker, besonders der Griechen*, 4 vols. (Leipzig: Heyer and Leske, 1810–12); Friedrich Majer, *Allgemeines mythologisches Lexicon*, 2 vols. (Weimar: Landes-Industrie-Comtoir, 1803–4); Joseph Görres, *Mythengeschichte der asiatischen Welt*, 2 vols. (Heidelberg: Mohr and Zimmer, 1810); and a variety of works on myth and folklore of the Middle East and India by Beethoven's acquaintance Joseph Hammer-Purgstall. A standard monograph in English is A. Leslie Willson's *A Mythical Image: The Ideal of India in German Romanticism* (Durham: Duke University Press, 1964); see also Raymond Schwab, *The Oriental Renaissance: Europe's Rediscovery of India and the East, 1680–1880*, trans. Gene Patterson-Black and Victor Reinking (New York: Columbia University Press, 1984). Both books overlook the Masonic aspects of the subject.

46. Heiligenstadt Testament, 6–10 October 1802, *Briefe*, vol. 1, p. 122 (no. 106), *Letters*, vol. 3, p. 1352 (appendix A). Letter to Wegeler of 29 June 1801, *Briefe*, vol. 1, p. 80 (no. 65), *Letters*, vol. 1, p. 60 (no. 51).

47. Letter written before 6 August 1808, *Briefe*, vol. 2, p. 21 (no. 332), *Letters*, vol. 1, p. 197 (no. 175). "Beethoven . . . is presently indeed composing an opera by Schikaneder, but he himself told me that he is seeking rational *[vernünftige]* librettos." Georg August Griesinger, letter to Gottfried Christoph Härtel, 12 November 1803, in *"Eben komme Ich von Haydn . . . ": Georg August Griesingers Korrespondenz mit Joseph Haydns Verleger Breitkopf & Härtel, 1799–1819*, ed. Otto Biba (Zürich: Atlantis, 1987), p. 212.

48. William Warburton, *The Divine Legation of Moses Demonstrated on the Principles of a Religious Deist, from the Omission of the Doctrine of a Future State of Reward and Punishment in the Jewish Dispensation*, 2nd ed. (London, 1778), reprinted in *The Works of the Right Reverend William Warburton, D.D., Lord Bishop of Gloucester*, 12 vols. (London: Cadell and Davies, 1811), vol. 4, p. 375.

49. See Ernst Cassirer, *Mythical Thought*, vol. 2 of *The Philosophy of Symbolic Forms*, trans. Ralph Manheim (New Haven and London: Yale University Press, 1955), pp. 3–4.

Chapter 9. The Shape of a Journey

1. See chapter 1. For a possible parallel to Dante's use of the vernacular in his "sacred poem," see Erich Auerbach, *Introduction to Romance Languages and Literature*, trans. Guy Daniels (New York: Capricorn, 1961), p. 125.

2. Romain Rolland follows August Halm in viewing the Alla marcia as "la vraie première" variation. The Alla marcia is "more than just a variation, it . . . annuls Diabelli's theme." Rolland, *Beethoven: Les grandes époques créatrices* (Paris: Albin Michel, 1966), p. 987.

3. The "maestoso" indication may have a religious as well as a royal connotation, as in Beethoven's setting of Gellert's "Die Ehre Gottes aus der Natur," op. 48, no. 4, which is designated "majestic and sublime *[majestätisch und erhaben]*."

4. Joseph Kerman, *The Beethoven Quartets* (New York: Knopf, 1967), pp. 195–222.

5. Wilhelm Lenz observed that in three crucial movements of his late works Beethoven used unusual titles drawn from Italian song genres: Arioso (op. 110), Arietta (op. 111), and Cavatina (op. 130). Wilhelm von Lenz, *Beethoven, eine Kunst-Studie: Kritischer Katalog sämmtlicher Werke Ludwig van Beethovens mit Analysen derselben* (Hamburg: Hoffman & Campe, 1860), vol. 5, part 4, pp. 93–94. See also Ludwig Nohl, *Beethoven's Leben*, vol. 3 (Leipzig: Günther, 1877), p. 279.

6. Northrop Frye, "New Directions from Old," in *Myth and Mythmaking*, ed. Henry A. Murray (New York: Braziller, 1960), p. 123.

7. Northrop Frye, "The *Koine* of Myth: Myth as a Universally Intelligible Language," in *Myth and Metaphor: Selected Essays, 1974–1988*, ed. Robert D. Denham (Charlottesville and London: University Press of Virginia, 1990), p. 14.

8. Kalidasa, *Sakontala*, trans. Georg Forster (Mainz and Leipzig, 1791), p. 123 (act 4).

9. William Kinderman, *Beethoven's Diabelli Variations* (Oxford: Clarendon Press, 1989), p. 96; Eric Blom, *Classics: Major and Minor* (London: Dent, 1958), p. 66; see also Tovey, *Essays in Musical Analysis: Chamber Music* (London: Oxford University Press, 1944), p. 135.

10. According to G. F. Fort, *Early History and Antiquities of Freemasonry* (Philadelphia: Putnam, 1875), "three strokes by a Master convened all the members of that Degree; two strokes by the Pallirer called the Fellows, and by a single blow each member was assembled in Lodge." Quoted by Albert G. Mackey, *Encyclopedia of Freemasonry*, revised and enlarged by Robert I. Clegg and H. L. Haywood, 3 vols. (Chicago: Masonic History Co., 1946), vol. 1, p. 551.

11. [Johann Heinrich Faber, ed.,] *Der ächte Illuminat oder die wahren, unverbesserten Rituale der Illuminaten* (Edessa [Frankfurt]: Hermannische Buchhandlung, 1788), pp. 189–90; Josef Irmen, *Mozart: Mitglied geheimer Gesellschaften* (Zülpich: Prisca, 1988), chapter 2.4, passim.

12. Blom, *Classics,* p. 70.

13. Jürgen Uhde, *Beethovens Klaviermusik I: Klavierstücke und Variationen* (Stuttgart: Reclam, 1980), p. 543.

14. For the reminders of Bach in variations 24 and 32, see Kinderman, *Beethoven's Diabelli Variations,* p. 106, and Martin Zenck, "Rezeption von Geschichte in Beethovens 'Diabelli-Variationen': Zur Vermittlung analytischer, ästhetischer, und historischer Kategorien," *Archiv für Musikwissenschaft* 33 (1980): 61–75.

15. In the nineteenth century, Hans von Bülow observed that variation 23, Allegro assai, "imitates the idiom of an étude in the style of Johann Baptist Cramer," a view recently enlarged on by Kinderman, who sees the variation as a "Cramer parody" to go with the Mozart parody that preceded it, and who shows similarities between the variation and the opening of the first étude of Cramer's *Studio per il pianoforte* (1804). See Kinderman, *Beethoven's Diabelli Variations,* pp. 104–5, quotation on p. 105. Uhde, however, thinks it more likely that Carl Czerny was the "godfather of this variation," and he too cites a conceivable prototype; see Uhde, *Beethovens Klaviermusik I,* pp. 543–44. Neither the Cramer nor Czerny examples are wholly convincing, for they lack Beethoven's disjunctive features—syncopations, contrary motion, and dynamic contrasts.

16. Bülow's commentary on the "Diabelli" Variations is quoted from the French translation, *Édition instructive d'oeuvres classiques pour le piano . . . Sonates et autres oeuvres pour le piano par Ludwig van Beethoven,* ed. Hans von Bülow, trans. Ernest Closson (Stuttgart and Berlin: Cotta, 1902), vol. 5, part 2, pp. 158–205, at p. 194. See also pp. 184, 196; Nottebohm, *Zweite Beethoveniana,* p. 571.

17. Kinderman, *Beethoven's Diabelli Variations,* p. 59.

18. For a telling description of the transition from the fugue to the final variation, see Max Rudolf, "Improvised Thoughts on the 33rd Variation in Beethoven's Op. 120," in *Max Rudolf, A Musical Life: Writings and Letters,* ed. Michael Stern and Hanny Bleeker White (Hillsdale, N.Y.: Pendragon, 2001), pp. 303–4. I am indebted to maestro Rudolf for calling my attention to the "pilgrim's walk" tempo of episodes in late Beethoven.

Chapter 10. Intimations of the Sacred

1. Ignaz Xaver von Seyfried, untitled article, *Caecilia: Eine Zeitschrift für die musikalische Welt* 9 (1828): 226, reprinted in Kunze, p. 449, quoted by Warren Kirkendale, "New Roads to Old Ideas in Beethoven's *Missa Solemnis,*" *Musical Quarterly* 56 (1970): 665–701, at p. 679.

2. Parenthetical page numbers in the text refer to Kirkendale, "New Roads to Old Ideas."

3. Erich Schenk, "Barock bei Beethoven," in *Beethoven und die Gegenwart: Festschrift [. . .] Ludwig Schiedermair,* ed. Arnold Schmitz (Berlin and Bonn: Dümmler, 1937), pp. 177–219, at p. 216. Schenk has described the extensive use of tone-painting in *Fidelio,* including leitmotif techniques and numerous word-music equivalencies, in "Über Tonsymbolik in Beethovens 'Fidelio,'" *Beethoven-Studien,* ed. Erich Schenk (Vienna: Böhlaus, 1970), pp. 223–52.

4. William Kinderman, "Beethoven's Symbol for the Deity in the *Missa solemnis* and the Ninth Symphony," *19th-Century Music* 9 (1985): 102–18; see also Kinderman, *Beethoven* (Berkeley and Los Angeles: University of California Press, 1995), pp. 238–52. Kinderman builds upon parallel observations about the significance of the E-flat sonority in Wilfrid Mellers, *Beethoven and the Voice of God* (London: Faber and Faber, 1983), pp. 334, 342.

5. Mellers, *Beethoven and the Voice of God,* p. 344. Subsequent page numbers are given in parentheses in the text.

6. Karl Holz recalled that Beethoven "wanted to write choruses in the ancient modes" for the proposed oratorio on Saul to a text by Kuffner. See Thayer-Deiters-Riemann, vol. 5, p. 326. In a conversation book for mid-April 1826, Holz wrote, "Here it would be very good to introduce a chorus in the Lydian mode, as you wanted." *Konversationshefte,* vol. 9, p. 204 (Heft 108, 44r). See also Beethoven's Tagebuch entry, "In order to write true church music go through all the ecclesiastical chants of the monks etc." (no. 168).

7. Northrop Frye wrote the defining explorations of the symbolism of ascents and descents in myth, theology, and literature; see *The Secular Scripture: A Study of the Structure of Romance* (Cambridge, Mass.: Harvard University Press, 1976), pp. 97–157; "The *Koine* of Myth: Myth as a Universally Intelligible Language," in *Myth and Metaphor: Selected Essays, 1974–1988,* ed. Robert D. Denham (Charlottesville and London: University Press of Virginia, 1990), pp. 3–17; "New Directions from Old," in *Myth and Mythmaking,* ed. Henry A. Murray (New York: Braziller, 1960), pp. 115–31; and *Anatomy of Criticism: Four Essays* (Princeton: Princeton University Press, 1957).

8. Nottebohm, *Zweite Beethoveniana,* p. 191.

9. Earlier examples of kindred scenarios may be found in the Fantasia for Piano in G minor, op. 77; the Choral Fantasia, op. 80; and the finale of the *Eroica* Symphony. See also the Variations in E-flat for piano trio, op. 44, with its slow *minore* variation setting up a rollicking ending.

10. Donald Francis Tovey, *A Companion to Beethoven's Pianoforte Sonatas (Bar-to-bar Analysis)* (London: Associated Board of the Royal Schools of Music, 1931), p. 229.

11. Kirkendale, "New Roads to Old Ideas," p. 165. Rosen called attention to additional compositional means by which motionlessness can be simulated: "the fastest *perpetuum mobile* can appear immobile, and a long silence can be heard *prestissimo.* . . . This power to suspend motion, seeming to stop the movement of time, which is measured only by action, . . . became one of Beethoven's most personal traits." Charles Rosen,

The Classical Style (New York: Viking, 1971), pp. 446–47. Mellers sees some sources of Beethoven's time-stopping effects in "the vast, often overlapping, span of the melodic phrases; other sources are the harmony's frequent elisions of tonic, dominant and subdominant triads . . . [and] the prevalence of drones and pedal notes within the texture." Mellers, *Beethoven and the Voice of God,* p. 345.

12.   In his "Dissertation on the Chronology of the Hindus," Sir William Jones refers to Hindu theologians who say, *"Time . . . exists not at all with God."* Jones et al., *Dissertations and Miscellaneous Pieces Relating to the History and Antiquities, the Arts, Science, and Literature of Asia* (Dublin: Byrne and Jones, 1793), p. 211. Beethoven read and copied materials from a German-language edition of Jones's collection, translated by J. G. C. Fick and published at Riga in 1795.

13.   Schenker, *Beethoven: Die letzten Sonaten. Sonate C moll, op. 111,* ed. Oswald Jonas (Vienna: Universal, 1971), p. 48.

14.   Tovey, *A Companion to Beethoven's Pianoforte Sonatas,* p. 277.

15.   Joseph Kerman and Alan Tyson, "Beethoven," *New Grove,* vol. 2, p. 387, reprinted in Kerman and Tyson, *The New Grove Beethoven* (New York: Norton, 1983), p. 129; Denis Matthews, *Beethoven* (New York: Vintage, 1988), p. 99; Bekker, *Beethoven,* pp. 140–41; Kinderman, *Beethoven,* p. 234.

16.   Rolland, *Beethoven: Les grandes époques créatrices* (Paris: Albin Michel, 1966), p. 804.

17.   Jürgen Uhde, *Beethovens Klaviermusik,* 3 vols. (Stuttgart: Reclam, 1968–74; reprint, 1980–91), vol. 3, p. 616.

18.   Theodor W. Adorno, *Beethoven: The Philosophy of Music. Fragments and Texts,* ed. Rolf Tiedemann, trans. Edmund Jephcott (Stanford: Stanford University Press, 1998), pp. 175–76 (no. 366).

19.   William James, *The Varieties of Religious Experience: A Study in Human Nature* (New York: Longmans, Green, 1902; reprint, New York: Modern Library, n.d.), pp. 28–29.

20.   Letter 24, "Über die ästhetische Erziehung des Menschen, in einer Reihe von Briefen," in *Schillers sämtliche Werke in zwölf Bänden* (Leipzig: Max Hesse, n.d.), vol. 12, p. 70, *Letters on Aesthetic Education,* quoted in *The Works of Friedrich Schiller: Aesthetical and Philosophical Essays,* ed. Nathan Haskell Dole (New York: Bigelow, Brown, 1902), vol. 1, p. 89.

Chapter 11. The Sense of an Ending

1.   Letter of ca. 19 March 1819, *Briefe,* vol. 4, p. 262 (no. 1295), *Letters,* vol. 2, pp. 804–5 (no. 939).

2.   Thayer-Deiters-Riemann, vol. 5, p. 298, n. 3; Wilhelm von Lenz, *Beethoven: Eine Kunst-Studie,* 6 vols. (Kassel and Hamburg: Hoffmann & Campe, 1860), vol. 5, part 4, p. 219; and Solomon, *Beethoven,* pp. 422–23.

3.   For the revisions of the early quartets, see Sieghard Brandenburg, "The First Version of Beethoven's G Major String Quartet, Op. 18 No. 2," *Music & Letters* 58 (1977):

127–52; Janet M. Levy, *Beethoven's Compositional Choices: The Two Versions of Opus 18, No. 1, First Movement* (Philadelphia: University of Pennsylvania Press, 1982).

4.   In a discerning paper, Kropfinger argues that the resistance of audiences, critics, colleagues, and publishers to the Grosse Fuge persuaded Beethoven to replace it. He does not, however, take into account Beethoven's customary disregard for negative reception of his works. Klaus Kropfinger, "Das gespaltene Werk—Beethovens Streichquartett Op. 130/133," in *Beiträge zu Beethovens Kammermusik: Symposion Bonn 1984,* ed. S. Brandenburg and H. Loos (Munich: Henle, 1987), pp. 296–335, esp. pp. 317–20.

5.   Emil Platen, "Beethovens Autographen als Ausgangspunkt morphologischer Untersuchungen," in *Bericht über den internationalen musikwissenschaftlichen Kongreß: Bonn 1970,* ed. Carl Dahlhaus et al. (Kassel: Bärenreiter, 1971), p. 535. See also Lewis Lockwood, "Beethoven and the Problem of Closure: Some Examples from the Middle-Period Chamber Music," in *Beiträge zu Beethovens Kammermusik,* p. 270.

6.   Lewis Lockwood, "On Beethoven's Sketches and Autographs: Some Problems of Definition and Interpretation," *Acta Musicologica* 42 (1970): 34.

7.   Levy, *Beethoven's Compositional Choices,* p. 3.

8.   Otto Jahn, *Gesammelte Aufsätze über Musik* (Leipzig: Breitkopf & Härtel, 1866), p. 244, trans. Thayer-Forbes, p. 381.

9.   Nottebohm, *Zweite Beethoveniana,* p. 182 n.

10.   Leopold Sonnleithner, "Ad vocem: Contrabass-Recitative der 9. Symphonie von Beethoven," *AmZ,* new series, 2 (6 April 1864): cols. 245–46; Kerst, vol. 2, pp. 78–79; Thayer-Deiters-Riemann, vol. 5, pp. 65–66. My translation. Sonnleithner's entire letter is translated by Max Rudolf, "A Question of Tempo in Beethoven's Ninth Symphony," *Beethoven Newsletter* 4 (Winter 1989): 56–57.

11.   Joseph Kerman, *The Beethoven Quartets* (New York: Knopf, 1967), p. 262; Nottebohm, *Zweite Beethoveniana,* pp. 179–82. The main thrust of Nottebohm's evidence has always been widely accepted both by the standard biographers and by the leading scholars of Beethoven's compositional process. See Thayer-Forbes, pp. 890–91; Heinrich Schenker, *Beethoven's Ninth Symphony,* trans. John Rothgeb (New Haven: Yale University Press, 1992), pp. 271–75; Paul Mies, *Beethoven's Sketches,* trans. Doris L. Mackinnon (London: Oxford University Press, 1929), pp. 7–8; Sieghard Brandenburg, "Die Skizzen zur Neunten Symphonie," in *Zu Beethoven: Aufsätze und Dokumente,* ed. Harry Goldschmidt, 3 vols. (Berlin: Neue Musik, 1979–84), vol. 2, pp. 108–9, 128–29; Douglas Johnson, Robert Winter, and Alan Tyson, *The Beethoven Sketchbooks,* ed. Douglas Johnson (Berkeley and Los Angeles: University of California Press, 1985), pp. 410 and passim. In "The Sketches for the 'Ode to Joy,'" in *Beethoven, Performers, and Critics,* ed. Robert Winter and Bruce Carr (Detroit: Wayne State University Press, 1980), Robert Winter found the evidence to be "rather softer" than Nottebohm allowed (pp. 197–98), but closer examination of the sketches (including Autograph 8/2 [Kraków]) has essentially settled the question, showing that the sketches for an instrumental finale were more extensive than Winter or even Nottebohm had known. Brandenburg summarized the situation:

The theme that eventuated in Opus 132 appears in many passages in the sketchbooks, essentially more often than, for example, Winter thought. It is encountered at the beginning of work on the finale, when the decision for the vocal version had not yet been settled on: "Vielleicht doch den Chor. . . ." Then again, Beethoven himself designates it as "instrumental finale." Finally it appears again at the end of the sketches for the finale (in pocket sketchbook aut. 8/2), after everything had already been composed.

(letter to the author, 3 October 1984)

"The theme," writes Brandenburg, "must have been always present in Beethoven's mind during the composition of the symphony." Brandenburg, "Die Skizzen zur Neunten Symphonie," p. 129. Still, alternatives to Nottebohm's interpretation of the evidence continue to be offered; for example, by Nicholas Cook, *Beethoven: Symphony No. 9* (Cambridge: Cambridge University Press, 1993), pp. 17–19. Such interpretations do not take account of Czerny's reports of Beethoven's dissatisfaction with the choral finale and his idea of replacing it with an instrumental finale.

12. Henry James, "The Art of Fiction," in *The Future of the Novel: Essays on the Art of Fiction,* ed. Leon Edel (New York: Vintage, 1956), p. 8.

13. Robert S. Winter, *Compositional Origins of Beethoven's Opus 131* (Ann Arbor: UMI, 1982), p. 137; Joseph Kerman and Alan Tyson, "Beethoven," in *New Grove,* vol. 2, p. 380.

14. Friedrich Nietzsche, *The Birth of Tragedy out of the Spirit of Music,* in "*The Birth of Tragedy*" *and "The Genealogy of Morals,"* trans. Francis Golffing (Garden City, N.Y.: Anchor, 1956), p. 117.

15. Frank Kermode, *The Sense of an Ending: Studies in the Theory of Fiction* (London: Oxford University Press, 1967), p. 64.

16. Alejo Carpentier, *The Lost Steps,* trans. Harriet de Onís (New York: Knopf, 1956), p. 93.

17. See Otto Baensch, *Aufbau und Sinn des Chorfinales Beethovens neunter Symphonie* (Berlin and Leipzig: Walter de Gruyter, 1930); Maynard Solomon, "The Ninth Symphony: A Search for Order," in Solomon, *Beethoven Essays,* pp. 3–32.

18. Prose jotting to *Die Kunst und die Revolution,* in *Richard Wagner's Prose Works,* trans. W. Ashton Ellis, 8 vols. (London: Routledge and Kegan Paul, 1893), vol. 8, p. 362.

19. See Nottebohm, *Zweite Beethoveniana,* pp. 189–91, and Thayer-Deiters-Riemann, vol. 5, p. 29; my paraphrase.

20. Kerman points out that none of the ten surviving sketch possibilities for a concluding movement to the original version of Opus 130 "has any suggestions of fugal treatment or any signs of a certain four-note configuration." See Kerman, "Beethoven Sketchbooks in the British Museum," *Publications of the Royal Musical Association* 93 (1966–67): 83–84.

21. See letters of September 1800, 10 September 1800, and 21 October 1800, *Schillers Briefwechsel mit Körner,* 2nd ed., edited by Karl Goedeke, 2 vols. (Leipzig: Veit, 1878), vol. 2, pp. 356–59. See also Solomon, *Beethoven Essays,* p. 209. For a critical edition of

the two versions of "An die Freude," see *Schillers sämmtliche Schriften,* ed. Goedeke et al., 15 vols. (Stuttgart: Cotta, 1867–76), vol. 3, pp. 1–5, 351–52.

22. Samuel Beckett, *Endgame: A Play in One Act* (New York: Grove, 1958), p. 3.

23. Letter to Franz Anton Hoffmeister, 8 April 1802, *Briefe,* vol. 1, p. 105 (no. 84), *Letters,* vol. 1, p. 73 (no. 57).

24. In his fragments and texts for a never-completed book on Beethoven, Adorno offered a parallel interpretation:

> In Schiller's "Ode to Joy," the text of the Ninth Symphony, any person is included in the circle provided he is able to call "even a single soul his own in this wide world;" that is, the person who is happy in love. "But he who has none, let him steal weeping from our company." Inherent in the bad collective is the image of the solitary, and joy desires to see him weep. . . . The loneliness punished by Schiller . . . is no other than that produced by his revellers' community itself. In such a company, what is to become of old maids, not to speak of the souls of the dead?

Theodor W. Adorno, *Beethoven: Philosophie der Musik. Fragmente und Texte,* ed. Rolf Tiedemann (Frankfurt: Suhrkamp, 1993), trans. *Beethoven: The Philosophy of Music. Fragments and Texts,* ed. Rolf Tiedemann, trans. Edmund Jephcott (Stanford: Stanford University Press, 1998), p. 33. A variant of this interpretation appears in a draft entitled "Fortschritt," also published posthumously in T. W. Adorno, *Gesammelte Schriften,* ed. Gretel Adorno and Rolf Tiedemann, 20 vols. (Frankfurt: Suhrkamp, 1970–86), vol. 10, part 2, and reprinted in *Beethoven,* p. 212 n. 87.

25. Schiller's poem is translated from Beethoven's own adaptation.

26. Otto Fenichel, "Brief Psychotherapy," *Collected Papers,* ed. Hanna Fenichel and David Rapaport, 2 vols. (London: Routledge & Kegan Paul, 1954), vol. 2, p. 253.

27. Hans W. Loewald, "The Waning of the Oedipus Complex," *Papers on Psychoanalysis* (New Haven: Yale University Press, 1980), pp. 401–2.

28. Totalitarian implications in Beethoven's Ninth Symphony were recognized by Adorno: "Works like the Ninth Symphony exert a mesmerizing influence; the power they have by virtue of their structure is translated into power over people." T. W. Adorno, *Aesthetic Theory,* trans. C. Lenhardt (London: Routledge & Kegan Paul, 1984), p. 347, *Beethoven,* pp. 222–23 n. 169; see also p. 77 (no. 193). The regressive and authoritarian potentialities of some of Beethoven's heroic-style compositions, and especially the triumphalist stance of their recapitulations, have also been noted by Bekker and Kerman. Of the "shattering . . . overstatements" in the closing pages of the String Quartet in C, op. 59, no. 3, and the Fifth Symphony, Kerman writes, "These are the accents of the hero turned demagogue; Beethoven, who had torn up a title page in 1804, remained unable to meet the Napoleonism latent in his own work for quite a few more years." Kerman, *Beethoven Quartets,* pp. 144–45. For Goethe's and Nietzsche's remarks about the regressive implications of Beethoven's musical affirmations, see above, pp. 35 and 133–34.

29. For a list of exemplary papers on the finale's form, by Ernest Sanders, Michael C. Tusa, James Webster, and William Kinderman, see Solomon, *Beethoven*, p. 507.

30. Whatever its suspicions of Beethoven, the imperial court had not forgotten his patriotic and uncharacteristically obsequious Congress of Vienna works—*Der Glorreiche Augenblick*, op. 136, *Germania*, WoO 94, and the "Chorus to the Allied Princes," WoO 95, which begins "You wise founders of fortunate states *[Ihr weisen Gründer glücklicher Staaten]*"—and it might well have viewed the Ninth Symphony as the latest of Beethoven's *pièces d'occasion*, a view that would not be contradicted by the subsequent dedication of the symphony to Friedrich Wilhelm III of Prussia. In October 1822, only seventeen months before the premiere of the Ninth Symphony, Beethoven's music for the festspiel *Die Weihe des Hauses* was performed to honor Emperor Franz's nameday as well as to celebrate the opening of the Josephstadt Theater.

31. Bertolt Brecht, *Aufstieg und Fall der Stadt Mahagonny*, vol. 2 of *Bertolt Brecht: Werke, Berliner und Franfurter Ausgabe*, ed. Werner Hecht et al., 30 vols. (Berlin and Weimar: Aufbau; and Frankfurt: Suhrkamp, 1988–), pp. 349–50.

Chapter 12. The Healing Power of Music

1. Jahn, letter to G. Hartenstein, 12 December 1852, in *Otto Jahn in seinen Briefen. Mit einem Bilde seines Lebens von Adolf Michaelis*, ed. Eugen Petersen (Leipzig and Berlin: Teubncr, 1913), p. 83.

2. Otto Jahn, "Ein Brief Beethovens," *Die Grenzboten: Zeitschrift für Politik und Literatur* 26, no. 2 (1867): 100–105, at p. 101; see also the extract published in Thayer-Deiters-Riemann, vol. 3, pp. 214–15, Thayer-Krehbiel, vol. 2, p. 179.

3. Letter from Antonie Brentano to Bettina Brentano, Vienna, 11 March 1811 (Sammlung Varnhagen, Biblioteka Jagiellońska, Kraków), published by Klaus Martin Kopitz, "Antonie Brentano in Wien (1809–1812): Neue Quellen zur Problematik 'Unsterbliche Geliebte,'" in *Bonner Beethoven-Studien*, vol. 2, ed. Sieghard Brandenburg and Ernst Herttrich (Bonn: Beethoven-Haus, 2001), pp. 115–44, at p. 128.

4. Mathilde Marchesi, Marquise de la Rajata de Castrone, *Aus meinem Leben* (Düsseldorf: Felix Bagel, n.d. [ca. 1888]), p. 12, quoted by A. C. Kalischer, *Beethoven und seine Zeitgenossen*, 4 vols. (Berlin: Schuster & Loeffler, n.d. [1908–10]), vol. 3, *Beethovens Frauenkreis*, part 2, p. 125, trans. George Marek, *Beethoven: Biography of a Genius* (New York: Funk & Wagnalls, 1969), p. 291. See also Mathilde de Castrone Marchesi, *Erinnerungen aus meinem Leben* (Vienna: Carl Gerolds Sohn, 1877), p. 7. Ertmann's son, Franz Carl, died 19 March 1804, according to information in Viennese death registers located and generously communicated by Klaus Martin Kopitz.

5. Letter to Mendelssohn's mother, 14 July 1831, in Felix Mendelssohn-Bartholdy, *Reisebriefe aus den Jahren 1830 bis 1832*, 4th ed., edited by Paul Mendelssohn Bartholdy (Leipzig: H. Mendelssohn, 1862), p. 195. See also Thayer-Deiters-Riemann, vol. 2, p. 415, trans. Thayer-Forbes, p. 413. Antonie Brentano's account echoes the latter phrase, "said

everything and brought comfort *[alles gesagt und Trost gegeben hatte]*," possibly suggesting that either she or Jahn was familiar with Mendelssohn's letter.

6.   Adamberger, quoted by Thayer-Deiters-Riemann, vol. 3, p. 583.

7.   de Castrone, *Erinnerungen aus meinem Leben,* p. 12, trans. Marek, *Beethoven,* p. 291.

8.   See Lisa Feurzeig, "Heroines in Perversity: Marie Schmith, Animal Magnetism, and the Schubert Circle," *19th-Century Music* 21 (1997): 223–43; Harry Goldschmidt, "Schubert und kein Ende," *Beiträge zur Musikwissenschaft* 25 (1983): 288–92.

9.   Goldschmidt, "Schubert und kein Ende," pp. 290–91.

10.   Goldschmidt favors the song paraphrase in the middle of the "Wanderer" Fantasia, ibid., p. 291.

11.   Feurzeig, "Heroines in Perversity," pp. 231–32.

12.   Phyllis Greenacre, *Emotional Growth: Psychoanalytic Studies of the Gifted and a Great Variety of Other Individuals,* 2 vols. (New York: International Universities Press, 1971), vol. 2, p. 628. Leonard Meyer reached a similar conclusion via a different route, holding that "a patient's belief in the efficacy and power of music to heal may be a significant element in the success of music therapy." Leonard B. Meyer, "Learning, Belief, and Music Therapy," *Music Therapy* 5 (1955): 27–35, at p. 33; see also Meyer, *Emotion and Meaning in Music* (Chicago: University of Chicago Press, 1956), pp. 73–75.

13.   For "the image of Bach as healer" see Walter Frisch, "Bach, Brahms, and the Emergence of Musical Modernism," *Bach Perspectives,* vol. 3, ed. Michael Marissen (Lincoln and London: University of Nebraska Press, 1998), pp. 127–29.

14.   We are reminded also of the dying Hezekiah, "sick unto death," who in despair had "turned his face towards the wall": but his prayer was answered, his health restored, his days lengthened by fifteen years, and his people delivered from the hand of the Assyrians (2 Kings 20.1–6, Isaiah 38.1–6). The Lutheran composer Johann Kuhnau told the story in one of his Biblical sonatas for keyboard, titled "Hezekiah, mortally ill and then restored."

15.   Zarlino, *Institutioni harmoniche* (Venice, 1558), p. 303, quoted by Warren Kirkendale, "New Roads to Old Ideas in Beethoven's *Missa Solemnis,*" *Musical Quarterly* 56 (1970): 677. Kirkendale records several references to Zarlino in Beethoven's conversation books for December 1819, *Konversationshefte,* vol. 1, p. 108 (Heft 3, 52r) and p. 196 (Heft 6, 31v).

16.   Tovey found a close analogy in the opening of the second half of the Goldberg Variations: "Bach's sixteenth variation bursts forth, after the sombre tones of the fifteenth, with a 'feeling of renewed strength,' not unworthy to be regarded as a foreshadowing" of the Heiliger Dankgesang. Tovey, *Essays in Musical Analysis: Chamber Music* (London: Oxford University Press, 1945), p. 56. The healing powers of music were a serious topic in music journals of Beethoven's time; see, for example, the lengthy article by Dr. F. W. Weber, "Von dem Einfluße der Musik auf den menschlichen Körper und ihrer medicinischen Anwendung," *AmZ* 14 (26 May 1802), cols. 561–69 (2 June 1802), cols. 577–89 (9 June 1802), cols. 593–99 (15 June 1802), cols. 609–17; see also the article

by Beethoven's erudite friend Friedrich August Kanne, "Über die Harmonie in der Tonkunst in Beziehung auf ihre Verwandtschaft mit der Malerey, Plastik und Dichtkunst," *Conversationsblatt: Zeitschrift für wissenschaftliche Unterhaltung* 3 (Vienna, 1821): 836, in which he writes that those "who are convalescent from a sickness begin to sing as soon as they again become conscious of their strength." Translated by Kirkendale, "New Roads to Old Ideas," p. 701 n. 151.

17.   Wilhelm von Lenz, *Beethoven: Eine Kunst-Studie* (Hamburg: Hoffmann & Campe, 1860), vol. 5, part 4, p. 217; another account by Holz is in Ludwig Nohl, *Beethoven, Liszt, Wagner. Ein Bild der Kunstbewegung unseres Jahrhunderts* (Vienna: Braumüller, 1874), p. 112. The inscription *Inter Lacrymas et Luctum* (Amid tears and sorrow) written on the lost dedication copy of the Cello Sonata in A, op. 69, is probably not a description of the music but of Beethoven's melancholy state of mind in 1809, perhaps in connection with his unhappy courtships or the vicissitudes of the war and the French occupation of Vienna.

18.   Nottebohm, *Zweite Beethoveniana,* p. 190.

19.   Kerman, *The Beethoven Quartets* (New York: Knopf, 1967), p. 277.

INDEX OF COMPOSITIONS

Preceding the index is a Classified List that identifies by opus number the works mentioned in this book. For works without opus numbers, it gives the WoO or Hess number. The index lists the works in numerical order, with complete titles and page numbers, for each of these three groups. Projected works are listed alphabetically at the end of the index. Italicized page numbers indicate music examples.

CLASSIFIED LIST

GENERAL INDEX

Page numbers in italics refer to music examples.

Abrams, M. H., 48, 51, 133, 253n26; on
    Romantic crises, 62
Acacia, symbolism of, 146
Adagio Cantique, proposed, 124
Adagios, 195–96; of Cello Sonata in D,
    op. 102, no. 2, *66–67*; in "Ham-
    merklavier" Sonata, op. 106, 195,
    203; Mozart's, 196; of Ninth
    Symphony, 239; of Sonata for Violin
    and Piano in G, op. 96, 79, *80–82*,
    81–82, 86, 87, 203; of String Quartet
    in A minor, op. 132, *235*, *237*; of
    "Waldstein" Sonata, op. 53, 204
Adamberger, Antonie, 230
Adorno, Theodor W., 120; on Ninth
    Symphony, 297n28; on "Ode to Joy,"
    297n24; on Sonata in C minor, op.
    111, 211
Aesthetics: Beethoven's views on, 92–101,
    125, 224, 263n44; of Romanticism,
    38; Schiller's, 41, 98
Akademie der Wissenschaft (Vienna), 162
Albumblätter, Beethoven's, 157
Alexander I (czar of Russia), 141, 278n35
Alfieri, Vittorio, 60
Alienation: in art, 47; imagery of, 56;
    Romantic imagery of, 62; in Sonata
    for Violin and Piano in G, op. 96, 88
Alienation and restoration: Rousseau on,
    23, 78; Schiller on, 23, 78

Allanbrook, Wye J., 72, 74
Allegory, tonal, 46
Allgemeine musikalische Zeitung (Leipzig),
    33, 34, 35, 271n52, 299n16
Amenda, Karl, 256n61, 269n43
Anacreon, 121
Analogies, musical: to poetic genres, 8, 79,
    126; to text images, 201
Anapestic meter, in Seventh Symphony,
    107, 266n14
An die ferne Geliebte, op. 98 (Beethoven),
    50, *66*; breeze imagery in, 49–50;
    celebration in, 237; nature in, 64;
    pastoral imagery in, 56, 75; Romanti-
    cism of, 40; text of, 132, 273n68,
    289n24. *See also* Distant Beloved
André, Johann Anton, 142
Antiquity: Apollonian model of, 128;
    Dionysian model of, 128; evocations
    of, 124–25; festivals of, 121, 123, 125;
    the heroic and, 124–25; Laocoönian
    elements in, 128; pastoral poetry of,
    71, 258n1; primordial harmony in,
    130; religions of, 8–9; revalidation
    of, 129; revivals of, 126–28; rituals
    of, 148, 150, 165; Schiller's view of,
    8; yearning for, 272n67. *See also*
    Classicism; Music, Greek; Mysteries,
    ancient; Prosody, classical
Apollo, Beethoven on, 280n45

Compositor:	Integrated Composition Systems
Text:	11/14 Bembo
Display:	Filosofia Grand Bold
Printer/Binder:	Malloy Lithographing, Inc.
Music setter:	Mansfield Music-Graphics
General index:	Roberta Engleman